NATO's SOUTHERN ALLIES:
Internal and External Challenges

An Atlantic Institute for International Affairs
Research Volume

Other Research Volumes from:

The Atlantic Institute for International Affairs

Towards Industrial Democracy: Europe, Japan and the United
States
  edited by Benjamin C. Roberts

Japanese Direct Foreign Investment
  by Sueo Sekiguchi

Banks and the Balance of Payments: Private Lending in the
International Adjustment Process
  by Benjamin J. Cohen in collaboration with Fabio Basagni

National Industrial Strategies and the World Economy
  edited by John Pinder

The Public and Atlantic Defense
  edited by Gregory Flynn and Hans Rattinger

New Limits on European Agriculture
  by François Duchêne, Edward Szczepanik and Wilfrid Legg

NATO's Northern Allies: The National Security Policies of
Belgium, Denmark, the Netherlands and Norway
  edited by Gregory Flynn

Soviet-East European Relations as a Problem for the West
  edited by Richard D. Vine

NATO'S SOUTHERN ALLIES:
Internal and External Challenges

Edited by
JOHN CHIPMAN

An Atlantic Institute for International Affairs
Research Volume

ROUTLEDGE
London and New York

First published in 1988 by
Routledge
11 New Fetter Lane, London EC4P 4EE

Published in the USA by
Routledge
in association with Routledge, Chapman & Hall, Inc.
29 West 35th Street, New York NY 10001

Printed and bound in Great Britain by Mackays of Chatham Ltd, Kent

British Library Cataloguing in Publication Data

NATO's southern allies: internal and external
    challenges. — (An Atlantic Institute for
    International Affairs research volume).
    1. North Atlantic Treaty Organisation
    2. Security, International   3. Europe,
    Southern — Strategic aspects
    I. Chipman, John   II. Series
    355'.031'091821   UA646.3
    ISBN 0-415-00485-3

Library of Congress Cataloging in Publication Data

ISBN 0-415-00485-3

Contents

Preface

This is a study of the domestic sources of defence and foreign policy in Portugal, Spain, Italy, Greece and Turkey. With the exception of Italy, these countries have had recent experiences of authoritarian rule and significant internal turmoil that have affected both the perceptions of external threat and the manner in which policy is formed within the Atlantic Alliance. Each of the national studies was commissioned from a citizen of the country concerned. Meeting in Paris in early 1985, the authors decided that each should address four points: first, the historical constants which have affected the formation of security policy; second, the domestic tensions that determine the nature and form of defence and foreign policy; third, the relationship between the domestic and international environment with a view to examining the interplay between the two; and, fourth, the future changes in security policy which may be expected and how these may be influenced by internal developments. Each of the authors has, in his own fashion, followed this agenda thus assuring both consistency between the chapters and the preservation of national perspectives. As this book was conceived largely as a comparative examination of the other countries in NATO's Southern Periphery, the chapter on Italy is intentionally narrower in scope and approach: it concentrates on recent developments and analyses the Italian debate on the question of whether Italy could or should come to play a larger role in Mediterranean security. In addition, an attempt is made to describe the general security situation for the Alliance in the Mediterranean and to compare the national attitudes of these countries towards Western security problems in the Southern Region.

The chapter drafts were discussed at a conference in Castel-gandolfo, Italy in 1985. The Institute is grateful to the U.S. Mission to NATO which contributed to the costs of this meeting. The conference brought together government officials, diplomats, academics and journalists from the countries under study as well as from other Alliance nations. The drafts were revised on the basis of the discussions and later rewritten after an authors' workshop in 1986.

John Chipman would like to thank Dr. Gregory Flynn for

helping him organize both the study as a whole and his own chapters. Numerous NATO officials and leading personalities of the countries examined in this book gave him their impressions of the situation in southern Europe during interviews held in 1985 and 1986. Mr. Diego Ruiz Palmer of the BDM Corporation helped to correct a number of errors in successive drafts of chapters 1 and 2. Andréa Hecht and Ann Proctor, of the Atlantic Institute, did some editing and the in-house typing of materials. Thelma Black reviewed the manuscript and made final corrections. Although the editor received considerable support in the preparation of this book, none of the individuals who kindly assisted can be made responsible for its contents.

The Atlantic Institute for International Affairs is particularly grateful to the Rockefeller Foundation for the grant that made this book possible.

Andrew J. Pierre

Glossary

ACE	Allied Command Europe
AD	Democratic Alliance Party (Aliança Democrática) (Portugal)
AFSOUTH	Allied Forces Southern Europe
AIRSOUTH	Air Forces Southern Europe
AMF	Allied Mobile Force
AMAG	American Mission to Aid Greece
ANAP	Motherland Party (Anatavan Partisi) (Turkey)
ANZUS	Security Treaty between Australia, New Zealand and United States
AP	Popular Alliance (Alianza Popular) (Spain)
ASALA	Armenian Secret Army for the Liberation of Armenia
ASW	Anti-Submarine Warfare
ATAF	Allied Tactical Air Force
AWACS	Airborne Warning and Control System
C3	Command, Control and Communication
CDS	Democratic and Social Centre Party (Partido do Centro Democrático Social) (Portugal)
CDS	Democratic and Social Centre (Centro Democrático y Social) (Spain)
CECMED	Commandement en Chef pour la Méditerrannée
CENTCOM	Central Command
CENTO	Central Treaty Organization
CINCIBERLANT	Commander-in-Chief Iberian Atlantic Area
CINSOUTH	Commander-in-Chief Allied Forces Southern Europe
CNAD	Conference of National Armaments Directors
COB	Colocated Operating Bases
COMAIRSOUTH	Commander Air Forces Southern Europe (Naples)
COMLANDSOUTH	Commander Land Forces Southern Europe (Verona)
COMLANDSOUTH-CENT	Commander Land Forces South-Central Europe (Larissa)
COMLANDSOUTH EAST	Commander Land Forces South-Eastern Europe (Izmir)
COMNAVSOUTH	Commander Allied Naval Forces Southern Europe (Naples)
COMSTRIKEFOR SOUTH	Commander Naval Striking and Support Forces Southern Europe (Naples)
CP	Popular Coalition (Coalición Popular) (Spain)
CPX	Command Post Exercise
CVBG	Carrier Battle Group

DC	Christian Democratic Party (Partito della Democrazia Cristiana) (Italy)
DCS	Defence Communications Systems
DECA	Defense and Economic Cooperation Agreement
DICA	Defense and Industrial Cooperation Agreement
DISK	Confederation of Revolutionary Workers (Turkey)
DLP	Democratic Left Party (Turkey)
DPQ	Defence Planning Questionnaire
DYP	True Path Party (Dogru Yol Partisi) (Turkey)
EDA	United Democratic Left (Eniaia Demokratike Aristerá) (Greece)
EDSA	European Distribution System Aircraft
EC	European Community
EEZ	Exclusive Economic Zone
EFA	European Fighter Aircraft
EFTA	European Free Trade Association
EK	Centre Union Party (Enosi Kentrou) (Greece)
EPC	European Political Cooperation
ERE	National Radical Union (Ethniki Rizopastiki Enosis) (Greece)
EUREKA	European Research Coordination Agency
FAR	Force d'Action Rapide
FIR	Flight Information Region
FIR	Forza di Intervento Rapido (Italy)
FLA	Liberation Front of the Azores
FMS	Foreign Military Sales
FNLA	National Liberation Front of Angola
FOPI	Forza di Pronto Intervento
FRELIMO	Mozambican Liberation Movement
FTX	Field Training Exercise
IBERLANT	Subordinate Command of SACLANT
ICAO	International Civil Aviation Organization
ICBM	Intercontinental Ballistic Missile
IEPG	Independent European Programme Group
INF	Intermediate-range Nuclear Forces
IRBM	Intermediate-range Ballistic Missile
JEMAD	Chief of the General Staff
JSP	Joint Strategic Plan
JUSMAPG	Joint United States Military Advisory and Planning Group
KKE	Communist Party (Kommunistiko Komma Ellados) (Greece)
LANDSOUTH	Land Forces Southern Europe (Verona)
LANDSOUTHCENT	Land Forces South-Central (Larissa)
LANDSOUTHEAST	Land Forces South-Eastern Europe (Izmir)
LORAN	Long-range Aids to Navigation
MAC	Military Airlift Command

MAP	Military Assistance Programme
MFA	Movement of the Armed Forces (Portugal)
MFO	Multinational Force and Observers
MNF	Multinational Force
MPAIAC	Movement for the Independence of the Canary Islands
NADGE	NATO Air Defence Ground Environment
NAEW	NATO Airborne Early Warning
NAMSO	NATO Maintenance and Supply Organization
NATO	North Atlantic Treaty Organisation
NAVOCFORMED	Naval On-Call Force Mediterranean
NAVSOUTH	NATO Subordinate Navy Command (Nisida Island, Naples)
NBC	Nuclear, Biological and Chemical
ND	New Democracy Party (Nea Demokratia) (Greece)
NDD	National Defence Directive
NDP	National Defence Plan
NIAG	NATO Industrial Advisory Group
NOTAM	Note to Airmen
NSP	National Salvation Party (Turkey)
OAU	Organization for African Unity
OECD	Organisation for Economic Cooperation and Development
OPEC	Organization of the Petroleum Exporting Countries
PAIGC	African Party for the Independence of Guinea and Cape Verde
PASOK	Panhellenic Socialist Movement (Panellinion Socialistikou Kinema) (Greece)
PCE	Spanish Communist Party (Partido Comunista de España)
PCI	Italian Communist Party (Partito Comunista Italiano)
PCP	Portuguese Communist Party (Partido Comunista Português)
PDP	People's Democratic Party (Partido Demócratico Popular) (Spain)
PLO	Palestine Liberation Organization
PRD	Democratic Renewal Party (Partido Renovador Democrático) (Portugal)
PRI	Italian Republican Party (Partito Repubblicano Italiano)
PS	Socialist Party (Partido Socialista) (Portugal)
PSD	Social Democratic Party (Partido Social Democrata) (Portugal)
PSI	Italian Socialist Party (Partito Socialista Italiano)
PSOE	Spanish Workers' Socialist Party (Partido Socialista Obrero Español)

RPP	Republican People's Party (Cumhuriyet Halk Partisi) (Turkey)
RPR	Rassemblement pour la République (France)
RPV	Remote Pilotless Vehicle
RRP	Rapid Reinforcement Plan
SACEUR	Supreme Allied Commander Europe
SACLANT	Supreme Allied Commander Atlantic
SALT	Strategic Arms Limitation Talks
SAM	Surface-to-Air Missile
SBA	Sovereign Base Area
SDI	Strategic Defense Initiative
SDHP	Social Democratic Populist Party (Sosyal Demokrasi Halkçi Partisi) (Turkey)
SEATO	Southeast Asian Treaty Organization
SETAF	Southern European Task Force
SLOC	Sea Lines of Communication
SNLC	Senior NATO Logisticians Conference
STRIKEFORSOUTH	NATO Subordinate Naval Striking and Support Forces Command (U.S. Sixth Fleet, home ported at Gaeta, Italy)
TSMA	Theatre of Strategic Military Action
UCD	Union of the Democratic Centre (Unión de Centro Democrático) (Spain)
UNCLOS	United Nations Conference on the Law of the Sea
UNIFIL	United Nations Interim Force in Lebanon
UNITA	Union for Total Independence of Angola
WESTLANT	Western Atlantic Command (Norfolk, Virginia)
WEU	Western European Union
WTO	Warsaw Treaty Organization

Tables

Introduction

John Chipman

While Western security is normally regarded as indivisible by those responsible for its maintenance, politicians, military planners and analysts have methodically divided the 'West' into regions and categories. NATO authorities pay hommage to this tendency both formally and informally: for practical needs, through the elaboration of command structures, and, of more dubious utility, through the development of loosely 'military' terms that refer to prospective areas of engagement. Thus, within Europe, attention is paid in varying degrees to the defence of the Central Front and to the Flanks, both Northern and Southern.

Most time has traditionally been spent in the analysis of defence of the front line in West Germany, largely because that line corresponds precisely to the division of Europe: the ideological and juridical reality that makes conflict possible. The fact that Europe is divided at the place named the Central Front, and that opposing forces are most heavily concentrated there, has prompted people to presume that conflict is more likely to occur in the centre than in any other area of the continent. It is probable, also, that because any aggression against the Central Front is (almost by definition) likely to be clear and easily verifiable, planners have necessarily emphasized the importance of that area. Since NATO was established with the aim of defending the status quo in Europe, it makes sense to concentrate on the place where a change would be most evident and have the deepest political ramifications.

It is by no means evident that the Soviet Union would necessarily choose the front line in Germany as the place to begin a military aggression against the West, or that instability in other areas in Europe, whether fomented by the Soviets or not, would be of less importance to the maintenance of Western unity. Any Soviet attack on NATO's Central Front would quite quickly involve the Flanks; and were the Soviets to invade a Flank country first, the West would have to be in a position to contain immediately any initial Soviet successes. The individual states of the Mediterranean region must also be able to deter aggression coming from other sources in the area for the sake of overall security in Europe.

1

It would be impossible to say that the Soviet military threat to the Central Front has declined in recent years, and therefore unwise to argue that the security problems at the Central Front are insignificant or imaginary. Instability in Eastern Europe and tensions between leaders of East and West are recurrent, yet the types of problems that exist, even if potentially very dangerous, contrast sharply with problems elsewhere, which may be more modest in scale but also less easily controllable.

This is especially the case for NATO's Southern Region[1] — for those countries facing south and directly concerned by events in the Mediterranean and North Africa. Many of the non-NATO countries that lie along or near the Mediterranean are particularly susceptible to political drama and outbreaks of violence on a continuous basis. The quickly changing politics in the Middle East are difficult to control and inevitably spill over to other, essentially more stable, countries in the Mediterranean region. Even when there is no immediate prospect of violence in the area, the wide perception of regional volatility conditions the policies of the more stable countries and makes their leaders highly sensitive to the vicissitudes of local politics. Moves towards crisis prevention or attempts to regulate nascent conflict are often considered counterproductive, and a degree of instability is generally thought unavoidable.

If the divide in Germany constitutes the principal symbol of East-West tension, it is also the object of the most sophisticated and controlled form of crisis management. In the Mediterranean, for reasons that are psychological and cultural more than strategic, there is not the same sense of proximity to ultimate disaster. Thus, things become possible in the Southern Region that cannot be contemplated in Central Europe where the major powers have carefully demarcated their policies in the area and generally accept that, given the military situation and the vigilance with which changes in that situation are observed, there is only limited room for action.[2] The Mediterranean, as a region, does not benefit from the same all-encompassing regulatory system of 'deterrence' as do the countries of continental Europe, which play out their tensions according to well-established rules of the game.

Faced as they are with immediate problems in the Mediterranean, where political change rather than maintenance of the status quo is the rule, the states of NATO South can look north to the Central Front and believe in the relative stability of the military situation. Added to the general threat of a possible Soviet aggression against their countries, felt unevenly throughout the south, are a number of threats born of local instability that have various origins and different actors. The variety of the problems that obtain in the Mediterranean, and the complexity of the political perspectives brought to bear on them, make it especially difficult to isolate security challenges that could be the object of *collective* Western policy. Individual defence approaches were thought both appropriate and inevitable. This helps explain why, in the past, there was less concern with the Southern Flank than there is at present, owing to the growing understanding that changes in the nature of the threat require a more collaborative approach. Once the forgotten area of NATO, the Southern Region is benefitting from increasing attention, even if the Central Front inevitably has a certain priority.

One important reason why the organization of Western defence at the Central Front has traditionally been kept the focal point of NATO attention is the ability of the West European powers most immediately implicated to insist on proper attention. The fact that most of the states of NATO South are both poor and inconsistently represented in the various Western fora, makes it more difficult for them to argue their concerns and needs persuasively than is the case with Western Europe's major powers, or even the states of NATO North whose special perspective is perhaps better understood.[3] Many of the states in NATO South, moreover, have dramatically individual views of their security needs. They have differing opinions as to the nature, extent and origins of the challenges that may confront their societies. There is little that links them together. Separated by large distances, the southern member states of NATO share no common frontier. They all, with the exception of Portugal, possess coasts on the Mediterranean but this fact is not a significant unifying factor. The Mediterranean is a geographical entity, yet this does not make it either a political or strategic whole. The Mediterranean is, after all, the only area in the world where Western democracies, communist regimes, non-aligned states, rich oil producers and poor developing countries live side by side.[4] Nevertheless, at a time when people are speaking of 'European security' in almost autonomous terms it now seems vital to analyse its southern aspect more closely.[5]

The difficulty is that to speak of Mediterranean security is to presume a coherent view on the sorts of political or military developments that are acceptable and on the threats to certain areas which would require either individual or collective responses. Leaving aside the specific NATO concerns about a Soviet attack on the Southern Flank — that area in the eastern Mediterranean for whose defence Turkey, Greece and Italy are primarily responsible — there is no general definition of Mediterranean security that can be satisfactory to all NATO members of the Southern Region, and none, *ex hypothesi,* to which all littoral states would agree. While the broad aims of NATO in the Central Front are roughly coextensive with the fears of those NATO powers that lie on the East-West divide (especially West Germany), the security concerns of many states in the Southern Region are perceived as not fully met by NATO. This is so because many of the threats appear to be 'out-of-area' in their origins — even if not in their eventual impact — and for this there is virtually no actual planning. Equally, some of the Southern Region states often consider certain security concerns of the United States in the area to be irrelevant to their special needs, or even counterproductive to their foreign policies. The NATO states in the Southern Region — and those outside the area, such as Britain and the United States which maintain influence in it — may not always be very far apart in their analysis of 'the nature of the threat,' but the expression of their views remains highly individual. The analysis of security problems in the Southern Region is therefore inseparable from an analysis of the political perspectives of the countries having a stake in the Mediterranean.

For NATO, the principal military problem in the Southern Region derives from the fact that because the area constitutes neither a geographic nor a political whole it cannot be the subject of a single military strategy. It is barely possible to speak of a strategy for the Southern Flank, which itself is little more than a juxtaposition of at least four operational theatres. If all countries in NATO South felt that they were prospective victims of the same fate that would already be an advance towards easier internal management of NATO affairs in the region; but this is unlikely to be the case for some time and cannot be the case in certain circumstances. If it is true that the United States and the Soviet Union use the Mediterranean, at least partly, to support and advance their policies elsewhere, it is

4

also true that countries like Portugal, Spain, France, Italy, Greece and Turkey, at different times, in varying degrees, and for a range of motives, also concern themselves with evolving and actual threats in the Third World rather than with those inside NATO's constitutional area of responsibilities. Understanding the individual attitudes of all these countries is therefore an essential precondition for analysing what types of defence preparation properly lie within each state's own hands, and which must be the responsibility of NATO as a whole. The coordination of national policy with NATO strategy represents a challenge that is greater in the Southern Region than in any other area of the Western Alliance.

Any analysis of the Western security situation in the Mediterranean must therefore go beyond an assessment of the sources of foreign threat and the balance of military force. It must examine the roots of national security policies in a region where policy making is highly individual. In a number of these countries, national security refers primarily to security against internal tensions or uprisings rather than external intimidation or direct attack. The balance of power between right and left, or between civilians and the military, is perceived as something that requires careful management, not to say manipulation. Foreign and defence policies must build on a carefully forged national consensus, and equally they help to strengthen a sense of community and statehood. The image that government leaders present to the outside world is crafted to help create an internal sense of purpose and must often be seen in this light. On the other hand, the nature of foreign policy choices and the international relations managed by government leaders also have domestic consequences. This is generally accepted to be the case for all states, but the dynamic between domestic and external ambitions is particularly acute in the countries that form the object of this study given their especially turbulent recent histories.

From time to time, when a spirit of compromise and negotiation characterizes internal politics, this is transposed to the international arena, where the search for détente is seen as a natural extension of the domestic need for stability. More often, the battles that dominate the search for internal order find their complement in foreign policies that appear intransigent and narrow. Relations with an ally, principally the United States, may be more difficult to manage and control than relations with traditional or new enemies, since relations with the United States often become an important issue of domestic politics. For the Southern Periphery countries (Portugal and Spain at one extremity of the Mediterranean, Greece and Turkey at the other), dealings with the United States are a major foreign policy preoccupation; just as these countries would be horrified to find themselves dominated by the Soviet Union, they have a residual fear of becoming partial satellites of the United States. This instinct for 'resistance' against a large power exerting influence in the Mediterranean has its historical roots. To understand the causes of the often very frustrating relationship that the United States has with the countries of this region which it is seeking to protect, it is important to take these roots into account.

This book seeks to do two things. First, it attempts to assess the place of the Southern Region of NATO in the strategic perceptions of both the Soviet Union and the Western Alliance as a whole. The degree to which the peacetime activities of both the United States and the USSR are related to current political needs and ambitions is analysed, and the relevance of these activities to potential wartime goals is examined. The book assesses the political and the military difficulties in arranging for a proper coalition defence against both the Soviet threat and threats coming from other sources. The impact on Alliance cohesion of changing attitudes amongst Alliance members regarding their place in NATO and the nature of Mediterranean security is also analysed. Second, the book looks at the domestic determinants of foreign and security policy in the countries under examination. Debates and struggles between the civilian and military sectors of society and amongst political parties (as well as other important groups where appropriate) are reviewed in an attempt to discover the sources of external policies that may sometimes appear strange or illogical to outsiders. The evolving strengths and weaknesses of various influential élites are assessed with a view to identifying new trends in foreign and defence foreign policy making.

This dual approach allows for an appropriate evaluation of the tensions between national and Alliance-wide priorities in NATO's Southern Region. Leaders in most of the countries under study do not believe that they can have a major impact on the Alliance decision-making process as a whole, yet they can have a quite dramatic influence over the methods and means of local defence in the Southern Region. As these countries emerge from difficult periods of national political and economic development, they may become more assertive in NATO councils as well as in their bilateral relations with other NATO countries. The form and substance of such new confidence, if it does indeed begin to manifest itself, will have implications for a whole range of issues associated with the management of Western security interests in the Mediterranean. The chapters that follow suggest, against the background of recent history, that the NATO allies in the Southern Region will begin to impose their national interests more effectively on other allies, thus making the development of a coherent Western policy for Mediterranean security both more necessary and more complex than has heretofore been the case.

NOTES

1. Throughout the Introduction and the succeeding chapters there are references to NATO's Southern Region, NATO's Southern Periphery and NATO's Southern Flank. While the explanation of these terms is made in the text it seems appropriate to set out in advance the meaning of these distinctions. NATO's Southern Region refers to those NATO states that lie at the southernmost points of NATO's area of responsibility. This groups together Portugal, Spain, France, Italy, Greece and Turkey. NATO's Southern Periphery is used to refer to those states whose strategic concerns are primarily centred on events taking place within the Southern Region, which are economically weaker than the other NATO states and which have traditionally not been as politically active in the full range of Alliance activities as other NATO states. This term roughly groups together those states that are the focus of this study: Portugal, Spain, Greece and Turkey. NATO's Southern Flank refers to those states that have principal responsibility for the defence of the southeastern area of the Southern Region and which are within the Allied Forces Southern Europe (AFSOUTH) area of action. This includes only Italy, Greece and Turkey.

2. Umberto Cappuzzo, 'The New Italian Perception of Security,' *The International Spectator*, XIX, no. 3/4 (July-December 1984): 135.

3. Luigi Caligaris, 'La Defensa del Mediterraneo,' *Revista Ideas*, vol 1 (Madrid, 1984): 366.

4. Contre-Amiral Henri Labrousse, 'La Sécurité en Méditerranée,' *Défense Nationale* (June 1981): 65.

5. Caligaris, 'La Defensa del Mediterraneo': 365.

1

NATO and the Security Problems of the Southern Region: From the Azores to Ardahan

John Chipman

The defence of the NATO countries of southern Europe was not a central concern of Alliance planners who were 'present at the creation' in 1949, even if Portugal and Italy were founder members of the Alliance. The inclusion of Greece and Turkey in NATO (1952) symbolized not a shift in emphasis, but a recognition that these states, which were vulnerable to communist and specifically Soviet threats, would have to be included in the Alliance if the West's interests in the Mediterranean were to be secured. For many, the defence of the Mediterranean was largely conceived to be a necessary condition for the defence of continental Europe. At present, it is no longer correct to think of the Southern Region as an ignored or neglected part of NATO. In the late 1970s and early 1980s numerous high-ranking government and NATO officials warned that insufficient attention was being paid to the area. By the mid-1980s, this problem was largely solved, as analysts began to devote time to the Southern Region. In 1985, NATO itself formally recognized that the relative weakness of Portugal, Greece and Turkey was one of the 'critical deficiencies' that the Alliance had to repair.[1] It will be long before this has an effect on NATO planning, but at least the problems of the Southern Region are officially on NATO's agenda.

These problems are very largely political, but they also have important military and operational aspects. The difficulties of preparing for coalition warfare in the Southern Region are various. The NATO nations of the Mediterranean do not have a long history of operating in wartime alliances which is, no doubt, one of the many psychological root causes of the difficulties encountered by NATO planners in coordinating

Alliance and national plans for the defence of the south. Moreover, the fact that the Southern Region does not present a unified theatre of potential war for which a single strategy can be elaborated is an important practical impediment to full coordination. The Alliance is organized to conduct a defence of the south, but this is still largely dependent on national (and sometimes nationalistic) defence policies and capabilities.

Creating the conditions for a more efficiently integrated defence in the south will require all NATO countries to demonstrate an interest in the area's defence that is proportional to their proximity to the region and their relative size. This chapter assesses the evolving Soviet threat, the continued relevance of U.S. naval power in the Mediterranean, and steps that may be taken to create a more impressive area defence for the numerous theatres of NATO's Southern Region. Engaging the states of the Southern Region in a more openly collective defence is a political challenge that is essential because of the need for a sound policy of deterrence throughout the NATO area. This does not diminish the priority of the Central Front; it is simply that if the Alliance does not appear to take account of threats to the Southern Region, this area may well become the 'liability' some Western leaders once feared.

THE SOVIET UNION AND NATO: MILITARY PERCEPTIONS OF THE SOUTHERN REGION

The Soviet Union's military perception of the Southern Region must be seen in the context of its overall vision of areas of potential military action outside the country. The USSR organizes its military thinking and operational plans into theatres of war and theatres of strategic military action (TSMAs) which correspond to its own strategic priorities and administrative needs. Each of the TSMAs falls within a theatre of war and each, naturally, has a different level of potential military importance for the Soviet Union. This is reflected in the category and readiness of Soviet/Warsaw Pact troops responsible for taking action in these areas. From the Soviet perspective, NATO's Southern Region falls within two different theatres of war and three TSMAs. The first and most important TSMA is the Western one, which is in the most critical area within the Western theatre of war.[2] On the Soviet side, this TSMA takes in

Czechoslovakia, East Germany, Poland and the Baltic and covers the Carpathian, Belorussian and Baltic military districts. On the western side it includes NATO's Central Front, the Baltic exits, and extends to Britain, France and the Iberian peninsula as well as their maritime approaches. The northern part of this TSMA cuts across the south of Sweden and Norway, while the southern part runs down the Alps and includes part of the Algerian and all of the Moroccan coasts. Of the approximately ninety-three Soviet and Warsaw Pact divisions concentrated on the Soviet side of this TSMA, about fifty are considered combat ready. The countries of the Iberian peninsula, therefore, find themselves operationally in the same region as the NATO countries of the Central Front. This does not make these countries central or even ultimate objectives of Soviet political or military strategy, but it implies, at a minimum, that in war, operational lines of attack for the Soviet Union would implicate these countries.

The Southwestern TSMA is widely considered next in importance and is also within the Western theatre of war. It is broadly orientated towards the Balkans, Turkey and the Mediterranean.[3] The Soviet side of the area comprises Bulgaria, Hungary, Rumania and the Odessa and Kiev military districts. The western side covers Italy, Greece and the western part of Turkey as well as that part of the Mediterranean that does not fall within the Western TSMA. Most of the twenty Soviet divisions in this area are stationed inside the Soviet Union, while the twenty-six Warsaw Pact divisions are at a very low level of readiness. This naturally has an effect on the Soviet capacity to launch a major offensive in the area without drawing from forces committed, in principle, to other areas. Military action in this area would consist of joint Warsaw Pact operations in accordance with a general concept for the defeat of NATO forces. Possible lines of operations would be direct attacks on Turkish and Greek Thrace; actions in the Dardanelles, incorporating advances from Bulgaria; and naval operations in the Black Sea to destroy U.S. carrier forces.[4]

Considered separately from these other TSMA's is the Southern TSMA, which is in the Southern theatre of war, but does include some NATO territory. The Southern TSMA begins in the Caucasus and Turkestan and extends to the eastern part of Turkey, Iran, Afghanistan and Pakistan, continuing down through India.[5] In the Soviet perception, Turkey is therefore divided; one part belonging to the Southwestern TSMA, and the other to the Southern TSMA. The Southern TSMA ranks extremely low in Soviet strategic priorities, largely because in almost the whole of this area the Soviet Union does not face a direct, organized threat. Possible lines of operations here would include front operations against eastern Turkey, operations against Iran alone, or a full-scale operation against a combination of states including Turkey and Iran.[6]

It is notoriously difficult to establish from military dispositions precise intentions in war and it would be dangerous to presume, for example, that because the Soviet Union has divided its potential theatres of operations, it believes that activities in that area, which NATO calls the Southern Region, can be insulated one from the other. Rather, this merely indicates that while the Western TSMA is of prime importance, the Southwestern TSMA (which forms part of the Western theatre of war) and the Southern TSMA (which is a different theatre of war) are all possible areas of opportunity for the Soviet Union whose planning does not divide so 'neatly' as does that of NATO, between in-area and out-of-area activity.

If NATO and the Warsaw Pact naturally have asymmetrical views as to how the area should be divided operationally, both would agree on the *importance* of the stake. It is sufficient simply to state the level of international maritime traffic in the Mediterranean to see this: more than 1,500 ocean-going ships and 5,000 smaller craft travel it each day. It is a vital route for the international oil trade, especially for Europe as over 50 percent of its petroleum imports arrive via the Mediterranean. It is economically vital for the Soviet Union, since 50 percent of its imports and 60 percent of its exports pass through the Mediterranean.[7] The Mediterranean basin is also likely to become more important as a source of hydrocarbon materials.[8] The economic resources of the Sea are potentially vast and have unfortunately often been an object of conflict between the riparian states rather than a subject for cooperation.

From a purely military perspective, it is a truism that during any conflict in Europe or the Middle East, control of the Mediterranean would be a precondition of military success for the NATO or Warsaw Pact powers. This fact is recognized by all states concerned; whether external ones seeking political influence, or local ones understanding the value of what they can offer in terms of promises of neutrality or commitments to

11

act. It is impossible, especially in the case of generalized conflict in Europe, that the Southern Region be accorded less priority — to the extent that one can speak in these terms given the nature of modern warfare — than the Central Front. The resupply of Western Europe as well as the prevention of certain Soviet gains would depend on an ability to keep open (or to close) the relevant choke points. In war, it would be very important for the Soviets to control the Turkish Straits (which the West would want to prevent); while NATO would be especially concerned to ensure that the Straits of Gibraltar would be secure so that necessary reinforcements for Greece, Italy and Turkey would be assured (an objective that the Soviets would wish to hinder). Of course, it is in the nature of the special rivalry between the superpowers that there are general political advantages to be gained, separable from eventual military contingencies, in seeking to win friends and influence others throughout the Mediterranean.

It is this political competition that gives some meaning to the idea of 'Western security' in the Mediterranean; but it is not an idea uniformly held or powerfully shared by all Western countries in the south. While in the Central Front there is an almost perfect identity of interests between the United States and its West European allies (although not perfect agreement on the methods to defend them), this cannot be the case in the Mediterranean. For both superpowers, their activity in the Mediterranean is related as much to their own individual interests beyond Europe as it may be to the protection of their Alliance partners. Because of this, if conflict arose between the two superpowers in the Mediterranean, it would probably be related to a political problem to which the members of the two alliances feel alien.[9] It is awareness of this fact that makes many countries in NATO South assert their own individual and local concerns with particular energy; and the implication of these assertions is often that NATO does not adequately provide for their security. There is also a generalized feeling among these states that U.S. policy in the Mediterranean region is sometimes irrelevant or contrary to their needs. This is not simply out of a fear that they will be dragged into a conflict in which they have no interest, but also, more positively, a desire to show that their own foreign policies need not be subservient to the logic of the East-West competition. Precisely because it is at the Central Front where that competition is most strongly felt, there is a natural tendency amongst the countries of the Southern Region, that surfaces from time to time, to argue that they need not be implicated in all aspects of the East-West struggle. It is perhaps not an historical accident, but a geographical and political inevitability, that it is in NATO South where ideas of a 'Third Force' and national 'independence' are often the strongest.

However, Western planners are now coming to realize the artificiality of separating the Flanks from the Central Front and the principal dangers of an East-West conflict. In terms of nuclear war, it is true that there are no military targets in the Mediterranean or nuclear weapons systems (at present) crucial for U.S. *strategic* capacities in nuclear war (with the exception, perhaps, of cruise missiles stationed in Sicily).[10] Nevertheless, most Mediterranean countries, because of their location, are certainly of strategic importance in the case of conventional conflict, wherever it may begin, especially given the rising need, because of the development of new technologies, for appropriate land-based forces in sea conflicts.[11] The possible use by the Soviet Union, in the event of a general East-West conflict, of facilities in that part of the Mediterranean lying outside the NATO area means that just as the distinction between Central Front and Southern Region contingencies is likely to be blurred, so is the separation of NATO and non-NATO problems.

For practical purposes, NATO naturally divides the area it has to defend into specific regions. Within Allied Command Europe's (ACE) military areas, the Southern Region is the largest, comprising about four million square miles. The immediate responsibility for the NATO defence of the area lies at Allied Forces Southern Europe (AFSOUTH) in Naples, whose wartime mission is to defend Italy, Greece and Turkey, as well as the sea lines of communication throughout the Mediterranean and Black Seas. Five Principal Subordinate Commands (two land, two naval and one air) have been established to fulfil this purpose: AIRSOUTH (Naples), LANDSOUTH (Verona), LANDSOUTHEAST (Izmir), NAVSOUTH (Nisida Island, Naples), and STRIKEFORSOUTH (U.S. Sixth Fleet, home ported at Gaeta, Italy) (see Table 1.1).

The duties of each of the commanders are vast. COMAIRSOUTH must defend the airspace along a 3,600-kilometre border stretching from the Italian Alps to eastern Turkey, and does so through the 5th Allied Tactical Air Force (ATAF) at

Table 1.1: NATO military command structure — Elements in the Mediterranean and adjoining area

North Atlantic Council (Brussels) and Defence Planning Committee

Military Committee and International Military Staff (Brussels)

```
Supreme Allied Commander Atlantic,           Supreme Allied Commander Europe,
SACLANT (Norfolk, Virginia)                  SACEUR (Casteau, Belgium)

Commander Iberian                            Commander-in-Chief Allied Forces
Atlantic Area,                               Southern Europe,
COMIBERLANT                                  CINCSOUTH (Naples, Italy)
(Oeiras, Portugal)

Island Commander
(Madeira)
```

Commander Allied Naval Forces Southern Europe, COMNAVSOUTH (Naples)

Commander Naval Striking and Support Forces Southern Europe (Naples)

Commander Land Forces Southern Europe (Verona) COMLANDSOUTH

Commander Air Forces Southern Europe COMAIRSOUTH (Naples)

Commander Land Forces South-Eastern Europe, COMLANDSOUTHEAST (Izmir)

Commander Land Forces South-Central Europe COMLANDSOUTHCENT (Larissa)

Commander 5th ATAF (Vicenza)

Commander 6th ATAF (Izmir)

Commander 7th ATAF (Larissa)

Western Mediterranean Area, MEDOC (formerly Toulon, now exercised by NAVSOUTH directly)

Central Mediterranean Area, MEDCENT (Naples)

North Eastern Mediterranean Area, MEDNOREAST (Ankara)

Maritime Air Mediterranean, MARAIRMED (Naples)

Gibraltar Mediterranean Area, GIBMED (Gibraltar)

Eastern Mediterranean Area, MEDEAST (Athens)

South Eastern Mediterranean Area, MEDSOUEAST (formerly Malta, now exercised by NAVSOUTH directly)

Submarines Mediterranean SUBMED (Naples)

Key:
——— chain of command
– – – new commands proposed in Rogers plan
· · · co-located headquarters

Vicenza, and the 6th ATAF at Izmir, while a 7th ATAF in Greece is still a subject for negotiation. AIRSOUTH is the only command in the Southern Region that has NATO forces under its control perpetually in peacetime. COMLANDSOUTH is responsible for the defence of the western portion of the Southern Flank: the Veneto-Friuli plain. His wartime mission is to defend the area as far forward as possible (to ensure that the Southern Region does not become 'separated' from the Central Front), and, most importantly, to prevent oncoming forces access to the Po plain, Italy's most industrialized area. COMLANDSOUTHEAST has the task of protecting the Turkish flank, and particularly the 600- kilometre border with the Soviet Union, which the USSR might decide to cross if ever it wished direct access to Middle East oil supplies. The staff, as in all other AFSOUTH headquarters, is composed of Turkish, British, Italian and American personnel (LANDSOUTHEAST and 6th ATAF in Izmir are the only AFSOUTH headquarters in which Greek personnel do not also participate). Because of the sometimes extraordinary age of much of Turkey's armaments, LANDSOUTHEAST is most in need of more sophisticated weaponry of almost all types.

COMNAVSOUTH has responsibility for six geographical areas: Gibraltar-Mediterranean, central Mediterranean, eastern Mediterranean, northeastern Mediterranean, western Mediterranean, and southeastern Mediterranean. The latter two areas are under his direct command while the other four are under other naval commanders who have specific authority over each zone. Among NAVSOUTH's more important tasks is coordinating on a twenty-four hour basis the surveillance of Soviet bloc maritime forces from its surveillance coordination centre in Italy. NAVSOUTH works closely with STRIKEFORSOUTH. COMSTRIKEFORSOUTH is responsible for largely the same area as is COMNAVSOUTH and has the general task of deterring all forms of aggression against the NATO states in the Mediterranean. STRIKEFORSOUTH has three subordinate commands at its disposal: Task Force 502 (Carrier Striking Forces), Task Force 503 (Amphibious Forces) and Task Force 504 (Landing Forces). Although the two naval commands have similar areas of action, in practice, COMNAVSOUTH would be responsible in wartime for the safeguard of supply lines in the Mediterranean while STRIKEFORSOUTH's mission would be directed more towards the projection of power ashore.[12] In general, NAVSOUTH is geographically orientated: it must assure the security of the Mediterranean through anti-submarine warfare and protection of convoys; STRIKEFORSOUTH is functionally orientated: it must be prepared to take measures of various kinds to defeat the Soviet presence in the Mediterranean and assist in the land battle in Europe.

Since the late 1970s, AFSOUTH has been concerned about the relatively slow reaction by NATO powers to the Soviet buildup in the Mediterranean, both on land and at sea, and by the fact that NATO planners have been most concerned by the possibility of a Soviet threat on the Central Front. At the Central Front, the Soviet Union is heavily opposed not only by ground forces, but also by tactical nuclear forces and the strategic deterrents of three NATO powers. A war on the Southern Flank is probably inconceivable outside the context of a general European conflict, but if the Soviet Union merely wanted to test Alliance solidarity, it would probably be more profitable to attempt this in the south rather than at the centre.[13] Most allies have not been too concerned about the prospect of a threat in the south. Had the United States been truly concerned about this threat, it probably would not have instituted an arms embargo against Turkey from 1974 to 1978 after the latter's invasion of Cyprus. The period of détente, that coincided roughly with this embargo, made it easy to believe that the progressive weakening of defences in Southern Region countries (through old age, insufficient modernization, and an increase in enemy capacities) need not be a cause for immediate alarm. Paradoxically, the approximate 'end of détente' coincided with the end of Soviet naval (if not land or air) buildup in the Mediterranean area. The need remains, however, for NATO powers to develop their capacities to deter a threat that has increased, if stabilized, in the last decade.

THE EVOLVING SOVIET THREAT AND NATO STRATEGY

Traditionally, as strategists have turned their minds to the security situation in the Mediterranean, they have concentrated on its naval aspects. The rise of Soviet naval power in the Sea in the 1970s reinforced the natural and inevitable tendency to see in naval power the barometer of military security and political stability. This increase in Soviet naval power has now levelled off. At sea, the Soviet Union has a presence that removes from the United States its former near monopoly of naval-based military influence in the Mediterranean region. The Soviet Union, too, can now 'show the flag.' But as this naval power has established itself, other Soviet improvements, notably in land-based air power, have made the USSR a more credible threat in the south. The Soviet Union now has a capacity to threaten, at a distance, the whole Southern Region, so that the long coastlines of the NATO Mediterranean states and their forces at sea cannot remain immune to Soviet power.

The specific nature of U.S.-Soviet political competition strengthens the idea that the struggle for power in the Southern Region takes place at sea. The history and nature of Soviet sea power in the Mediterranean must therefore be analysed, but more to prove that, having established a basic presence, the Soviet Union has seen fit to control its growth and it is in other areas that Soviet military power challenges the West. Perhaps this more diversified and generalized capacity to threaten Western interests in the south will force NATO to take a more comprehensive and collective view of what constitutes security in the Southern Region.

The Soviet Navy and the Politics of Presence

The development of a Soviet naval interest in the Mediterranean dates from the period 1957–1958 when Soviet leaders made political decisions to increase their conventional abilities to project power abroad. Procurement programmes were established that would make it possible, ten years later, for the Soviet Union to indulge in coercive naval diplomacy. The Cuban missile crisis of 1962 showed the superiority of American naval power and reinforced, from the Soviet perspective, policies that were already underway for the expansion of naval capacities. The presence in the Mediterranean of the U.S. Sixth Fleet able to launch nuclear attacks against the Soviet Union was a threat which the Soviets felt had to be dealt with; just as the decline of British and French power in the Levant and North Africa created a political vacuum that the USSR wanted to fill.[14]

While it is true that Soviet submarines were stationed at Valona Bay in Albania from 1958 to 1961 (a Soviet cruiser and

17

two destroyers had first paid a port call to Albania in 1954), these did not perform any important political or military roles.[15] The new naval programme launched by Nikita Khrushchev in the late 1950s was aimed at ensuring that Soviet naval forces could properly carry out a true internationalist mission in every major body of water over the globe. From 1965, the Soviets began deploying detachments from their Black Sea Fleet in the Mediterranean, and the size of the Soviet Mediterranean squadron (Sovmedron, or Fifth Eskadra as it is often called) grew steadily over the ensuing years. This presence has always been justified on the (curious) grounds that the Soviet Union is a littoral state — since its access to the Mediterranean is direct through the Black Sea, which in the Soviet view forms a distinctive gulf of the Mediterranean. According to Soviet declarations, this is in contrast to the American position: the Sixth Fleet, for the Soviets, is an 'alien' or 'foreign' presence in the region.

These statements aside, it is clear that the decision to deploy a relatively large naval force in the Mediterranean was a result of a perceived need to show the flag. The succinct statement of Admiral Sergey Gorshkov in 1962, to the effect that 'the Soviet Navy ... is obliged to be prepared at any moment and at any point of the globe to secure the protection and interests of our state,' suffices as a general explanation of why the Soviets chose to develop a greater naval presence.[16] In the Mediterranean, these deployments were initially also intended to counter U.S. ballistic missile submarines operating in the Sea, although Soviet anti-submarine detection capability was so low as to make this mission almost impossible. More significant was the growing importance of the Soviet fleet's mission to counter U.S. cruisers, with surface-to-surface missile armed submarines, cruisers and destroyers.

This presence in the Mediterranean quickly became a source of some concern for the West; though the mere fact of a Soviet presence must be distinguished from a latent Soviet military threat to Western states or challenge to Western political and economic order. Certainly the improvement in Soviet naval capacities did not in and of itself signify a heightened threat to the West.[17] Initially, the Sovmedron was exclusively a symbolic and defensive force. Up to 1967, in fact, the Soviets frequently called for the denuclearization of the Mediterranean and the creation of a zone of peace in the area. These statements reflected concern over the strategic threat posed by the Sixth Fleet and the corresponding incapacity of the Sovmedron to offer a credible counter to the Americans in the area.[18] But after the Middle East war of June 1967, the Soviets became engaged in making dramatic improvements both in their force levels and in their operational tactics, thus giving themselves a wider range of political and military options.

The main obstacle to the projection of Soviet power in the Mediterranean has remained the terms of the 1936 Montreux Convention, which limit the size of the ships that can be brought through the Black Sea into the Mediterranean and require the Soviet Union to give the Turkish government eight days notice of transit through the Straits by warships (see Table 1.2). These requirements persist to this day, but the Soviets, in increasing the size of their squadron in 1967, also initiated the practice of

Table 1.2: Soviet naval transits of the Turkish Straits 1964–1985

Year	Auxiliary transits	Surface combatant transits	Total
1964	56	39	95
1965	80	49	129
1966	71	82	153
1967	149	93	242
1968	113	117	230
1969	142	121	263
1970	149	122	271
1971	154	123	277
1972	140	114	254
1973	159	126	285
1974	145	93	238
1975	146	79	225
1976	63	69	132
1977	103	82	185
1978	121	107	228
1979	129	94	223
1980	124	111	235
1981	158	160	318
1982	134	94	228
1983	132	113	245
1984	137	86	223

Source: Western European Union, 'European security and the Mediterranean,' Assembly, 32nd Ordinary Session (second part), Document 1073 (14 October 1986), 11. Figures for 1981, which do not appear in the WEU report, are taken directly from: République de Turquie, Ministère des Affaires Etrangères, *Rapport Annuel sur le mouvement des navires à travers Les Detroits Turcs*, 1981, 45th year (Ankara, 1982).

'contingency declarations,' stating that a ship would transit, but sending it only if a diplomatic or military need arose. This practice allows the Soviets to send forces more rapidly into the Mediterranean at the outbreak of a crisis.[19] Of course, a rapid egress of ships from the Black Sea is difficult, and a dramatic increase in declarations and consequent transits would not be conducive to strategic surprise.[20] Furthermore, in time of general war the Soviets must assume that passage through the Straits will be denied them unless they are able to occupy the Dardanelles, free the Straits from mines, and control the airspace above.[21]

The Turks are careful to apply the terms of the Montreux Treaty as rigorously as circumstances allow. Although Turkey is subject to continuous pressure from the Soviet Union for more liberal and 'modern' interpretations of the Treaty it must be presumed that it is in the Turkish interest, as well as that of the West, for Turkey to maintain as much control over the Straits as possible. Equally, Soviet policy is to do by stealth what cannot be done overtly, and recently the USSR has been successful in introducing larger and more sophisticated warships into the Mediterranean by carefully defining their characteristics so as to conform to the terms of the Montreux Treaty. The Soviet Union's ability to do this is central to its political strategy; in circumstances short of general war, movements of the Black Sea Fleet into the Mediterranean can still serve very important objectives. It is doubtful whether the Soviets could legally bring a fully fledged aircraft carrier through the Straits. However, there has always been concern that if the Soviets did attempt to bring such a ship through, the Convention might not be invoked. This worry has mounted ever since the Soviets developed their Kiev-class carrier in 1976 and has intensified because of speculation that a large carrier is now being developed at the construction yard in Nikolaev and may eventually be brought into the Mediterranean.[22]

Despite the constraints of the Montreux Convention, the experience of Soviet naval activity during the June 1967 war — when the Soviet Union assigned combatants to follow each major Western carrier group, mounted a resupply and airlift to the Arabs, and discreetly threatened a direct military intervention — gave the Soviets a sense of the value of their navy in the exercise of coercive diplomacy.[23] By the time of the Jordanian crisis of September 1970, when King Hussein's regime was threatened by Syria and by a range of Palestinian groups, the Fifth Eskadra had grown sufficiently in size to allow it to inhibit U.S. freedom of action. From September to October 1970, the Soviets increased the size of their squadron from forty-six to sixty ships and had sufficient cruise-missile-equipped combatants and submarines to match the two Sixth Fleet attack carrier groups.[24] As it happened, Soviet ambitions in the Jordanian crisis were ambiguous, but the presence of the Eskadra affected the mobility of the Sixth Fleet and made clear that Soviet interests in the region would have to be considered carefully by the United States before any major operation (such as a shore landing) was considered. The presence of Soviet naval forces during the Jordanian crisis also helped give substance to the Soviet claim that it was protecting the Arab world from Western imperialism.[25]

The height of Soviet naval activity in the Mediterranean in defence of political interests in the Middle East came with the war of 1973. During the crisis month of October, Soviet warships began by simply shadowing American ones, but by the end of the month, after the American defence alert, the Soviets initiated anti-carrier exercises against the Independence task force. To the extent that this threat was credible, it was so only because of the high state of tension between the two superpowers at the time. In less dramatic circumstances a Soviet threat of this kind would probably be discounted, as such an act of war could well lead to a general outbreak of hostilities unjustifiable by the local interests at stake. The threat of 1973 was probably the most intense signal the Soviets have ever transmitted with their naval forces.[26]

Throughout this period, much of Soviet political activity in the Mediterranean was linked to the need to acquire appropriate facilities that would make this sort of naval diplomacy easier. Most of Soviet access diplomacy in the 1950s, 1960s, and early 1970s, was related to the Soviet effort to build and sustain influence with the Arab states. However, the importance, for general political purposes, of maintaining a force in the Mediterranean was certainly as vital for the USSR as was a specific capacity to aid militarily any given Middle Eastern state.[27] Given that the Soviet Union has no national ports in the Mediterranean, access to the facilities of others was a necessary precondition to any prolonged Soviet naval activity in the area. Furthermore, the fact of easy access, in certain circumstances, to foreign ports helped make the Soviet presence in the Mediterranean appear normal; this normalization of the Soviet presence in turn assisted the Soviet Union gain rights elsewhere. The success of its access policy has, nevertheless, been mixed: the Soviets have lost facilities in Albania and in Egypt, and have never succeeded in gaining full base rights in any Mediterranean port. Donor states have traditionally been wary of granting the USSR facilities that could not be unilaterally revoked.

By the same token, the forced departure of Soviet submarines from their enclave in Valona Bay in 1961, after Soviet-Albanian relations had soured owing to the Sino-Soviet split, made the USSR particularly leery of entering into agreements on which it could not rely. All facility agreements that the Soviet Union has made with Mediterranean states have been the result of a mutual perception of shared security interests, and these can be subject to radical redefinitions. There are no *natural* local donors to the Soviet Union, and its ability to preposition in the area, or to reinforce rapidly, is thus compromised by a need perpetually to negotiate adequate rights on the basis of political expedience. The principal problem for the Soviet Union is that the nature and the extent of rights that it is able to acquire in the Mediterranean directly affect decisions on both the size and composition of the Soviet Mediterranean squadron. It is generally acknowledged that there is a strong correlation between the nature and magnitude of the Soviet naval presence in the Mediterranean and the navy's ability to meet its requirements for sea- and land-based support.[28] When the Soviet surface navy began to make its presence felt in the Mediterranean in 1964, it did so when various technological developments had made the fleet easier to protect. The possession of the shipborne surface-to-air missile (SAM), for example, made it realistic to send combatants without separate air cover. Even more important, however, was the fact that the Soviet Union was able to introduce sophisticated submarines into the Mediterranean that very much complicated the tasks of Western navies. Access to various Egyptian facilities in the wake of the June 1967 war allowed the Soviets to become much more daring in their Mediterranean deployments.

These rights, which were codified in the Soviet-Egyptian agreement of March 1968, included virtually exclusive use of seven airfields in Egypt, though, in fact, Soviet fighters based in this country did not operate a great deal in the Mediterranean for fleet air defence.[29] Possibly more important for the Sovmedron was the fact that Egypt offered it the use of four harbours along the Mediterranean coast: Port Said, Alexandria, Mersa Matruh, and Sollum, as well as Berenice in the Red Sea. The squadron's combatants were given anchorages at Sollum, and its amphibious warfare contingent was for some time accommodated at Port Said. Much of the fleet's maritime patrol and surveillance aircraft were based at Mersa Matruh. Alexandria, the centre of Soviet naval activities from 1968 to 1972, provided mid-deployment repair and maintenance of the squadron's conventional submarines.[30] Many of these facilities were withdrawn in July 1972 when President Sadat decided to nationalize all foreign military installations. He also expelled Soviet advisors serving in the Egyptian armed forces. In May 1975, Soviet combatants were denied access to the Sollum and Mersa Matruh harbours and, by March 1976, the USSR was formally asked to leave Egypt and to remove all remaining units from Alexandria.

The Soviet Union's early hopes of creating in Egypt the infrastructure necessary to support fully the operations of its Mediterranean fleet were therefore destroyed within a few years of their formation. The loss of Eygptian facilities affected both the structure of Sovmedron and Soviet policy towards other potential donors of facilities. From 1972 onwards, in fact, the Soviet Union began to reduce the number of surface combatants it brought into the Mediterranean as if aware that their maintenance at Egyptian facilities could not be assured. At the same time — since Eygpt was still willing to service Soviet submarines during this period — submarine deployments (primarily from the northern fleet) increased, in partial compensation for a decline in the Eskadra's surface combatant strength.[31]

After the 1973 conflict and in view of the new Egyptian attitude, the Soviet Union sought expanded access to the Syrian ports at Tartus and Latakia. This shift to Syrian facilities was accompanied by a decision to develop an elaborate arms transfer policy to that country. From 1973 to 1976 the USSR transferred to Syria MiG 23 and SU 20 fighters, Scud surface-to-surface missiles, SAM-3, 6 and 7, T-62 tanks, modern artillery and armoured personnel carriers. There were several motives for making these transfers, but an important one was the desire to show other states the advantages that might accrue to them for providing the Soviet Union with strategic access.[32] These arrangements were in no sense guaranteed, however, and during the Lebanese crisis of 1976 Soviet naval access to Syrian ports was cut and arms transfers to that country declined drastically before being taken up seriously again in 1982.[33] In the late 1970s the increase in Soviet arms shipments to Libya can perhaps be traced to a desire to gain air and naval facilities at Tobruk and Benghazi.

Further west in the Mediterranean, the Soviet Union has been interested in acquiring rights in the Maghreb that would facilitate the Eskadra's manoeuvrability. As early as 1966, Soviet naval units made operational visits to the ports of Oran, Algiers and Annaba, but the Soviets have been unsuccessful in gaining full rights at the principal port of Mers el-Kebir, evacuated by the French in 1968.[34] This failure has occurred despite considerable arms transfers to Algeria in support of its position in the western Sahara conflict. For the Algerians, there is no perceived benefit in partly releasing to the Soviet navy a prize they only recently regained from the French.

Of all the littoral states with which the Soviets have dealt for access rights over the years, only Yugoslavia offered facilities that were not directly connected either to special arms shipments or to (even temporarily) shared security interests in the area. While it is true that during the late 1960s and early 1970s Yugoslav leaders made repeated reference to the threatening nature of the Sixth Fleet, and the concomitant right of the Soviet Union to establish a defensive presence in the Mediterranean, the decision in 1974 to allow the Soviets certain privileges at Yugoslav ports and shipyards was taken largely for economic reasons. In 1974, the Soviet Union began to have its diesel submarines refitted at the modernized Tivat naval yard and arranged for the maintenance of various naval auxiliaries at the civilian shipyards of Trojir and Bijela. These facilities were granted to the Soviets on a purely commercial basis — though not for hard currency. The Yugoslavs were at all points concerned to gain financially from the Soviet use of their facilities without tarnishing their non-aligned image. Accordingly, when in 1976 the Soviet Union began to request an enlargement of these privileges, as well as a more liberal attitude towards overflight rights, Yugoslavia categorically refused any modification of the policy established in 1974.[35] A Balkan strategy that would bring Yugoslavia and Albania more enthusiastically into the Soviet orbit would naturally improve the USSR's ability to sustain a force in the Mediterranean. Although this may continue to be a long-term aim of the Soviet Union, it seems equally far from being realized.[36]

The history of its access diplomacy suggests the difficulty the Soviet Union has had in maintaining rights to important ports and shipyards in the Mediterranean. Since the loss of facilities in Egypt, no significant progress has been made towards finding suitable alternatives. It may well be the case that the Soviet Union has accorded a lower priority to its access diplomacy in the 1980s than before, in the belief that such rights are now less important owing to various technological advances made by the armed forces. It may also have run out of possible options. Over the last decade the Soviet Union has been effectively pushed out of the 'inner ring' of Mediterranean states and forced to look towards such countries as Syria, Libya, Yemen, Aden, Ethiopia, and (to a lesser extent and at different times) Iran and Iraq. The few Soviet successes among these states (notably with Ethiopia) have had a greater impact on Soviet capacities in the Indian Ocean than in the Mediterranean.[37] Although the Soviet navy, like other major navies, will probably improve its ability to sustain its principal combatants with various support ships and protect them with land-based armaments, there are still natural limits to these sorts of half-measures.

For the moment, the Soviet Union has to satisfy itself, in peacetime, with a rather modest level of activity in the Mediterranean. The size of the Sovmedron has stabilized to an average of seven combatants, six submarines and thirty-one auxiliaries (a total average of forty-four vessels) on any given day. Currently the ship days of the Sovmedron have levelled off at approximately 16,000 ship days per year from a high of 21,000 in 1973. Except in times of crisis this presence is also not very active. In fact, the Mediterranean squadron spends most of its time at anchor. These anchorages are in protected places in the open sea, off the coasts of various countries, but beyond the limits of the territorial sea. The most important anchorages are in the Gulf of Hammamet off the Tunisian coast, the Gulf of Sollum off Libya, one to the east of Crete, and another off Lemnos in the east Aegean. During exercises the Sovmedron also uses anchorages off Kithera in southern Greece and south of Cape Passero off Sicily.[38] Manoeuvres and steaming from one port to another take up less than a quarter of the Sovmedron's time,[39] but Soviet submarines in the Mediterranean (which are becoming increasingly quieter and do not have to snorkel so often) spend about 90 percent of their time at sea.

The Role of the U.S. Sixth Fleet

It remains the case that so long as the U.S. Sixth Fleet continues to maintain the rights in the Mediterranean that it has acquired over time, it will continue to have an important comparative advantage over the Soviet Union in the area, though for a number of reasons it can no longer consider itself as secure as before. Current Soviet military options have to be examined in the context of the Sixth Fleet's changing role.

At least until the mid-1960s, the Sixth Fleet's position within the Mediterranean was clearly paramount; the only other warships in the Mediterranean being either allied or insignificant.[40] Until 1963, there were no Soviet warships in the Mediterranean.[41] Although the Soviet Union did have submarines that could move into the area, and possessed Tu-16 naval bombers that were within striking range of U.S. carrier forces in the eastern Mediterranean, the military threat posed by these instruments was largely discounted owing to the perceived impossibility that they could be used except in the most extreme of political circumstances. Certainly neither Soviet submarines, nor Soviet naval bombers, could be used as forces of political persuasion or blackmail. The Sixth Fleet was therefore able to move within the Mediterranean, and show the flag with full confidence that its political weight would be felt by those it wished to influence. Its main advantage was its flexibility. It could control sea lanes, project power ashore, land troops and shell coastal targets. The Soviet Union had only a dramatic option: strategic attack against the United States, or unimpressive ones: anti-shipping tasks against third parties or coastal defence on its own behalf.[42]

This advantage of the Sixth Fleet in the Mediterranean was one the United States exploited in both overt and subtle ways. When, on 20 April 1957, 1,800 U.S. marines anchored off the coast of Beirut in readiness for a possible intervention in Jordan to support King Hussein, the Sixth Fleet carried out manoeuvres in the eastern Mediterranean, thus adding credibility to the

United States' position. Similarly, in July 1958, the Sixth Fleet assisted the landings of almost 15,000 U.S. troops in Beirut to support, in President Eisenhower's words: 'the independence and integrity of Lebanon.'[43] Both operations were successful. Thereafter, the Sixth Fleet in the Mediterranean was understood to be a deterrent force which had to be taken into account by anyone whose actions might adversely affect U.S. interests in the area; the nature of U.S. interests as well as the capacities of the Fleet meant that the area in question included the entire Middle East. Also, in the late 1950s and early 1960s, U.S. carrier forces sustained the entire naval contribution to the American strategic deterrent and the eastern Mediterranean was their most advantageous location.[44] By the late 1960s and early 1970s, much of this had changed. The prospective wartime activity of the Sixth Fleet became limited to a number of narrowly defined roles: air power support to local (Greek and Turkish) troops during the first stages of a defensive battle; air strikes against the southern part of the Soviet Union as part of a counterattack; or direct support for NATO defenders in the Central Front in the event of a Soviet assault there.[45]

For most of its existence, up until 1979, the Sixth Fleet was composed of about forty ships including escorts and replenishment vessels. The surface forces operated as three distinct groups: two carrier battle groups (CVBG) and an amphibious task group. In theory, operations covered the whole Mediterranean, but usually one CVBG operated in the central Mediterranean, and the other in the western Mediterranean.[46] After 1979, only one CVBG was kept in the Mediterranean, though from time to time there were two as rotations took place. Following events in Afghanistan and Iran, it was decided to deploy more naval forces in the Persian Gulf/Indian Ocean area, and this came largely at the expense of the Sixth Fleet in the Mediterranean. Since March 1986, there has been a return to the old policy, with usually two CVBGs in the Mediterranean. Clearly, with two aircraft carriers in the Mediterranean, the U.S. Sixth Fleet represents a potent force. Yet even with two CVBGs, the variety of useful missions related to power projection that the Sixth Fleet could perform is limited. Over the years the Fleet has learned to operate alongside other Western navies deployed in the Mediterranean and collaboration between these forces is quite good. It is certain, however, that if events in the Gulf

27

region require an increased American naval presence, this may result in a drawdown of Sixth Fleet assets, significantly reducing the capacity to perform certain missions.

The realistic military role of the Sixth Fleet for purely intra-Mediterranean contingencies is very different from what it was earlier, as countervailing Soviet power, based both on land and at sea, has made its presence felt. Questions can now reasonably be asked as to exactly what role the Sixth Fleet could be expected to play in a generalized European conflict. Would the one hundred or so aircraft at the Sixth Fleet's disposal (added to the 4,000 land-based NATO aircraft that would be expected in the European continent during a war) make any real difference between victory and defeat, especially since most of the Sixth Fleet's aircraft are required for its own defence?[47] At least some analysts have argued that if prepositioning and forward defence is an appropriate strategy for a land theatre that lacks geographical depth, this is not necessarily the case for naval forces. The paradox of the NATO role of most naval forces is that, in the words of Admiral Bagley, 'the innate strategic flexibility of ships in the Mediterranean is exchanged for the immobility of land-based forces in whose stead they serve.'[48] Is it right for an inherently mobile force to assume a fixed posture similar to that of foot soldiers on the ground in central Europe? If war did break out in Europe, it is likely that the Sixth Fleet would wish to move throughout the Mediterranean and conduct, from wherever it might be located, a perimeter defence in depth coupled with appropriate counterattacks against any enemy forces within its reach. Such action would not necessarily mean defence *for* the Central Front, or defence *in* the eastern Mediterranean. Probably the principal contributions that carrier-based U.S. air power could make to NATO's conventional forces in the eastern Mediterranean are twofold. First, it could bring to bear extremely sophisticated air defence assets (F-14 and F-18 fighters and E-2C airborne early-warning aircraft) to bolster the limited and somewhat obsolescent air defence forces of Greece and Italy. Second, there is some capacity to deploy offensive air support (in the form of A-6 light bombers) that have a large combat radius, a large payload and an all-weather flight capacity. Use of these assets is still very dependent on what is available after the specific defence needs of the Sixth Fleet have been provided for, and, as indicated, it will be difficult, given the rise of Soviet air power, to release much Sixth Fleet aircraft for offensive purposes. Clearly in its one carrier battle group formation the Sixth Fleet would have more difficulties carrying out its missions in the eastern Mediterranean than would be the case if two carriers were deployed.[49]

Despite the Soviet naval buildup in the Mediterranean, most naval strategists believe that the Sixth Fleet would carry the day in a strictly naval exchange with the Soviet Eskadra. But the Fleet's capacity to assist in the land battle has certainly decreased, and the threat that Soviet land-based air power poses for it is such that its freedom of operation in the Mediterranean is less than it once was. The primary mission of the Sixth Fleet in a NATO/Warsaw Pact contingency might therefore be more orientated towards sea control than towards power projection; unless the Soviet air threat were neutralized, in which case, the Sixth Fleet might be able to provide some assistance to the conventional battle in Europe. A nuclearization of the naval conflict in the Mediterranean would in all likelihood drive the Sixth Fleet and other allied navies out of the Sea.

What the Sixth Fleet (or STRIKEFORSOUTH) may do in the event of a European war should, in any case, be distinguished from what it can do in peacetime, and from what both allies and potential enemies believe it might do in various other contingencies. Because of the increase in Soviet naval power in the Mediterranean, it is true that the general *political* utility of the Sixth Fleet in time of peace has now been challenged. The Sixth Fleet, nevertheless, remains the principal symbol of the U.S. guarantee to its Mediterranean allies, just as U.S. troops in West Germany give substance to the U.S. commitment to defence of the Central Front. To the extent that the Fleet is vulnerable, this vulnerability is a symbol of American willingness to provide a forward naval defence for Europe at the risk of American lives. Yet, because in peacetime the Sixth Fleet has obvious missions outside Europe, it is not seen in the same light as U.S. troops in continental Europe. Its role in support of U.S. policy outside the NATO area is a source of friction with Southern Region allies, especially given the general perception throughout the Southern Region that U.S. ground and air forces based in the area are more useful for the defence of what are thought to be particular American interests than they may be for the immediate defence of the Southern Region itself. The air raids launched against Libya in April 1986 reinforced this perception in many sectors of public opinion in the Southern Region.

The Alliance's Mediterranean flank is inevitably the operational bridge between the military security of Western Europe and the defence of the Gulf states, either against Soviet attacks or against local insurgents. Since the United States sees itself responsible for both these missions, and in fact serves as the strategic link between the two areas, its own definition of Southern Region defence is necessarily wider than that of any of the NATO countries that are part of the area. The need for the United States to defend Israel and the usually very close nature of U.S.-Israeli defence collaboration in the region add to the variety of purposes for which U.S. naval power in the Mediterranean may be used. The special role of the Sixth Fleet in defence of the United States' Middle Eastern interests makes its NATO role seem ambiguous to many. However, if the Sixth Fleet were not in the Mediterranean this would clearly be to the great advantage of the Soviet Union and, therefore, the place of the Sixth Fleet in the East-West confrontation must still be seen in relation to Soviet military options.

Soviet Military Options

Generally, the Sovmedron's existence is closely linked to that of the Sixth Fleet: it was introduced into the Mediterranean to counter American naval activities and ostentatiously to display the Soviet Union's interest in the Mediterranean. Naval *presence* is a mission like any other. This was the original (and will probably prove to be the most enduring) Soviet purpose in the Mediterranean. In the early years, the squadron was used in moments of crisis in the Middle East to hinder the Sixth Fleet's capacity to defend American interests and also to support whatever initiatives the Soviet Union wished to take in the region. The squadron continues to exist as a deterrent to U.S. military action and is equipped to strike against U.S. forces in order to contain their capacity to escalate the level of conflict.

If, originally, it was largely presumed that many of the ships in the Soviet task force were deployed to shadow American carrier forces and hamper an American nuclear strike, it is clear that this is no longer either a primary or even an important option. This is so if only because the growth of the Soviet

Mediterranean squadron coincides with the declining significance to the United States of the Sea as a nuclear launching area. Most of the current seaborne strike potential of the United States and 90 percent of the submarines that carry nuclear weapons normally lie outside the Mediterranean. Even if the Sixth Fleet still has a nuclear strike role its destruction would hardly materially affect the ability of the United States to devastate the Soviet homeland.[50]

While it is probably correct to presume that strategic defence (in this sense, the establishment of a defensive perimeter to the south of the Soviet Union) must be included amongst the squadron's missions, a number of specific military roles are of importance in the case of crisis or conflict. The minimum Soviet objective would be to prevent the Sixth Fleet from entering the Black Sea. The squadron is primarily designed, therefore, for anti-submarine and anti-carrier operations and has a minimal ability to effect beach landings. However, the naval infantry brigade attached to the Black Sea Fleet based at Sevastopol is trained to seize the Straits and prevent Turkey from controlling them in wartime.[51] In the early 1980s, the Soviets conducted an amphibious assault exercise in Syria with Syrian collaboration, but there is no indication that the Soviets are confident in their naval intervention capacities.

Outside the context of a general war, the role of the Sovmedron is to complicate the tasks of the Sixth Fleet. In the conflicts that broke out in the Middle East in the 1970s, the Soviets were careful to deploy their ships in such a way as to make it more difficult for the Sixth Fleet to project power ashore. Although during the Yom Kippur War three Alligator tank landing ships with naval infantry were attached to the Sovmedron, actual intervention by the squadron remained militarily infeasible.[52] The Sixth Fleet was reinforced to challenge Soviet air and sea lines of communication, thus making any Soviet move on land, at best, costly, at worst, disastrous.[53] The stabilization in the growth of the Sovmedron since around the mid-1970s is testimony to the fact that the Soviets are aware of the military limitations to the use of their sea power in the Mediterranean. This being said, the distinction between the peacetime political effects of the general Soviet presence and the wartime military capacities of the squadron must always be kept in mind. It is necessary at least to acknowledge that the Soviet Union has learnt to exert political influence in times of both peace and crisis with forces that would prove militarily inferior in actual war.[54]

The Soviet Union's naval strategy in the Mediterranean must therefore be seen as more political than military: its mission is to modify the behaviour of other actors by its mere presence, as much as by any potential combat action. The wartime role of the squadron would naturally be determined by the circumstances of actual conflict. In the case of a long conventional war, Soviet naval forces would have to ensure the interdiction of NATO's transatlantic lines of communication to prevent the successful reinforcement of forces at the Central Front. In a long war, equally, the Soviets would be burdened with the task of protecting their sea-based nuclear deterrent — insignificant as it may be in comparison to its land-based arsenal.[55]

In these circumstances, naval forces *located* in the Mediterranean are not ideal for the performance of *either* of these missions. The Mediterranean squadron would be useful in a short war — to knock out U.S. carrier forces — but if a long war were expected the Soviet Union would no doubt prefer to deploy its naval forces in seas other than the Mediterranean (if this could be accomplished) where they would be both more useful and less vulnerable. Some analysts have even suggested that because Soviet surface ships in the Mediterranean are unlikely to retain combat ability beyond the first few days, and because Soviet undersea forces would have almost no ability to rearm while deployed, NATO interests would not necessarily be best served by denying the Soviet navy access to the Mediterranean; its forces would be more accessible targets there than they would be in the Black Sea.[56] The converse of this argument is contained in the cynical view that a sign of the outbreak of war in the Southern Flank would actually be the *withdrawal* of the Sovmedron from the Mediterranean, rather than its reinforcement from the Black Sea. From the Soviet perspective, the dilemma could perhaps be stated as follows: if the Soviets were to withdraw the Sovmedron they would limit their options in the Mediterranean and perhaps send a signal that they were abandoning a political presence, thus risking misinterpretation; if they were to move in completely they might send a more obviously aggressive signal but would have a serious problem of resupply.

In considering any move on the Southern Flank, Soviet forces would have to take into account not only land forces reinforced by troops from NATO countries outside the region but also the special power and position of the U.S. Sixth Fleet. Soviet strategy in the Mediterranean in the past could not go much beyond trying to destroy as much of the Fleet as possible while necessarily sacrificing its own Eskadra. Because of new Soviet land and sea deployments, as well as the U.S. navy's decision to give more attention to its squadron in the Indian Ocean (so that often there is only one U.S. carrier group in the Mediterranean), the Sixth Fleet is not as self-subsisting as it once was. The commander of the Sixth Fleet can remain confident about the Fleet's fighting capacity in the eastern Mediterranean, but it would, of course, be safer in the western Mediterranean from Soviet aircraft which would have to overfly a number of NATO countries and their air defence systems in order to attack U.S. ships. The West must be careful to ensure that, in war, the Sixth Fleet will be able, in collaboration with other NATO navies in the Mediterranean, to maintain a forward posture in the Sea in order to destroy the Sovmedron and ensure that the diverse sectors of the Southern Flank are reinforced and resupplied.[57] Certainly, if the Soviet Union were ever to obtain important bases in North Africa from which it could launch air strikes, the Sixth Fleet might have to leave the whole Sea if it wished to be sure of its safety, though, of course, these Soviet bases themselves might be vulnerable to attack, and the Soviet Union could never be certain that they would have unimpeded access to them in times of tension.

The fact remains that the Soviet navy in the Mediterranean is not in a position to act effectively as an autonomous force. It can harrass the Sixth Fleet (and other allied naval forces), it can prevent the Fleet from being exactly where it would prefer to be, but an attempt to prevail over the Americans would probably be suicidal. The Fleet still has a powerful advantage over the Sovmedron and, in any case, its special configuration makes it especially hard to target. At the same time, the Fleet's wartime tasks of battle management and the enhancement of theatre air superiority[58] are threatened by improvements made by the Soviet Union in its major ground-based air assets.

The deployment of Soviet Backfire (TU-26s) and Blinder (TU-22s) bombers in the Crimea is the principal new threat to Western forces in the Mediterranean, particularly to aircraft carriers. The air challenge now posed to AIRSOUTH will require important measures to be taken in order to achieve a greater integration of Southern Region air forces and to plug some of the important gaps and weak points that now exist. COMAIRSOUTH is committed to operate in a multifront theatre and must be prepared to conduct the full spectrum of air warfare — from air defence and defensive counter-air to offensive air support and counter-air interdiction, as well as tactical air support of maritime operations. The command, control and communication (C3) challenge to ensure that the land and maritime principal subordinate commanders of AFSOUTH are in proper contact with each other is therefore vast.[59] If the Soviet bombers are the most important actual threat to the Sixth Fleet and other NATO forces, planning in the region is complicated by the fact that the USSR has, over the last four or five years, added hundreds of heavily armed attack helicopters, such as the MI-24 Hind D and MI-8 Hip E, to its inventory, thus increasing the Soviet advantage at the front line while releasing tactical fighters for deeper interdiction missions.[60] It is the growing variety of Soviet air power, as well as its strength and quality, which is likely to make NATO organization in the Southern Region more complicated.

Aside from complicating tasks for the Sixth Fleet, Soviet military options in the Southern Region are various and must be examined fully when considering how to organize Western defence in the region. A victory at sea would be irrelevant if NATO forces could not ensure the defence of continental Europe. Not only is it important to consider the nature of the land threat, but also its likely direction. It has often been suggested, for example, that the Soviet naval presence in the Mediterranean and its access diplomacy in North Africa is directed towards creating the circumstances by which an attack on the soft underbelly of Europe would be possible. The fear is that the Soviet Union might acquire the capability to attack NATO forces in the south from African airfields, as well as put at risk transatlantic convoys or reinforcements and supplies.[61] Such an attack, if successful, would prevent NATO from grouping to attack Warsaw Pact forces at the Central Front and divert important Western forces from other tasks.

Whether the Soviet Union would want to divert *its own* forces to this end is a subject of dispute. Many of the missions that might be assigned to Soviet aircraft based in Africa could probably now be fulfilled by aircraft located within the Soviet Union. The fact that there is considerable Soviet air power concentrated in Libya must be a matter for concern, but whether Libya, or any other country in Africa, would permit the Soviet Union to use national airfields for attacks on Europe is questionable, or at least should not be taken for granted. It is true, nonetheless, that if Libyan airfields could be used, they would be enormously useful to the Soviet Union for the recovery and turnaround of Soviet aircraft launched from Warsaw Pact bases. An attack on the Southern Region from Africa, however, would still pose considerable problems for the Soviet Union. Such a forward area is not a favourable operating environment for the Soviets in a major war. In the specific case of Libya, it is arguable that the USSR may become increasingly reluctant to 'preposition' expensive equipment where its use probably appears wasteful to the Soviets. (In 1987, Libya lost hundreds of millions of dollars worth of Soviet and East European equipment in Chad). Also, the Soviet Union would have to go to elaborate ends to protect such far-flung forces, and in so doing would tie up forces potentially more useful elsewhere and, moreover, would not cause major problems for NATO. From the few facilities that the Soviets might be able to maintain in Africa, they are unlikely to pose a direct threat to the West.[62] Soviet naval aviation Backfire bombers operating from airfields in Libya would, for example, be more exposed and vulnerable to NATO counterattack than if they flew wartime missions into the Mediterranean from safer havens in the Crimea. If, in a general European war, the Soviets' use of whatever facilities in Africa they controlled is a contingency for which NATO must plan, a Soviet assault on southern Europe from Africa (unconnected to a more general struggle) seems out of the question. The immediate, most realistic aim of the Soviet Union in the Southern Region is to ensure a capacity to project itself effectively into any crisis that may involve a prime client in the eastern Mediterranean, the North African littoral, or the Yemeni part of the Arabian peninsula.[63]

The degree of Soviet penetration in some of these littoral countries is a problem Western defence planners must take into account — since that penetration makes *some use* of these facilities conceivable at *some time,* the task of NATO armed forces in the region is made more complicated. Political/ military influence in the relevant countries is also an added general challenge to Western predominance in the Mediterranean area.

In the southern European land theatre other more direct options remain which Western countries must take into account as they modernize their forces and capacities. The Warsaw Pact forces are able to deploy some thirty-five divisions on the Greek-Turkish border, while NATO forces (mostly infantry units) number about thirty-two divisions. Most Warsaw Pact divisions are mechanized, armoured and could be reinforced by at least two airborne/airmobile divisions.[64] These comparisons do not immediately reveal anything in particular, as the quality of the available Warsaw Pact and NATO forces varies considerably. More important is the environment in which these forces may have to fight. Turkey's mountainous and rugged terrain favours its defence, though the inadequacy of Turkish anti-tank weapons, radar, and armoured attack helicopters makes of geographical inaccessibility a necessary virtue rather than a useful luxury. In the special case of Turkey, NATO is at a slight advantage in that a defence in depth is both possible and advisable. The main advantage that the Warsaw Pact has against Greek and Turkish forces in this area is tactical mobility. Once a Warsaw Pact breakthrough was made, it would be difficult for Greece or Turkey to withdraw and establish new lines of defence. This puts a premium on individual NATO countries in the region increasing their capacities for area defence through the use of light infantry.

A Soviet attack through the Gorizia Gap, possibly using Hungarian divisions, has been the traditional fear in the northeast of Italy. But such an attack would depend on the Soviet Union being able to pass through neutral Austria and rely on a passive Yugoslavia. All this would require time and would provide strategic warning for NATO forces to react. The Gorizia Gap remains the most operationally valid way to invade Italy and has for long been the focus of Italian defence planning, but few analysts consider that the various improvements made by the Soviet Union and Warsaw Pact countries to their armed forces in recent years have made any qualitative change to the threat in this area.

More concern has surfaced over possible Soviet interests in thrusting southwards towards Iran. The Soviet Union has a history of involvement in Iran which it occupied both in the 1920s and during World War II. Iran's northern provinces are ethnically similar to Soviet Azerbaijan and it can be presumed that if Iran were to break up in civil war, or if certain Western powers (the United States in particular) were to establish bases in the country, the USSR may consider it necessary to intervene. The Soviet Union has, in fact, refused to acknowledge Iran's renunciation of the 1921 Treaty of Friendship under whose terms the Soviet Union could occupy Iran if it perceived a security threat.[65] Clearly the fact that 60 percent of Soviet troops in the Transcaucasus Military District of the Soviet Union are only at a very low level of readiness (Category 3) at present militates against the likelihood of any serious military adventure in the region. Equally, given that the United States would consider a Soviet 'grab for oil' as a *casus belli*, restraint will be the operative word in respect of Soviet policy towards the area and especially Iran.[66]

The facts of geography, as well as information about past Soviet military planning, make it clear that the USSR's possible invasion routes towards Iran would not necessarily include any part of NATO territory. Theoretically, there are routes from either side of the Caspian Sea that would allow the Soviet Union to reach Tehran without having to take Turkey into account.[67] However, it is probable that the Soviet Union would not wish to leave its border with eastern Turkey undefended in the event of a move towards Iran and might also seek, in such a contingency, to conduct a front offensive against Turkey at least to ensure Turkish neutrality. It is therefore conceivable that a conflict with Turkey would not have Ankara as an objective and may take place outside the context of a general European war.[68] The Turkish military seems implicitly to have accepted this possibility as indicated by the fact that its most recent improvements have been in the defence of the east.[69] In any case, the fact that the Soviet Union has important interests in Iran and other areas in the Middle East reinforces the argument that the West should not distinguish too clinically between in-area and out-of-area threats, particularly in the special case of Turkey, which can easily become embroiled by conflicts and instability in such areas as the Persian Gulf and Near East. The problem for NATO strategists is to assess the various risks that exist in the Southern Region and establish a military strategy that takes these into account. This will help to reinforce the sense of political solidarity amongst NATO states in the south, so essential to a general policy of deterrence.

FUTURE COURSE OF NATO STRATEGY

While the individual states of NATO South have elaborated defence policies considered by them to be roughly sufficient to deal with the specific threats to their territories, a stronger deterrent in the south would require a more evidently collective effort on the part of these states. Naturally, there are Alliance-wide plans for the defence of the Southern Region, just as there are plans for the Central Front and the north. But these plans do not presume as high a collaborative effort as do those for other Alliance areas, and, in some instances, have not been entirely absorbed by national planners. Both these problems now have more severe consequences than before. The more diversified Soviet threat to the region means that Southern Region states need to be able to work together at an early stage in a conflict, and incorporate reinforcements in a timely fashion. As states work on their national defence plans in the coming years, it will be necessary to find instances where a joint defence can become truly collective. To achieve this, various modifications to land, air and sea that would substantially improve the current military balance can be envisaged (see Table 1.3).

The general NATO problem in the area has long been recognized as deriving from the natural difficulty in defending four separate theatres: Italy, Greece and western Turkey, eastern Turkey and the Mediterranean Sea. Communications over this area are extremely thin, partly because national systems remain inadequate and also because those that exist are not perfectly compatible. Geographically, NATO is at a disadvantage in so far as its ability to move ground troops throughout the area is lower than the Warsaw Pact's ability to present a significant threat to them. Recent Warsaw Pact manoeuvres in 1982 (Shield '82, a field training exercise or FTX) and 1984 (Soyuz '84, a command post exercise or CPX) have shown that Soviet strategy to gain access to the Middle East and the Indian Ocean probably includes plans to overrun the Turkish First Army in Thrace, and to force the Bosporus with at least nine divisions supported by air and sea elements and a number of Bulgarian tank regiments staging from Varna and Burgas.[70] The aim would be to split the Greek and Turkish units in order to leave the defence of the Straits and the west coast of the Bosporus exclusively to Turkish forces.

Any defence in the Southern Region must be aimed at ensuring

Table 1.3: Comparison of NATO and Warsaw Pact forces

I. Naval forces comparison			
Southern Region	NATO	Warsaw Pact	(France)
Carriers	1	—	(2)
Cruisers	5	3	(1)
Destroyers/Frigates	60	8	(13)
Submarines	37	9	(11)
Amphibious	24	1	(—)
Other	70	27	(19)

II. Air forces comparison		
Southern Region		
Fighter/Bomber		
Ground/Attack	615	695
Interceptors	295	1560
Reconnaissance	90	195

III. Land forces comparison		
Eastern Turkey		
Divisions	12	20
Tanks	1000	2435
Artillery/Mortar	1800	4800
Balkan Front		
Divisions	25	34
Tanks	3000	6570
Artillery/Mortar	2800	6400
Northeastern Italy		
Divisions	8	17
Tanks	1250	4340
Artillery/Mortar	1400	2860

Note: Spanish forces have not been included in NATO figures, nor have French air or land forces.
Source: AFSOUTH Headquarters Italy (unclassified).

that the Soviet Union does not realistically believe that it can outflank NATO forces in a drive either to the Middle East or through the southern area of the Mediterranean in an attempt to disrupt allied control of the Sea. Given the divided theatres of possible battle, it is clear that initial defence in the Southern Region must be national. The forces of each country must be able to resist an aggression at least long enough for reinforcements to arrive or for NATO authorities to warn an aggressor that continued action could lead to the use of nuclear weapons. Clearly, the priority must be on improving local defence capacities and the ability to integrate reinforcements efficiently.

To counter a possible Soviet land attack, the Greek and Turkish armies maintain in peacetime quite large forces, totalling roughly ten divisions stationed in a very narrow area. This represents the largest concentration of force in any operational sector of NATO's forward defence.[71] However, these forces are mainly traditional infantry, weak in anti-tank equipment and feeble in logistics and infrastructure. Both Greece and Turkey have pledged themselves to the modernization of their armed forces, but it is clear that as long as they keep large forces it will be difficult to afford the technological improvements that are necessary. A choice is clearly imposed between size and quality, and as long as the former remains a priority, the latter is sacrificed. Since there is in the Southern Flank an especially great need to incorporate reinforcements, these states will have to concentrate not only on the modernization of equipment, but also on improvements of their host nation military facilities — particularly transportation and communications networks to assist incoming forces, and petroleum pipelines to resupply vehicles and aircraft engaged in combat. More effort also has to be put into such areas as air defence and runway repair capacities.

The most important outside instrument of Southern Flank security (dependent for its success on the implementation of such improvements) is to be found in the Rapid Reinforcement Plan (RRP) adopted by NATO's Defence Planning Committee in its ministerial session of December 1982. The plan sets down the strategy for the reinforcement of Europe in time of crisis or war. It envisages the involvement of over 2,000 U.S. combat aircraft,[72] up to 700 of which could probably be made available for a contingency in the Southern Region. Even given significant improvements in base support, airlift and rapid reinforcement training experience, it is expected that it will take several weeks for large reinforcements to arrive. Some of these problems could be solved if there were more prepositioning of equipment in the Southern Flank. For some time the Senior NATO Logisticians Conference (SNLC) has recommended that a major stockpile of matériel be built up in the Southern Flank and placed under the control of a NATO command. But this has not yet been decided on, and therefore there are considerable local weaknesses that must be repaired. This not only puts a premium on local forces holding out until reinforcements arrive but also makes it essential that NATO be able to signal appropriately early in a crisis that there will be a military response to aggression, so that conflict may be avoided.

In the case of the Flanks, NATO's principal military means of signalling concern lies in the ACE Allied Mobile Force (AMF). Established in 1960, the force's declared purpose is to come rapidly to the aid of NATO states on the Flanks, particularly Norway, Denmark, Greece and Turkey. The land component comprises infantry, artillery helicopters, armoured reconnaissance, combat support and administrative units from Belgium, Canada, West Germany, Italy, Luxembourg, the United Kingdom and the United States. Most units are based in their home countries. The air component comprises squadrons from Belgium, Canada, West Germany, Italy, the Netherlands and the United States. The AMF regularly participates in exercises on the Flanks. The force's role is primarily a deterrent one, but if deterrence fails the AMF is intended to fight alongside host country troops to help contain any enemy advance. Such participation by a NATO force in a Flank country would help to multilateralize the conflict and show the enemy that NATO as a whole was concerned about the security of the invaded country.

Unfortunately, the Allied Mobile Force is more symbolic in peacetime as a sign of political will to come to the assistance of a NATO country than as a credible defence force in time of conflict. The AMF is not truly a fighting force: it is intended primarily 'to show the flag.' It should not be considered a force capable of providing reinforcement, but rather as an immediate reaction unit which the Supreme Allied Commander Europe (SACEUR) would call upon for political reasons, to signal concern. It is not organized or equipped to be one of SACEUR's regional reinforcements, and the size and combat capability of the force is deliberately constrained so as not to be too provocative. But even given its limited mission, the AMF has problems which make it less efficient than would be desirable. Turkey's geographic isolation poses serious logistical problems and in any case the force is too small to be decisive in battle.[73] While its headquarters are in Heidelberg, few of the troops are permanently on station, and in fact some elements of the AMF are not winter equipped. It might be able to deploy rapidly *once assembled*, but this would take some time. While the air element could go to both Flanks, the land element could only go to one or the other. It would certainly be useful if the composition of the land element was increased so that it could simultaneously be deployed to both Flanks. This would naturally raise the costs of the force, and would depend on the availability of more transport capacity, but it would be a useful reassurance to the local states that others were interested in their security.

On the Southern Flank there are additional reasons why the force has not developed as fast as it should. According to current planning the AMF could deploy to five contingency areas: northern Italy, northern Greece, Turkish Thrace, eastern Anatolia and southern Anatolia. While the AMF has been able to work closely with Italian forces, neither Greece nor Turkey has incorporated the AMF into its general defence plans. If the force were to deploy to the Southern Flank in a deterrent capacity, it would spread itself out throughout the threatened territory to reassure the local population and signal resistance to the enemy. But if this deterrence failed, the force would have to quickly integrate itself into the national armed forces to participate in national defence until reinforcements arrived. This would not be possible unless the host countries agreed to allow the AMF to exercise according to national defence plans. Current AMF exercises in the south are hampered by the fact that the Turks do not allow the AMF to mix with the local population — a necessary activity of the force in its deterrent capacity — nor do they allow the AMF to work very closely with Turkish forces as they would deploy in a wartime contingency — which would be useful training for the AMF given its possible utility in an immediate reaction role.

Another problem is primarily budgetary in nature. Countries contributing to the air element of the AMF have committed themselves to transporting both troops and matériel by air; yet when the AMF is exercised, matériel arrives by ship. Exercises under more realistic conditions would add to the AMF's deterrent value. If deterrence fails, the AMF has a residual combat role, therefore improvement of the force's anti-air and anti-armour capabilities, and its command, control and communications (so that it can be in perfect contact with SACEUR) would be highly desirable. But finding money for these sorts of ameliorations is difficult, not least because the force requirements of the AMF must be merged with those of the major NATO commands and can get easily lost in the process. Some have argued that because of the very special nature of the AMF, its land commander should be allowed to negotiate directly with the nations involved to secure needed force improvements. Though it would be unrealistic (and inappropriate) to expect the general composition and dual mission of the AMF to change, improvements can be envisaged that would simultaneously enhance the force's deterrent and combat capacity.

Given that after any attack to the Southern Flank, NATO would need mobile forces more than any other sort of capability, it is unfortunate that little has been done to improve the AMF's in-theatre mobility, currently very limited. This is all the more striking because of the fact that many individual members of the Alliance have increasingly given attention, in their own armed forces, to rapidly mobile divisions. Aside from the U.S. decision to create the Rapid Deployment Force that eventually became a new U.S. command named CENTCOM, the British sought, especially after the Falklands conflict, to increase the capacity of 5 Airborne Brigade and to add further air transportable elements to their armed forces.[74] The French in the 1984–1988 Military Programme Law reorganized their paratroop forces and created the *Force d'Action Rapide* (FAR).[75] The Italians in the 1985 Defence White Paper argued for the creation of a *Forza di Intervento Rapido* (FIR) and have since moved to establish a small force.[76] Many of the smaller members of the Alliance, including Spain, Portugal, Greece and Turkey, have affirmed their own need to develop forces with a 'firefighting' capability that could be used rapidly in times of crisis.

These policies have emerged in recognition of the fact that air or sea transportable armed forces can serve as important and credible conventional deterrents. If there is a place where easily mobile, light infantry is especially necessary, it is the Southern Flank. It is impossible to make great improvements in the AMF without changing the nature of its largely political mission, but unless it is made to look more effective even its role as a symbol may appear illusory. Drawing on the experience of national rapid deployment forces, NATO planners should look to strengthen the AMF, if only to remove doubts among some Flank countries about its capacity to fulfil its combat mission. There are already deep suspicions, for a variety of historical and sometimes contradictory reasons, amongst the Greeks and the Turks about the reliance that can be placed on the 'West' for their country's defence. As noted above, both countries contribute to this by not exercising with the AMF in the most efficient way possible and in not distinguishing carefully between the deterrent and combat roles of the force. Over time these misunderstandings are bound to decrease, but it is clear that if improvements can take place, they will be for naught unless the host nation's support (both psychological and logistic) for the AMF makes commensurate advances.

Improvements in the capacity to signal concern (through the AMF) or to reinforce the Flanks (through the RRP) would be irrelevant if there was no advance by NATO in upgrading its air defence capacities in the south. Without effective air and anti-missile defence American and other allied air and naval operations become extremely risky.[77] Some improvements have taken place, such as the introduction of Airborne Warning and Control Systems (AWACS) at three forward operating bases — at Trapani in Italy, Preveza in Greece and Konya in Turkey — as part of the NATO Airborne Early Warning (NAEW) programme.[78] This upgrading of local air defence will provide over-the-horizon and low-level radar coverage beyond the current capabilities of the NATO Air Defence Ground Environment (NADGE). But it would be useful if more could be done to widen the operational area of air defence forces so that NATO could provide at least a semblance of a true, forward defence of its air space. This would require a much higher degree of cooperation amongst individual NATO states and movement towards a true integration of Alliance air force capacities.

Successful air defence also depends on procuring more modern aircraft. Western land-based tactical aircraft located in southeastern Europe, particularly in Greece and Turkey, must be improved to ensure the protection not only of the Sixth Fleet, but also of land forces.[79] In fact, almost all NATO aircraft in the region are in serious need of modernization or replacement. The average age of these aircraft is still well over twenty years. Near vintage jets such as the F-84, F-104 and the F-100 are still being maintained and flown. The F-104 is one of the few planes that is common throughout the region and when a new generation of planes is put into service, attention will have to be paid to the need for improved standardization and interoperability. At the moment, there are too many different types of aircraft requiring different sorts of support elements. If interceptor aircraft are an urgent necessity, planning equally must go ahead for the development and purchase of longer-range aircraft to attack the Warsaw Pact threat at source. These improvements in air assets are necessary especially to offset the recent gains the Soviet Union has made in equipping its planes with stand-off missiles. Reliance on anti-air missiles to counter Soviet air power is no longer sufficient.

At sea, NATO's position is strong (see Table 1.4). Even if analysts have often concentrated on naval balances, the strictly Soviet naval threat is not of a kind that requires more ships to meet it. The nature of the unique American presence in the form of the Sixth Fleet, however, is such that more allied naval cooperation would be useful, if largely for psychological reasons. Aside from the AMF, NATO's only other immediate reaction force is the Naval On-Call Force Mediterranean (NAVOCFORMED) which provides a deterrent and quick intervention capacity and is composed of combatant warships of several NATO members, usually Italy, Turkey, the United Kingdom and the United States. When the force is exercised, other NATO states provide support. It is called together to train twice a year for about thirty days, and responsibility for detailed planning of these exercises rests with COMNAVSOUTH.

Table 1.4: NATO ships in the Mediterranean 1986/87 (approximate average figures)

Type	Greece	Italy	Turkey	France (1)	Spain (1)	US (2)
Submarines	10	10	16	17	8	3
Aircraft Carriers				2	1	1
Light Aircraft Carriers		2				
Helicopter Carriers				1		
Cruisers	2			1		2
Destroyers	14	4	14	15	10	8
Frigates	2	16	4	24	11	
Corvettes		8				
Fast-Attack Craft	20		26	3	12	
Hydrofoils — Missiles		7				

Note: (1) Total numbers; the numbers for the Mediterranean vary.

(2) Average over the period of one year.

Source: AFSOUTH Headquarters Italy (unclassified).

There have often been appeals to upgrade this to a standing (from an on-call) force but the disputes between Greece and Turkey — both of which would naturally have to contribute to such a force — have made it impossible to create a more multi-lateral permanent sea presence for NATO in the Mediterranean. This is unfortunate, because a standing force could work more efficiently with elements of the Sixth Fleet and better signal a collective Alliance concern.

The contribution that NATO can make to strengthen the Southern Region states' sense of solidarity with the Alliance is to make more obvious its military commitment to this region's defence. At the moment, local defence is locally organized and is the responsibility of the individual countries aided directly by the United States and indirectly by NATO infrastructural support. But there is no strong sense in the Southern Region that NATO will 'come to its defence.' NATO, as it were, has 'prepositioned' in the area, and has promised to reinforce in time of war, yet this assurance is dependent on there being forces available to come to the area. A real capacity to bring substantial conventional power to bear on the Southern Flank in time of crisis would strengthen NATO's capacities for internal management of political relations between the various NATO states, as well as offer a more credible deterrent to possible aggression. The local states and NATO, as a whole, must therefore consider ways to make Western forces in the region (and those that must be brought to the area) lighter and more mobile. Commensurate improvements in the quality of NATO exercises in the region would strengthen allied solidarity (see Table 1.5).

This chapter has argued that the growth of Soviet military power in the Southern Region has been important, but that the Soviet threat *specific* to it is not unmanageable. Yet, if the actual Soviet threat to the Southern Region itself is not as high as sometimes feared, it is certainly true that the specific Southern Region deterrent to Soviet aggression is not as high as it should be. The real deterrent to Soviet action in this area remains the general Western deterrent (still mainly nuclear) to Soviet action anywhere in Europe. It is meaningless to speak of the Southern Flank as having been converted, by virtue of Soviet military improvements, into a front, if only because this has always been the case. It is a wholly different argument, however, to say that Western defensive capabilities in the Southern Region have been in relative decline. This decline does require remedial

Table 1.5: Southern Region NATO Exercises

I. Exercise Display Determination Series

Held annually for about one month in the autumn to exercise the employment of land, sea, and air forces of the Southern Region, deployed external forces, and forces made available to the region. This is a major exercise which is part of the NATO 'Autumn Forge' series and is conducted by CINCSOUTH. The goals of the exercise are to improve combat readiness, enhance crisis management capabilities, and demonstrate allied solidarity and preparedness. Nations participating in the 'Display Determination' series each year are shown in the table. France, which does not belong to NATO's integrated military structure, often participates with air and naval forces as part of its normal training relations with its allies.

Southern Region ground and air forces practise land and air combat operations in northern and northeast Italy and Turkish Thrace. Power projection training is conducted by amphibious forces and carrier-based tactical aircraft. Marines and naval infantry carry out amphibious training in Sardinia, Italy, and Turkey. Maritime forces practise all facets of naval warfare while supporting ground and air forces. External reinforcements join regional forces in northeast Italy and Turkish Thrace.

Participating Nations Display Determination

Year								
1980	TU	US	IT	PO	UK	FR	NL	
1981	TU	US	IT	PO	UK	FR		GR
1982	TU	US	IT	PO				GR
1983	TU	US	IT	PO	UK			
1984	TU	US	IT	PO	UK	FR		
1985	TU	US	IT	PO		FR		
1986	TU	US	IT			FR		

II. Exercise Dawn Patrol/Distant Hammer Series

Held annually in the spring for about two weeks. It is a major exercise conducted by CINCSOUTH. Air forces, supported by deployed external forces, practise air combat operations in Italy and Turkey. Power projection is conducted by amphibious forces and carrier-based tactical aircraft. Maritime forces practise all facets of naval warfare in the Mediterranean supported by, and in support of, air forces in Italy and Turkey.

Particular emphasis is on protection of sea lines of communication and on cooperation of maritime and land-based air forces. Participating nations are shown in the table.

Participating National Dawn Patrol/Distant Hammer

Year						
1980	US	IT	FR	UK	NL	TU
1981	NOT HELD					
1982	US	IT	FR	UK	NL	TU
1983	US	IT	FR	UK	NL	TU
1984	US	IT	FR	UK	NL	TU
1985	US	IT	FR	UK	NL	TU
1986	US	IT	FR	UK	NL	TU

Key: TU = Turkey, US = United States, IT = Italy, PO = Portugal, UK = United Kingdom, FR = France, NL = Netherlands, and GR = Greece.

Source: AFSOUTH Headquarters Italy (unclassified).

action, both in terms of local force modernization and improvements in the capacity of the Alliance to bring outside force quickly to bear on the region, so that, as elsewhere in the Alliance, a conventional deterrent exists that does not make the nuclear one appear mythical.

Strengthening the conventional deterrent in the Southern Region would ensure what is already a probability: that the Soviet Union will not attempt to control the Southern Region totally except in the circumstances of a direct and European-wide conflict between the two alliances. At the moment, it is unlikely that a conflict could take place in the Mediterranean as the result of an aeronaval confrontation between the forces of the United States and the Soviet Union. War may occur as an extension of military activity in other areas of Europe or as a result of a crisis that is initially external to the two alliances, such as a conflict in the Middle East.[80] Improvements in the deterrent specific to the Southern Region would help to guard against both possibilities. As long as it is absolutely clear that military activity in the Southern Region by the Soviet Union, or any other power, will be met by Western forces, both European and out-of-area disturbances could be limited in their scope.

All this points to the fact than an improved defence of the Southern Region can only occur if there is a successful balance between national and Alliance-wide approaches to regional security. The paradox of the security situation in the Southern Region is that individual national approaches to defence have been necessary because of the facts of geography — countries may be left alone to defend themselves longer in the south than elsewhere and therefore need to be able to hold out — yet purely national approaches are highly inefficient, particularly, as noted above, in the field of air defence. Furthermore, some of the states in the region may wish to adopt more national approaches to defence to counter those threats that are specific to them, but the domestic consensus needed to support such efforts has to be developed quite differently than that for support of Alliance-wide efforts. In all this, the role of the United States is crucial. As the principal external provider of security to the allies in the Southern Region, it is the United States with which the NATO countries of the Mediterranean must bargain, both to encourage a greater contribution to the area's defence and to allow for more 'national' approaches to regional security.

NOTES

1. See generally, David M. Abshire, *NATO on the Move*, The Alliance Papers, no. 6 (Brussels: U.S. Mission to NATO, September 1985).

2. Michael MccGwire, *Military Objectives in Soviet Foreign Policy* (Washington, DC: The Brookings Institution, 1987), 128. I have adopted the term TSMA (not used by MccGwire) as it appears to be a more useful acronym for an English reader to describe the Russian term 'teatr voennykh deistvii.' TVD is the Russian acronym used by many Western specialists including MccGwire.

3. Ibid., 139.

4. Phillip A. Petersen, 'Turkey in Soviet Military Strategy,' *Dis Politika* (Foreign Policy) (Ankara), 13, nos. 1-2 (1986): 80.

5. MccGwire, *Military Objectives in Soviet Foreign Policy,* 183.

6. Petersen, 'Turkey in Soviet Military Strategy': 82.

7. Jed Snyder, *Defending The Fringe: NATO, the Mediterranean, and the Persian Gulf,* SAIS Papers in International Affairs, no. 11 (Boulder: Westview Press, 1987), 7.

8. See generally, Giacomo Luciani, 'The Mediterranean and the Energy Picture,' in *The Mediterranean Region: Economic Interdependence and the Future of Society,* ed. Giacomo Luciani (Beckenham: Croom Helm, 1984), 1-40. (Hereafter cited as: *The Mediterranean Region*).

9. Maurizio Cremasco, 'NATO's Southern Flank in the East-West Balance,' *The International Spectator,* XIV, no. 1 (January–March 1979): 14-15.

10. Ciro Elliot Zoppo, 'American Foreign Policy, NATO in the Mediterranean, and the Defence of the Gulf,' in *The Mediterranean Region,* ed. Luciani, 299.

11. Ibid., 300-301.

12. See generally, Colonel Norman L. Dodd, 'Allied Forces Southern Europe,' *The Army Quarterly and Defence Journal,* 114, no. 2 (April 1984): 178-187; and NATO, *Allied Command Europe,* (Brussels: NATO Information Office).

13. Captain G.R. Villar, 'Trends in Maritime Warfare: The Need for Power Overseas?' in *Royal United Services Institute for Defence Studies Yearbook* (London: Brassey's, 1984), 282.

14. Keith Allen, 'The Black Sea Fleet and Mediterranean Naval Operations,' in *The Soviet Navy: Strengths and Liabilities,* ed. Bruce W. Watson and Susan M. Watson (Boulder: Westview Press, 1986), 219. (Hereafter cited as: *The Soviet Navy*).

15. Richard B. Remmek, 'The Politics of Soviet Access to Naval Support Facilities in the Mediterranean,' in *Soviet Naval Diplomacy,* ed. Bradford Dismukes and James McConnell (New York: Pergamon, 1979), 362.

16. James Cable, *Gunboat Diplomacy 1919–1979: Political Applications of Limited Naval Force,* Second Edition (London: Macmillan, 1981), 162. (Hereafter cited as: *Gunboat Diplomacy*).

17. Alvin Z. Rubenstein, 'The Soviet Union and the Eastern

Mediterranean 1968–1978,' *Orbis*, 23, no. 2 (Summer 1979): 299.

18. Paul J. Murphy, ed., *Naval Power in Soviet Policy*, Studies in Communist Affairs, vol. 2 (U.S. Air Force, 1978), 237.

19. Anthony R. Wells, 'The June 1967 War,' in *Soviet Naval Diplomacy*, ed. Dismukes and McConnell, 167.

20. Allen, in *The Soviet Navy*, ed. Watson, 218.

21. Paul H. Nitze, Leonard Sullivan, Jr., and the Atlantic Council Working Group on Securing the Seas, *Securing the Seas: The Soviet Naval Challenge and Western Alliance Options* (Boulder: Westview Press, 1979), 60. (Hereafter cited as: *Securing the Seas*).

22. Allen, in *The Soviet Navy*, ed. Watson, 218.

23. Wells, in *Soviet Naval Diplomacy*, ed. Dismukes and McConnell, 166.

24. Abram N. Shulsky, 'The Jordanian Crisis of September 1970,' in *Soviet Naval Diplomacy*, ed. Dismukes and McConnell, 171.

25. Ibid., 177.

26. Cable, *Gunboat Diplomacy*, 264-265.

27. Thomas H. Etzold, 'The Soviet Union in the Mediterranean,' *Naval War College Review* (July–August, 1984): 6.

28. Robert G. Weinland, 'Land Support for Naval Forces: Egypt and the Soviet Escadra: 1962–1976,' *Survival* (March/April 1978): 73.

29. Ibid., 75.

30. Ibid., 76-77.

31. Exact figures of Soviet submarine strength during this period are not available, but it is probable that the USSR adopted this strategy. See Weinland, Ibid., 79.

32. Robert E. Harkavy, 'The New Geopolitics: Arms Transfers and the Major Powers' Competition for Overseas Bases,' in *Arms Transfers in the Modern World*, ed. Stephanie G. Neuman and Robert E. Harkavy (New York: Praeger, 1980), 137.

33. See generally, Cynthia A. Roberts, 'Soviet Arms Transfer Policy and the Decision to Upgrade Syrian Air Defences,' *Survival* (July/August 1983): 154-164.

34. Remmek, in *Soviet Naval Diplomacy*, ed. Dismukes and McConnell, 388.

35. Ibid., 386.

36. J.F. Brown, 'The Balkans: Soviet Ambitions and Opportunities,' *The World Today* (June 1984): 253.

37. Etzold, 'The Soviet Union in the Mediterranean': 6.

38. Western European Union, 'European Security and the Mediterranean,' Assembly, Document 1073, Revised Report, Mr. Kittelmann rapporteur (Paris, October 1986), 10.

39. Nitze, *Securing the Seas*, 68.

40. Edward N. Luttwak and Robert G. Weinland, *Sea Power in the Mediterranean: Political Utility and Military Constraints*, The Washington Papers, no. 61 (Washington, DC: CSIS, 1979), 7.

41. CSIA European Security Workshop Paper, 'Instability and Change on NATO's Southern Flank,' *International Security*, 3, no. 3 (Winter 1978–1979): 151.

42. Luttwak and Weinland, *Sea Power in the Mediterranean*, 8.
43. Cable, *Gunboat Diplomacy*, 78.
44. Ibid., 156.
45. Jan S. Breemer, 'De-Committing the Sixth Fleet,' *Naval War College Review* (November–December 1982): 27-28.
46. Snyder, *Defending the Fringe*, 16-17.
47. Ibid., 30.
48. Worth H. Bagley, *Sea Power and Western Security: The Next Decade*, Adelphi Paper, no. 139 (London: IISS, Winter 1977), 22.
49. Snyder, *Defending the Fringe*, 17.
50. Cable, *Gunboat Diplomacy*, 156-7.
51. Michael J. O'Hara, 'The Naval Infantry,' in *The Soviet Navy*, ed. Watson, 52.
52. Ibid., 53.
53. Luttwak and Weinland, *Sea Power in the Mediterranean*, 90.
54. Etzold, *The Soviet Union in the Mediterranean*, 12.
55. Robert Weinland, 'Soviet Strategy and the Objectives of Their Naval Presence in the Mediterranean,' in *The Mediterranean Region*, ed. Luciani, 273-274.
56. Etzold, *The Soviet Union in the Mediterranean*, 16.
57. Philip A. Karber, 'NATO Doctrine and National Operational Priorities: The Central Front and the Flanks: Part 1,' in *Power and Policy: Doctrine, the Alliance and Arms Control*, Part Three, Adelphi Paper, no. 207 (London: IISS, 1986), 21.
58. Etzold, *The Soviet Union in the Mediterranean*, 16.
59. Lieutenant General W.E. Brown, Jr., 'Instant Readiness AIRSOUTH,' *NATO's Sixteen Nations* (June–July 1983): 53.
60. Ibid.
61. Richard B. Remmek, 'Soviet Military Interests in Africa,' *Orbis* (Spring 1984): 128.
62. Ibid., 132, 142.
63. Alvin Z. Rubenstein, 'The Changing Strategic Balance and Soviet Third World Risk-Taking,' *Naval War College Review* (March–April 1985): 14.
64. James Brown, 'The Southern Flank: Political Dilemmas and Strategic Considerations,' unpublished paper (Dallas: Southern Methodist University, 1984), 5.
65. Ralph King, *The Iran-Iraq War: The Political Implications*, Adelphi Paper, no. 219 (London: IISS, 1987), 49.
66. Paul Dibb, *The Soviet Union, The Incomplete Superpower* (London: Macmillan, 1986), 132.
67. Marshall Lee Miller, 'The Soviet General Staff's Secret Plans for Invading Iran,' *Armed Forces Journal International* (January 1987): 28.
68. Petersen, 'Turkey in Soviet Military Strategy': 82.
69. It is likely that some of these improvements and new deployments are also intended to counter the internal Kurdish threat.
70. Lawrence L. Whetten, 'Turkey's Role in the Atlantic Alliance,' *Atlantic Quarterly*, vol. 2, issue 3 (Autumn 1984): 262.
71. Karber, in *Power and Policy: Doctrine, the Alliance and Arms Control*, 20.

72. General Larry D. Welch, 'NATO Rapid Reinforcement — A Key to Conventional Deterrence,' *NATO's Sixteen Nations*, Special Issue, 'NATO's Air Forces,' 32, no. 1 (1987): 114.

73. Duygu Bazoglu Sezer, *Turkey's Security Policies*, Adelphi Paper, no. 164, (London: IISS, Spring 1981), 27.

74. Early news to this effect can be found in *Defence* (London, November 1983): 700.

75. For an analysis of French capabilities, see John Chipman, *French Military Policy and African Security*, Adelphi Paper, no. 201 (London: IISS, Summer 1985).

76. Ministero della Difesa, *La Difesa, Libro Bianco*, vol. 1 (Rome, 1985), 59.

77. Stefano Silvestri, 'The Consequences of the Evolving Italian Defence Model for Italy's Defence in NATO,' Paper presented in Rome at a Seminar sponsored by the Centro Alti Studi per la Difesa, Istituto Affari Internazionali and C&L Associates. 19–20 March 1987, 11.

78. Salvador Mafe Huertas, 'Mediterranean Exchange' *Aviation News*, 13, no. 8 (25 January–7 February 1985): 688. I am grateful to Diego Ruiz Palmer for providing me with this reference.

79. Brown, 'The Southern Flank,' 4.

80. Maurizio Cremasco and Luigi Caligaris, *Italian Rapid Action Force*, IAI Paper (Rome, February 1985), 9.

2

Allies in the Mediterranean: Legacy of Fragmentation

John Chipman

Sea powers are naturally drawn to the Mediterranean and, traditionally, great powers operating in the Sea have sought to control the local residents. When Britain was weighing up what remained of its status as a great power in 1946, it was deemed essential that a presence in the Mediterranean be maintained in order to influence the countries of southern Europe. In a memorandum written on 13 March 1946 on defence in the Mediterranean, the Foreign Secretary Ernest Bevin argued:

> If we move out of the Mediterranean, Russia will move in and the Mediterranean countries, from the point of view of commerce and trade, economy and democracy, will be finished. We have a chance of holding Italy in the Western civilisation, and although Yugoslavia is really under Russian control at the moment, the position there is very uneasy and one wonders how long as a Mediterranean people Yugoslavia will put up with Russian control. ... It is essential from our point of view that Greece remains with us politically ... [1]

These assessments did lead Britain to continue maintaining, for a time, a military presence in the Mediterranean that served as a unifying factor in the Sea. Now, the British presence is considerably less — though two Sovereign Base Areas (SBAs) are maintained in Cyprus, protected by the 4,000-strong British Forces Cyprus — and the United States has taken over as the principal external provider of security and unification. But a legacy of fragmentation exists — the national policies of all the NATO Mediterranean states are still very strong, and as the Alliance considers the question of regional security in the area, the challenge is how to make the allies work together before they, again, risk drifting apart.

The predominant military power of the United States in the Mediterranean is a result not only of the capacities of the Sixth Fleet but also of the extensive facilities and rights that it enjoys in the Mediterranean. In the event of war involving the NATO Alliance, most of these installations would come under the direction and command of NATO authorities. In peacetime, however, these facilities are used by the United States exclusively or in collaboration with the host allied country. In addition to managing these facilities, the United States distributes very large amounts of aid to the Southern Region countries as part of its defence agreements with each state (see Table 2.1). The nature of these arrangements has created a close, but often very awkward, relationship between the United States and its allies. Any change towards a more collective approach to regional defence will have to take place both with the aid and the acquiescence of the Americans. The United States will have to help, as it has already done, in providing some of the means by which these states can better defend themselves and collaborate with their allies. But it will also have to acquiesce, in so far as it may be forced to accept that the increased regional organization of defence in the south (just as for more efficient European defence generally) will detract from the special relationship that the United States maintains with each of its allies in the Southern Region. The extent of the U.S. military presence and the nature of national defence policies are, at present, questions that have to be assessed together so that a politically robust and militarily useful cooperation between the United States and its European allies can be prepared for the future. A better spirit of collaboration between the United States and its southern European allies is a pre-condition for these allies to take a more important position within the Alliance and particularly in building up its European pillar.

POLITICAL CHALLENGES AND THE U.S. MILITARY PRESENCE

As the postwar era unfolded after 1945, the United States was relatively quick to react to events in the Mediterranean and assume political responsibilities that helped to define the first years of the Cold War. When the British government decided,

Table 2.1: U.S. military aid to southern region nations

U.S. fiscal year	1980	1981	1982	1983	1984	1985	1986
Greece							
Credit	145.0	176.5	280.0	280.0	500.0	242(T) 258(C)	83.546(T) 347.104(C)
MAP	.58	.869	1.455	0.55	0.97	—	—
IMET	1.186	1.135	1.237	1.238	1.387	1.370	1.244
Portugal							
Credit	—	—	45.0	52.5	45.0	55.0	43.065(T)
MAP	37.8	53.6	23.5	37.9	60.0	70.0	66.9
IMET	1.794	1.807	2.286	2.027	2.9	2.96	2.336
Spain							
Credit	120.0	120.0	125.0	400.0	400.0	400.0	382.8(T)
MAP	3.913	2.834	.543	.325	.071	—	—
IMET	2.119	2.450	2.016	2.402	3.014	2.926	2.351
Turkey							
Credit	202.9	250.0	343.0	290.0	285.0	235(T) 250(C)	79.288(T) 330.165(C)
MAP	2.104	1.043	57.0	110.0	130.0	215.0	206.0
IMET	1.303	1.622	3.070	2.592	3.256	3.562	3.194

Key: MAP = Military Assistance Program; IMET = International Military Education and Training; (T) = At U.S. Treasury rates of interest; (C) = At concessional rates of interest.

Source: Comptroller of the U.S. Defense Security Assistance Agency, 'Foreign Military Sales, Foreign Military Construction Sales and Military Assistance Fact Book,' September 1985 as updated, AFSOUTH for 1986.

in February 1947, that it was no longer economically in a position to support Greece and Turkey nor, thereby, to stall any prospective moves towards the establishment of communist regimes in these countries, the American government, through the Truman Doctrine (which had long been in development), stepped in to fill the gap. The Doctrine provided for the support of 'all free peoples who are resisting attempted subjugation,' and was a policy that immediately benefitted the United States' future allies in the eastern Mediterranean. Already, in April, July and September 1946, the Sixth Fleet had made its presence known near Turkey and Greece, and generally in the Adriatic, to support friends of the United States.[2] On 30 September 1946, the U.S. government formally announced that henceforth units of the U.S. navy would be permanently stationed in the Mediterranean to help carry out American policy and reinforce diplomacy. The Marshall Plan for Europe that followed the Truman Doctrine was a natural extension of these initial political and military démarches. The policy that eventually became known as containment had its first manifestations in the Mediterranean.

It is interesting to observe, however, that formal treaty commitments to the eastern Mediterranean did not immediately follow. It is not simply that the inclusion of Greece and Turkey in NATO was not considered until 1951 (both became members in 1952), but that in the early debate on NATO within the United States there were serious concerns about what military commitments the government should be prepared to give in the Mediterranean. Dean Acheson, at the Senate hearings on the NATO pact in 1949, explicitly felt it necessary to testify that no one 'at the present time' contemplated following NATO with a 'Mediterranean pact and then a Pacific pact and so forth.'[3] In the early years, a large group of American strategists, as well as many of their West European counterparts, believed that NATO would be a more defensible alliance if it did not include potentially highly vulnerable members in the eastern Mediterranean.[4]

These initial hesitations aside, the U.S. commitment to Mediterranean security evolved rapidly during the 1950s, not just through the general machinery of NATO, but also through U.S. unilateral military deployments and U.S. bilateral treaty arrangements with the Southern Region states. These agreements, establishing a special relationship of sorts with all the signatory states (Portugal, Spain, Italy, Greece and Turkey), for all practical purposes made these countries consider that 'Western security' really meant U.S. base rights and assistance rather than a general commitment to NATO, or at least that U.S. security concerns and those of NATO were inseparable, a conviction that persists to this day. The fact that the Sixth Fleet possesses both a national and a NATO role (as STRIKEFORSOUTH) has added to this tendency to identify the unique American contribution to Mediterranean security with the general one of NATO. This view of the U.S. role is perhaps strongest in Spain, which was not a member of NATO until 1982, and much less the case with Italy, which has traditionally distinguished its relationship with the United States from its general commitment to NATO in a way not true of the Southern Periphery states: Portugal, Spain, Greece, and Turkey.

The role of the United States in the Mediterranean is one that is welcomed, but also treated with some circumspection by the local NATO states. The form this circumspection takes is another mark of distinction between the southern NATO states and their counterparts in central Europe. While budgetary constraints sometimes lead U.S. leaders to call for the reduction of U.S. troops in Europe and periodically to warn NATO allies that it will reduce forces unless a greater effort is made by Europeans for their own defence, in the context of the Southern Region, the United States fights tenaciously to keep the presence it has. The states of the Central Front most often express concern about the possible reduction of U.S. troops in Europe, while the states of the Southern Region periodically *call* for the withdrawal of the U.S. presence. Since the American presence in the Mediterranean is largely a 'rented' one, the content of base negotiations can often stray from the narrow parameters of security concerns; and because there is no perfect alignment between U.S. and local state security interests, the 'landlord' states reasonably believe that they can afford to make firm demands concerning the territory which they give over to U.S. military use.

The extent of U.S. rights throughout the region is impressive and compares favourably with the few facilities of military significance that the Soviet Union can exploit for use in the Mediterranean region. In the western approaches to the Mediterranean the most important facility is Lajes airfield in the Portuguese island of Terceira in the Azores. This base was used by the United States during the October 1973 war primarily as a refuelling stop for resupply operations to Israel, and was, at the time, the only unrestricted available facility. During the crisis the U.S. Military Airlift Command (MAC) was able to route forty-two flights through Lajes in a twenty-four hour period.[5] If the United States again asked Portugal to give it the same rights in similar circumstances, the government would probably refuse, unless the North Atlantic Council and the Defence Planning Committee agreed that the use of Portuguese facilities was vital for 'NATO security'; but it is not something automatically to be expected. The Lajes airfield is, however, extremely important to NATO for a number of in-area tasks. It would be vital for the resupply of Europe in the event of hostilities.[6] It is a major centre for anti-submarine warfare (ASW) operations for which the United States has supplied its most sophisticated equipment. From facilities located in the chain it is possible to track Soviet submarines operating within a 1,000-mile radius. Thus, the Azores installations permit the United States to maintain extensive surveillance of Soviet activity in and around the Straits of Gibraltar, as well as to monitor the mid-point of the 4,000-mile sea lane that links the Sixth Fleet with its major supply depots in the American east coast.[7]

In Spain, the use of Spanish facilities by the United States is governed by the five-year Defense Economic and Cooperation Agreement (DECA) signed in 1982, ratified in 1983 and currently under renegotiation. The agreement allows for the stationing of up to 12,545 U.S. military personnel and 1,669 civilian personnel at thirteen different bases and establishments, four of which are particularly important.[8] The aeronaval base at Rota is central to the United States for surveillance and control of the western Mediterranean Sea and the Atlantic Ocean. It is a very important communications centre for the Sixth Fleet, and stores ammunition and equipment that may be used by the United States in the region. In the 1970s it acted (like Holy Loch in Scotland) as a base for Poseidon submarines, though since 1979, at the demand of the Spanish government, this has no longer been the case. Torrejon, near Madrid, has become significant as an air base since the Sixth Fleet began concentrating its manoeuvres in the eastern part of the Mediterranean. Elements of the 401st U.S. Tactical Fighter Squadron based there are responsible for air control of the western Mediterranean area, a task for which aircraft of the Sixth Fleet were previously responsible. The 72 F16s based there could support Italy and Turkey in time of war and if needed, could pick up nuclear weapons in these countries to perform a nuclear mission. The base is a major staging, reinforcement and logistic airlift base for U.S. forces. The runway at Torrejon is the longest to which the United States has access in southern Europe and can be used by Galaxy heavy transports. The Torrejon base was at the centre of bilateral negotiations conducted between Spain and the United States on the reduction of the U.S. presence in Spain in 1986–1987, during which the United States consistently emphasized the importance of the base for NATO defence. The base at Zaragoza houses KC 135 tankers, the only U.S. tankers deployed in the Southern Region, and it is also an important air-to-ground and air-to-air weapons training centre for the U.S. air force in Europe. The Bardenas Reales firing range is also extremely important. Moron is a small air base providing further necessary logistic support,[9] and houses a terminal for naval communications which connects it and Rota to other U.S. bases in the Mediterranean.[10] The relative freedom of action that U.S. forces have had at these bases over the years has sharpened and confused the debate in Spain on the relative value (and exchangeability) of the U.S.-Spanish military relationship and active Spanish participation in NATO. After the March 1986 referendum in which Spain voted to remain in NATO — though out of the integrated military command — the government began pressing the United States for a reduction of its presence in the country, which the referendum had cited as part of Spanish policy. The Spanish government is determined eventually to eliminate the American presence in Torrejon as part of its commitment to the public regarding the 'progressive reduction' of U.S. forces in Spain.

In Italy, the U.S. military presence serves a variety of purposes, but perhaps the most important is the coordination of all U.S. activity in the Mediterranean. There are numerous U.S. nuclear weapons units in Italy spread throughout the country and a variety of communications units that form part of the U.S. Defense Communications Systems (DCS). Ten NADGE centres are located throughout the country. In northern Italy at Vicenza, the Southern European Task Force (SETAF), which is part of the U.S. army in Europe, has several functions: it administers the U.S. nuclear custodial units attached to the Italian army; it is intended to provide support to Italian ground forces; it would provide logistics support for operations in the

59

Southern Region; and it hosts the 4th Battalion (Airborne) 325th Infantry — which is earmarked to the AMF. This battalion is now a forward element of the 82nd Airborne Division, the leading component of the U.S. Rapid Deployment Force.[11] This change constitutes, at a minimum, an important symbol of the continued weight that the United States attaches to its south European bases for the performance of out-of-area tasks.

The natural concentration on naval forces as the primary means to confront the Soviet Union in peacetime has meant that a large number of U.S. military personnel in Italy are involved in this task. Aside from the principal naval base at Gaeta, which serves as the home port of the Sixth Fleet flagship, there are also two important bases serving ASW functions: Sigonella near Catania in Sicily, for maritime patrol aircraft, and La Maddalana off the northeast coast of Sardinia, used by nuclear attack submarines. Aircraft based at Torrejon air base outside Madrid are often deployed to Aviano air base. Intelligence operations are conducted from San Vito dei Normanni near Brindisi. The U.S. army has two bases (Camp Ederle and Darby) which are used by several army and air force units.[12] The range of U.S. military operations in Italy is considerable and it is evident that from these bases U.S. troops are able to perform many NATO-related tasks, while also remaining available to defend U.S. interests outside the NATO area.

In Greece, the current five-year DECA governing the use of Greek bases by the United States dates from 1983 and will remain in force at least until 1988. The government of Andreas Papandreou has pledged not to renew this agreement when it expires, though the economic advantages of maintaining a special link with the United States, as well as the fear that any American reaction would inevitably be in some respects 'pro-Turkish,' will make the government pause, once the day of reckoning arrives. The principal U.S. facilities in Greece serve primarily to support U.S. air and naval action in the Southern Flank. The most important facility is the Souda Bay complex on the northwest side of the island of Crete. This houses fuel and ammunition and its anchorage is almost large enough to accommodate the whole Sixth Fleet. The airfield is used for military reconnaissance by U.S. forces, and can accommodate any U.S. navy or air force tactical aircraft, as well as (though with difficulty) air force C-141 and C-FA cargo planes.[13] At Heraklion, also on Crete, the United States conducts intelligence operations and the air station there supports air tanker refuelling operations. Five NADGE centres are dispersed in northern Greece. A large military communications centre is located at Nea Makri just north of Athens.[14] The Hellenikon air base complex provides a full range of support activities for U.S. military aircraft operating throughout the Mediterranean and aircraft deployed from this base also perform intelligence missions.[15]

Greek bases are vital intelligence gathering centres for the U.S. armed forces and their loss would seriously constrain the capacity of the Sixth Fleet to operate effectively in Mediterranean waters. All Greek governments have usually considered that U.S. facilities on their territory serve *exclusively* U.S. and not (to the extent these can be separated) NATO interests. The reduction of the U.S. presence in Greece (as in Spain) seems to be a political inevitability, but the extent and form of that reduction must be negotiated so that general NATO interests are preserved.

U.S. installations in Turkey have increased in importance since the collapse of Iran. The DECA dating from 1980 was renegotiated in 1986. Throughout the agreement special mention is made of the fact that Turkish facilities are put at U.S. disposal 'in support of NATO defence plans,' and the agreement as a whole draws an especially close link between economic and defence assistance.[16] Its renegotiation was, in fact, delayed largely because the Turks desired further concessions on trade matters. The major facility that is vital to both the United States and NATO is Incirlik air base, which provides forward basing for U.S. tactical fighter bombers in rotation from Spain. Fighters based here are the most forward deployed landbased U.S. aircraft in the eastern Mediterranean.[17] Other facilities are: Sinop, used for electromagnetic monitoring; Kargabarun, for radio navigation; Belbasi, for seismic data collection; and Pirinclik for radio warning and space monitoring. There are also several other storage depots, communications sites and fourteen NADGE early warning sites. Information from these systems would help the Sixth Fleet know of Soviet air attacks in the eastern Mediterranean and give it warning of the need to deploy further west if necessary. These intelligence gathering sites in Turkey are also very important for monitoring the Soviet Union's military activity in its southwestern military districts and the development of weapons systems in the Black Sea region, as well as collecting data on Soviet tests pertinent to strategic arms limitations agreements.[18]

At least 20 percent of the Sixth Fleet's Mediterranean-based fuel is kept at Turkish installations. The U.S.-Turkish agreement of October 1982 on colocated operating bases (COB) provides for the modernization of several Turkish airfields and the building of two new ones capable of receiving transport planes and long-range bombers. These improvements will eventually give the United States, and NATO generally, an enhanced capacity for the forward defence of Turkey.[19] U.S.-Turkish cooperation on all clearly Alliance activities is likely to remain strong even if Turkish governments will always be especially concerned about the impact of these relations on their own regional policies, which must be carefully managed.

This is, in fact, the case for all the states of the Southern Region, for each of which the out-of-area question poses problems. The United States' allies in the Southern Region are all very concerned about not promising the United States the use of any national facilities for action in the Middle East in advance of any actual crisis there. It is a reasonable presumption that in the current political climate, automatic use of such facilities would not be forthcoming unless events in the Middle East were judged to impinge directly on national security and the proposed U.S. military response to these events was thought to be appropriate. As the simultaneous presence of these two conditions must be assumed unlikely, U.S. planners cannot expect to receive the necessary support from Southern Periphery countries in the event of a U.S. military response to a Gulf crisis. Unless Soviet power, particularly Soviet power based in the Mediterranean, was directly brought to bear on the Middle East, Southern Periphery states — all of which have special relationships with the Arab States — would be adverse to harming the sometimes delicate balance of their Middle East foreign policies by directly supporting the military action of the Western superpower.

The U.S. raid against Libya in April 1986 raised concern in southern Europe, more than in any other area of Europe, about American unilateralism in the area. This concern receded once it was clear that there would be no 'backlash' from the Middle East, but the action did seem to reinforce the view that, owing to the U.S. base presence in the Mediterranean, NATO's southern allies can be implicated against their will in U.S. Middle East policy. Though various recent NATO communiqués have recognized the prospective danger of out-of-area developments to Western security, the interpretation of the relevance of Middle Eastern events to national security necessarily remains both subjective and a matter of the moment. Even if in the view of the United States the Southern Flank of Europe extends beyond Turkey to the Gulf, there is not an automatic acceptance of this link between south European and Middle Eastern security by any of the NATO countries closest to both regions.

In any case, through these various agreements most of the countries of NATO South have forged a special relationship with the United States that sets them apart from the majority of their West European counterparts. The purposes to which U.S. bases are put in Portugal, Italy and Turkey are such as to keep the link between U.S. and NATO activities very strong. In Spain and Greece, for a number of historical and also geographical reasons, U.S. bases serve more obviously U.S. interests — there are in fact no NATO headquarters in either of these countries — and the 'NATO element' of the U.S. presence seems weaker, and therefore creates problems in the management of bilateral relations. In the specific case of Greece, it may be that the establishment of LANDSOUTHCENT/7th ATAF at Larissa would have beneficial pyschological implications for NATO by legitimizing the U.S. military presence in Greece as part of a larger Alliance set-up. Yet, this still would come up against some resistance. Taken as a whole, the Southern Periphery countries define their relations with the 'West' primarily as a function of the agreements which they have with the United States. As their views of their place in the Western world are partly derivative of the early deals they struck with the United States, their defence perspectives are based largely on a tradition of bargaining with the Western superpower, rather than on a will to build general designs for future security.

This may change, and the southern states may move from a uni-dimensional Atlanticism to a less anachronistic and broader vision of their place in Western security. But this will require both enlightened management of the necessarily persistent special link with the United States and perhaps a new round of special bargaining with the other countries of Western Europe. As has happened in the economic field (especially with the entrance of Spain and Portugal into the European Community), similar, if not entirely complementary, moves are likely to be made towards a Europeanization of defence perspectives. Turkey and Portugal have established close bilateral links with

63

the Federal Republic of Germany; just as Greece and Spain have done with France. In all these cases these bilateral links have served as a limited counterweight to the predominance of the United States. How the countries of NATO South will develop their defence policies depends on their own perceptions of the Soviet threat, on the NATO analysis of security problems in the Mediterranean, and on the links that they will gain or break with the non-NATO states of the Mediterranean littoral. Their perception of the contribution they can bring to NATO defence is in every case individual, and this represents both the strength and the weakness of the NATO position in the Southern Region.

INDIVIDUAL SOUTHERN REGION DEFENCE POLICIES

Portugal and Spain: Western Area Partners?

Portugal and Spain have traditionally had rather different security perspectives and have only recently begun to share the same interests. As both are now members of NATO and the EC their foreign policy 'options' are precisely the same for the first time in history. If Portugal naturally has a much more Atlantic vocation, and Spain a Mediterranean one, the sources of potential tension in dividing responsibilities for the defence of the western approaches to the Mediterranean persist. A more active cooperation between the two states in security policy is symbolized by the existence of a defence pact that calls for yearly meetings of the two armed forces and is continually strengthened by joint exercises and programming. Each country, however, is developing and redesigning its armed forces to deal with contingencies of special national importance.

Despite Portugal's current interest in developing closer ties with other West Europeans, as evidenced by its application to join the Western European Union, its army is not yet in a position to contribute significantly to continental security. The earmarking in 1976 — after the end of the colonial wars in Africa — of a brigade to NATO AFSOUTH was a symbolic move towards a more European-orientated policy, but the brigade now only provides a strategic reserve for the southern land theatre, and lacks the lift capacity to make an adequate contribution to Central Front defence.[20] Much effort has been made to modernize the army, which has been reorganized and reduced in size in the last ten years, from 190,000 to about 45,500 men.[21] As time goes on, Portugal is likely to show an attachment to continental security, and to further cooperation with the states of the Central Front. The air base that the Portuguese have put at the disposal of the West German air force for training purposes, at Beja in the southern Alentejo region, is a symbol of this commitment. But until Portugal is able to modernize its quite old equipment (the army still relies on very old M-48 tanks), the country will not be able to help NATO's defence substantially at the centre.

Although it will be necessary for Portugal to play its European card as strongly as its more traditional American one, it is nevertheless true that the American connection will continue to dominate Portuguese strategic thinking. Portugal's primary responsibility — the defence of the Portugal-Azores-Madeira triangle — necessarily requires close collaboration with the Americans. The prime Portuguese mission is to help preserve NATO's sea lines of communication in the Atlantic that are likely to be threatened by submarine elements of the Soviet navy. Anti-submarine warfare in the Atlantic is therefore Portugal's first task in the event of a major East-West conflict. In order to improve its capacity to undertake this role the Portuguese navy arranged (with NATO support) for the purchase of three frigates that would have an ASW capacity, and is also attempting to develop its fleet of minehunters and minesweepers. As Portuguese ships would be the only naval units immediately available in the IBERLANT area in the event of hostilities, considerable improvements are necessary to make these into a credible force. The three minesweepers currently in Portugal's inventory are not actually operational as such and are only used for coastal surveillance. To increase the capacity for manoeuvre in the huge Atlantic zone in which the navy operates, Portugal seeks to establish appropriate naval support installations at Praia da Victoria near Lajes air base, and is improving the facilities at the Ponta Delgada harbour.[22] Similarly, efforts are being made, again with NATO support, to improve the Porto Santo airfield near Madeira, a potentially important facility for the reinforcement of Europe, that would also be vital for the defence of the Portuguese islands. With Spain and Italy, Portugal is also participating in the latest

NATO project for the upgrading of Southern Region radar air defence.

The modernization of Portugal's armed forces, as well as of its military and civilian infrastructure, is a priority that helps to maintain Portugal's essential attachment to NATO and especially American defence policies. This does not, however, extend to an acceptance of some of the arguments advanced regarding the out-of-area threat to NATO security, and Portuguese authorities who have their own out-of-area concerns, are reluctant to allow the United States to be the primary interpreter of these. Certainly, in respect of the Middle East, Portugal does not wish to acknowledge that a military presence there, composed of any special combination of NATO powers acting even on their own initiative, is an appropriate way to deal with the various conflicts that upset the region. The decision by Portugal not to send a peacekeeping contingent to Lebanon was taken in part because of an innate reluctance to send forces abroad after the Portuguese African debacle, but also because of a desire not to give credence to the idea that events in the Middle East require military responses by NATO powers.

While there is much discussion in Portugal as to what role will be played by that country in the event of an outbreak of hostilities, there is less debate as to how war may begin and against what special threats it must be prepared. There is, at present, no definition of a threat to Portugal within the concept of national defence. There is a perceived need to prepare against possible contingencies: a conventional Warsaw Pact attack against the Portuguese metropole; or commando attacks against special military facilities or the various archipelagos. But the Warsaw Treaty Organization (WTO) threat is still considered extraordinarily distant; the declaration of Libya's Colonel Muammar Muhammed Gadaffi that the various Portuguese islands are really part of Africa, and the presumption that a Morocco, in the post-Hassan II era, may be a more hostile neighbour, raise concerns that are both geographically and pyschologically more immediate. Certainly if the western Sahara were under Soviet influence, or subject to pressures from other hostile or revolutionary states, this might well have an effect on the separatist movements in the Canary Islands, and as a consequence on the Portuguese possessions off the coast of Africa.[23] Portuguese diplomacy is therefore especially concerned to strike an appropriate balance of influence in the states of North

Africa, and to establish a rhythm of economic and other cooperation that would make hostile acts by these countries counterproductive.

If this is true in the case of Portugal, it is all the more so for Spain. Spain's entrance into the Alliance does not mean that its military preparations will necessarily be concentrated on defending against a Soviet threat. While much of what Spain hopes to do in the military field in the next five to ten years will help the Alliance in the event of Soviet aggression, its military policy is not by any means exclusively directed against this threat. One of the principal points of the Joint Strategic Plan (JSP), in which the government has recently elaborated the main strategic objectives of the armed forces, is that the Spanish military should be in a position to neutralize whatever threat may present itself (outside the East-West conflict) without receiving any assistance from the United States or other allies.[24] This independent defence policy has been developed in the full knowledge that the Alliance could not undertake to protect Spain in the event of an attack on the Spanish enclaves of Ceuta and Melilla (off Moroccan territory) which is perceived as one of the more realistic threats to Spain. The JSP provides for collaboration with the Alliance in order to defend the Straits of Gibraltar with units operating from the Canary and Balearic Islands. Military reforms under way reveal that the threat from the south is still of primary concern.

Defence plans developed since the JSP was established have aimed at reorientating the Spanish armed forces towards the south of the peninsula. In 1984, the Defence Ministry decided to reorganize the internal deployment of the Spanish ground forces. The nine Spanish military regions inherited from the Franco regime have been reduced to six, with headquarters in Madrid, Seville, Valencia, Barcelona, Burgos and La Coruna.[25] The 2nd military region in the south will be reinforced to prevent any attack on Spain's southern flank. Four large bases will be strategically distributed throughout the southern province of Andalucia at Almeria, Granada, Cordoba, and Campo de Gibraltar. The operational command for these bases will be in Seville. Two motorized infantry brigades and one mechanized brigade will be placed in the south making it the most heavily armed military area in Spain.[26] A Special Operations Group, composed of three companies, has also been allocated to the south. The 414 Roland anti-air missiles, which the Spanish armed forces received in 1984, will almost all be placed in this zone. The seventy-two F-18A aircraft acquired by the air force in the same year were chosen primarily because of their utility in an attack role against North African targets.[27] Many of these decisions form part of the government's army modernization plan whose general aim was to convert the Spanish army from a 'force of occupation' to one having a direct role against potential external threats.[28]

These new deployments, offensive as they may seem, have not damaged relations with Morocco. The Spanish have explained these changes as ensuring their capacity to control the Straits of Gibraltar, and to keep protected, in the event of war, the link between the Canary Islands and the metropole. The two countries have even held joint exercises, and the Spanish government has sold Morocco military equipment including at least one corvette and several patrol boats.[29] Morocco is hoping to add F-16, F-20 or Mirage 2000 planes to its inventory, whose only realistic role would be in intercepting F-18As. King Hassan has publicly declared that if Spain were ever to recover Gibraltar from the British, he could not tolerate Spanish control of three important points at the entrance to the Mediterranean (including Ceuta and Melilla) and would not be adverse to seeking whatever help was required to recover the enclaves. The Spanish government, however, seems to have put the need to expand its arms exports (which have also included transfers to such countries as Paraguay and Libya)[30] above either the fear that these may be used against Spain or the political nature of the receiving country. Nonetheless, the Spanish-Moroccan relationship is likely to remain unsteady despite efforts by both sides to build confidence between the two countries.

The question of Spain's contribution to NATO has always been affected by the fact that the threat from the East is not paramount in Spanish eyes. Since the March 1986 referendum on NATO, however, the special terms of the referendum have served as guiding principles for government policy. In late 1986, a series of negotiations began with NATO to establish the means of Spanish military collaboration with NATO while staying out of the integrated military command. The government has demonstrated its intention to be widely represented in NATO military fora (for example, the Military Committee, the Defence Planning Committee and the Nuclear Planning Group) without committing forces to the Alliance, an attitude that has led to charges of ambiguity by Spanish opposition leaders.[31] While the government has insisted on non-integration, it is interested in alignment, as indicated by the fact that Spain has chosen to organize its own force planning cycle to correspond with that of NATO. Clearly Spain will be willing to perform military missions that are relevant to NATO security but will not prefer to commit itself to deploying forces outside Spanish territory. Though it may be possible for Spain to negotiate agreements with NATO calling for Spanish force deployments in case of war far from Spanish territory, the tendency will remain to concentrate on local and regional defence.

Where a military mission may be confined to protecting areas important to Spain, notably the strategic axis, formed by the Balearic Islands, the peninsula and the Canary Islands, a full commitment by Spain is only to be expected, as the defence of this area corresponds precisely to national interests as defined by the Spanish. Missions that constitute support for actions taken by other powers elsewhere are inevitably seen as less important and may even be excluded. The Spanish navy, for example, is well placed to add to NATO's security in the Mediterranean as it has important shore facilities that can help support forces throughout the region.[32] Even if Spain is not integrated into the Alliance, many would hope that memoranda of understanding could be arrived at which would give Spain a role in the defence of the western Mediterranean. While some have argued that it would be useful if Spain were to contribute land forces to the AMF, for example, or commit itself to other specific NATO military missions, such options seem to be ruled out by the referendum conditions. Certainly, there will be very great reluctance to assist in the performance of out-of-area tasks. Any collaboration of Spain with other allies is likely to be pragmatic and on a bilateral basis, justified by the nature of Spanish defence interests. The wider the interpretation of Spain's security interests, the greater will be its contribution to Alliance security. The probable trend is for more bilateral agreements with other Mediterranean countries. Whatever policies Spain adopts it will resist being seen simply as an area that increases the depth of the Central Front, a place from which arms and equipment can be redeployed, a less vulnerable storage centre for necessary supplies, or a trampoline for action elsewhere — all 'defence analyst' visions of Spain which the Spanish resent.[33]

The decision by Spain to keep out of the integrated military command has removed (at least temporarily) one of the major difficulties between Spain and Portugal. For years Portugal has been concerned that Spain might wish to play a role within IBERLANT (the subordinate command of SACLANT in which Portugal exercises its military responsibilities), and have especially feared that Spain might be granted command of IBERLANT. Clearly Spanish interests do not lie exclusively in the Mediterranean, and some compromise would have to be worked out which included a role for Spain in the IBERLANT area as currently constituted. Even if Spain stays out of the integrated command, Spain and Portugal will have to debate between themselves complementary security roles in the Atlantic/Mediterranean region. A discreet rivalry between the two countries certainly persists and affects the nature of relations with the United States. In mid-1987, for example, Portugal watched with interest the base negotiations which the United States was holding with Spain, and remained cautiously uncommitted on the question of whether it would accept extra U.S. bases if Spain were to expel the Americans from Torrejon. It is only to be hoped that important security tasks for each country will eventually evolve because of a need to share duties with each other, rather than simply to negotiate work loads with the United States.

France and Italy: Central Mediterranean Leaders?

The French and the Italians, for different geopolitical reasons, have both recently developed foreign and defence policies that emphasize the Mediterranean dimension of their power and influence. In the process, neither has devalued the quite special contribution each brings to continental or Central Front security, but rather have sought to build on natural geographic advantages to solidify a type of political strength that would allow them to act as arbiters in the various latent and actual conflicts of the Mediterranean basin. Both the French and the Italians have sought to establish a military presence for broad political reasons, rather than to counter any well specified military threat, and in this way have followed the examples of the two superpowers, which have established a military presence for political reasons.

70

The beginning of an active French Mediterranean policy was in the early 1970s when President Georges Pompidou increased French political activity in the Middle East and chose to give the Mediterranean a 'privileged' status within French foreign policy. There were three principal political axes to this new orientation. First, the Pompidou government sought to push the European Community southwards by openly supporting the candidacy of Spain to the EC, and defending the idea of *latinité* in various proclamations. Second, Pompidou began a more active policy in the three states of the Maghreb — Tunisia, Algeria and Morocco — with which he increased trade and political contacts. Third, the government decided to resurrect long-standing French interest in the Middle East, and began to present France as the main interpreter of European interests in the region. From the beginning of his presidency, Pompidou embarked on a declaratory policy that called for the desirability of returning the 'Mediterranean to the Mediterraneans,' and supplemented the expression of this wish by increasing French arms sales throughout the area. Throughout the Pompidou period, several large military exercises were held in the Mediterranean that displayed a growing French interest in the political advantages that could be derived from the overt use of sea power.[34]

The formal military extension of this policy did not truly come about until 1976, when under President Valéry Giscard d'Estaing, the French navy moved its aircraft carriers Foch and Clemenceau from their base at Brest to Toulon.[35] A very much enlarged French Mediterranean squadron was created to establish an important 'third force' in the area that gave a military complement to France's general political discourse in this sense. The policy of 'separating the superpowers,' and the refusal to accept the 'logic of the blocs' received its strongest (and safest) manifestation in the Mediterranean. When the British left their base in Malta in 1977 (dissolving the Royal Marine Commando Group), the French could claim to be the most important European power in the Sea. The interest of the navy in strictly 'Mediterranean problems' has grown because of increased instability in the Middle East, a continuingly volatile energy market, a dramatic rise in Islamic fundamentalism, and the persistence of conflict in the Maghreb.

As a consequence, since at least 1976, the French navy in the Mediterranean has collaborated very closely with its NATO

71

counterparts with which it regularly holds joint exercises. The Commandement en chef pour la Méditerrannée (CECMED) has signed a memorandum of understanding with NAVSOUTH that delineates ways in which the French navy can cooperate with NATO forces in time of war. Despite the 'politics of independence' that govern the French presence in the Mediterranean, it is probable that the French Mediterranean squadron is *de facto* the most 'NATO integrated' of all French armed forces. Several agreements exist with NATO AFSOUTH which establish the basis for French participation in Mediterranean defence. While it is true that as long as they are not engaged with allied forces, French ships and naval aviation serve a strictly national deterrence policy, the belief that the central and eastern parts of the Mediterranean constitute a vital transition area between Europe and various other external theatres has led the French to work extremely closely with their NATO allies to defend the sea lines of communication in the Mediterranean.[36] From time to time French maritime patrol aircraft collaborate with other NATO forces in the surveillance of Soviet naval vessels in the Mediterranean.[37]

Following the reorganization of the French armed forces that has taken place pursuant to the terms of the 1984-1988 Military Programme Law, the French Mediterranean squadron (composed of roughly 100,000 ship tons, or 40 percent of the French navy) has begun to work especially closely with French intervention forces. It is supported by a flotilla of light craft, a squadron of attack submarines, and a variety of naval aircraft including Breguet Atlantic patrol planes, Super Etendards and helicopters (based at Saint Mandrier). In June 1985, the *Force d'Action Rapide* participated, for the first time, in major manoeuvres in the Mediterranean, in which both the Foch and Clemenceau aircraft carriers, their support ships and France's nuclear attack submarines took part.[38] These types of exercises are symbolic of the nature of France's interest in the Mediterranean and will continue to increase in scope.

Unwilling to let the Sixth Fleet be the sole defender of Western interests in the Sea, the French navy seeks to demonstrate a capacity to act independently within the Mediterranean in order to project power effectively outside it. France's participation in the multinational peacekeeping force in Lebanon could not have taken place without important (national) sea-based support, especially given the French decision to stay on after other Western powers had left. France's substantial presence in the Mediterranean and the closeness of French naval ties to NATO very much complicate Soviet planning in the Mediterranean, especially in the west. The care France has taken to adopt a flexible and balanced policy in the Maghreb has been perhaps the most important obstacle to the deep penetration of Soviet influence in North Africa, which if ever established, would clearly totally change the perception of Soviet power in southern Europe. France's independent political strategy in North Africa and its self-sustaining naval presence in the Mediterranean are healthy additions to the Western position in the Southern Region.

Italy's evolving Mediterranean design is not nearly so overtly ambitious, but it serves comparable ends. In the 1980s Italian Defence and Foreign Affairs Ministers have tended to put greater emphasis on the geopolitical link between European and Mediterranean security, a link which naturally makes of Italy a key, rather than a marginal, factor in ensuring stability within southern Europe.[39] But more importantly, Italy has recently argued (what so many other Southern Region states have traditionally seen as an elemental truth) that the Western Alliance cannot provide satisfactory answers to all possible national security problems. Defence Minister Lelio Lagorio put this view in dramatic terms when, on 13 October 1982, he said to the Parliamentary Defence Commission that the Alliance 'no longer offered a total guarantee of the defence of our country.' This statement was not interpreted to mean that the importance of the Alliance in deterring the Soviet Union from attack had in any sense declined, but rather was thought to imply that as threats to Italian territorial integrity could come from elsewhere — notably the south — it was Italy's responsibility to defend against threats not formally recognized by NATO.[40]

Few Italian officials have specified, for diplomatic and political reasons, exactly whence the southern threat comes, though potential Libyan aggressiveness against Mediterranean shipping or Italian islands is clearly a concern. The desire to *reinsure* Italian security by taking specifically national measures to defend the peninsula from commando attacks or other forms of low-scale violence stems precisely from the fear that any threat against Italian security interests is likely to take modest forms and will therefore be insufficiently serious to trigger full-scale Alliance-wide measures. In this, Italy

73

is typical of the states of the Southern Region, in its increasing concern that while NATO may have prepared itself well and consistently for the most awe-inspiring of possible threats — a full-scale Soviet attack across the Central Front — more minor forms of assault must be matters of national responsibility.

The perceived need to do more for national defence has made it appear that Italy wishes to have more autonomous power within the Mediterranean. Modest steps have been taken to increase the degree of Italian power facing south. A squadron of interceptor aircraft has been placed in Sicily, a certain redistribution south of the armed forces (especially engineer batallions) has taken place in order to deal better with possible commando attacks, and military facilities in many of the southern islands have been upgraded. With the modernization of NADGE, several new radars will be placed in the south. Now that the proposed Italian intervention force is in place, Italy will have an increased ability to defend national interests beyond its national territory, especially to protect its citizens in other countries. The deployment of the new Garibaldi aircraft carrier with a task force orientation will also give Italy an increased sea control capacity.

But these reforms in no way suggest that Italy wishes to become the Mediterranean policeman in an out-of-area role. The FIR has now been fully established with headquarters in Florence and includes (among others) the Folgore airborne infantry brigade, the Friuli motorized infantry brigade and the San Marco naval infantry battalion. There is still much internal debate in Italy, however, about how such a force could be used. There is no specific 'historical' or other mission for which the Italian intervention forces would be relevant. It would be most useful as a force to defend Italian territory, keep the peace elsewhere, or form part of a strategic reserve for AFSOUTH forces. It would not have more than a 'firefighting role' in any conflict and certainly could not sustain itself for very long. Even if there is some internal discussion in Italy concerning improvements in Italian naval capacity that would make it possible for Italy to relieve the Sixth Fleet of some of its burdens, it would be unrealistic and unproductive to consider ways to *replace* American naval power in the Mediterranean. At the moment, there is no clear political requirement for Italy to improve dramatically its capacity to project power in the Mediterranean, and as a consequence there will be insufficient political will to establish some of the more radical reforms that have been put forward to upgrade Italian military power in the south. A clear ability to defend the northern land border and possibly come to the aid of Austria or Yugoslavia in time of conflict will remain the chief Italian defence priority.

The fact that there exists substantial internal debate in Italy on these questions is, nevertheless, a healthy sign for the Alliance. Rather than concern itself largely with what can be done (at a minimum) to fulfil the Alliance's defence needs, Italy is beginning to take several security initiatives which even if they have specifically national motivations are of general utility to the Alliance. Since the defence of AFSOUTH is, in any case, primarily a *national* responsibility, individual defence measures are in the collective interest. Because the threat to AFSOUTH countries does not issue exclusively from the Soviet Union, but also from the Mediterranean littoral states which may develop specific military objectives in times of political crisis, defensive deployments southwards have a deterrent value that is broadly stabilizing; just as do political undertakings, such as Italy's guarantee of Malta's neutrality. Like the naval forces of the United States and France, those of Italy are able to play a political role that is useful in peacetime. The challenge for both Italian and NATO defence planners in the near future is to ensure that the new security measures taken by Italy are adequately coordinated with those of other Southern Flank countries, as well as of NATO countries outside the region that have responsibilities within it. The hope of President Pompidou that the Mediterranean become a 'lake of peace' was never shared by Italian leaders of the time. Even if Italy would like now to play a greater role in Mediterranean security, nothing would displease it more than to be alone in defending the Alliance's front line in the south.[41] This is why many outsiders hope that Italy may be ideally placed to play a brokerage role in the Southern Region, convincing the Spaniards of the need to participate more in collective defence, or mediating between the Greeks and the Turks.

Greece and Turkey: Eastern Mediterranean Disputants?

Two of AFSOUTH's land sub-theatres are under the direct control of Greece and Turkey: Greek-Turkish Thrace and eastern Turkey. If Warsaw Pact ground and air forces were able to defeat land forces in one of these areas in wartime, it would become extremely difficult for other NATO forces to act later to recover lost territory. Any naval supremacy that NATO forces may be able to maintain, even in the eastern parts of the Mediterranean, would be insufficient for Western defence if it proved impossible for the local armies (with whatever outside assistance might immediately be available) to hold the land front in either Greece or Turkey. The lack of territorial depth in Greek-Turkish Thrace (about 25 kilometres at its narrowest point, and 180 on average) puts a premium on territorial defence and on a high concentration of forces in this area, but the political disputes between Greece and Turkey have made coordination of policy difficult. Since neither country sees the Soviet Union as the only source of its insecurity (Greece considers Turkey a threat, and Turkey is concerned about the implications of regional instability in the Middle East), strategic thinking on how to defend against a potential attack has not developed sufficiently, and has been held hostage to a number of extraneous political factors.

The PASOK government of Andreas Papandreou in Greece formally announced, at the end of 1984, a New Defence Doctrine that made the threat from the east (Turkey) the official primary security concern of Greece. In so doing, the government has merely given sanction to the popular view (which has existed at least since the Turkish invasion of Cyprus in 1974) that the threat from the Soviet Union or from Warsaw Pact armies is not as urgent as the threat from Turkey. The elaboration of this defence doctrine has not led to significant changes in force structure or doctrine. Greek forces remain distributed throughout the country as they have been for about a decade. Arms purchases and modernization programmes in no special way indicate that capacities are being developed that would be more relevant for conflict with Turkey than with Warsaw Pact forces. The principal new developments in Greek armed forces — the shift to a much more fully mechanized infantry, the purchase of new tanks to replace aging M48s, the improvements in the Greek navy's ASW capacity, and the purchase of new radars and fighter planes — are as important (if not more so) for the fulfilment of NATO-orientated tasks as for a limited conflict with Turkey arising from a dispute over an Aegean island or seabed rights. The declaratory policy of the

Papandreou government is therefore not fully translated into military improvements that reflect an ostensibly increased concern for potential Turkish belligerency. Though it is hardly an obsession, Greek military planners still concern themselves with the fact that Bulgarian armed forces, were they to choose to do so, could pose a major threat to Thrace, and occupy the whole area within forty-eight hours.

Politically, the attitude of the PASOK government, as a matter of objective fact, has not served to decrease tensions in the Aegean, or between Greece, the United States and NATO. The aim of Papandreou's declaratory diplomacy is in part internal, to mollify sections of the church and the left, and partly external, to increase Greek bargaining power within the Alliance and to keep the Aegean issues high on the NATO agenda.[42] In this latter sense, the PASOK policy has been successful, but it is limited in so far as it is a tactic that is not subsumed in a wider strategy. The solution of the various Aegean issues does not lie, after all, in NATO or in U.S. hands, but rather in bilateral negotiations with Turkey in which external actors would have a proper role to play only at the end, rather than at the beginning. After the June 1985 elections, Papandreou seemed to adopt more conciliatory tones within NATO, negotiated with the United States for the sale of F-16 aircraft, and appeared to take a less strident attitude on the issue of U.S. bases in the country. Relations with Turkey, however, have remained tense and in March 1987 Greece and Turkey almost came to blows following a dispute over oil drilling in the Aegean, thereby demonstrating the fragility of relations between the two countries.

Individually, the issues that divide Greece and Turkey (except for the special case of the resolution of the Cyprus problem) are not major, but taken together they form a package of problems that can easily be exacerbated and serve to reinforce mutual suspicions. The four principal issues are the dispute about sovereign rights over the continental shelf, the question of territorial sea limits claimed by each country, the dispute over military and civil air traffic control zones in the Aegean area, and the problem of the remilitarization of the Greek islands in the eastern Aegean.[43] The detailed position of each side in these disputes has not changed substantially since they were first established. The Greek view is reinforced by the fact of the Turkish invasion of Cyprus, and the establishment of the

Fourth Army at Izmir, which seem to serve as proof of continuing Turkish belligerency; and the argument of the Turks is strengthened by the recent refusal of the Greek government to come to the negotiating table, on the grounds that international law favours Greece on each issue, which taken in a larger historical perspective is seen by Turkey as representing an abuse of rights that has allowed Greece to expand its operational 'control' over the whole Aegean area.

Without entering into the details of these highly complex issues, it is possible to state that this dispute has generally complicated NATO military planning in the Aegean, and in some respects made it impossible. NATO exercises in the area are hampered by the dispute and the coordination that would be necessary in time of war cannot be put to the test. The establishment of COMLANDSOUTHCENT and 7th ATAF at Larissa remains subject to the resolution of outstanding problems related to the Aegean questions. Diplomatically, tensions between the two countries have put NATO in a difficult position; it has had to respond to the entreaties of both Greece and Turkey and is regularly accused of supporting one side against the other. Only in its economic policy towards the countries has NATO escaped relatively unharmed. The Economics Directorate, since 1977, has sought to coordinate aid to Greece and Turkey (as well as Portugal), in order to support economic development in these countries which is viewed as a necessary precondition to any successful military modernization programme. The United States is also caught in the dilemma, notably because of the Congressional practice to keep aid for Greece and Turkey at a seven to ten ratio, a policy which Turkey would prefer abandoned and Greece would like maintained.

Military modernization is very important for Turkey whose needs in certain areas are urgent. At the moment, Turkish forces have no protection against nuclear, biological and chemical (NBC) weapons, almost no anti-tank guided weapons or night-vision equipment is in service, little air defence exists (though British *Rapier* systems have recently been bought), and command control and communications equipment are generally in poor shape.[44] These problems have taken on special significance in the past few years as the countries surrounding Turkey have appeared especially unstable, a fact that has made Turkish leaders insist on the importance of diplomatic, as much as military, measures to guarantee Turkish territorial integrity.

The 'National Security Concept' developed under the government of Bulent Ecevit is, in its essence, still part of Turkish foreign and security policy.[45] The proximity of the Soviet Union, the war between Iran and Iraq, the military buildup in Syria, and the general instability of the southeastern Mediterranean region have made it necessary for Turkey to base its security policy on maintaining good relations with all countries of the area. This policy has not only resulted in a Turkish form of *Ostpolitik*, but also in balanced policies towards Iran and Iraq and in moves to enhance mutual confidence with other bordering states.

The present government of Prime Minister Turgut Ozal clearly considers the Soviet Union the primary external threat (unlike the government of Ecevit that, in 1978, formally declared the Soviet Union no longer a challenge to Turkish security), but believes that any army modernization must be managed so as not to be too provocative. Turkish leaders wish to maintain carefully the special relationships that they have established with their Middle East neighbours and, to some degree, with the Soviet Union (primarily in the trade field).[46]

While the United States is Turkey's principal aid donor, Turkey is seeking to diversify its military suppliers within the Alliance, not only because of the unfortunate experience of the U.S. arms embargo of 1974-1978, but also in the interest of promoting its relations with the countries of Western Europe. This is unlikely to harm its now very close relations with the United States and, in any case, decisions that serve to distinguish bilateral U.S.-Turkish relations from general intra-NATO ones are beneficial to an alliance whose notions of collective security have become fragmented. As the front-line state in NATO's Southern Flank, Turkey has a special claim on the Alliance that few other countries, aside from West Germany, can better. This is something well understood by Turkish leaders, who use what leverage is possible to extract what they can from Alliance partners. But it also requires of Turkey's NATO partners an appreciation of the fact that the management of regional security in the southeastern Mediterranean requires Turkey to fashion a foreign policy that may not be in perfect conformity with typical Western theses about the sources of threat in the area.

THE SOUTHERN REGION: IN SEARCH OF COHESION

In assessing what type of security policy NATO should have in the Southern Region, the Alliance must struggle with the fact that the *individual* defence policies conducted by the NATO states in the area are also *autonomous* ones. The fact that the Alliance has not been able to reduce the degree of nationalism in the defence efforts of the Southern Region states has effects that are both benign and troublesome. As long as defence efforts remain clearly national they are likely also to be serious. When states believe that their defence requirements can only be satisfied by their own policies, then they can be counted on to do their utmost to provide for their own security. The states of the Southern Region are forced to adopt purely national defence policies for a number of reasons. First, the terrain to be defended makes the development of region-wide defence strategy very difficult — geography creates disincentives to coordination. Second, as these states do not share common conceptions about the origins of possible military threats to their territories, national incentives to cooperate are not automatically great — assets that cannot be pooled need not be collected. Third, since many of these states consider some of the Alliance's concerns to be separate from their own, the Alliance is not a body to which defence can be entirely entrusted — in these political circumstances, special needs may be ignored, and responsibilities imposed that have no relation to immediate fears.

These resolutely national policies of defence, however, are sometimes inefficient and create unfortunate impediments to collaboration. The aim of improving the prospects for regional defence is essentially twofold. First, the Soviet Union must be deterred from thinking that NATO South can be politically or militarily decoupled from the Central Front. The whole Alliance must be willing and able to display a firm commitment to the region's defence. Second, all NATO allies must be aware of the inevitable link between the security of the Southern Region and the situation in the Middle East and the Gulf, and develop more of a common approach in dealing with the problems of these areas. For the states of NATO's Southern Region the problems of the Middle East and the Gulf are central to their concerns; a strong defence for the Southern Region will make it more difficult for problems to 'spill over' into the NATO area. While both these aims can be achieved, in part, by close consultation and further planning with European allies, the relationship with the United States will remain the most important determinant of whether progress can be made.

Over time it can only be hoped that a more balanced relationship can be developed between the United States and the states of NATO South. American out-of-area policy produces tension that is difficult to resolve. On the one hand, the states of the Southern Periphery, which see their capacity to bargain with the United States as a key element in their security policy, recognize their special utility to the United States lies, in some degree, in what can be offered to that country in terms of bases or facilities which it may wish to use for out-of-area activities. They bargain, or so it often seems to them, less for their own security than for the interests of the United States outside the Southern Region. This means that when foreign policies on out-of-area issues differ — as they often must, precisely because issues that are out-of-area for the United States are often local ones for the states of the Southern Region — the place of the United States within the Mediterranean is questioned. On the other hand, the U.S. position cannot be rejected, since it is the U.S. connection that for many of these countries gives meaning to their membership in the Alliance. When relations with the United States are good, 'NATO' itself seems irrelevant; when relations are bad, NATO is seen as part of the problem. Since the United States, through its bases agreements, is seen as the 'federator' of the south, disputes with the United States are direct challenges to the Alliance, a fact that is truer in the Southern Region than it may be at the Central Front. At the centre, problems are shared, whereas in the south, for geographic and political reasons already referred to, they are individual. The important political challenge that must be confronted in the next few years is for the United States and the countries of the Southern Region to come to a better understanding of where their mutual interests lie in the Mediterranean area.

It is probably right to expect that these mutual concerns can only be expected to produce truly collaborative action — or at least no very major disagreement — on purely NATO-related questions. None of the U.S. allies in the Southern Region is likely to consider favourably requests for the use of U.S. facilities on their territories for out-of-area contingencies. All have made clear that this issue is to be decided on a case-by-case

81

basis and that the cases where agreement can be expected are going to be rare. Difficulties in the relationship between the Southern Region states and the United States can also arise because of the expectations that these agreements bring. Portugal, Spain, Greece and Turkey all expect increasing American security assistance in return for continued use of host-country military facilities. These countries have all succeeded during base negotiations to extract an agreement from the U.S. executive that 'best efforts' would be made to convince the U.S. Congress that it should approve security assistance which the executive believes appropriate.[47] On the other hand, it may be that Congress, from time to time, chooses to attach to the offer of further or increased security assistance, flexibility on the behalf of the host countries in the interpretation or implementation of existing agreements. This dynamic is bound to lead to frustrations and it is desirable that the United States and its partners in southern Europe establish, as clearly as possible in negotiating extensions of agreements, enduring principles on which these agreements can be based.

Despite these tensions, NATO will continue, at least pyschologically, to have a comparative advantage over the Warsaw Pact in the Southern Region, if only because six NATO states have an easily verifiable stake in the defence of the area, while the bulk of the Warsaw Pact countries have a much more nebulous interest in southern European affairs. The principal NATO challenge in the Southern Region, whatever the exact dimensions of Soviet capabilities in the area or the ambitions of other non-NATO states, will remain one of internal management. The variety of political interests and national concerns amongst countries whose territory stretches from the Azores to Ardahan necessarily means that Alliance debates on the management of Western security are open ended and difficult to manage. Many of the NATO states in southern Europe consistently hold internal debates on the role that they should play within the Alliance, and on what the Alliance can do for them. This indicates that in dividing responsibilities for Western defence in southern Europe, the Alliance will continue to discover that there exists between member states a tension in general defence requirements and individual aims. This makes an understanding of the internal policies of these countries, the subject of the following chapters in this book, all the more necessary.

NOTES

1. Memorandum by Bevin on defence in the Mediterranean, Middle East and Indian Ocean, 13 March 1946. DO(46)40, CAB 131/2 Public Records Office, London. Quoted by David Dilks, in 'The British View of Security: Europe and the Wider World 1945-1948,' in *Western Security:The Formative Years*, ed. Olav Riste (Oslo: Norwegian University Press, 1985), 37.

2. Edward N. Luttwak and Robert G. Weinland, *Sea Power in the Mediterranean: Political Utility and Military Constraints*, The Washington Papers, no. 61 (1979), 10.

3. Walter LaFeber, *America, Russia and the Cold War, 1945-1980*, 4th Edition (New York: John Wiley and Sons, 1980), 84.

4. Coral Bell, *The Diplomacy of Détente: The Kissinger Era* (London: Martin Robertson, 1977), 140.

5. Foreign Affairs and National Defense Division, Congressional Research Service, 'United States Foreign Policy Objectives and Overseas Military Installations,' report prepared for Committee on Foreign Relations, U.S. Senate (Washington, DC, 1979), 52. (Hereafter cited as: 'United States Foreign Policy'). See also Foreign Affairs and National Defense Division, Congressional Research Service, 'U.S. Military Installations in NATO's Southern Region,' report prepared for the Committee on Foreign Affairs, U.S. House of Representatives (Washington, DC, October 1986), 4-5. (Hereafter cited as 'U.S. Military Installations').

6. Alvin J. Cottrel and Thomas H. Moorer, *U.S. Overseas Bases: Problems of Projecting American Military Power Abroad*. The Washington Papers, no. 49 (Washington, DC: CSIS, 1977), 12-14.

7. Congressional Research Service, 'United States Foreign Policy,' 52.

8. See, Ministerio de Asuntos Exteriores, *Convenio de Amistad, Defensa y Cooperacion Entre Espana y los Estados Unidos de America* (Madrid, 1982).

9. Alberto Santos, *La Péninsule Luso-Ibérique: enjeu stratégique*, Les Cahiers de la Fondation pour les Etudes de Défense Nationale, no. 18 (Paris,1980), 40-41.

10. Congressional Research Service, 'United States Foreign Policy,' 56.

11. William M. Arkin and Richard Fieldhouse, 'American Military Forces in Italy,' in *What the Russians Know Already and the Italians Must Not Know*, Istituto di Ricerche per il Disarmo, lo Sviluppo e la Pace, (Rome, March 1984), 9.

12. Congressional Research Service, 'United States Foreign Policy,' 58.

13. Congressional Research Service, 'U.S. Military Installations,' 35.

14. Ibid., 61.

15. Greek Foreign Ministry, *Agreement on Defense and Economic Cooperation Between the Government of the Hellenic Republic and the Government of the United States of America* (Athens, 1983).

16. See, U.S. State Department, Annex of *Cooperation on Defense*

and Economy, Agreement Between the United States of America and Turkey, signed at Ankara, 29 March 1980, Treaties and Other International Acts Series 9901, (Washington, DC).

17. Congressional Research Service, 'United States Foreign Policy,' 64.

18. Congressional Research Service, 'U.S. Military Installations,' 49.

19. Bruce R. Kuniholm, 'Turkey and NATO: Past, Present and Future,' *Orbis*, 27, no. 2 (Summer 1983): 438-439.

20. General A. Garcia dos Santos, 'A New Army for Portugal,' *NATO's Sixteen Nations*, 28, no. 5 (Special 1/1983): 73.

21. Western European Union, 'European Security and the Mediterranean,' Assembly, Document 1073, Revised Report, Mr Kittlemann rapporteur, (Paris, October 1986), 13.

22. Admiral Antonio Egidio de Sousa Leitao, 'The Strategic Relevance of the Azores,' *NATO's Sixteen Nations*, 29, no. 2 (Special 1/1984, April-May 1984): 80.

23. Alvaro Vasconcelos, 'Vision Portuguesa Sobre la Seguridad de la Region Peninsular y Norteafricana,' in *Estrategia del Mediterraneo Occidental y del Maghreb*, Instituto de Cuestiones Internacionales (Madrid, 1983), 254.

24. Miguel Angel Liso, 'Asi es el Plan Estratejico Conjunto,' *Cambio 16*, no. 705 (6 March 1985): 36.

25. Stanley G. Payne, 'Modernization of the Armed Forces,' in *The Politics of Democratic Spain*, ed. Stanley G. Payne (Chicago: The Chicago Council of Foreign Relations, 1986), 186.

26. Miguel Angel Liso, 'Cuatro Bases para la Defensa de Espana,' *Cambio 16*, no. 706 (10 June 1985): 41.

27. See *El Pais*, 4 November 1984.

28. See *El Pais*, 9 January 1985.

29. Payne, 'Modernization of the Armed Forces,' 191.

30. Ibid.

31. Anabel Diaz, 'El Gobierno mantiene su ambiguedad sobre la aportacion a la Otan,' *El Pais*, 14 April 1987.

32. David J. Salusbury, 'Spain: The Challenge for NATO,' *Journal of the Royal United Services Institute for Defence Studies* (September 1983): 20.

33. Maurizio Cremasco has argued that this has been a traditional view of Spain (and of Portugal) held by other Alliance members. See his article 'The Mediterranean, the Atlantic and the Indian Ocean: A Difficult Strategic Equation,' *Lo Spettatore Internazionale*, 15, no. 1 (January-March 1980): 14.

34. Daniel Colard, 'La Politique Méditerranéenne et Proche Orientale de Georges Pompidou,' *Politique Etrangère*, 43, no. 3 (1978) passim.

35. Announcement of this change in policy is in *Le Monde*, 8 May 1975.

36. Admiral Yves Leenhardt, 'The Role of the French Navy in the National External Action Policy,' *NATO's Sixteen Nations*, 29, no. 2 (Special 1/1984, April-May 1984): 38.

37. WEU, 'European Security and the Mediterranean,' 16.

38. *Le Monde*, 5 June 1985.

39. Lelio Lagorio, 'From the Alps to the Mediterranean: Italy's Defence Posture,' *NATO's Sixteen Nations*, 28, no. 3 (June/July 1983): 60.

40. IAI Report, 'The Evolution of the Major Factors Influencing International Politics and Italy's Options for the 1980s,' *The International Spectator*, 19, no. 3/4 (July-December 1984): 183.

41. François Puaux, 'Regards sur la Politique Etrangère de l'Italie,' *Politique Etrangère*, no. 2 (June 1981): 308.

42. See generally, John C. Loulis, 'Papandreou's Foreign Policy,' *Foreign Affairs* (Winter 1984/1985): 375-391.

43. See generally, Andrew Wilson, *The Aegean Dispute*, Adelphi Paper, no. 155 (London: IISS, Winter 1979/1980).

44. Gregory Copley. 'Turkey's Bold New Strategic Initiative,' *Defense and Foreign Affairs* (November 1984): 10.

45. For an analysis of the Ecevit policy see, Michael M. Boll, 'Turkey's New National Security Concept: What it Means for NATO,' *Orbis*, 23, no. 3 (Fall 1979).

46. George Capopoulos, 'La Turquie, entre Orient et Occident,' *Etudes Polémologiques*, 31, 3rd Trimester (1984): 125.

47. Congressional Research Service, 'U.S. Military Installations,' 58.

3

Portuguese Defence Policy: Internal Politics and Defence Commitments

Alvaro Vasconcelos

INTRODUCTION

Located on the Western periphery of Europe and removed from the Western front, Portugal was a non-democratic member of NATO for twenty-five years. This anomalous situation has now changed. An analysis of Portugal's present role in the Western security system must be based on an historical evaluation of internal Portuguese politics. Three factors stand out. First, between 1949 and 1974 (and especially after 1961) defence and security policies were not centred on the Euro-Atlantic theatre. Second, from 1974 to 1975, the country lived through a unique experience in postwar Western Europe that contributed to the formation of a strong anti-Soviet and pro-Atlantic national consensus. The attempt of the Communist Party to take power during this period forced democratic elements to rally around a new sense of Atlantic solidarity. Third, until 1982 political power was supervised by a politico-military body — the Council of the Revolution — created by the constitution. Only after this date was the principle of the subordination of military forces to duly elected political power incorporated into a revised constitutional text.

Today, thirteen years after the coup d'état of 25 April 1974 which brought about democracy in Portugal, the Portuguese people are coming to grips with the various problems associated with this transition. It would seem logical that Portugal's entry into the European Community on 1 January 1986 should have ended a difficult period of integration into the international system. Similarly, its adoption of democratic government and foreign policy guidelines parallel to those of other Community members established it as a more valuable contributor to the Alliance's ideals. Uncertainty about the fundamental options of Portuguese society was resolved by the time Portugal became an EC member state.

However, despite sharing common geostrategic concerns with its European partners, Portugal's economic difficulties, the evolution of its domestic politics and the particular role of the military within its society still differentiate it from other West European democracies. Its political and economic situation and its policy-making process in defence and security link Portugal more closely with peripheral European countries of the Mediterranean.

Foreign and security policies have been undergoing a process of redefinition since 1976, when NATO and the EC began to figure prominently on the Portuguese government's agenda. As yet, successive governments have not elaborated policies that would reflect this increased concern for European defence. 'Coexistence' with Spain, with which Portugal now shares fundamental options regarding foreign policy, NATO and the EC, is one of the important issues to be addressed in the policy redefinition process. With respect to NATO, Portugal has been able to demonstrate positively its role as an ally. A favourable domestic political climate created by the gradual strengthening of democracy and the victory of pro-Atlantic political parties is to thank for this. Negotiations are taking place on how to extend U.S. rights to the mainland; facilities had formerly been granted only in the Azores. In the years to come Portugal will have to define more carefully its military relationships with the United States, Spain and its European partners in NATO.

This redefinition must of course be based on certain facts of geography as well as on less immutable political considerations. In global strategic terms, Portugal is part of the Atlantic-Mediterranean region that stretches from the Azores to the eastern Mediterranean and the Persian Gulf. From the NATO perspective, this region reaches as far as Ardahan in Turkey, a few miles from the Soviet border. The increasing geostrategic importance of Portugal, especially in the out-of-area context, is becoming evident. It is also apparent, however, that military forces are ill-equipped, both structurally and in terms of matériel, to handle adequately the tasks which the new foreign and defence policies of Portugal may require them to perform. Furthermore, although there is a pro-NATO consensus that binds together democratic parties and the public, there is no similar agreement over the need to modernize the Portuguese armed forces. Both the public and certain important sections of the political leadership are sceptical about the extent to which a modernization of the armed forces would contribute to deterrence since they perceive a threat against Portugal as highly unlikely and, moreover, they feel that, given the shield already provided by NATO, a Portuguese deterrence apparatus would be redundant. In addition to this, military expenditure is generally perceived as an extravagance given Portugal's severe economic difficulties. Political instability and economic troubles have also led to the emergence on the left and reemergence on the right of nationalist opposition to the foreign and security policies (interpreted as a 'surrender' of the country to the allies) adopted since 1976. Furthermore, however unrealistic it may seem, the threat from Spain is often invoked by conservatives who are still haunted by António de Oliveira Salazar's prophecy that once deprived of its colonies Portugal would in turn fall under Spanish colonial rule.

Two essential objectives have dominated Portuguese politics over the centuries: the maintenance of its colonial empire, and the affirmation of its national identity within the Iberian peninsula — a term disliked and used as little as possible by most Portuguese in anything other than its strictly geographical sense. An alliance with the dominant maritime power (first Britain, and later the United States) has always been regarded as essential for fulfilling these two objectives. During World War II, even if Salazar's political beliefs drew him close to the Axis, geostrategic and political constraints forced him to adapt his neutrality policy to the requirements of the Anglo-Portuguese alliance and later to join NATO.

Portugal has abandoned its isolationist attitude vis-à-vis Europe and now wants to play an active role within NATO. It does not wish merely to assume the role of a large airport at the gates of Europe, and seeks to be more assertive within NATO councils. Portugal, the 'faithful ally' as it was once called by Joseph Luns, has begun to feel that it has not always been treated well by the allies. Some Portuguese recall the period of the African wars when Portugal received little support, others refer to ingratitude shown for Portugal's role in facilitating U.S. military action in the Middle East during the Yom Kippur War, while still others consider that the country has not received sufficient help to modernize its armed forces. Some people, therefore, wonder if a more 'prodigal son' attitude, similar to that taken by other peripheral countries, would not, all things considered, be more advantageous.

HISTORICAL AND GEOGRAPHICAL CONSTRAINTS ON PORTUGAL'S SECURITY POLICY

Portugal's foreign and security policies reflect, to a certain extent, the geographical position of the country and the shape of its territory (a rectangular strip of land, plus the Atlantic archipelagos — Madeira and the Azores). Situated on the Atlantic flank of the Iberian peninsula, Portugal is clearly on the periphery of the European continent, from which it stretches out towards Africa and the Americas.[1] The Algarve, the southern coast of Portugal, is 220 kilometres from the Moroccan coastal line. The Atlantic archipelagos of the Azores and Madeira and the Spanish Canary Islands reach out even further towards the African and American continents. If their marginal position isolated Portugal and Spain from the great changes wrought by the industrial revolution in Europe and allowed the peninsular states to maintain a comparatively neutral position during World War II, their projection towards Africa and the Americas explains their involvement in the affairs of those regions.

While in terms of climate, flora, level of economic development, culture and especially language, Portugal is a Mediterranean country,[2] in terms of geographical position and geopolitical options, Portugal belongs to the Atlantic theatre. Its Atlantic dimension, especially vis-à-vis Spain (which, for the Portuguese, belongs more to the Mediterranean theatre), has always been central to Portuguese strategic thinking, although Portugal's special relationship with the Arab countries, particularly with Morocco, has recently added a new dimension to its strategic outlook.

In spite of common traits that differentiate the peninsula as a whole from the rest of Europe, the resemblance between Portugal and Spain is only superficial. Some experts and decision makers consider fallaciously that the Iberian peninsula is a uniform (although not homogeneous) entity, a notion which may have been reinforced by the simultaneous entry of Spain

89

and Portugal into the European Community. Drawn in the twelfth and early thirteenth centuries, Portugal's national borders remain the oldest and most stable in Europe. The individual shape of Portugal is easily identifiable, detaching itself from the heart of the peninsula, the *meseta*, the massive high plain from which Castille integrated all the peripheral units with the sole exception of Portugal.[3]

Traditional Alignment with Sea Powers

For evident geostrategic reasons, Portugal has always created alliances with leading maritime powers: first Britain, then the United States and NATO of which Portugal was one of the founding members. Portugal's membership in NATO, therefore, is consistent with its traditional alliance policy. The Anglo-Portuguese Treaty of Alliance was signed in 1373 and renewed through complementary treaties from the fourteenth to the twentieth centuries. It was applied frequently in the interests of both countries, although there have occasionally been harmful side effects. After the Napoleonic Wars, for example, the English general, Beresford, remained in Portugal as pro-consul while the Portuguese king, John VI, was in Brazil. During this period Beresford, in his capacity as commander-in-chief of the Portuguese army, violently suppressed the liberal revolution and was eventually expelled by the victorious insurgent movement. The treaty was not applied, however, during the Goa crisis of 1961.[4] It was, of course, implemented successfully as recently as the Falklands War, when Santa Maria and Porto Santo were used for refuelling by Britain.

The mutually beneficial character of the Anglo-Portuguese alliance is evident. Formally, it was a guarantee of Britain's hegemonic Atlantic position and of the integrity of Portugal's national boundaries and colonial empire. Britain did, however, interfere with Portugal's colonial policy on one occasion. On 11 January 1890, it issued an ultimatum against Portugal's plan to link Angola and Mozambique by land (which would have included what was eventually to become Rhodesia) — an incident which sparked a profound crisis in the Anglo-Portuguese alliance and led to the development of anti-British and nationalistic sentiment, as well as republican ideas which contributed eventually to the abolition of the Portuguese monarchy in

1910. Portugal complied with Britain's ultimatum and did not carry out its designs. But, paradoxically, it was only after 1890 that the actual colonization of Mozambique and Angola took place and Portugal established itself as the fourth world colonial power, counting among its possessions Angola, Mozambique, Guinea, Cape Verde, Sao Tomé e Príncipe, Timor, Goa, Damão and Diu. During the First Republic (1910–1926) the protection of colonial possessions became a dominant concern of Portuguese politics and remained so until 1974. It was so dominant that, even in spite of resentment towards Britain because of its 'breach of contract' in 1890, Portuguese republicans allied with Britain during World War I primarily in order to protect the overseas empire.

The tradition of basing security policy on alliances is still evident in present day Portuguese politics. The policy owes its success largely to the tactic of forging flexible alliances that are neither exclusive nor irreversible. Portugal has consistently sought compensations for a dependence on outside powers that might become unmanageable, drawing a balance between the Atlantic and European dimensions of its foreign policy.[5] The management of 'dependencies' is the central feature of Portuguese foreign policy.

Because no wars have been fought on Portuguese soil against a foreign power since the beginning of the nineteenth century (following the Napoleonic Wars), a notion has emerged that it is possible to 'neutralize' national territory. War is regarded as something only remotely possible, in spite of recent painful experience with colonial wars, and this belief in some way affects public attitudes to defence policy. Despite a general popular consensus in favour of the alliance with Britain and the United States, and a tendency to support military action taken by allies (for example, the clear public support of British intervention in the Falklands in 1982 and the only mild criticism of the American intervention in Libya in 1986), increasing distrust and resentment towards the allies is becoming evident among political leaders and military circles. From the experience, sometimes negative, of the presence of British troops in Portugal,[6] some have drawn the conclusion that 'invasions by the allies are often more harmful to a country than enemy invasions.'[7] By 'invasions' these critics (mostly in the army) refer to the possible presence on Portuguese territory of allied troops, American or Spanish, to face threats with which the

Portuguese army would not be able to cope. This naturally would diminish the autonomy of Portugal within NATO. It is often recalled that during World War II ground forces in the Azores were Portuguese.[8] This 'historical tradition' is used as an argument by the army to justify its position that the presence of foreign troops in the country, even in its protection, should be resisted.[9] That is not to say that in the case of aggression against Portugal allied troops would not be welcome; rather, it is to argue that at present there is no perception of threat that would justify the stationing of foreign troops.

Portugal's strategic position has become vital — especially because of the geographical situation of the Azores — in terms of war scenarios in the European or the Mediterranean theatres in which the United States may become involved. It is widely accepted that Portuguese positions in the Atlantic are of the utmost importance to U.S. power projection towards Europe. This fact was already evident during World War I, when Portugal granted use of facilities in Ponta Delgada (Azores) to the United States, and it became even clearer with the development of U.S. naval and air power in the period immediately before and during World War II. To Americans, the Azores became, as Admiral Sterling put it in 1938, an 'advanced strategic border' of the North American continent, with a similar position in the north Atlantic to that of the Hawaiian Islands in the Pacific Ocean.[10]

The strength of U.S. interest in the Azores was incompatible with the policy of Iberian neutrality (Portuguese *and* Spanish) which Salazar sought to maintain at all costs through intense diplomatic activity in London, Berlin and Madrid prior to and during the course of World War II. A friendship and non-aggression treaty designed to maintain the status quo in the peninsula, and subsequently known as the Iberian Pact, was signed between Portugal and Spain in Lisbon in March 1939, and as a result, Salazar later played an important liaison role between Spain and the allies.

Portugal's difficulty in reconciling its desired neutrality with the interests of its maritime ally also became apparent when the United States actually decided to occupy the Azores. In a meeting held in Washington on 11 May 1943, in which both Franklin D. Roosevelt and Winston Churchill took part, 'Operation Lifebelt' was decided upon. The advocates of military occupation argued that the Azores were indispensable for the surveillance of a wide portion of the Atlantic in the performance of anti-submarine warfare tasks and that the islands were critical to the link between the United States and Britain, the European continent and Africa. 'Operation Lifebelt' was the code name for the military occupation of the Azores which, in fact, never took place. Political considerations, diplomatic pressures and the fact that the British were convinced that the Anglo-Portuguese alliance would work, finally solved the problem without need to resort to military action. After negotiations, facilities were granted to the British and extended to the Americans (as British allies). The American negotiator of this agreement, Chargé d'Affaires, George Kennan was right in stating that: 'Salazar ... fears association with us only slightly less than with the Russians.'[11] The Americans arrived in the Azores in the beginning of 1944 and never left.

U.S. interest in the Azores did not diminish after the war ended. In the opinion of U.S. military planners, the Azores, together with Greenland and Iceland, were the most important American bases outside the United States.[12] Although Salazar eyed the United States suspiciously after the wartime pressures — especially because of its policy of rejecting the inclusion of colonial possessions (Algeria excepted) in the NATO area — he had to face the fact that Britain was no longer the leading maritime power in the world. Despite the opposition of a strong group of Salazar's followers to any form of involvement in 'European disputes,' the reality of Soviet advances and the emergence of the United States as a global Atlantic power left Salazar with limited options. Domestic pressures prevailed and eventually, Salazar accepted to join NATO, despite tensions with the United States.

The end of the war fed the hopes of the Portuguese democratic opposition that the allies would bring democracy to Portugal. But because he could claim membership in an alliance of democratic nations 'determined to safeguard the freedom ... of their peoples, founded on the principles of democracy, individual liberty and the rule of law,' Salazar was able to boost his own public image (both at home and abroad) without satisfying the aspirations of the democratic opposition.[13] The opposition reacted by making vain appeals to the democratic states to reject Portugal's membership in NATO.[14] The communists, conversely, used Portugal's acceptance in the Alliance to expose the latter's 'reactionary and imperialist' character.

During the Cold War, Salazar made ideological use of NATO membership in his crusade against the Soviet communist threat which he projected onto the domestic theatre in order to fight against internal opposition, whether it was communist-inspired or not. The term 'crusade' was actually used in the recommendation of the Câmara Corporativa (Portugal's second legislative house composed of representatives appointed from professional bodies) to the National Assembly in support of the ratification of the NATO treaty. Salazar was unable to make the most of Portuguese participation in NATO to improve Portugal's external public image, since this image was damaged by his policy of proceeding 'proudly alone,' as the last symbol of Catholic values surrounded by 'devilish' democracies.

The isolationist doctrines of self-reliance contained in Portuguese foreign policy were not only unrealistic, given the growing interdependence between states in the postwar system, but a certain recipe for disaster. This became evident when, a year after Salazar refused the Marshall Plan for Portugal (and even offered financial aid to help other European countries recover from wartime disruption), he was forced, because of a large national debt, to revise his position and apply for an extension of the Plan to Portugal, subsequently approved for the year 1949–1950.[15]

Neither the Anglo-Portuguese alliance nor the Iberian Pact (Portugal's most important international commitments) were inconsistent with the NATO option. However, although Spain itself was shifting towards an alliance with the United States and adapting to postwar changes, it objected to Portugal's membership in NATO arguing that it undermined the Iberian Pact. The Portuguese denied this and made some weak attempts to convince their NATO allies that Spain ought also to become a member. However, the Portuguese nurtured suspicions about Spain which, during the period of Salazar's rule, turned into outright anti-Castillian hysteria much encouraged by official propaganda. The mentality of generations which have learned history from school books of that period is still tainted by such sentiments. Throughout the regimes of Salazar and Franco, mutual suspicion persisted in ironic contrast to the ideological proximity of the two dictators.

On 5 January 1951, the Mutual Aid and Defense Agreement between Portugal and the United States was signed. On the basis of this agreement, a defence agreement was signed on 6

September 1951, whereby Portugal granted the United States use of military facilities in the Azores (Lajes base). The integration of Portugal into the military structure of NATO went smoothly since there was no question of Spain joining the Alliance. Portugal fell under SACLANT, although the Azores were not included in the IBERLANT (activated in December 1966) whose headquarters are in Oeiras, near Lisbon, but in WESTLANT, which is stationed in Norfolk, Virginia.

Until 1974, Portugal's defence policy and consequently its policy of alliances were primarily motivated by the need to defend the overseas empire. When the wars in Africa broke out in 1961, Portugal became further alienated from its American and European allies. In the following period, the country's military effort focused largely on those wars. As a result, responsibility for defence of Portuguese territory was effectively entrusted to other NATO members. The truth is that a military threat to the mainland or the Atlantic archipelagos has never been taken seriously by Portugal and membership in NATO served, in the 1960s and 1970s, primarily as a means to gather political and military support for the war effort in Africa.

In spite of Salazar's warnings against the threat posed by the Soviet Union in Europe, the country's military expenditure was not increased when Portugal joined the Alliance, even if a significant process of modernization was undertaken in the 1950s within the NATO framework. The budget increased substantially only when the war in Angola broke out in 1961. Although, between 1953 and 1961, Portugal contributed a division for the defence of central Europe, its overall participation in NATO military forces was relatively insignificant.

The wars in Africa caused Portugal to become even more estranged from its European allies, whom Salazar accused of conspiring against Portugal's presence in Africa just as they had done in giving no help to Portugal when India occupied Goa in 1961. Relations with the United States were also extremely tense throughout this period, especially during the Kennedy administration, when both the Mozambican Liberation Movement (FRELIMO), led by Eduardo Mondlane, and Holden Roberto's National Liberation Front of Angola (FNLA) were receiving U.S. support. In 1961, an arms embargo was passed against Portugal by the U.S. Congress. Salazar responded by refusing to renegotiate the 1951 defence agreement, thus hoping to make the Americans fear for their bases in the Azores. Following this, the United States made some concessions on its African policy. Relations with the United States improved further during Premier Marcelo Caetano's government which came to power in 1968 after Salazar's death. As a consequence of growing U.S. involvement in Vietnam, the political stances of the Nixon administration and the Portuguese government became more similar even though there was sustained Congressional criticism of Portugal. In a memorandum addressed to the President in 1970, Kissinger recommended the relaxation of the embargo through the selling of 'equipment which has dual civilian and military uses.'[16] During the Yom Kippur War, the Caetano government was put in an awkward position by the Nixon administration which demanded overflight rights from Portugal for U.S. aircraft proceeding to the Middle East. While Caetano initially hoped for various *quid pro quo's* for this concession, the Nixon government succeeded in pressuring the Portuguese government by implying that the United States would take a firmer public stance in the United Nations and elsewhere against Portugal's colonial policy. The Caetano government, therefore, eventually acceded to Nixon's request on the understanding that the United States would provide Portugal with support should it be the object of economic or even military reprisals from the Arab countries.

NATO's attitude towards Portugal, prior to 1974, did not have a negative influence, as it did in Greece, on the formation of democratic political parties or on Portuguese public opinion. This was partly because the non-communist opposition was very weak and was constituted mainly of moderate socialists and republicans whose ideal model of society was reflected in the Western democracies of the other NATO member countries. And if Mário Soares, founder and leader of the Socialist Party, was critical of the support — even if minimal, and often reluctant — lent by some NATO members (France, Germany, and the United States) to the Portuguese war effort, this criticism was never very strong.[17] Furthermore, the Socialist Party (PS), the only democratic party that existed before 25 April 1974, was founded in Germany in March 1973, with some support from the German Social Democratic Party which was then in power. The two other democratic parties in existence before 1985, the Social Democratic Party (PSD) of liberal orientation, and the Democratic and Social Centre Party (CDS) of Christian

Democrat leanings, were both led by people who had been linked to Caetano's policies of overture. Both parties adopted pro-European and pro-NATO attitudes and benefitted from the support of German foundations.

The Growing Weight of the Military Forces

Although the military instigated the movement that eventually overthrew parliamentary democracy in 1926 and brought Salazar to power, there were many opponents to the regime within the armed forces, sympathetic especially towards Britain, and who welcomed participation in NATO as a means for cooperation with the allied democracies. Participation in NATO eventually served to 'democratize' the Portuguese military and throughout the Salazar regime members of the armed forces expressed their dissatisfaction. As early as 1946, General Marques Godinho and General Ramires, both governors of the Azores during World War II, led an abortive military revolt against the regime. In 1949, General Norton de Matos, who had been governor of Angola prior to 1926, ran for Presidency against the official candidate of the regime, another army general, Oscar Carmona. Later, in 1958, a military man, Air Force General Humberto Delgado, a former military attaché in the United States, was the opposition candidate in the Presidential election held in that year. He was murdered by the political police in 1965. In 1961, Defence Minister, General Júlio Botelho Moniz, openly expressed his disapproval of the regime. He was promptly removed from office. Overall, however, Salazar was able to keep rebellious members of the military under control. In any case, a sense of duty and discipline prevailed until 1974, reinforced by the common feeling that it was an inappropriate time for disunity since the first and foremost duty of each soldier was to help sustain the empire.

The war in Africa restored much of the lost influence and power of the armed forces and gave them a greater degree of autonomy vis-à-vis civilian political power. The military asserted its views more and more strongly on the crucial problem of the Portuguese nation: how to end the colonial war. Among those in favour of a political solution to the African problem was General António de Spínola, Commander-in-Chief of the armed forces in Guinea, who tried to persuade

97

Premier Caetano to negotiate with the liberation movement, the African Party for the Independence of Guinea and Cape Verde (PAIGC). Even if he may have been inclined to listen to General Spínola, Marcelo Caetano could not, in turn, convince the ultra-conservative political and military sections, who had the support of the President of the Republic (1958–1974), Rear Admiral Américo Tomás.

NATO member states had different individual approaches towards the situation in southern Africa. These differing policies, however, created a generally negative attitude towards NATO within Portugal where the domestic debate on this issue was divided between two radically opposed groups. On the one hand, the *ultras* could never forgive NATO for what they considered its ambiguous or even treacherous positions: its rejection of the Portuguese thesis of 'enlargement' of the Alliance towards the south Atlantic; and the support lent by European and NATO countries to the liberation movements in Portugal's former colonies. On the other hand, those sections permeated by communist influence and most of the younger officers, who had adopted the ideological beliefs of the liberation movements they were supposed to be fighting, could not forgive NATO for what they considered to be all-out support for Portugal in the colonial wars. The latter were the founders and organizers of the Movement of the Armed Forces (MFA, also termed 'movement of the captains'). The central issue in the formation of the MFA in 1973 was the opposition of a group of junior officers (captains with four years training in the Military Academy) to the government's decision to offer full military careers to graduates of a six-month course. Led by a group of young army captains, engaged in the colonial wars, the movement was soon to become more political. Like General Spínola, the captains realized that the colonial wars had no military solution and strove to find a political solution to the colonial question. On 25 April 1974, the MFA overthrew the regime in a swift military coup in Lisbon that had general public support. Premier Caetano and President Tomás were to surrender to General Spínola.

Portugal's interaction with the European economy, culture and society has been increasing steadily since 1949. At the beginning of 1974, more than one million Portuguese were working in France and some 200,000 in Germany. This brought badly needed foreign exchange into Portugal. Foreign trade was

carried out primarily with Europe. Britain was the main impor-
ter of Portuguese products (23.7 percent of total Portuguese
exports in 1973), and during the first enlargement of the EC,
Portugal negotiated an agreement with the Community, signed
in June 1972, that further linked the economies of Portugal and
those of other Western European countries.[18]

This rapprochement with Europe was opposed by a sector of
Portuguese businessmen (accustomed to special privileges in
Africa) who defended a more protectionist view. The majority
of leading businessmen, however, (who had benefitted from
Portuguese membership since 1955 in the European Free Trade
Association, EFTA) were sympathetic to a liberalization
process that would bring Portugal politically closer to the rest of
Europe. In a book that had a large influence on the military
leadership and other sections of Portuguese society, General
António de Spínola — who was to become the first President of
the Republic following the 1974 coup — praised the European
Community and said there was no alternative for the Portuguese but integration into a 'European space' that 'might accept
us if we behave predominantly as Europeans.'[19]

EMERGING DIFFERENCES ON DEFENCE AND SECURITY

When Portuguese military involvement in Africa ended, the
Communist Party (PCP) and the left-wing in the military tried
unsuccessfully to impose a position of neutrality within NATO
and of pro-Third World non-alignment in Portugal's foreign
and security policies. Nevertheless, many of those who questioned, after the 1974 coup, the use of the Alliance to
guarantee Portugal's security, came to realize fully through
their own experience in 1974-1975 how important allies
could be. In the late 1980s, attitudes towards security issues
and decision making on national defence matters are still
determined by events that immediately followed the coup.
Domestic political events have played a decisive role in
shaping perceptions in foreign and defence policy matters.

Anti-Soviet and pro-Atlantic Sentiment

In Portugal there is a broad national consensus in favour of
NATO and an anti-Soviet strategy, comprised of the

99

democratic political parties, the armed forces, leading figures in the media and the public as a whole. The Communist Party has a strong influence, however, over the workers in and around Lisbon and the rural workers of the large southern estates nationalized by the land reform.

The impact of the 1974–1975 crisis on the Portuguese people cannot be overemphasized. While Europe was welcoming détente and the outcome of the Helsinki conference, Portugal was undergoing what Mário Soares described as a communist effort at 'the final assault on power, even reaching the stage of an attempted siege on the Assembly of the Republic, as if to take the Winter Palace in St. Petersburg in 1917.'[20] Fortunately enough, Mário Soares never became the 'Portuguese Kerensky,' the gloomy role which Henry Kissinger had predicted for him, nor was Portugal a 'lost cause' or the 'anti-communist vaccine of Europe.'

In 1974–1975, the communists were able to integrate into their political front an important group of the MFA and thus radicalized the democratic process. They were able to force the pro-Western President, General António de Spínola, to resign and to replace him with General Francisco da Costa Gomes. With the subsequent nationalization of banking and major industries, and the land reform, the communists gained control of important sections of the state apparatus. Finally, in the summer of 1975, since they had almost complete control of the cabinet led by the decidedly pro-communist Vasco Gonçalves, the government was practically in communist hands. In order to thwart the communist onslaught, the democratic forces were compelled to unite. They had to reject any possibility of compromise with the Communist Party, and to fight it decisively in every area identified as a 'key area' by Soviet ideologist Boris Ponomarev (in his work published in June 1974 to draw lessons from the defeat of communism in Chile). These areas were the media (deeply infiltrated by the communists, where politico-ideological blackmail was the rule), the armed forces and the state bureaucracy.[21]

In the nineteen months between 25 April 1974 and 25 November 1975 — when a group of military officers became disgruntled with what they perceived as a putschist and totalitarian left-wing regime — Portugal underwent profound changes, the consequences of which are still strongly present in all aspects of Portuguese society. During that period, moderate representatives of the military, led notably by General António de Spínola, were outside the government. The Council of the Revolution, a politico-military body entrusted with the supervision of the MFA and the political parties, was established to act, in the words of the constitution, as 'guarantor of the enforcement of the Constitution and of the faithfulness of the spirit of the Portuguese Revolution of 25 April 1974 and as political and legislative body in military affairs.'[22] The 1976 constitution was drafted in 1975 in a tense atmosphere — during which the Assembly was under siege by communist and leftist workers — that led to considerable bargaining and compromise. This is the reason for the explicit mention of the armed forces as the guarantors of democracy.

From the unity achieved in the defeat of the totalitarian forces, the Socialist Party, the Social Democratic Party and the Christian Democrats reached common stands on such issues as membership of the European Community (which was the first priority in foreign policy from 1976) and the necessity of Portugal's participation in NATO and in the defence of the West. For the Portuguese political leaders who dominated the political scene up to the 1985 general election, loyalty to the Atlantic Alliance became a fundamental factor in Portuguese politics. This was due to internal reasons and to the need for external support (particularly financial aid) to fund the deficit of the balance of payments. These same leaders have been generally more opposed to appeasement towards the Soviet Union than their counterparts in Europe, favouring a hard line in international negotiations with the USSR: 'The Portuguese government is in favour of consensus and negotiation, but with one limit: that they be actually feasible and not a mere excuse for softness and giving-in on the part of the West.'[23] Public opinion in Portugal follows quite closely the views of the political leadership, although there is a clear lack of public interest in international issues.

A possibly more important opinion leader, in times of crisis, is the Catholic Church, the ideologically predominant force in Portuguese society. The Portuguese Catholic Church is a traditional church, that generally supported the previous regime until 1974. Although strongly anti-Soviet, it is more than cautious in expressing opinions on international matters. Its stance is not dissimilar from certain forms of isolationism that seek to protect Portuguese Catholics from atheist ideas. In 1974–1975 the

101

Church demonstrated its great influence. Feeling threatened by the communists, it mobilized a large part of the population against the Communist Party. Some observers identify the turning point during the 1974–1975 crisis as the time when the Catholic Church was under direct and open attack from the communists and was compelled to respond. The most spectacular aspect of this mobilization was perhaps the assault against communist headquarters, some of which were burnt down, after an appeal for Catholic resistance made by the Archbishop of Braga, D. Francisco Maria da Silva.

Isolationism and pro-Atlanticism

Any analysis of opinion polls taken in the last few years shows that the Portuguese people are relatively uninterested in major international issues, even in those directly related to the country. The share of non-respondents ranges from 20 percent in the IEEI 1983 poll on NATO,[24] to some 45 percent in *Euro-baromètre* polls of April 1985 on the EC (which dropped to 30 percent in October 1985, after enlargement was already decided). The non-respondent average in other European countries is, according to *Euro-baromètre* polls taken in October and November 1985, 5 percent (see Table 3.1). On the other hand, people in Portugal express what sociologists have called 'localism,' focusing their concern largely on domestic issues. There is a general lack of enthusiasm displayed with respect to Community membership.

The Portuguese people's ignorance and lack of concern with regard to international issues is a consequence not only of historical and geographical factors, but also of the lack of attention paid to these questions in public discussions, whether in electoral campaigns, parliament or in the media. It is also a result of a general lack of information: only about 19.7 percent of the population read the newspapers.[25] The radio (except for one broadcasting station owned by the Church) and the television are state owned and generally under permanent financial strain which affects the quality of their services.

Despite general indifference to international issues, however, in a crisis situation the Portuguese would be likely to respond. Opinion polls show that the Portuguese are among the Europeans who are most 'willing to fight for their country': 65

Table 3.1: General attitudes of the Portuguese
(October–November 1985)

	Portugal %	Spain %	EC %	Greece %
Preparedness to fight for one's country				
— yes	65	69	48	76
— no	21	18	37	16
(non-respondents)	(14)	(13)	(15)	(8)
Support the movement for European union				
— very much in favour	28	36	28	24
— in favour	28	35	48	43
— against	4	3	9	12
— very much against	3	2	5	7
(non-respondents)	(37)	(24)	(24)	(14)
Membership in the EC is				
— a good thing	42	57	60	39
— not good or bad	18	20	23	26
— a bad thing	10	7	12	23
(non-respondents)	(30)	(16)	(5)	(12)

Source: *Euro-baromètre*, no. 24, December 1985.

percent, against an EC average of 48 percent, ranging from a maximum of 69 and 76 percent in Spain and Greece to a minimum of 36 and 33 percent in Belgium and Germany, respectively. Willingness to defend one's country appears as proportional, in the same *Euro-baromètre* poll, to the feeling of national pride, with the notable exception of Portugal (the share of 'very proud' being 33 percent in Portugal, 64 and 72 percent in Spain and Greece, 26 and 20 percent in Belgium and Germany, respectively).

The analysis of the few opinion polls taken on defence and security issues portrays a decidedly pro-Atlantic Portuguese public, especially in comparison with opinions expressed in countries like Spain and Greece. The majority of those who know what NATO is are in favour of the Alliance (64 percent in favour, 16 percent against).[26] In July 1983, only 17 percent of the Spaniards were in favour of NATO.[27]

Domestic Politics and the Perception of Threats

The 1974–1975 domestic political experience strongly influenced the Portuguese public's threat perception. Even if an

103

external threat was not apparent at that time, because of the massive political and financial support received by the PCP from the Soviet Union, Portuguese public opinion does not distinguish greatly between the PCP and the USSR. The PCP is in fact the most openly pro-Soviet communist party in the West and has explicitly condemned Eurocommunism. The negative image of the Soviet Union held by a large number of the Portuguese is a direct consequence of their clear opposition to the PCP.

Two other factors help to account for the presence of anti-Soviet and pro-NATO sentiment in Portuguese society. The first was the Soviet-Cuban intervention in Angola, which directly affected the lives of hundreds of thousands of Portuguese who had to flee from Angola and return to their homeland. This is why the Union for Total Independence of Angola (UNITA) has the sympathy and complicity of so many people in Portugal. In fact, notwithstanding the importance (including economic relations) of Angola for Portugal, the Portuguese government has always resisted repeated pressures from the Angolan government and has never taken strong measures against UNITA leaders in Portugal, and several leaders of the PSD and the CDS have made no attempt to conceal their good relations with the movement. (The situation in regard to Mozambique is altogether different, since there was no civil war and the FRELIMO seems determined to defend broadly defined national interests.) The second factor is the official rhetoric of the old regime which closely identified African liberation movements with the USSR, perceiving them as agents of Soviet communism. As the Soviet Union was, indeed, one of the main supporters of the liberation movements, it was perceived as the enemy of the Portuguese army in the African colonies.

When the public was confronted with political programmes and styles that reflected a Soviet model, a non-aligned Third World model, and a Western or European model, the Portuguese public was generally favourable towards NATO. Politicians used their external contacts in political discourse so that, when the leaders of the Socialist International came to visit to offer Mário Soares their support, the Portuguese Socialists claimed, 'Europe is with us.' Soviet support to the Communist Party was evident to everyone, as was the assistance lent by NATO countries to the major democratic parties. The PS, the

PSD and the CDS were known to have close ties with German foundations. The public appearance made by François Mitterrand at a Socialist Party rally and the overt support given Mário Soares by American Ambassador Frank Carlucci had a strong and favourable public impact.

These basic, and relatively easy, choices of foreign policy orientation, however, do not satisfy all security concerns given that most Portuguese consider the internal threat to security greater than any coming from abroad. The question of internal and external threats was brought up during the discussion in parliament of the National Defence Law[28] (October to December 1982) and again during the parliamentary debate on the Internal Security and the Intelligence Services Laws in 1984. During the course of these debates, differences between both the right- and left-wing sections of the military and the political leaderships of the democratic parties came to light. The democratic parties had two altogether different attitudes towards internal threat. During discussions of the National Defence Law, they were totally against any mention of an internal threat and even refused to discuss its existence. Two years later, when the Internal Security and the Intelligence Services Laws were debated, they stressed the dangers ensuing from indirect strategy (unmistakably meaning Soviet indirect strategy) and the need to be prepared to defend against such threats.

The reason for this apparent paradox is quite simple: the fundamental issue of the National Defence Law was not to create an instrument for prompt and effective action against an external threat, but rather to end the period of transition that had lasted since 1974 and to define the tasks of the military forces strictly as those of defence of national sovereignty. The mission of the armed forces, as defined in the National Defence Law, is to defend the country against an external threat. The authors of this legal text were fully aware that they were going against the opinion of influential military men, who stood for a 'broader concept of national defence, encompassing protection in relation to an internal threat, one that would almost coincide with the notion of internal security.'[29] The main issue was therefore the same one that had been central in Portuguese security and defence policy in previous years: 'normalization' of the military forces by their subordination to political authority. The National Defence Law was designed primarily to counter that specific internal threat to democracy resulting from the

105

manipulation of the armed forces by 'anti-democratic minority groups.' Although an inefficient and inconsistent enforcement of the National Defence Law meant that there was no thorough 'normalization' of the armed forces (as the majority would have wished), the military did withdraw from the political arena.

When the Internal Security and the Intelligence Services Laws were first discussed (and generally approved by the same PS-PSD-CDS majority as for the National Defence Law) the objectives were totally different and the question of internal threat was considered of central importance. The words of the then Vice Premier and Defence Minister Carlos Mota Pinto (who was also the leader of the PSD at the time) could not be more explicit in exposing and condemning the activities of 'fifth columns': 'external aggression against national independence, against the integrity and security of the Portuguese can be perpetrated by forces within ... we all know such things as the so-called 'indirect strategies' exist.'[30]

In official strategic concepts, indirect strategy is evaluated as a basic threat that can take primarily two forms: it can be psychological, and seek to curb national will; or military, through the use of internal agents to commit acts of sabotage with or without the support of commando groups that have infiltrated national territory. The importance attached to the internal threat in military planning is justified, in part, by the size of NATO infrastructure on Portuguese territory, which could be the object of attacks. For the Chief of Staff of the Armed Forces:

> 'at the military level ... it is in our interests ... to take effective measures of protection not only against possible acts of sabotage and destruction of installations and infrastructures of significant military relevance, but also we must stay on the alert against any attempts aiming at the erosion of national determination in the field of defence and security.'[31]

However, concern is not centred solely on possible acts of sabotage supported by the Soviet Union implementing a 'strategy of denial' in Portugal. There are also fears stemming from the appearance of terrorist activities (extreme-left terrorism and Arab terrorism), inefficiency of police forces against organized crime, and the non-existence of intelligence services that could combat the threats. The focus on internal threat indicates how important domestic issues still are in Portugal's defence policy, and are generally indicative of the low priority attached to external threats.

A major concern in military circles is the so-called 'separatism,' the independence movements in the archipelagos of Madeira and, especially, of the Azores. During the 1974–1975 crisis 'separatism' developed as a way to put pressure on the central government and had some American support. In the Azores, 'separatism' has a long tradition owing to the support received from the Azorean community living in the United States. This community is larger than the population, totalling 250,000, of the nine islands forming the archipelago, a fact which has a decisive economic impact on the life of every family. The existing system of autonomy recognized by the constitution has isolated 'separatism' and reduced the Liberation Front of the Azores (FLA) to virtual non-existence. But regional autonomy is regarded with suspicion by sectors of the Portuguese armed forces who are inclined to think that it contains the seeds of 'separatism.' Regional autonomy grants the regional government the right to take part in international negotiations concerning the islands. This gives cause for suspicion that these rights may be used by external forces to put pressure on the Portuguese government. In 1986, a fierce debate between the armed forces and the regional government of the Azores took place. The law on regional autonomy that had been passed containing an article to the effect that the regional flag would have the same honours as the national flag in public or military ceremonies held in the Azores was vetoed by the President. This illustrates that the armed forces are very much concerned with the unity of the state and are inclined to intervene publicly every time they feel the options of the democratic state do not uphold the 'vital interests of the nation.'

Given the situation of continued political instability in Portugal, many consider that the existing political parties will never be able to stabilize democracy. The military naturally sees political instability as a national defence problem. Some even go so far as to consider that the first priority in a strategic concept of national defence should be 'to strengthen political power at the centre.'[32] Others regard economic development as the top priority. But the continued open expression by sectors of the military about appropriate policies for national stability shows that there has not been a thorough 'normalization' of the military in

Portuguese society, a concern both of civilian politicans and large sections of the military who are in favour of a thorough normalization process.

Paradoxically, the lack of a clear perception of an external threat is also one of the reasons for the comparative immunity of the younger generation to pacifist ideas. Furthermore, because nuclear weapons are not an issue in Portugal (a country where geography demands *de facto* de-nuclearization for theatre nuclear weapons), anti-nuclear movements are virtually non-existent, except for one group — the World Peace Council — that is a feeble echo of its counterparts in central Europe and so openly communist controlled that it has no credibility.

The importance still attached to the internal threat and a general disbelief in the existence of any external threat have a number of implications for defence policy making. The first seriously negative consequence is the unwillingness to bring defence expenditure anywhere near the levels required for an adequate deterrent capacity. Another consequence, especially among the younger generation, is a gradually increasing rejection of compulsory military service. Despite the young people's anti-Sovietism, they do not understand the purpose of compulsory military service and consider that it is a waste of time. The youth organizations affiliated to democratic political parties have advocated a shorter term for military service. The Communist League was the only group not to do so. The Communist Party in Portugal will support the armed forces in each and every circumstance or issue. They know from the experience of 1974–1975 that they can only hold power with the support of the armed forces. In 1986, the point of view held by the Young Socialists, Social Democrats and Christian Democrats was finally accepted (against the opinion of the armed forces) and the present term of service is twelve months. One other symptom of the rejection of compulsory military service is the large number of conscientious objectors: in 1984, for example, 4,580 young men filed applications as conscientious objectors, representing 4.32 percent of those figuring on the enrollment lists. According to the law, approved conscientious objectors must perform civil defence duties in lieu of military service.

Most Portuguese, including members of parliament, conceive the role of national defence as bearing a likeness to that of the coast guards, equipped with appropriate vessels and aircraft to patrol the Exclusive Economic Zone (EEZ) and to make sure foreign fishing fleets are kept away from Portuguese seas. Given the vastness of the Portuguese EEZ, that kind of problem is easily understood, but it is unlikely that the public will easily accept a broader or more sophisticated definition of an external role for the Portuguese armed forces.

Broad National Consensus: For How Long?

The existing broad consensus in favour of NATO has remained unquestioned because of the dominant role played by the three major democratic parties from 1976 to 1985. This consensus exists despite the inability of the major parties to work together and the main problem faced in Portugal remains the achievement of greater internal political stability. The PS, PSD and CDS have tried every possible combination of two-party coalitions, none of which managed to stay in power until the end of their respective mandates. Since the October 1985 general election, the PSD has formed a one-party minority government. The electoral system is one of the reasons why it so difficult to reach more lasting solutions. The present system is based on proportional representation. Given the comparatively large number of important political parties (four in 1983, five in 1985), the party that wins the election is almost sure not to have a large enough majority to avoid a minority or a coalition government. Recent reports show that if a non-proportional scheme had been adopted in the 1983 general election, the Socialist Party would have obtained a full majority in parliament, and the coalition with the PSD would have been unnecessary. During the 1985 Presidential campaign the electoral system was a central issue. The elected candidate, Mário Soares, was opposed to changing the proportional system. The parties in favour of changing the system — the PSD and CDS — represent less than 40 percent of the votes in parliament. Since a two-thirds majority is required, there are slim chances of changing the established system in the near future.

Apart from political instability, profound economic difficulties have engendered the spread of pessimism among intellectuals and the general public. It must be borne in mind that Portugal embarked upon modernization programmes economically weakened by fourteen years of war and under the impact of the 1973 oil crisis. Portugal is still a poor country by European economic standards: the GDP per capita was 1,905 U.S. dollars in 1985. This compares unfavourably with figures from Spain (4,192) or Greece (3,380) but is higher than Turkey (1,018). Most of the obstacles to development are structural: a huge bureaucracy (employing 530,000 people, over 5 percent of the population), an enormous nationalized sector accumulating growing deficits every year (equalling 11.3 percent of the GDP in 1982), and a lack of competitiveness in the public and private sectors. Moreover, constant political instability has made long-term economic planning difficult.

As dependence on foreign supply for such essentials as energy and food is considerable (85 percent of energy and 65 percent of foodstuffs are imported), foreign debt grows steadily and becomes increasingly difficult to service. Up to 1984, it totalled approximately 18.5 billion U.S. dollars, against reserves of some 7 to 8 billion dollars. Unemployment rose from 2 percent in 1974 to 11 percent in 1985 and this, in the public mind, tended to reflect badly on the democratic parties. Inflation, measured by the consumer price index, reached a peak in 1983 of 33.9 percent and declined to 21.2 percent by the end of 1984. The annual foreign debt in 1983 was 1.75 billion, but dropped in 1984 to 500 million dollars. Owing largely to favourable external factors, most macroeconomic indicators now show an apparent improvement. Although still provisional, official figures for 1986 indicate a 12 percent inflation rate and a 4 percent GDP growth rate.

Political leaders are hoping that EC membership will be a catalyst to boost the economy. Meanwhile, the incapacity they have demonstrated in finding solutions for political and economic problems has opened up new possibilities for other kinds of solutions. In the Presidential elections of 1986, two of the major candidates to the left and to the right of Mário Soares, (Maria de Lourdes Pintasilgo and Diogo Freitas do Amaral) frequently cited General de Gaulle in their advocacy for greater Presidential intervention in domestic politics. They have also argued that referendums should become a more important feature of Portuguese politics, and that this vehicle would help to solve political instability. Mário Soares, who held different views on the role of the President, won the election.

During this period a new political party also emerged — the Democratic Renewal Party (PRD) — that presented new ideas to the public. Drawing on the prestige of President António Ramalho Eanes (1975–1986), the PRD tried to portray itself as the champion of the discontented multitude. It combines the populist propositions of the non-communist left of the MFA with large doses of regionalist nationalism, and has been criticized by other parties for lacking a clearly defined ideology. It is perhaps curious to note that the PRD belongs to the same group as the French Rassemblement pour la République (RPR) in the European Parliament.

The PRD made its formal public appearance at the general election of October 1985 when it drew a 19 percent share of the vote mainly from the socialist areas of the electorate (see Table 3.2). In this election the Socialist Party dropped to 21 percent of the vote from 36.3 percent in 1983, the PSD increased to 30 percent from 27 percent, and the CDS dropped to 10 percent from 12.4 percent. The Presidential election in January 1986 seems to have proven that anti-communism is still widespread and outspoken. The two principal candidates — Amaral and Soares — supported by the PSD, CDS and PS received 71 percent of the national vote in the first round of the election.

Political parties have recently undergone substantial leadership transformations. These are bound to re-shape party politics profoundly, especially since the new leaders are either junior members or did not play a major role during the 1974–1975 events. In general, they are less influenced by external events, more technocratically minded, more concerned with economic development and European economic integration than with sustaining a great anti-Soviet campaign. The leaders who fought the 1974–1975 political struggle — Mário Soares, Sá Carneiro and Freitas do Amaral — are no longer, for different reasons, the leaders of their own parties.

The new leader of the PSD, Aníbal Cavaco Silva, is an economist concerned with the liberalization of the economic system, who sees foreign policy in terms of the financial impact it may have on the country's economy. He chose as Foreign Minister a former member of the board of directors of a nationalized company. Foreign and defence policies are not the top priorities of the present government. Cavaco's foreign policy displays a more nationalistic, less cosmopolitan approach to international relations than was the case with his predecessors. Other changes have occurred in the Socialist Party after former Secretary General Mário Soares was elected President and

Table 3.2: General elections in Portugal since 1974

Parties or coalitions	1985 %	1985 S	1983 %	1983 S	1980 %	1980 S	1979 %	1979 S	1976 PCP %	1976 S	1975 PCP/MDP %	1975 S
APU	15.55	38	18.20	44	16.92	41	18.96	47	15.91	41	7.65	16
CDS	9.74	22	12.38	29	0.23	(a)	0.40	(a)	—		—	
PRD	19.04	38	—		—		—					
PS	20.81	57	36.35	100	—	FRS	27.43	73	34.97	106	37.86	115
PSD	29.79	88	27.04	73	2.49	(a) 8	2.38	(a) 7	24.03	71	26.38	80
AD	—		—		44.40	123	42.24	118	—		—	
FRS	—		—		27.13	71	—		—		—	
MDP	—		—		—		—		—		4.12	5
PCP	—		—		—		—		14.56	40	12.52	30

Key:

S = Seats; AD = Aliança Democrática (CDS + PSD + minute monarchist party with no electoral significance); APU = Aliança Povo Unido (PCP + MDP); CDS = Partido do Centro Democrático Social; FRS = Frente Socialista Revolucionária (PS + minute extreme-left parties with no electoral significance); MDP = Movimento Democrático Popular; PCP = Partido Comunista Português; PRD = Partido Renovador Democrático; PS = Partido Socialista; PSD = Partido Social Democrata. Parties in upper part of Table fought the last general election and their percentages are quoted throughout the text. Coalitions and parties in lower part fought previous elections, indicated by the years in which results are shown, and have either disappeared as such (FRS, AD) or exist in different arrangements. These parties are represented in parliament.

Note: (a) = Results in the autonomous regions of Madeira and Azores. The AD (CDS + PSD) was formed for all constituencies *except* those in the autonomous regions. This explains the (a) figures for the PSD and the CDS in 1979 and 1980.

chose for himself a 'monarchical, above party politics role.' The dominant group in the PS today is in favour of a more European option. Vítor Constâncio (who gave up his position as chairman of the Bank of Portugal to become the new party leader), reaffirmed the pro-NATO policy of Mário Soares, although most of his followers are critical of what they consider excessive pro-Americanism. General Eanes was reelected President with this group's support although they were the losing 'minority' against Soares in the 1983 PS congress.

The emergence of the PRD, growing nationalistic trends, and General Eanes' and the military's criticism of the 'internationalism' upheld by certain political leaders have weakened the broad consensus that emerged out of the 1974–1975 crisis. Even the PCP has shaken off its negative image as the years go by, and shows slow but steady gains in the successive general elections: 12.5 percent of the vote in 1975, 14.6 percent in 1976, 18.2 percent in 1983, and 15.5 percent in 1985. This last result gives a 2.7 percent swing to the PRD, which represents a numeric loss and a political gain for the PCP. The PCP's shift towards Eurocommunism, considered to be out of the question while the present Secretary General, Alvaro Cunhal, is in charge, would also have a disruptive influence on the present reference points of pro-Atlanticism in Portugal.

Internal transformations will profoundly influence foreign and security policies in the future, as they have done in recent years. Appeals to nationalism grow louder as economic and political difficulties have to be confronted. In 1985, the year when the treaty for Community membership was signed, several nationalistic demonstrations were organized, culminating in the commemorations of the battle of Aljubarrota (1385), where the Spaniards were defeated and Portugal reaffirmed its independence.

PORTUGAL BETWEEN THE ATLANTIC AND MEDITERRANEAN

It is misleading to view Portugal as a country living in peace and tranquillity, 'safely' removed from the European front, shielded by U.S. nuclear deterrence (in return for a few facilities), a mere symbolic military participant in the defence of Europe, and a simple geostrategic contributor to the Atlantic Alliance. The

113

situation in peripheral regions, even in the European periphery, is dominated by differing tensions, and Portugal naturally has to incorporate this regional context into its own defence policy and strategy. Simultaneously, Portugal's democratic governments have set before themselves the objective of reinforcing the role of Portugal in Western security and adapting its strategic contribution to new foreign policy concerns.

When speaking of Portugal in geostrategic terms one must bear in mind that it is formed by a continental strip of land on the Atlantic coast of the Iberian peninsula, with a medium width of one hundred miles, and two archipelagos — the Azores, on the Atlantic coast of the Iberian peninsula, with a median width continent. These groups of islands and the mainland are in an intermediate position, geographically, between the Atlantic and the Mediterranean, and between Europe and Africa. From a strategic point of view, this geographical space is, for the most part, comprised within an Atlantic area defined by a group of archipelagos. This area can be referred to as the 'Atlantic-Mediterranean,'[33] region whose southern boundary is the Tropic of Cancer.

In the post-colonial period, the strategic importance of Portuguese territory increased, both in the East-West and North-South context. Portugal is a *plaque tournante* between North and South, between East and West, and this has been demonstrated on several occasions. Portuguese strategists define the functions of Portuguese territory by using the concept of a 'strategic triangle' — one that expresses both the importance of each component and of the international space encompassed — crossed by some of the most important sea and air lines of communication, such as those linking North America to Europe, the east coasts of South America to Europe, the Mediterranean to the north of Europe, and southern Africa to Europe.

The importance of the Portuguese strategic triangle in the context of the East-West confrontation is strongly stressed in Portugal. Its functions are usually defined as follows:[34]

a) to reinforce Europe rapidly in case of war, particularly the Southern Flank.
b) in the case of the Azores, to provide an ideal base for surveillance in the Atlantic and for anti-submarine warfare.
c) to provide a pivotal position in relation to another very

114

important strategic region formed by Greenland, Iceland, the Faroë Islands and Great Britain.

d) in the case of Madeira, to control the Straits of Gibraltar and, in particular, to provide an advanced position in relation to North Africa, where a growing hostile presence is expected by Portuguese military planners.

Generally, the strategic importance of Portugal may be said to have increased because of the rise in the deployment of Soviet naval power in the north Atlantic. Recently, there have been a number of occasions where Portugal's position was useful to allies having to project power southwards, as was the case during the Shaba conflict in Zaire, in April 1977, when the airfield of Porto Santo (Madeira) was used by the French, and during the Falkland crisis, when the Azores were used by the British air force. In a totally different context, the airfield of Santa Maria (Azores) was used in the winter of 1975 for the transport of Cuban troops to Angola in commercial Cubana Airlines flights.[35] The Portuguese positions are, naturally, also fundamental to the projection of power in the East-West direction, as became evident during the Berlin crisis.

The growing strategic importance of Portugal is largely due to its *en route* position for U.S. power projection outside the NATO area, in particular for the most probable scenarios: the western and eastern Mediterranean, and the Persian Gulf. The present U.S. maritime strategy, requiring the deployment from U.S. territory of important military forces by air and sea in the case of war, cannot take place without logistic facilities *en route*. It is worth recalling that in 1973, during the Yom Kippur War, the United States was denied the use of facilities in the United Kingdom, Spain, Italy, Greece and Turkey, and Portugal was the only country to agree to the U.S. request (the U.S. aircraft flew from Germany to the Lajes base, in the Azores and from there to Israel).[36]

The U.S. rapid deployment force (organized under CENTCOM) can draw great advantages from facilities in Portugal, Spain and Morocco. The United States has obtained facilities in Zaragoza, Moron, Torrejon and Rota (all in Spain), and in the aeronaval base of Kenitra in Morocco. Since Morocco is an Arab country, and owing to the uncertainty of the outcome of the current negotiations with Spain, there is increased U.S. interest in obtaining facilities on Portuguese territory. The Lajes base is only 2,500 miles from the U.S. east coast and 1,000 miles from Britain, while the Persian Gulf is 7,000 miles away from the United States. Given the flight range of carrier craft — 2,140 miles for the C-141, 3,250 for the C-5A — the access to bases in the Atlantic-Mediterranean region is clearly indispensable to U.S. force protection capacities. The general importance of the Southern Flank to American policy is often underlined by U.S. officials.

Portugal is not in the Southern Flank of NATO, but strategy binds it more and more closely to the south. As George Shultz has said: 'Our NATO allies, Turkey, Greece, Spain and Portugal, provide a shield both for the Mediterranean and the Southern Flank of Europe, as well as a bridge to the Middle East and Southwest Asia; and the Azores base is pivotal if the United States is to react effectively to military challenges in Europe or to threats to Western security outside NATO.'[37]

Security Relations with the United States, Germany and France

The agreement between Portugal and the United States, signed on 13 December 1983 and taking effect in February 1984 for a seven-year period, is seen in Portugal as a step towards the reinforcement of a mutual understanding between the two states in their commitment to Atlantic security. The agreement deals exclusively with the use of facilities in the Azores: Air Force Base no. 1 — Lajes, the airport of Santa Maria, and the seaports of Ponta Delgada and S. Miguel (fuel storage). This special agreement is a result of pressures from the regional government of the Azores which demanded that the Portuguese government allow for separate negotiations for the use of facilities in the Azores and the use of facilities in other parts of the country. Negotiations between Portugal and the United States are underway, and an agreement was signed in March 1984 whereby a U.S. 'geodss' system (space surveillance relevant to strategic defence) would be located in Portugal. This is now being reevaluated by the Portuguese government. Negotiations are also being undertaken to allow the United States access to home port facilities in Porto Santo on Madeira, and in the airfields of Ovar, Montijo and Beja on the mainland. The German air force has for some time had training facilities in the Beja air base and in Alcochete. The agreement with Germany, dating back to 1960, was renewed on 15 May 1980. France has a surveillance and guiding station for missiles on the isle of Flores in the Azores, as per the agreement between Portugal and France signed in 1964, renewed on 24 February 1977 and renegotiated in 1984.

Security Relations with Spain

With the transformation of Portugal and Spain into democratic countries, the old Iberian Pact was replaced by a Friendship and Cooperation Treaty signed in November 1977. This treaty provided for regular meetings of both general staffs of the armed forces, established the framework for common military manoeuvres to take place regularly, and also contemplated industrial cooperation which has not yet begun. Everything points to greater cooperation between the two Iberian states. This, however, would require a reduction of the imbalance in military power between the two countries and a precisely defined division of responsibilities within the Alliance.

Spain's adherence to NATO received Portuguese approval, although it sparked off a debate about how Spanish membership would affect Portugal's role within the Alliance and gave rise to fears that the United States or NATO might be tempted to entrust Spain with security tasks within IBERLANT for which Portuguese armed forces are not yet adequately equipped.

It is of immediate importance to establish the framework for aeronaval cooperation between Portugal and Spain. In the event of Spain joining the military structure of NATO, the prevailing opinion in Portugal is that the two countries should belong to two different major commands, Portugal to SACLANT and Spain to SACEUR. It is not possible, however, to disregard Spain's contribution to Atlantic defence and to IBERLANT through the Canary Islands/Gibraltar space. If the solution to this problem led to the removal from IBERLANT of the Gibraltar/Canaries area, Portugal would certainly impose the condition of integration of the Azores (presently under WESTLANT) into the new IBERLANT. Irrespective of the solutions to the command question, Spanish cooperation with IBERLANT (at present the CINCIBERLANT is a Portuguese admiral) is both necessary and possible. In the case of war, it is evident that both countries would have to cooperate in the reinforcement of European forces.

Out-of-Area Contingencies

Because of its great dependence on energy resources from the Persian Gulf area and its proximity to areas of tension in the south, Portugal cannot neglect its out-of-area responsibilities. Portugal and the United States have mutual out-of-area interests but they may have different views on how to defend these interests. In 1980, the Portuguese government made it clear that the use of facilities for out-of-area contingencies was subject to prior clearance on a case-by-case basis, and this was once again stressed during the negotiation of the present agreement. 'Under no circumstance can clearance for the use of the Lajes base be considered as automatic outside the NATO area.'[38] In the case of a Middle East conflict involving Israel and an Arab state such as Syria, it would be highly unlikely that Portugal would openly assist a U.S. intervention. Portugal has made it clear that its territory will never be used against Arab countries.[39]

The attitude of the Portuguese government in out-of-area contingencies is beginning to shift from one of outright support for American positions — as during the Afghanistan and Iran crises in 1979 when economic boycotts were imposed on both countries by the United States, and Portugal withdrew from the Olympic Games — to a much less ideological, more pragmatic and cautious position, motivated by economic interests (such as commercial relations with the Arab world) and by a desire to be part of a common European stand. This became evident in 1986 during the U.S.-Libyan confrontation. The Portuguese Foreign Minister deplored 'the use of force' by the United States.[40] Like the European countries generally, Portugal was reluctant to impose severe economic and other sanctions against Libya. The cases in which Portugal would be willing, in principle, to authorize the use of its military bases for out-of-area contingencies are understood to be those in which military support would be needed to ensure the security of the Arab states, particularly in the Gulf area. If Spain's position of not granting facilities under any circumstances for Middle East contingencies remains unchanged, it will be very difficult for

118

Portugal, especially as a member of the EC, to accept the fact that it would be the only European country to do so.

Policy makers think that only by implementing a Euro-Atlantic foreign policy based on relations with the EC, the United States, and Portuguese-speaking Africa and Brazil, can Portugal safeguard autonomous political action. The European option is regarded as a fundamental precondition for the development of Portugal and for preserving a certain degree of independence vis-à-vis the United States. In seeking to develop fully a European dimension in its foreign policy, Portugal applied for membership in the Western European Union in October 1984. It is also striving to increase its participation in all NATO European fora, and particularly in the Independent European Programme Group,[41] considered as an ideal platform for industrial defence cooperation and for research and development. Portugal is already participating in the AWACS programme.

A Strategy of Denial

Given the existence of NATO facilities on Portuguese territory, the most probable form of Soviet strategy in the region will be a strategy of denial. In the case of open conflict, Soviet strategy could take the form of sabotage or commando actions against coastal targets and existing facilities, mining of harbours, surgical bombing from aircraft or submarine-launched cruise missiles with conventional charges. The target goal of Soviet indirect strategy is to render impossible U.S. access to facilities in the region, or at least to make it as difficult as possible, and to create insecurity in sea and air lines of communication. For the Soviet Union, this is the reason for the immediate strategic importance of the conflict in the western Sahara. The defeat of the Moroccan king and the accession to power of populist groups (which would be the foreseeable consequence of a victory of the Polisario Front) would create an atmosphere of instability in the region with direct consequences in the Atlantic archipelagos of Portugal and Spain.

The situation thus created would be especially delicate for Spain, owing to the immediate threat that would be posed to the Spanish North African dominions, Ceuta and Melilla, and also because of the vulnerability of the Canary Islands, sixty-two miles away from the western Sahara. Portuguese territory could also be implicated as the western Sahara is only 360 miles from Madeira, 210 from the Selvagens, and 120 miles separate the coasts of North Africa and the Algarve. In February 1978, Gadaffi declared that 'there ought to be liberation movements in the islands occupied by Portugal' because 'the African islands belong to Africa, and their freedom is interdependent.'[42] An attempt was made to raise this issue at the Organization for African Unity (OAU) summit meeting at Khartoum, in July 1978, but the matter was never discussed, in part because Gadaffi's statements were given no credence (the Portuguese archipelagos were uninhabited at the time of their discovery), and partly because the leaders of the former Portuguese colonies refused to discuss the question. Nevertheless, the subject was raised again, in December 1981, by the Foreign Minister of Zimbabwe, Mangwende. In 1976–1978, contacts between Libya and the feeble separatist movements in the Azores and Madeira were reported, in the form of meetings of these groups with the President of the Islamic Bank for International Development in Paris.[43] Although the movements in the Azores and Madeira have been unsuccessful thus far, the Canary Islands have been subject to greater pressures, owing to their proximity to the Saharan conflict, to the greater significance of the separatist movement there (the Movement for the Independence of the Canary Islands — MPAIAC), and also to the discussion of the Canary question in the OAU, which has formally recognized the MPAIAC as a liberation movement. The MPAIAC has almost disappeared, but the people of the Canaries reject the so-called 'OTANization' of the territory. The neutralization of the Canary Islands would be seen as a form of indirect strategy aimed at limiting U.S. power projection capacities. The conduct of this type of strategy does not come exclusively from outside, it also issues from within, and it is today one of the objectives of the communist-controlled pacifist movement within Portugal. Its aim is the neutralization of Portugal within the Alliance, in particular for out-of-area contingencies. Membership of the Alliance has never been openly questioned, not even by Vasco Gonçalves in 1974–1975. This objective has been clearly defined by General Costa Gomes, who was President of the Republic from 1974 to 1976 prior to the first Presidential election and subsequently a member of the presidency of the World Peace Council: 'It is not

NATO policies that are keeping us from having healthy relations with the Arab world, but an inexplicable subserviency towards the Reagan Administration.'[44]

Neutralistic tendencies exist in leftist military circles and in pro-communist circles, but also exist, though in a less extreme form, in far more influential conservative sectors, which tend to reformulate the old anti-Europeanism that characterized Salazar's geopolitical options. Anti-Europeanism can, however, also reinforce a type of pro-Americanism. One observer has remarked that 'it is not surprising that Portugal, having completed the cycle of the empire, should now cling to the geostrategic capacity of her territory, to cooperation with Portuguese-speaking countries and to the historical alignment with the dominant maritime power, in order to survive and to keep her freedom of action and political weight, especially as she will have to accept something like a reversal of her history in joining the European Community.'[45]

Portugal and Challenges from the South

Portuguese defence decision makers are not concerned solely with the indirect implications of the geographical proximity of the south. They consider that in an increasingly multipolar world, regional strategy must take into account the greater probability of peripheral wars. They are aware of the fact that some of the North African states in the western Mediterranean have developed military capabilities matching those of neighbouring NATO countries. The technological developments and the military capabilities of countries such as Libya, Morocco or Algeria make it possible that a conflict in which these countries were involved would have military repercussions for both Spain and Portugal.

For military planners, an evolution in North Africa in favour of the Warsaw Pact would be the most nightmarish scenario of all — one that would greatly alter existing perceptions of external threat. Any form of strategic military planning in Portugal should take that eventuality into account. NATO is also becoming aware of the implications of such possible developments. SACLANT logistic positions and sea lines of communication are threatened by Soviet bombers and submarines based in the north, but could be attacked also by Soviet naval and air

121

capabilities based in the south, were the Soviets to succeed in obtaining facilities in Portuguese former colonies in Africa. In order to ensure that NATO retains control of this region, plans for the development of air facilities in Porto Santo (Madeira) are becoming a priority of IBERLANT.

The possibility of a conflict between a peripheral NATO state (such as Portugal) and a non-Warsaw Pact state should be considered. Though other European NATO countries may regard such a conflict as an out-of-area contingency, it would clearly be a conflict to which Article 5 of the NATO treaty would necessarily apply. Of course, Portuguese diplomacy tries to foster good relations, in an attempt to reduce the risk of disputes, with North African countries that in the past naturally opposed Portugal's colonial policies. Relations with Morocco form an especially important part in this regional diplomatic strategy. During his visit to Rabat in March 1984, the Foreign Minister reaffirmed that Portugal does not recognize the Democratic Arab Republic of the Sahara and in his meetings with King Hassan, he discussed the need for Atlantic strategic cooperation, as well as the importance of consultation and cooperation to solve the problems raised by the third enlargement of the EC.[46]

Aside from assisting the out-of-area activities of others, Portugal may, in the future, embark on military cooperation with the Portuguese-speaking African states. Economic cooperation is bound eventually to generate military ties. Not only would the former colonies welcome the presence of Portuguese military advisors, but now that these countries are negotiating military cooperation with France and Britain, Portuguese leaders may decide that closer links with the ex-colonies must be maintained.

DEFENCE POLICY MAKING AND THE MODERNIZATION OF THE ARMED FORCES

The two major priorities for the Portuguese armed forces are thorough normalization of their status and modernization of their equipment. Only by making major improvements will Portugal be able to perform its tasks in the NATO and regional contexts, and to develop any form of military cooperation with the African states. From a legislative point of view, the 1982

National Defence Law represented a turning-point in the integration of the military forces into the democratic state, made possible by the revision of the constitutional text. Once the National Defence Law had been approved, it was necessary to pass complementary legislation and regulations pertaining to the implementation of the law. This legislation included: The Strategic Concept of National Defence, intended to lay out the guide-lines for an adaptation of security and defence policies to the changes that had taken place after the end of the African wars; the multiannual military programme laws that would allow for some degree of parliamentary control of medium-term planning in military expenditure; and, finally, the organic law of the Defence Ministry, that would enable the government to actually carry out the tasks contemplated in the National Defence Law.

The most important aspect of the National Defence Law is that it put an end to the situation existing prior to 1982 in which the military had the power to make the laws ruling the armed forces, to define their budgetary and procurement policies and to approve international agreements in military matters. In other words, the National Defence Law deprived the armed forces of any political functions. All responsibilities in defence policy making and administrative matters were transferred to the government. The President is the Supreme Commander of the Armed Forces, a somewhat honorific role which would only acquire meaning in time of war. He has the power to declare war and appoint the Chiefs of Staff whose names are proposed by the government. He also chairs the National Defence Council, formed by a majority of cabinet ministers, two members of parliament, the four Chiefs of Staff and the two Presidents of the regional governments of Madeira and the Azores. Legislative and supervisory powers in defence matters are the responsibility of parliament.

However, the National Defence Law has not been imple-mented by the successive governments since 1982 as they have wanted to deal carefully with the armed forces and gain their confidence. The organic law of the Defence Ministry, the legal instrument necessary to provide the ministry with an operative structure, has not yet been approved; some people even say that the Defence Ministry does not exist but *de jure*. It should also be noted that the new provisions of the 1982 National Defence Law relating to the Chiefs of Staff have not been implemented so far, and consequently they still have practically the same powers as before. In reality, the coordination of foreign military aid, representation abroad and in international organizations, definition of strategic options and procurement are all powers which still lie with the Chiefs of Staff, even if, for matériel purchases, the signature of the Prime Minister, who then delegates this sort of power to the Minister of Defence, is legally required.

Ideal circumstances for the establishment of a framework for thorough normalization have been lacking. Several commanding officers (including the Chief of Staff of the Armed Forces) were potential candidates to the Presidency (paradoxically encouraged by party leaders) so that there is still considerable involvement of the military in politics. Furthermore, for several years Defence Ministers were also Deputy Prime Ministers and therefore could not devote enough time and attention to defence policy issues, a fact which naturally allowed the military greater freedom of action in defence issues.

The vast majority of the military wish to see the normalization process fully completed as a prerequisite for the definition of an integrated and consistent Portuguese military strategy. This would in turn facilitate the replacement of obsolete matériel and equipment which is necessary if Portugal wishes not to become a vulnerable NATO ally.

Until now, the role of parliament in the process of defence decision making has merely been to vote the defence portion of the state budget. The parliament and the public have, thus far, had no say in negotiations with foreign countries conducted by the government. The operating principle has always been: 'the less said, the better.' Neither public opinion nor the media (except in the Azores) has acted as a lobbying force in these issues. The democratization of the decision-making process through increased participation by parliament would contribute to a greater understanding of the need for modernizing the armed forces.

Normalization of the armed forces began on 25 November 1975, with the defeat of the military leftists and the Communist Party. The election of General Eanes — a prominent figure of the 25 November counter-insurgency — to the Presidency in April 1976 was viewed by those who favoured normalization as a form of institutional subordination of the military forces to an elected president. Against this stood the so-called 'operatives' who argued that General Eanes should have military power only. General Eanes insisted, however, that he would only agree to become President if he were also made Chief of Staff of the Armed Forces. At the time this condition was accepted. Eanes was the man whom people saw as having put an end to a situation of total instability, both political and military.

During the following years, however, General Eanes' influence in the armed forces declined. First, because he refused to take sides on the conflict between military factions in favour of normalization and the politico-military sections of the MFA. The latter group had a comfortable majority in the Council of the Revolution and it was from among them that General Eanes selected the Chief of Staff of the Army, General Garcia do Santos. Second, after the 1982 revision of the constitution (made by the PS, the PSD and the CDS) the President of the Republic was deprived of most of his military powers and, notably, of the exclusive power of appointing the Chiefs of Staff who were subsequently to be appointed by the President *after* the government had made a formal proposition.

Even if the National Defence Law did not entirely ban the military from political affairs, and moreover has largely not been implemented, this has not prevented left-wing sections of the MFA or the Council of the Revolution (grouped in the so-called 25 April Association) from persisting in their struggle to 'fight for the preservation of the ideas of April.' General Eanes is the honorary president of this association, the most radical sections of which publish the review *Liber 25* which advocates a policy of neutrality between the blocs.

The governments of the Democratic Alliance (AD) the PSD-CDS coalition 1979–1983, and the *Bloco Central,* the PS-PSD coalition 1983–1985, perhaps worried about a military backlash, were unable, or did not wish to set forth clearly the necessary changes implied in the 1982 National Defence Law. After much hesitation, General Garcia do Santos was replaced as Chief of Staff of the Army in 1983 and this is considered to be 'the sole political measure taken by the government' in military matters.

In 1986, because the PSD government was a minority government, the opposition introduced an article in the State Budget Law whereby expenses surpassing 1,000 million escudos in defence expenditure would have to be previously approved in parliament. This was a way of giving parliament an opportunity to discuss the programme of military contracts even if some of

125

these had already been signed and the corresponding decisions taken before the military programme laws for the 1986–1991 period were submitted. It is evident from the inordinate sums which the procurement programme gobbles up from the overall financial resources projected until 1991, that 'normalization' of the relationships between the armed forces, government and parliament has so far been unsuccessful. Already authorized or contracted purchases of matériel consume almost all the financial resources for the next few years and it seems, therefore, that neither the government nor parliament has had any role in the definition of fundamental defence options. Definition of a modernization or reequipment programme seems fruitless if money has already been irreversibly committed.

The Modernization Programmes and their Conceptual Basis

Many military leaders claim that the fear of a 'vacuum of power' is the most serious security problem facing Portugal. It is therefore imperative, they argue, to fill this 'vacuum' in Portugal's interterritorial space, otherwise its Spanish or American allies will surely move to fill it. Equipped to fight wars in Africa — wars of mines, guns and light armoured cars — the Portuguese military forces, especially the army and navy, are almost totally unprepared to guarantee the security of their own strategic space or to contribute to the NATO missions to which they are assigned.

A clear lack of military capabilities is evident in Portugal, in spite of the important infrastructures (especially air force) based there. From 1974 to 1985, modernization of the military forces made little if any progress due to economic difficulties, insufficient clarification of defence policy guidelines, and the absence of an adequate body designed to integrate the efforts of the three services and to arbitrate interservice rivalry, by deciding what priorities should be set for each one. The defence agreement recently signed with the United States has had principally two beneficial effects on the modernization of the armed forces. First, the resulting military aid made the first steps towards modernization possible. Second, each military service was compelled to define its own priorities in equipment and matériel. Thus, during the course of the negotiations with the United States a modernization programme was presented. It was still, however, an unsystematic amalgam of the requirements of each service, and by no means an integrated programme. The purchasing programme submitted to parliament in July 1986 was elaborated on the basis of these various lists of priorities.

The definition of the Portuguese strategic concept in the post-imperial period is to be found in three documents: *The Major Options of the Strategic Concept of National Defence,* approved by the Assembly of the Republic, the *Strategic Concept of National Defence,* approved by the government in February 1985, and *The Military Strategic Concept,* approved by the National Defence Council in December 1985. Of these *The Military Strategic Concept* is the most important.[47] It outlines Portuguese geostrategy and military roles. The National Defence Law accords the Joint Chiefs of Staff the powers to draft this document, and it therefore reflects the point of view of the armed forces, even if it has to be approved by the National Defence Council.

The doctrines incorporated in these documents elaborate on the concept of an interterritorial space, and the defence of the maritime area within the Portuguese strategic triangle. Several specific requirements emerge from these documents. The aeronaval component of Portuguese military forces needs to be emphasized in order to protect the communications between the Azores, Madeira and mainland Portugal. For this task the acquisition of anti-submarine naval capabilities, and the proper use of the 'angles' of the triangle as bases for military aircraft, are vital.

The navy and the air force emphasize the maritime threat and, more specifically, the threat posed by Soviet submarines and bombers. Portugal needs to obtain better means for attack and surveillance, and is ordering patrol boats and more fighters and frigates. These means are sought also to deter a potential threat coming from North Africa. It is also considered that with the acquisition of these types of capabilities, compatible with NATO requirements in the area, the risks are slimmer of tasks within the 'Portuguese interterritorial space' being assigned to forces other than the Portuguese even if Spain were to join the military organization. It is more difficult for the army to combine national and NATO requirements in the national territory. The only existing brigade has been equipped for use in the Southern Flank of NATO. For the army, 'interterritorial space' does not mean much, for it is concerned with the territorial defence of each one of its 'angles.' That should be, in the army's view, the first priority of Portuguese armed forces, and air and naval support from other allied forces should be accepted only as an unfortunate necessity.[48]

The structure of forces resulting from these contradictory concepts is not very clear. The Joint Chiefs of Staff are drafting a proposition for missions and forces. Protection and presence appear to be the most likely missions, together with increased mobility of forces between the mainland and the archipelagos.

The Army

Numerically and politically the most important section of the armed forces, the army has the greatest difficulties in defining a programme of modernization. The number of troops shrank from 194,300 in 1974, to 49,800, in 1975, and at present is 41,000 men. But the number of officers was not cut down in anything like the same proportion — at present the pyramid is upside down with comparatively more high- than low-ranking officers. The resulting distribution of the army budget is irrational, making it almost impossible to buy matériel. The distribution is the following: personnel 72 percent, civilian personnel 14 percent, equipment 14 percent (of which 33.49 percent is spent on logistical infrastructures, which leaves only some 9 percent of the total budget for matériel).

From a structural point of view, the Portuguese army is still organized for physical occupation of the national territory, with six regional commands and nineteen regiments (including twelve infantry regiments) scattered throughout the country. However, as a result of the African experience, the army has kept special forces highly operative. Anti-guerrilla training is still a part of military drilling for conscripts and is highly intensive for the special forces.

As far as modernization is concerned, the army wants to complete the equipment of the only existing brigade (a NATO-assigned brigade earmarked for action in the Southern Flank in the north of Italy: the First Mixed Brigade) and to form two other brigades, one of them mobile. The NATO brigade is the only really modern army unit, but it still needs improved transport capability, particularly helicopters. The approved programmes of reequipment of the armed forces contemplate an air-defence programme (Vulcan, Chaparral and Stinger Systems) for the First Mixed Brigade. The other services are not enthusiastic about the creation of a mobile brigade. Intended for action in the 'angles' of the triangle, it could jeopardize the predominantly aeronaval defence concept. In particular, the attack and reconnaissance helicopters, that no modern moblile unit can do without and which would obviously be needed by this brigade, are questioned by the other branches.

Portuguese experience with mobile forces, and also the fact that the Portuguese military are among the few in NATO who have participated in conflicts outside the NATO area, mean that Portugal could make a significant contribution to NATO mobile forces. Such a Portuguese force would in any case be useful for national Portuguese force projection requirements.

The Navy

In terms of real capabilities, the navy is becoming almost obsolete. Its seven ASW frigates were delivered between 1967 and 1969 and are not equipped with helicopters. There is not one single minesweeper, since the three existing minesweepers were converted into coastal patrol craft some time ago, and there are no oceanic patrol craft. In 1989, one half of existing capabilities will become obsolete, and the other half by 1995. It should be added that naval aviation ceased to exist in 1952. The navy has been the largest beneficiary of the reequipment programmes. The most important programme is the purchase of three Meko 200 ASW frigates (similar to those Turkey has bought from Germany), which is being financed through a multilateral NATO programme that will be completed in 1992. The two other main objectives of the navy, to buy minesweepers and cutters, have not thus far been scheduled.

The Air Force

The process of modernization in the air force is clearly ahead of the other two forces, due in part to the importance of the airfields and air bases to the United States and partly to the dynamic attitude of the air force leadership. The air force has recently bought two squadrons of A7P aircraft from the United States; one of these is assigned as a reserve for SACLANT, the other for SACEUR. Six maritime patrol P3 Orion aircraft with ASW capabilities, especially for detection, location and pursuit of submarines to be assigned to IBERLANT, are on order from the United States. A radar system is being put into operation, and completion is scheduled for 1989. To complete the present

129

reequipment programme, the air force still wants to purchase a squadron of interceptors and training aircraft.

Financial Constraints to Modernization Programmes

There are of course serious financial obstacles to the modernization of the Portuguese military forces. The defence share of the state budget has decreased over the past years (see Table 3.3). Military expenditure represented 2.44 percent of the GDP and 6.96 of total public expenditure in 1984, against 3.11 and 8.35 percent in 1981. The defence budget is currently smaller proportionally to total public expenditure, than it was in the 1950s, before the wars in Africa. On the other hand, the proportion of the total defence budget left for matériel purchases after expenses with military and civilian personnel, infrastructures, and so on, have been paid, is almost negligible, especially in view of the high costs of matériel and equipment (see Table 3.4). It would be futile to expect a substantial increase of the defence budget in the present economic situation of the country, especially since there is no strong perception of

Table 3.3: Portuguese military expenditure

Year	Total (in million Esc. 1974 constant prices)	% State Budget	% GDP
1959	2,490	25.00	3.80
1960	2,841	25.50	4.00
1974	23,428	31.71	6.85
1975	16,645	19.62	5.14
1976	12,647	12.41	3.70
1977	11,506	11.25	3.16
1978	11,409	10.44	3.04
1979	12,212	9.73	3.01
1980	12,860	9.26	3.12
1981	12,856	8.35	3.11
1982	11,809	8.38	2.84
1983	11,412	7.81	2.66
1984	10,349	6.96	2.44
1985	10,680	6.50	2.44

Source: *Livro Branco da Defesa Nacional, 1986*, (Ministério da Defesa Nacional, 1986), 151.

Table 3.4: Breakdown of Portuguese military expenditure
(1980–1986)

Year	Personnel		Material & equipment		Operation & maintenance		Total (100%) military expenditure
1980	22,753	62.4%	7,065	19.4%	6,624	18.2%	37,655
1981	25,593	60.7%	8,045	19.1%	8,522	20.2%	44,570
1982	28,676	59.7%	8,112	16.9%	11,210	23.3%	50,084
1983	34,760	59.9%	9,573	16.5%	13,665	23.6%	60,358
1984	40,849	61.0%	8,923	13.7%	15,228	23.4%	68,501
1985	48,362	61.6%	8,755	11.5%	21,083	26.8%	85,890
1986	63,054	63.0%	13,042	13.1%	23,956	23.9%	106,857

Note: All figures are in millions of Escudos in current prices, and all percentages are of the total military budgets for the given year.

Source: *Livro Branco da Defesa Nacional, 1986*, (Ministério da Defesa Nacional, 1986), for figures 1980–1985. Figures for 1986 were given by Brig. Mota Mosquita, in a paper presented at the 5th Spring Seminar organized by the IEEI (Lisbon: IEEI, 1986).

an external threat. Therefore, the main source of financial backing for the modernization programmes will have to come from foreign aid, through the existing defence agreements with the United States, Germany and France.

Although some progress may be observed in the compensatory U.S. military assistance (65 million dollars in 1982, 125 million in 1985), these figures are still far behind the requirements of modernization. The approved reequipment programmes will, over the next six years, exhaust total German aid and the 462 million U.S. dollars from U.S. military assistance (including the already negotiated U.S. grants plus a significant part of the credit). The question for Portuguese negotiators at the moment is whether the German and the U.S. military aid can be increased. The Portuguese think it can, given the noticeable imbalance between U.S. military aid to Portugal and to other allies in the Atlantic-Mediterranean area. In 1985, while Portugal received 125 million dollars in credits and grants, Spain received 400 million dollars in Foreign Military Sales (FMS) credits. U.S. aid to Greece and Turkey (785 million dollars have been proposed for 1986 in FMS credits) is more favourable to these countries, even taking into consideration the more exposed situation of the eastern Mediterranean. It is true

131

that, besides Turkey, Portugal is the only other case where a portion of U.S. aid takes the form of a grant, but FMS loans are usually made on excellent terms, and Portugal would like to benefit more largely from these.

The NATO Question

Being a poor country by NATO standards (Portugal has the lowest GDP per capita among NATO states except for Turkey), Portugal has, nevertheless, been spending a significant amount on defence and is in no position to increase military expenditure greatly. Although some degree of rationalization may be introduced, it will not be possible to modernize and reequip the armed forces without considerable allied aid.

In the present situation, the disproportion — unanimously recognized by civilian and military experts — between the relevance of facilities granted to NATO allies and the means of the armed forces is such that, as a highly placed commanding officer has pointed out, the position of Portugal is beginning to resemble that of Iceland. This position is not commensurate with the requirements of the country's national defence, nor with those of the Alliance; the 'vacuum' of military power creates the perception in Portugal that in a situation of crisis Portugal will have to rely entirely on foreign forces.

In 1982, during a NATO Defence Ministers' meeting the Portuguese Defence Minister, Diogo Freitas do Amaral (at the time the leader of the Christian Democrats and a strong presidential candidate) stated that: 'If the situation is not significantly changed, and soon, the Portuguese government will be compelled to review its attitude within NATO and to reconsider the facilities that have been and are at present granted to NATO members on national territory.'[49] Before he became Foreign Minister, the Socialist Jaime Gama once insisted that Portugal 'must not be regarded as an aircraft-carrier on the routes of the Atlantic and the Mediterranean.'

The process of European integration and increased nationalism are bound to cause Portuguese military demands to be expressed with increasing firmness. Everything points to a tougher round of negotiations with the United States, and a more pragmatic Portuguese stance. Portugal is becoming aware of the one power it has not lost: the 'functional power' resulting

132

from its geostrategic position. A more realistic approach to foreign relations will not necessarily mean a more isolationist attitude towards the Alliance; on the contrary, it can mean a greater role in common security.

CONCLUSION: EURO-ATLANTICISM VERSUS ISOLATIONISM

None of the existing democratic political parties opposes either the membership of Portugal in the Alliance or in the EC, nor a policy of privileged relationships with the Portuguese-speaking countries in Africa and Brazil. Underlying these generally accepted positions, however, many questions are being asked as to the real substance of these policies. This may well cause a wide and profound debate on the future of Portugal in the post-imperial period, with a *remise en question* of the European option.

This increasing debate proves that the consensus in foreign and defence policies was not so wide as it seemed, and was based more on domestic factors than external ones. As the impact of the 1974–1975 crisis fades away, the political issues are now secondary. The main government objective is becoming the increase of the GDP per capita. At the same time, anti-European tendencies, less important during the struggle against the Communist Party, are now a prevalent feature of the political landscape. That explains why, in a country where membership in the Alliance is strongly advocated, there is a revival of nationalistic, neo-isolationist tendencies in influential circles. Allies become potential enemies: Spain is seen as the 'historical enemy,' and the United States as an ally but all too powerful. The real target of neo-nationalists, however, is opposition to Community membership. Even if the economic advantages of the European option are not denied, emphasis is placed on the risks rather than the benefits of integration for Portugal.

As a result of the fact that economic priorities prevail over political and strategic objectives, a 'normalization' of the relationship between politicians and the military is only a secondary aim of the political leadership. On the other hand, influential sectors of the armed forces consider it essential to define a broad concept of *national security* that should be adopted in every aspect of political and social life.

133

It is doubtful, however, that neo-nationalism or defensive and pessimistic attitudes will succeed in dominating Portugal's political future. But all will depend once again, as it always has, on elements of domestic politics and whether moves towards political and economic modernization will succeed. Political modernization must be directed in order to streamline the bureaucracy, to revise the electoral system and stabilize party politics, to establish a better relationship between political power and the armed forces, and to define a more appropriate role for the armed forces. Economic modernization must aim towards a dramatic reduction of the role of the state and increased competitiveness for Portuguese enterprises while increasing prospects for regional development by strengthening the possibilities of successful membership in the EC. This would, in turn, have a positive effect in reassuring the political leadership, some sectors of which are fearful of integration, that the correct external choices have been made.

One way or the other, EC membership and a more active participation in NATO are bound to generate nationalist defences. But, if Portuguese governments succeed in adopting an attitude that is both European *and* Atlantic, in which the relationship with North America is not exclusive, and seek to promote a Euro-south Atlantic relationship in which the role of Brazil is stressed, then it will be possible to fend off more nationalistic approaches to foreign and defence policies.

In order that such a foreign policy can be developed, it will also be necessary for leaders to arrive at a precise definition of the powers and competences of the central and regional governments. This would remove a factor of potential internal tension, thus permitting defence policy to be formulated exclusively on the basis of external issues, relieving it of the intrusion of questions of internal order.

Managing Portugal's security policy poses a number of challenges. It is important to note that the use of facilities on Portuguese territory in out-of-area contingencies is subject to authorization by the government on a case-by-case basis. Any attempt to impose a situation similar to the 1973 events in connection with the Yom Kippur War would have unpredictable consequences, altogether different from those that were felt during the non-democratic regime. One foreseeable effect would be the emergence of vehemently anti-American sentiments, at present virtually non-existent. Such anti-Americanism would arise from existing ambiguities in U.S.-Portuguese relations in respect to out-of-area contingencies: the Americans feel sure that Portugal will, in no circumstance, fail to offer its support, as it has done in the past; the Portuguese do not want to be deprived of a bargaining option by the complete clarification of their position, which a public debate would most likely reveal as being similar to that of other European countries.

In a doctrinal perspective, and also in view of the reequipment of the armed forces, some people still hold the view that, for the most part, efforts should be directed inwards, to reequip the ground forces to enable them to operate in the archipelagos and on the borders with Spain (traditionally, the invasion line). Matériel procurement already scheduled, however, shows a tendency to meet specific NATO requirements in the region, notably in the area of aeronaval capabilities for anti-submarine warfare. .

Military cooperation with the Portuguese-speaking African countries, which is bound to become, in the near future, one of the important items in the defence and foreign policy agenda of the government, is for the time being only a slight possibility. It is quite difficult to venture on military cooperation with countries ravaged and divided by civil wars, about which the Portuguese are also divided. A full policy of military and economic aid by Portugal to its former colonies would depend on internal stability in these countries.

In spite of the many negative domestic factors that hinder the external projection of the country, there are many reasons for an optimistic attitude. In the last twelve years, many things have happened: decolonization has taken place, followed by the return of nearly one million homeless people; the country has overcome the first communist attempt to seize power in postwar Europe; and Portugal has joined the EC — which no one believed would be possible — showing a great amount of political energy and a remarkable ability to handle situations of crisis. Of course, many obstacles still remain that will have to be overcome in the next few years. The difficulties will have to be removed first and foremost by the Portuguese themselves. However, the allies have to be reminded that most of the countries in the Southern Periphery of the Alliance face a major challenge in economic growth, a challenge that reflects on the very stability of the region. Moreover, when peripheral wars are becoming predominant, the importance of the south increases from a security perspective. The reinforcement of NATO's presence in the region, namely through the modernization of armed forces equipped with obsolete matériel (some of which dates from World War II) is a non-negligible task. It should be remembered that the countries of central and northern Europe, having taken part for thirty-five years in a process of European economic and political integration, have gained a sense of their own national differences, but have not let national competitiveness prevent the process of European unification. Portugal, as the oldest nation of Europe, is inevitably the most resilient to the supra-national utopia.

The urge felt by political leaderships to affirm Portuguese national identity within the EC and the Atlantic Alliance has not, as yet, been reflected in specific foreign policy initiatives, although the role of Portugal in the formulation of a European stance towards South Africa or the importance attached to European Political Cooperation (EPC) can be interpreted as an indication of this new mood. Portuguese diplomacy, for all too obvious reasons, has been primarily concerned since 1976 with the problem of European integration. In the years to come, and if the present trend persists, its chief concern will be to maintain a balance between its commitment to Europe and its special relationship with the United States, while strengthening cooperation and relations with other Portuguese-speaking countries.

Whatever direction foreign policy takes, it is clear that political leaders are today aware of the favourable international conditions for a more active Portuguese participation in international fora. They know that the dark years in the 1960s and first half of the 1970s, when there was an almost complete estrangement between Portugal and most countries of the world, are now over. Also gone is the almost automatic alignment with the positions of other allies, which in the late 1970s and early 1980s characterized Portuguese diplomacy within NATO. Portuguese foreign policy, while remaining unquestionably Euro-Atlantic, is adopting approaches which reflect a more sophisticated appreciation of the state of international relations, especially where Portugal has specific national interests, as is the case in southern Africa, North Africa and South America. Portuguese leaders are aware of their greater freedom of manoeuvre in the international system and, therefore, the allies, and primarily the United States, would be seriously mistaken in taking for granted Portugal's automatic acquiescence to the policies of others.

NOTES

1. See Juan Vilà Valentì, *La Peninsula Ibérica* (Barcelona: Ariel, 1968), 22-23.
2. See Orlando Ribeiro, *Portugal, O Mediterrâneo e o Atlântico* (Lisbon: Sá da Costa, 1983).
3. Idem, *Introduções Geográficas à História de Portugal* (Lisbon: Imprensa Nacional-Casa da Moeda, 1977).
4. For Salazar's position on the Goa crisis, see Franco Nogueira, *Salazar*, Vol. V (Barcelos: Livraria Civilizaçao Editora, April 1984).
5. See Jorge Borges de Macedo, *Aproximação Histórica as Opções Estratégicas de Portugal* (Lisbon: Instituto de Estudos Estratégicos e Internacionais (IEEI), February 1985).
6. See José Alberto Loureiro dos Santos, Brigadier-General, *Fundamentos Históricos para um Conceito Estratégico de Defesa Nacional* (Porto, Congresso 'Os Portugueses e o Mundo,' May 1985). (Hereafter cited as: *Fundamentos Históricos*).
7. Idem, *Incursões no Domínio da Estratégia* (Lisbon: Fundação Calouste Gulbenkian, 1983), 290.
8. Telegram from the U.S. Minister in Portugal, Norweb, to the Secretary of State summarizing Kennan's interview with Salazar, dated 2 December 1943. *Foreign Relations*, vol. II (1943): 575.
9. Cf. Salazar Braga, letter to the Chairman of the Parliamentary Defence Committee, quoted in *Diário de Noticias*, 5 May 1986. General Salazar Braga was the Chief of Staff of the Army at that time.
10. Mário Mesquita, *Açores, Tímidos Ensaios de Desestabilização Neutralista* (Lisbon: IEEI, 1983), 3.
11. Telegram from the Chargé in Portugal (Kennan) to the Secretary of State, 20 October 1943. *Foreign Relations*, vol. II (1943): 559.
12. See Erlin Bjol, *Nordic Security*, Adelphi Paper, no. 181 (London: IISS, Spring 1983).
13. Later, the North Atlantic Council meeting in Lisbon in 1952 was decisive in redeeming the internal public image of Salazar's regime — a fact which the government-controlled media unabashedly exploited.
14. See Mário Soares, *Le Portugal baillonné* (Paris: Calman-Lévy, 1972).
15. See José Calvet de Magalhães, *Portugal e o Tratado do Atlântico Norte* (Lisbon: IEEI, 1984).
16. Cf. José Freire Antunes, *Os Americanos e Portugal* (Lisbon: Dom Quixote, 1986), 372-373.
17. See Soares, *Le Portugal baillonné*.
18. Cf. José Luís Cruz Vilaça, *L'économie portugaise face à l'intégration européenne*, thèse de doctorat, Université de Paris 1, 1978.
19. See António de Spínola, *Portugal e o Futuro*, 3rd edition (Arcadia, March 1974).
20. Mário Soares, 'Dez anos Depois,' *O Jornal*, 27 April 1984.
21. Boris Ponomarev, 'A Situação Mundial e o Processo Revolucionário,' *Revista Internacional Problemas da Paz e do Socialismo*, no. 6 (June 1974).
22. Article 42 of the Constitution of the Portuguese Republic

137

(1976). The Council of the Revolution was established after the 11th March Movement, in 1975, that led to the exile of General Spínola.

23. *Diário de Notícias*, 12 October 1983, quoting Vice-Premier Carlos da Mota Pinto.

24. Poll IEEI/NORMA, October-November 1983.

25. GEAR, European Group of Audience Researchers, 1983.

26. Poll IEEI/NORMA, October-November 1983.

27. Polls by the Centro de Investigaciones Sociológicas (CIS), June 1983. *Revista de Estudios e Investigaciones Sociológicas* (Madrid, June 1983): 188.

28. Law of National Defence and of the Armed Forces. Law 29/82 of 11 November 1982.

29. Speech of Vice Premier and Defence Minister Diogo Freitas do Amaral in parliament, 7 October 1982. *Diário da Assembleia da República, I Série* (Lisbon, 8 October 1982): 5626-5643.

30. Carlos da Mota Pinto (Vice Premier and Defence Minister) during the parliamentary debate of the Intelligence Services Law. *Diário da Assembleia da República, I Série* (Lisbon, 22 March 1984): 3858.

31. José Lemos Ferreira, 'Alguns Apontamentos sobre Defesa Militar Portuguesa no Contexto OTAN,' speech at the Lisbon American Club, March 1985. General Lemos Ferreira is Chief of Staff of the Armed Forces.

32. Loureiro dos Santos, *Fundamentos Históricos*, 30.

33. See Hervé Coutau-Bégarie, *Géostratégie de l'Atlantique Sud* (Paris: PUF, 1985).

34. Cf. Abel Cabral Couto, 'Um Contributo para a Definição duma Estratégia Estrutural Portuguesa,' *Revista Militar*, nos. 1/2 (January/February 1981): 44-88.

35. Cf. Mário Mesquita, 'O Valor Estratégico dos Açores numa Perspectiva Africana,' in *A Africa num Mundo Multipolar* (Lisbon: IEEI, 1983), 21-23.

36. Cf. Jeffrey Record, *The Rapid Deployment Force and U.S. Intervention in the Persian Gulf,* Special Report (Cambridge, MA: IFPA, February 1981), 29.

37. George Shultz, 'Foreign Aid and U.S. Policy Objectives,' speech before the House Foreign Affairs Committee, U.S. Congress, Washington, DC, 9 February 1984.

38. José Calvet de Magalhães, interview in, *Diário de Notícias,* 9 January 1984.

39. Jaime Gama, speech during official visit as Foreign Minister to Iraq, in January 1984.

40. Pedro Pires de Miranda, Foreign Minister (1985-), interview in, *Semanário,* 3 May 1986.

41. Cf. António Figueiredo Lopes, 'Portugal e a Cooperação Industrial Europeia,' speech delivered at the IEEI 3rd International Lisbon Conference, 'New Challenges Facing Europe: Defence and Integration,' 24-26 October 1983.

42. Quoted in Mesquita, *A Africa num Mundo Multipolar,* 14.

43. Mário Bettencourt Resendes, 'José de Almeida-Príncipe Gafoor: o Terceiro-Mundismo Açoriano,' *Diário de Notícias,* 3 March 1978.

138

44. Francisco da Costa Gomes, interview in *Liber 25,* no. 6 (January/February 1982): 40.

45. Virgílio de Carvalho, 'A Complementaridade Estratégica de Portugal e da Espanha,' paper presented at the IEEI/Instituto Espanõl de Estudios Estratégicos seminar in Oporto, April 1984.

46. There is no real competition between Portugal and Morocco, as opposed to that between Spain and Morocco in such products as vegetables and fruit. For instance, while Spain exported 1,162 million dollars worth of vegetables and fruit to the Community (1981), Portugal exported 29 million (1:40). Some problems may arise, however, in some areas as textiles, ready-made garments and shoes.

47. These documents were discussed by António Fuzeta da Ponte, Rear-Admiral, in a speech at the Graduate Institute for Political & Social Science Conference in Lisbon, 6 May 1985 (to appear in *Revista Militar*).

48. Salazar Braga, letter to the Chairman of the Defence Committee (see note 9).

49. Diogo Freitas do Amaral, *Política Externa e Política de Defesa (Discursos e Outros Textos)* (Lisbon: Cognitio, 1985), 38.

4

Spain and NATO: Internal Debate and External Challenges

Angel Viñas

Note: This chapter was written in cooperation with Miguel Angel Martinez, M.P. and Ambassador Fernando Alvarez de Miranda

Spain became a signatory to the North Atlantic Treaty on 30 May 1982 and is, therefore, the last country to have entered the North Atlantic Alliance. Spain's decision was taken in the midst of fierce political debate. In general, the centre and right-wing parties, both at the national and regional levels, supported entry into NATO. The parliamentary left, including the Socialists and Communists, and a great many left-wing extra-parliamentary groups opposed the decision, bitterly at times.

When, later in 1982, the Spanish Workers' Socialist Party (PSOE) announced its platform for the general election — which was moved forward by several months — it made two formal commitments: a Socialist government would freeze the process of integration into the NATO military structure and would submit Spain's NATO membership to a popular referendum. The extent to which the Socialist stand on NATO contributed to the PSOE's landslide electoral victory on 28 October 1982, is a matter for conjecture. However, the new government kept its electoral commitments. The Spanish presence in the Alliance was maintained more or less at the level existing when the PSOE took office, and the referendum was eventually held on 12 March 1986.

Alliance membership loomed large in the domestic political discussions leading up to the referendum — the first of this kind to have taken place in any West European country. That the Socialist government carried the day is to a large extent the

140

consequence of a change in attitude towards the Atlantic Alliance between 1982 and 1985. Spain's role in Western security (as well as in the process of European integration) continued to be the subject of considerable domestic debate. Isolated for a long time from many currents in Western development, Spain is now emerging as an important Western power, but the country's place in the West has naturally been conditioned by a unique history.

INTRODUCTION

Spain is now a constitutional monarchy, after having endured some forty years of dictatorship. Together with Portugal, it forms the Iberian peninsula, with coastlines on the Bay of Biscay, the Atlantic Ocean and the Mediterranean, while the Balearic and the Canary Islands — in the Mediterranean and the Atlantic respectively — are part of its national territory. The small towns of Ceuta and Melilla on the North African coast and some rocks and little islands nearby in the Mediterranean Sea (Velez de la Gomera, Alhucemas and Chafarinas) also belong to Spain. Early in the eighteenth century, Gibraltar — on the southern coast of the peninsula — was occupied by Britain.[1] With a surface area of about 195,000 square miles, Spain is the second largest West European country after France. It ranks fifth in Western Europe in terms of population, with 38.5 million inhabitants. After protracted negotiations, it entered the European Community (EC) on 1 January 1986. Membership in the EC was important for the Spanish, for whom outside acceptance of the successful transition to democracy served to confirm a process that had taken a long time to consolidate.

Spain's early and limited democratic experience ended with the bloody Civil War of 1936–1939 when it was placed in abeyance by the Franco regime. On Franco's accession to power, Spain was suffering severely from forms of both economic and social domestic instability. Until this regime ended in 1975, Spanish economic and security policies were oriented towards the tasks of economic recovery and growth, and countering internal threats to stability. The first of these tasks was particularly difficult given the shattered state of the postwar economy and also the resistance offered by the old-fashioned landowning and financial oligarchies which, bent on

141

preserving the old social order, were impervious to the challenges of modernization and change. State security was threatened by the exiled opposition in France which, throughout the postwar period, attempted to gain entry into Spain. Rising guerrilla activity tied down troops and police, although it never threatened the dictatorship itself.

The domestic orientation of policy may be explained also by the fact that, unlike other West European countries, Spain did not perceive a Soviet threat. The Soviet Union was, in fact, the only great power which effectively helped the Republic during the Civil War. This contributed to the growth of the previously minuscule Spanish Communist Party and to enormous friction within the republican camp — particularly with the anarchists and socialists. But the virulent anti-communism of the Franco dictatorship and its black and white propaganda portraying the Soviet Union as the source of all evil in the contemporary world, successfully dissipated memories of Soviet unfriendliness. The Spanish Communist Party was, in fact, one of the major forces opposing the Franco regime. Moreover, Spain had no experience of Allied liberation from the fascist powers. The United States became a firm ally of the Franco dictatorship in order to secure for itself the use of military bases and facilities that were established on Spanish territory after 1953. This arrangement provoked anti-American sentiment (and continues to be a source of anti-Americanism), although the personal experience of the intellectual elite, educated in the United States in the 1960s, attenuated hostility.

After the death of Franco, the path towards democracy was apparently strewn with obstacles. Foreign observers expected that the political transition initiated in 1976, after so many years of dictatorial rule, would plunge Spain into instability, but it was extremely successful. Francoist members of the armed forces failed to stop democratization, despite an abortive military coup on 23 February 1981. A terrorist threat is still posed, however, by Basque nationalist, left-wing radicals who desire independence from the Spanish state and are unwilling to play the political game within the limits of the constitutional order now firmly established in Spain. The consolidation of the democratic experience over the past few years has diminished the prospects of domestic insecurity. Spain is, however, exposed to the geostrategic and geopolitical tensions of the Mediterranean and is also enmeshed in the East-West confrontation.

Spain must therefore develop an external security policy that incorporates historical and geographical determinants, its international commitments and national interests reflecting the aspirations of the Spanish political parties, and which is able to generate broad support among the population. This effort to develop a comprehensive foreign and security policy will require Spain to break out of a long pattern of isolation and isolationism that preceded the Franco regime and was only partly (and cynically) altered by the Generalissimo. Current policy can only be understood against this background.

A HISTORY OF ISOLATION AND ISOLATIONISM

Despite having built a large empire in the sixteenth century, Spain withdrew from European affairs once it could no longer retain its European possessions.[2] Concern for maintaining the unity of the Spanish state became the prime goal of the Spanish leadership. Even with the establishment of a liberal monarchy at the end of the nineteenth century (1874), there was little movement away from a traditional society. A tacit pact, created during this period between Catalan industrialists, Basque mining interests and the landowning oligarchy, was directed towards the organization of domestic production to cover simply the requirements of domestic demand. The central government in Madrid likewise worked to protect the economy from competition.

Economic isolationism went hand-in-hand with introversion. A century-long experience of geographical, social and cultural isolation from a burgeoning Western Europe led to introspection and a refusal to participate actively in international politics. Spain's defeat in the war with the United States in 1898 was a tremendous shock which, nevertheless, had positive effects. It first bore fruit in the cultural field. French, German and British influences became increasingly important to intellectuals bent on modernizing the country.

In terms of power politics, however, Spain was a loser in the age of imperialism. The nation had to come to terms with a vastly diminished status in world affairs, and this adjustment did not come easily. Indeed, attempts were made to reestablish Spanish grandeur. Spain reembarked on new colonial adventures in North Africa, an enterprise that was seen as a necessary outlet for an overblown and inefficient army whose principal role in the nineteenth century had been to influence the course of domestic politics. The liberal army that had developed as a result of the war against Napoleon had become a bastion of conservatism and reaction. By 1923, the political strength of the liberal monarchy and governmental attempts to maintain a unified and strong Spanish state against devolutionist tensions were largely exhausted. The army had suffered humiliating defeats in Morocco. The economic euphoria existing during World War I had evaporated. Revolutionary class struggle took on violent forms, while there were moves for autonomy, notably in Catalonia. Following a military *pronunciamiento* by General Miguel Primo de Rivera, a mild dictatorship was established that lasted until 1930, but it did not succeed in solving the various social or political problems that afflicted Spain. Its main achievement was to bring the colonial war in Morocco to an end.

By the 1930s dissatisfaction with the monarchy had become generalized. Municipal elections were held on 12 April 1931. They led to a victory of those candidates in the urban areas who were overwhelmingly anti-monarchist. The King abandoned the country and the Second Republic (the First had a brief existence in 1873) was established. The republican experiment was carried out by large numbers of the urban bourgeoisie, regionalist parties and socialists. Its goal was to modernize Spain and to do away with outdated economic, political and social structures. The introduction of regional autonomy led to a right-wing outcry about national disintegration. Military reform was launched which met with resistance in an underequipped army with far too many officers and generals. The separation of church and state and secular public education generated intense friction with the Catholic hierarchy. An attempt at long-overdue land reform was received with outright hostility by the landowning oligarchy.

The class struggle became increasingly bitter. The powerful anarchist movement grew larger and became an important force outside the political spectrum. The right conspired to abort any substantial social or economic experiments which were regarded with suspicion by British and American diplomats and business people.[3] In an era of intense political polarization, a particular brand of European fascism grew up in Spain. The fear arose that the right-wing political parties, which since 1933 had

144

dominated parliament, would do away with the progressive reforms already undertaken. In 1934, socialists and anarchists staged a proletarian revolution in Asturias which was crushed by the army and resulted in further tensions between the government and the left.

The February 1936 general election was won by centre-left and left-wing parties grouped in a 'Popular Front' coalition. The new government, from which socialists and communists were excluded, was formed by republicans and attempted once again to pass reforms that previously had been blocked. This was enough for some powerful groups in the army and the civilian right to intensify their activities leading to a coup d'état on 17 July 1936. A new Popular Front government then armed the masses, although it could not prevent large areas of the country from falling to the insurgents. Nazi Germany and fascist Italy provided immediate help for the Spanish rebels out of fear that the republican government might change the balance of power in Western Europe by allying itself with France.

The Madrid authorities had, in fact, asked the French for war matériel. The possibility existed that events in Spain might lead to an international conflict, and the policy of non-intervention formulated by France and Britain was designed to prevent this conflict. This policy did serve to contain the Civil War, but could not impede further German and Italian involvement in Spanish affairs, which in turn led Stalin to support the Republic in October 1936. He acted by no means selflessly, and three-quarters of the considerable gold reserves of the Bank of Spain were sold to the Soviet Union. The better organization and discipline of General Franco's side, combined with the relentless support of the fascist powers, led to his victory in April 1939.[4]

The Civil War put Spain in the headlines for more than two years and caused great turmoil in Spanish society. It contributed to the political polarization in Europe and provided encouragement for those states whose political outlook was anti-liberal, anti-democratic and anti-communist. The Franco regime adopted fascist institutions and before long it appeared to align itself with Rome and Berlin.

EMERGENCE FROM ISOLATIONISM

Spain's traditional isolation from international affairs eventually diminished under the Franco regime, which in its early years was shunned by many Western countries. The improvements that took place were the result of a combination of three major phenomena: the need (over time) to compensate for Axis support during the Civil War (Franco's 'original sin'); the transformations brought about in Spain by economic and social changes; and the increasingly close relationship between West European countries and the United States.

In terms of its 'original sin,' the Franco regime had to atone, vis-à-vis the allies, not only for German and Italian help (which was decisive for Franco's victory) but also for the pro-Axis course of its foreign policy during much of World War II. Retribution came in several forms: the rejection of Spain's membership to the United Nations; a resolution by the United Nations in 1946 to withdraw the ambassadors of member countries from Madrid; and Spain's absence from the process of rapprochement of the West European economies (which culminated in the establishment of the European Economic Community).[5] During the first years under Franco, therefore, Spain entered a period of international ostracism vis-à-vis the indignant publics and governments of the Western democracies.

In the economic sphere, exclusion from the international scene led the regime to pursue policies of self-sufficiency which prevented the Spanish economy from becoming a part of the emerging international division of labour in postwar Western Europe. Economic isolation was initially imposed upon Spain since the dictatorship's lack of respectability prevented its participation in the European Recovery Programme (the Marshall Plan), a major factor in the internationalization of the European economies. Autarchy first and import-substitution later were also predicated, however, on the mistrust with which the regime viewed the international scene.

Nevertheless, efforts were made in Spain's foreign policy which reflected the dictatorship's desperate need to gain international respectability. Relations with most Latin American and Arab countries were carefully cultivated, and occasionally led to major returns, as in the case of the economic assistance provided by Argentina and the diplomatic support given in the United Nations to the Franco regime by some countries of both groups. Slowly, Spain began to enjoy better relations with the United States and later with Western powers generally. American interest in ensuring that some measures would be taken to liberalize the regime was met with British fears that the Spanish situation might become destabilized, and so the United States began to drop its objections to the Spanish dictatorship.

The outbreak of the Cold War worked to Spain's advantage in this respect, and facilitated its gradual emergence from isolation. Spain's value as a potential ally was not lost on U.S. security planners and Franco's strong anti-communism complemented the American need to deploy forces in Spain. Political difficulties at the United Nations were solved by 1950. The following year, President Truman, overcoming his personal distaste for General Franco, agreed to begin exploratory talks with the Spanish dictatorship. In August 1953, a new *Concordat* was signed with the Vatican whereby the Catholic Church lent Franco even more moral support. A month later, three executive agreements were signed with the United States. The aim of the U.S.-Spanish agreements was to strengthen Western security. Franco's government thereby authorized the Americans to establish, maintain and use bases, military and transit facilities, and oil pipelines on Spanish territory. This implicated Spain in the U.S. policy of containment vis-à-vis the Soviet Union and signified the effective end of Spanish neutrality in any conflict that might occur in Western Europe. In exchange, the Franco regime was guaranteed significant — though hardly generous — economic assistance by the United States.

The U.S.-Spanish relationship was not entirely free from strain. In a series of secret agreements (also concluded in 1953) Spain made heavy concessions to the United States and effectively limited its sovereignty in dealings with the agreed-to American presence on Spanish territory. A secret clause stipulating the possible activation of U.S. military bases in time of war or emergency, gave the United States *carte blanche* but left the Spanish government little scope for action. A secret technical agreement, four technical documents — also secret — and a non-public status-of-forces agreement for Americans and their dependants were also signed. Between 1954 and 1960, twenty-two procedural agreements were concluded, which also remained confidential. The practical implementation of the agreements contributed further to limiting Spain's room for manoeuvre.[6] The secret agreements and their purpose were not made public until 1981, when the democratic system had already been established. But during the time of the Franco regime, unsuccessful attempts were made by the Ministry of Foreign Affairs (which had been excluded from the negotiations of the politico-strategic and military issues during the years 1951–1953) and by other bodies in the Spanish civil service to modify the larger concessions — including the introduction of nuclear weapons onto Spanish territory at the Torrejon and Rota bases — made by Franco in favour of the United States.

The development of ties with the United States was a great political triumph for Francoism. It cleared the way for admittance into the United Nations (1955) and other international agencies. The opposition — both domestic and exiled — interpreted the 1953 agreements as the seal of approval by Washington of the Franco dictatorship. This certainly coloured the future perceptions of the United States that would be held by political groups persecuted by the Franco regime. The agreements gave sanction to a government that was anti-communist but which at the same time trampled on the basic freedoms and moral values that are fundamental components of Western political life and philosophy.

The Franco regime became a 'free rider' within the Western defence system: it contributed passively by placing facilities at the disposal of the United States. Once domestic guerrilla activity had been stamped out in the early 1950s, Spanish defence expenditure diminished considerably. Defence policy remained low-key and the erstwhile desire to create an industrial base for it became no longer applicable when the equipment of the armed forces with modern matériel was carried out by the United States, even though this matériel was often out-dated. It was not until the late 1960s, when the economy was booming, that an in-depth review of defence policy was undertaken.

In mid-June 1971, the navy general staff prepared a strategic study which stressed the territorial claims that were potential sources of conflict for Spain, and indicated the possibility that the divergence of interests between Spain and Morocco might lead to a confrontation. Therefore, Spain had to maintain a clear deterrent capacity in the event of a threat from the south. North Africa was identified as the area posing the greatest security risk for Spain.[7] The conclusions of this study were incorporated into the first Joint Strategic Plan drawn up by the Franco regime as it neared its end. They proved to be right:

shortly before the dictator's death, the regime became entangled in the last episode of its colonial experience, namely, the decolonization of the western Sahara, which was claimed by Rabat.[8] Morocco occupied the territory and engaged in continuous warfare against the indigenous population led by the Polisario Front intent upon defending their right to independence.

Meanwhile, during Franco's dictatorship, Spanish society had undergone deep social and economic changes. These were partly wrought by the experiences of the Civil War, but also by the economic growth patterns of the postwar decades. The autarchic and interventionist policies followed by the regime after the Civil War stunted the moderate but sustained economic growth curves of the pre-Civil-War period. These policies engendered repression, re-ruralization, and serious food shortages; industrial production and real per capita income stagnated in the 1940s. In the 1950s the situation changed. Industrial production and GNP increased in Spain between 1950 and 1958, as they did in other Mediterranean countries such as France, Italy, Greece and Yugoslavia. This was the result of more open trading policies, of intense migratory movements which kept wages low, of better agricultural performance, and of the relaxation of very tight administrative controls.

Nevertheless, a bottleneck in the balance of payments in 1958–1959 induced the Spanish dictatorship to undertake its only ambitious strategic operation in economic policy: a fairly thorough stabilization and liberalization plan under the auspices of the Organisation for European Economic Co-operation and the International Monetary Fund. This ended the impossible dream of substantial import substitution and considerably reduced state intervention in international economic transactions. A more liberal import policy, the elimination of the balance-of-payments deficits (thanks to tourist receipts, direct foreign investments — which had been practically prohibited in the 1950s — and workers' remittances from abroad), as well as the massive inflow of foreign know-how and technology enabled the Spanish economy to participate fully in the fruits of the golden age of Western economic expansion. By 1962, Francoism even sought to establish links with the European Economic Community. Industrial production developed between 1958 and 1969 at one of the highest rates in Europe. The real growth rate of GNP was also extremely rapid and brought about the transition from a largely underdeveloped economy to an economy of West European stature, in which international connections permeated all sectors and fields of activity.

These economic changes deeply affected Spanish society. High labour force mobility played an important role. Massive emigration to the EC countries exposed Spaniards to foreign influences and a different work ethic. Tourism did much to soften traditional attitudes, even those between the sexes. Spain became a consumerist society. These developments contributed to create a positive image of the regime, which was seen as capable of offering the benefits of economic growth (however unequally distributed) and of curbing 'subversive' political activity and unrest. More and more, Francoism enjoyed the mark of approval of the rapidly expanding middle class which was reaping benefits from changes in the economic environment.

Economic growth required improved skills and education. Spaniards began travelling freely throughout Western Europe and the United States. The dictatorship's hold over people's minds loosened and the opposition to the Franco regime grew rapidly. It was now supported by a generation that had not known the Civil War years and the subsequent brutal repression. During the 1950s and 1960s, Spaniards adopted patterns of political and social behaviour similar to those prevailing in other industrial Western societies. These changes would not have taken place so rapidly had it not been for a third and particularly important phenomenon, namely, the closer link between the West European countries and the United States, brought about by substantial advances in communications which enabled images and behaviour to be transmitted easily from one culture to another. For a country like Spain, that had followed an isolationist path for so many decades, it meant that the outside world was suddenly introduced to the people at large. Western Europe came to represent a model to be emulated. The closing of the historic gap that had begun in the sixteenth century became imperative for those political forces opposed to the dictatorship, and for social groups directly associated with Franco. The erosion of Francoism coincided with a burst of enthusiasm among the more modern-minded segments of a country which was changing significantly behind the apparent passivity imposed by the dictatorship.

150

SPANISH TRANSITION POLITICS 1975–1982

After General Franco's death in 1975, Spain was faced with the realities of adapting the rigid political structures left by the dictator to the changes in society that had already taken place. This process of adaptation, known in Spain as 'the transition,' constitutes one of the most important chapters in Spanish history. The success of the transition is indicated by the fact that, by 1982, the Socialist Party, harshly persecuted under Franco, was able to assume the responsibility of government.

The transition agenda comprised two major reforms: political reform, aimed at creating a consensus among all the political parties and groups opposed to the dictatorship, and military reform, designed to neutralize the armed forces and the Francoist extreme right so as to prevent their interference in politics. Economic affairs were essentially allowed to drift, even though since the economic shocks of 1973 the Spanish economy had been in a downturn compounded by indigenous factors inherited from the Francoist economic system. Social and political turmoil left the policy makers with only a small margin for manoeuvre.[9]

Political Reform

From the outset there were two conflicting strategies for political reform. The first, espoused by Prime Minister Carlos Arias Navarro, sought to preserve political Francoism without Franco to the extent possible. The second alternative, defended by the democratic opposition, advocated a clean break with the political system inherited from Franco. The democrats demanded that the Spanish people be given the right to choose the form of government (monarchy or republic) that they desired; they called for a decentralization of the Francoist state, and for a general amnesty absolving individuals who had been declared guilty of political 'offences' and sentenced under the dictatorship. Franco's successor as head of state, King Juan Carlos, made it quite clear in 1975 that he wished to follow the path of democratization but there were considerable institutional barriers. Until the first half of 1976, therefore, he followed the strategy of continuity. It soon became clear, however, that cosmetic reforms were grossly insufficient and Arias Navarro's successor, Adolfo Suarez (who had a Francoist background) undertook, with the King's support, the dismantling of the repressive powers of the dictatorship.

After the legalization of trade unions and political parties (hitherto banned) and the passing of a political reform law — ratified by the Spanish people in a referendum held in December 1976 — a dialogue was established between the government and the opposition. The intention of this dialogue was to achieve a political agreement that would remove the dead weight of the Francoist state and establish the conditions for future democracy. The more liberal *Franquistas* were grouped with the democratic opposition, forming the Union of the Democratic Centre (UCD) which in June 1977 won the first general parliamentary election to be held in Spain since February 1936. The PSOE came second and played a leading role in the new parliamentary opposition, whereas the Spanish Communist Party (PCE) won only a negligible number of seats in parliament. Factions of the Francoist right were soundly defeated in the election.

Well aware of the need to dismantle the institutional framework of the dictatorship while at the same time complying with the existing legal order, the UCD, PSOE and PCE, together with a number of regional political parties, implemented a policy of consensus in order to lay the foundations of a new constitution, eventually adopted in December 1978 by popular referendum.

This union bore fruit also in the elaboration of foreign policy, which successfully overcame obstacles encountered earlier by the dictatorship. Spain joined the Council of Europe and requested the start of negotiations for accession to the European Community. Diplomatic relations were established with Mexico and East European countries, including the Soviet Union. The Spanish left, which under Franco had condemned the bilateral relationship with Washington, ceased to question the principle of the U.S. military presence in Spain. In this way it demonstrated an extraordinary sense of political realism at a time when the highest priority was the reestablishment of democracy. In exchange, the UCD refrained from altering the status quo with regard to the Atlantic Alliance. The left understood that the process of modernizing Spain politically and institutionally demanded a certain respect for the existing system of global balances and alliances. The government feared, however, that an overly rapid Spanish rapprochement with NATO would lose it political support from the left, whose participation and sanction in the process of political reform was crucial.

Military Reform

Reform of the military was a prerequisite for the political transition process to succeed. During the Civil War, the armed forces had understood, or been made to understand, that they were crusaders fighting against liberalism and leftism (communism especially) and had become a highly privileged body within the state. Since the early days of the dictatorship they were imbued with a sense of authority, mission and pride, bred on a hypernationalistic ideology and moulded, by Franco, into a stable social entity, relatively isolated from civilian life. The armed forces became identified with an 'eternal' Spain, the only possible Spain, where disorder, regional autonomy or class struggle would not be tolerated. In the late 1960s, however, the monolithic bastion of loyalty began to disintegrate, as signs of dissidence appeared among groups of young officers.

Under Franco, the Spanish armed forces constituted the *ultima ratio* of the political system and continued to be deployed territorially to prevent internal revolt. Major military bases and facilities were kept around the large cities and in industrial areas where domestic troubles might most easily erupt. Indeed, internal security constituted the armed forces' most important task under the dictatorship. The left consistently, therefore, referred to the territorial army as an 'army of occupation.'

The Franco regime froze military modernization. Complex regulations concerning assignments and promotions meant that an officer's seniority was more important than his capacities. This favoured more and more the traditional imbalance at the top (there was an abundance of generals and high-ranking officers) and also tended to encourage late retirement. Franco needed loyal commanders, not efficient ones. He inflated the ranks of Civil War veterans with 'provisional' officers, who subsequently opted to remain in the services, and thus the ratio of officers to troops reached an abnormally high level.

The armed forces did not share in many of the benefits of Spanish economic expansion. Their wages were modest — even though wages absorbed the greater part of defence expenditure. Equipment and training were greatly neglected and the level of technical skills attained was comparatively low. In 1975, the armed forces were in no position to respond to an external challenge since the reforms undertaken during the late years of the dictatorship had yielded meagre results. Towards the end of the Franco era, the armed forces were very isolated within Spanish society. Corruption was rampant in certain sectors and the threat of losing political influence worried the military as much as the likelihood of losing personal privileges and perquisites.[10]

This was the situation when the democratic government began to elaborate plans for reform. It set three tasks before itself, all designed to raise military professionalism and expertise to levels never attained during Franco's time.

The first was to subordinate the armed forces to civilian power and induce them to accept the transition towards a constitutional order. It became necessary to curb incidents of military misbehaviour that had broken out after Franco's death. The second was to modernize military institutions. Under the careful and intelligent supervision of the King who was Commander-in-Chief of the Armed Forces, the Prime Minister, Adolfo Suarez, was to draw up and implement appropriate measures. These included enforcing restrictions on the active participation of the military in politics, reorganizing defence commands, and revising the promotion, retirement and training systems, without making too severe a break with past policies. There were no purges, although essential changes were made in the higher echelons. The third task was to provide the armed forces with the means to carry out the duties prescribed to them in the democratic constitution of 1978: the guarantee of Spanish sovereignty and independence, and the defence of Spain's territorial integrity and constitutional order. This required a shift in emphasis of security concerns from domestic to external threat, which would consequently improve Spain's deterrent potential by modernizing equipment and raise the efficiency and morale of military personnel. Accordingly, the defence budget was increased and a higher proportion devoted to investment in matériel.

During the 1976–1980 period Spanish military policy was directed towards the maintenance of absolute unity within the armed forces to ensure their neutrality during the transition.

Thus, some young officers who had shown an interest in contributing to political change were discharged from active service. They were penalized for what were held to be punishable offences under the then current code of military justice. But despite the government's efforts not to offend susceptibilities while carrying out military reforms, it was difficult to prevent political and institutional changes from arousing discontent in military circles, particularly after the Communist Party was legalized in April 1977. It was not always possible to appoint progressive-minded officers to responsible positions without angering hard-line sectors. Although key posts were given only to law-respecting officers, the threat of a military coup from the extreme right still remained. The government did not dare to abolish right-wing publications which were widely read in the barracks. Throughout this period the armed forces were under great stress because of attacks on them by Basque terrorists and this naturally affected the severity with which the government could deal with the soldiers.

Ultimately, therefore, democratic normalization (both political and military) failed to proceed without provoking antagonism on all fronts. By late 1980, Suarez (the principal architect of the process) had become unpopular both with the opposition *and* with members of his own party. Suddenly, in January 1981, he resigned. His appointed successor was Leopoldo Calvo Sotelo. On 23 February, during the second vote in parliament to confirm his inauguration as Prime Minister, some army officers and soldiers, together with members of the Civil Guard, seized the Lower House and took the members of parliament and the government hostage while awaiting news of a nationwide military uprising supported by all high-ranking officers. This did not, in fact, materialize, except in Valencia — where the commander of the garrison appeared to have joined forces with the rebels. The attempted military coup was a traumatic experience for the country and radically transformed the political scene. It proved that the armed forces had not been entirely neutralized: a militant group had developed which was opposed to the policy of general change, either for ideological reasons or because it wished to protect long-enjoyed privileges. The expression was then coined that the Spanish democracy was under surveillance, to which Calvo Sotelo replied — not too convincingly — that Spain was a 'watchful' democracy.

The public and media both submitted the military to scrutiny while legal proceedings were being brought in a military court against the officers who had planned and led the failed coup. It then became clear that, had it not been for the resolute intervention of the King who had categorically denied legitimacy to the rebels and rapidly ensured the loyalty of the higher military echelons, matters might have taken a very different turn. It was more or less explicitly recognized that many officers were loyal to the King, yet not necessarily to the constitutional order.

Prime Minister Calvo Sotelo initially enjoyed wide support and cooperation from all political parties, trade unions and business organizations. Mindful of the need to stabilize the democratic system and strengthen policies so as to deal with the severe economic crisis, the Socialist Party even suggested that a coalition government be formed. However, that same year, Calvo Sotelo's position rapidly deteriorated; his own policies being partially to blame. The government's handling of military problems provoked strong criticism. It was considered an indication of firmness that for the first time since the Civil War no military officer was a member of the cabinet, but, on the other hand, the appointed civilian Defence Minister was not considered by many as equal to the challenge. His policy of assignments and promotions was sharply criticized; officers who demonstrated loyalty to democracy received little recognition and, in general, he seemed weak in his handling of the 'military question.'

Another major difficulty was the trial of the officers arrested in connection with the attempted coup — the non-commissioned officers involved were inexplicably readmitted to the services. Procedural mechanisms and protection of the defendants' rights considerably delayed preparations. Had summary procedures — abolished prior to the attempted takeover — been in force in 1981, the trial would have been conducted much more expeditiously and in a less tense atmosphere. Many felt that it would never take place, and the government appeared too passive. Yet, eventually, the trial was held from February to May 1982.

The significance of the trial depended, in part, on the harshness of the sentences, since it was inevitable that the trial itself would be judged by the public in terms of the vigour with which it defended democratic principles. In general, the sentences given in June 1982 were less severe than requested. Two leaders of the coup were given the maximum penalty — thirty years imprisonment — and discharged from the service. Other officers were also discharged, but many were acquitted. The State Prosecutor requested another hearing, which later culminated in more severe sentences. A third major coup leader was then sentenced to the maximum penalty.

Indecisive government policies raised the level of political polarization. After the so-called social democratic faction had split off from the Centre Party, Adolfo Suarez himself left UCD in July 1982 and formed his own political group. Calvo Sotelo no longer had the necessary parliamentary majority to face the challenge of renewed parliamentary activity in September, and was forced to dissolve parliament. The general election, originally planned for March 1983, was moved forward to October 1982.

SPAIN, THE UNITED STATES AND THE ATLANTIC ALLIANCE DURING THE TRANSITION

By the time of Franco's death, Spanish and American negotiators had been engaged for some time in one of their periodic reviews of the bilateral relationship. The conclusion of the negotiations was delayed until January 1976. It was then agreed that American nuclear submarines ought to leave the Rota naval base by July 1979, that Spanish territory would remain free of nuclear weapons, and that a geographical area of common interest would be defined to which the agreement would apply. For the first time, the U.S. Congress acknowledged that the relationship with Spain could be codified in a formal treaty. This was widely understood to be a way of supporting the incipient process of Spanish democratization. In some respects, the 1976 treaty was a clear improvement over the preceding agreements, but it had obvious deficiencies, particularly concerning the firmness of the Spanish controlling procedures over the facilities used by the United States.

Spanish concessions were not insignificant at that time, although this was not always acknowledged by the Americans. The receiving and transmitting unit at the Rota naval base and its relay at Moron are among the few facilities used by the U.S. navy to control world maritime, surface and submarine traffic. At Maspalomas there are facilities for substantial control of outer space. Seismic movements from underground nuclear

157

explosions are detected with precision at Sonseca. Effective command of the 16th U.S. air force is exercised from Torrejon. The significance of these facilities for assuring communications and control is considerable. It is true that on the strategic level their importance has dramatically decreased, although their contribution to the refuelling of aircraft *en route* to the East should not be underestimated. From Rota and Moron, moreover, there are control facilities for the Straits of Gibraltar and its approaches. The bases have retained their importance in the event of a crisis involving the Warsaw Pact, and their substitution would require much time and heavy expenditure by the United States.

The process of negotiating a new agreement was long and difficult. It began on 25 May 1981, after the attempted coup, and required ninety-six working sessions. Under the new political and social circumstances, the Spanish authorities were able to argue successfully in favour of a new kind of agreement that was more balanced and, in many technical aspects, more precise than any of its predecessors. It was necessary to obtain parliamentary consent for an extension of the 1976 treaty in order not to allow the defence nexus between the United States and Spain to lapse. This negotiation did not provoke severe criticism from political parties, but an entirely different situation arose when the government hinted that it might seek a rapprochement with the Atlantic Alliance.

The UCD platform for the 1977 and 1979 general elections had, indeed, referred to the desirability of Spanish NATO membership and, on several occasions, high-ranking members of the cabinet had expressed their support for such a move. Thus, in March 1978, the Foreign Minister, Marcelino Oreja, stated in the Senate that the government rejected neutrality and would stage a debate on the pros and cons of joining the Alliance.

Factors relating both to domestic politics (the desire to avoid further confrontation, and Adolfo Suarez's tarnished image) and foreign affairs (the aspiration to hold the Conference on Security and Cooperation in Europe meeting in Madrid in 1981) hindered the development of an Alliance-oriented policy. Suarez also made some spectacular gestures that demonstrated his wish not to align Spanish foreign policy prematurely: Spanish observers attended the Havana Non-Aligned Conference in 1981, and Yasser Arafat was warmly received in Madrid.

Foreign policy remained firmly bipartisan throughout this period, in which government and opposition learned their trade through experience.

Spanish NATO policy underwent a profound change with the appointment of the new Prime Minister. Calvo Sotelo had already made it clear in his inaugural address just before the coup that he intended to begin consultations with the parliamentary groups to obtain a majority, following which he would seek to define the terms and conditions under which Spain would be willing to participate in the Alliance. This line of action was consistent with the resolution of the second UCD Congress in which it had been mentioned that UCD support for the Atlantic Alliance would be brought before both houses of parliament before the next general election.

As a result of this proposal the confrontation over the Alliance — which so far had remained at a low level — between the right and centre, on the one hand, and the left, on the other, rapidly grew more heated. At the twenty-ninth PSOE Congress held in October 1981, a number of arguments were put forward against Spanish NATO membership. It was argued that entry into NATO did not guarantee defence of the full territorial integrity of Spain, as Ceuta and Melilla remained outside the confines of the North Atlantic Treaty. Moreover, any North African security problem that challenged Spain would be considered by the Alliance to be outside its area of responsibility. The view was put forward that participation in NATO would imply a higher nuclear risk for Spain and that the expansion of NATO to the south might provoke a reaction from the Warsaw Pact. Many individuals were concerned that Spanish entry into NATO could set in motion a process of 'militarization' because of the need to modernize substantially the armed forces. Others insisted that Spanish entry would only further strengthen the East-West confrontation. Finally, those who wavered on questions of principle insisted that Spanish NATO membership should not be undertaken unless suitable trade-offs could be obtained over Gibraltar and in the negotiations for entry into the EC.

The left's general opposition to NATO was based on four separate factors. First, during the Franco dictatorship, progressive public opinion in Spain had always identified Western Europe with democratic ideals, pluralism and respect for human rights. The Alliance, on the other hand, had glossed over the

Portuguese dictatorship and the Greek military regime. NATO, thus, seemed willing to subordinate the democratic ideals of the West to security requirements. Second, the Alliance was seen as a U.S.-dominated entity which had lent support to the Franco dictatorship and had not hesitated to countenance unacceptable military regimes in Latin America and elsewhere. The maintenance of bilateral security relations with Washington was not envisaged as an eternal feature of Spanish foreign and defence policies. It might, however, be more difficult to withdraw from NATO membership. Third, Spanish public opinion did not have any clear perception of a Soviet threat against Spain. Communism was widely seen as a gimmick used by Franco to attack the republican regime, establish his dictatorship and justify it for over forty years. This did not mean that there was a special Spanish sympathy for the East, but simply that the left could not easily be moved by questions relating to East-West rivalry. Finally, defence and security issues had not figured prominently in Spanish political debates: the Franco regime was not anxious to allow the public to comment on them and the left had other issues to worry about.

Against this background, the minority UCD government was prepared, for reasons which it never properly explained, to break the tacit understanding (among Spanish political parties) not to move significantly towards NATO membership. Despite its weak parliamentary base, once the UCD cabinet had speeded up the process of accession to the Atlantic Alliance, the left's room for manoeuvre was considerably curtailed. The Socialists were unwilling, for domestic political reasons, to bring down the government. However, it seemed wrong not to oppose a measure that was not widely supported and which destroyed the tacit understanding maintained until early 1981.

Under these circumstances, the Socialists followed a strategy designed to make the government aware of the scant popular support that NATO membership would command. Massive demonstrations were staged which served as rallying points for all the Spanish left. The Socialists also sought to prolong the parliamentary process of accession. This strategy did not succeed. On 20 August 1981, the cabinet agreed to submit NATO membership to parliamentary approval. The Lower House began to consider the issue on 15 September. It was debated in committee on 6–8 October, by the full House on 27–28 October and was passed by a majority of 186 votes to 146, with the left opposing. The Upper House debate was held on 24–26 November. The government won by a majority of 106 votes to sixty. Rarely in contemporary Spanish history had a foreign policy issue stirred so many emotions. Government polls in September 1981 revealed that 43 percent of the population would vote against, and only 13 percent for, entry into NATO.[11] Nevertheless, indifference to NATO was widespread and perhaps as important as outright opposition. NATO membership was not a priority concern for the Spanish, nor was it a problem that, in the public's perception, required an urgent solution.

It is likely that domestic concerns motivated the UCD government to accelerate NATO accession. First, it is probable that the government felt that participation in the Alliance would take the armed forces out of their ideological and emotional ghetto, by offering them many attractive professional opportunities and providing a special reason for the continuance of necessary technical and organizational reforms. However, this argument was never made explicit. Second, given the growing disintegration of the UCD, the NATO issue might have served for some time as an element of self-identification and unity within certain sectors of the party. Third, it was believed that if Spain under the UCD government did not accede to NATO, a Socialist or Socialist-supported government would be very unwilling to countenance such a move. This consideration clearly played a role in Calvo Sotelo's calculations. Fearful that his party would lose power, he felt it important to ensure that Spain enter NATO before domestic problems would make such a move too difficult. Forecasts of forthcoming regional elections did show that the UCD would not fare well.

When the government submitted the NATO issue to parliament, elections had already been called in Galicia for October 1981 and a date had been fixed for elections in Andalusia in May 1982. The latter were particularly significant, and after the Socialists won easily, the government's days were numbered. The cabinet, therefore, decided that Spain should become a member of NATO before it was too late. In a letter, dated 3 December, the Foreign Minister José-Pedro Pérez-Llorca informed the NATO Secretary General that Spain was willing to receive an invitation to join the Alliance. The protocol of invitation was signed on 10 December. Ratifications by the parliaments of the NATO member countries were concluded by

161

25 May. Five days later, the Spanish embassy deposited the instrument of accession in Washington.

The Spanish government wasted no time in formulating its relations with NATO. The Prime Minister attended the spring meeting of the Atlantic Council in early June and measures were swiftly taken to ensure a Spanish presence in the various bodies and committees of the Alliance. After a number of preliminary contacts, exploratory talks were soon under way with a view to incorporating Spain into the military structure. For the first time, the Alliance was able to make an exact analysis of the strengths and weaknesses of the Spanish armed forces.

The Socialists, on the other hand, were left in disarray. Accession to NATO had placed the PSOE before an entirely new situation in which Spain had assumed very important international obligations. Facing an electoral challenge, the PSOE decided to alter its position on NATO when preparing its election platform. Two major stands were taken: the PSOE would suspend integration into NATO's military structure; and, once in power, would call for a referendum on Spanish membership in NATO. There was a long tradition behind the second commitment: ever since the debate had started concerning NATO membership, the PSOE had asserted that a measure of such importance should not be taken without first consulting public opinion, which would almost certainly be against it. In 1982 it would have been impossible to go back on this pledge.

In the 1982 election campaign — in contrast to those of 1977 and 1979 — the NATO issue played an important role. Many citizens who had been surprised at the way in which the UCD government had carried out the accession, undoubtedly gave their votes to the Socialists, in the belief that the PSOE would take Spain out of the Alliance. In the heat of the campaign, some Socialists exaggerated the very precise commitments of the platform, which made no specific mention of a Socialist desire to leave NATO. After intense debate, the PSOE leadership had decided that since Spain's signature on the North Atlantic Treaty had substantially changed the terms of reference upon which Spanish foreign and security policies were based, policy on the Alliance had to take into account the difference between choosing not to enter and deciding to leave NATO. Since the platform excluded the possibility of neutrality, in the event of the Socialists winning the election, the new government would be left with two strategic options: either to remain in the

Alliance with a status yet to be determined; or to leave NATO whilst maintaining (at a cost) the relationship — whether modified or not — with the United States. It was recognized that Alliance membership had, in fact, helped to overcome some of the difficulties encountered in the U.S.-Spanish negotiations over the 1976 treaty.

A new agreement had, in fact, been signed with the United States on 2 July 1982. It was wider ranging than its predecessor and was explicitly based on a broader range of common interests. It consisted of the basic agreement on friendship, defence and cooperation, seven complementary agreements, nine annexes, two appendices and eight notes exchanged between the U.S. embassy in Madrid and the Ministry of Foreign Affairs. The agreement contained several new features.

The notions of 'operational and support installations' and of 'authorizations of use' were introduced in order to define precisely the many nuances that had previously been brought together under the overall term 'facilities.' A new complementary agreement was signed to this end. No fewer than seven annexes minutely detailed the working of both installations and authorizations. The goal was to enhance Spanish control and to guarantee the transparency of American activities in Spain. For the first time, also, clear definitions were adopted which rendered the execution of the agreement less prone to misinterpretation.

U.S. military aid and cooperation for updating the equipment of the Spanish armed forces were confirmed and provisions were established for how aid would be increased. Technical deficiencies of the 1976 treaty were either removed or resolved. The level of financing for the purchase of military equipment from the United States was increased and a complementary agreement on defence industrial cooperation was introduced.

A new agreement concerning the statute of the U.S. forces in Spain was also adopted. It was in line with many others entered into between the United States and other West European countries, and it was based on the status of forces agreement of 16 June 1951 signed by the United States and its European allies within the context of NATO. The importance of this new agreement can hardly be exaggerated. The Franco dictatorship had accepted provisions concerning the U.S. forces in Spain which were incompatible with national sovereignty. A general exemption from the application of provisions of the Spanish criminal code had been instituted for the American forces, and was bitterly resented by both the Spanish bureaucracy and the population.

From the military point of view, it was agreed that in the event of a threat of external attack against either of the two parties, the use of support facilities was to be a matter of urgent consultation between both governments. In this the Americans succeeded in introducing a reference to the alleged bilateral and multilateral objectives of the agreement, which implicitly linked it to NATO. The notion of a geographic area of common interest which had surfaced in the 1976 treaty was no longer maintained. For the first time, it was formally recognized that respect of the full territorial integrity of both countries was in the interest of both parties. The inherent Spanish right to self-defence was not derogated by any clause of the bilateral agreement. Spain was in a position to take any measures deemed necessary to safeguard its own national security in an emergency. On the basis of these provisions, a clear case could be made that the 1982 agreement did not interfere with Spanish freedom to develop a security policy not covered by the North Atlantic Treaty. By the time of the October 1982 elections, however, this new agreement had not been ratified.

Shortly before the election, it was discovered that some military officers had planned a coup for 27 October. The Spanish electorate, therefore, went to the polls well aware that there were still hardliners within the armed forces who did not approve of the consolidation of the democratic system. On 28 October 1982, the Spanish people voted massively for the PSOE, which obtained a landslide victory of just over 10 million votes — almost twice as many as those gained by the right-wing coalition. It was the first time in Spain's parliamentary history that such an overwhelming majority had been secured. The UCD collapsed, so that the right came second in a coalition in which conservative Christian Democratic elements that had created the People's Democratic Party (PDP), participated with others more closely affiliated with the Francoist tradition. Led by the Popular Alliance (AP), the coalition, called the Popular Coalition (CP) took a completely pro-Atlantic stance, calling for, *inter alia,* the full and immediate integration of Spain into NATO.

The first purely socialist government in Spanish history took office under the leadership of Felipe Gonzalez in December

1982. In his inaugural address, the new Prime Minister announced his intention to review, with all necessary rigour, the previous government's attitude towards the Alliance.

DOMESTIC TENSIONS CONCERNING NATO AFTER THE SOCIALIST VICTORY

The Socialists' 1982 landslide electoral victory ushered in a new political era for Spain. Later, in the April 1983 municipal elections, the PSOE made further local gains. It was the first time in Spanish history that the Socialists wielded such widespread political power. Socialist economic policies designed to bring down inflation and restructure industry created a clear cleavage with the political and the economic right. Since Socialist economic policy turned out to be quite moderate, it did not lead to major conflicts with the opposition. It was other aspects of social policy that caused more tension, notably the government's attitudes towards abortion, private schools and social change in general.

After election, the government hoped to give a new impetus to foreign policy by establishing a clear conceptual framework for it that would not subordinate national interests either to a search for international respectability or to the maintenance of domestic tranquillity. Those goals had been priorities of the Franco era and had not served Spain well. The Socialist government established, therefore, a number of basic axes around which foreign policy was to revolve. First, the modernization of the Spanish economy. Second, development of the means to contribute generally to continental security. Third, maintenance of the status quo in Spain's immediate security environment. Fourth, the creation of the means by which Spain could more efficiently project its influence. Specific policies were developed to give substance to each of these general aims. The effort to gain membership in the EC was intensified in the belief that more than anything else, EC membership would symbolize a growing affinity between Spain and other West European countries. The government also sought to develop a more global approach towards its North African neighbours. Rather than continue the tradition of making alternate overtures to Algeria and Morocco, the government wished for a more generalized strategy that would allow for the emergence of more fruitful

165

cooperation between Spain and the Maghreb. Finally, the new political formation that came to power equally hoped to deepen Spain's influence in Latin America, where the Socialist government believed it could have an important influence on regional developments.

Within this emerging context, the NATO issue became one of the most important bones of contention between the Socialist government and the right-wing and Communist opposition. The new government, concerned not to tamper with the agreed international alignment of Spain or to upset the European security scene at a time of increasing tensions between the superpowers, immediately began talks with a view to ratifying the 1982 agreement with the United States. A protocol to this agreement, in late February 1983, emphasized that the agreement itself could not affect the nature or form of Spanish participation in NATO. The protocol was approved in parliament almost unanimously with only the four Communist members of the Lower House and some others opposing.

During 1983–1985, the NATO issue continued to hold media interest. Confusion in public opinion was fuelled by contradictory statements on the Alliance by certain members of the government and the PSOE, and by the fact that no date was fixed for the referendum promised in the election platform. Public opposition to NATO grew considerably. By March 1983, government polls revealed that 57 percent of the population had a negative attitude, as against 13 percent which favoured NATO membership. On the other hand, the government's stance was openly criticized by the right-wing opposition which urged the cabinet to forego the referendum and proceed to integrate Spain fully into NATO's military structure.

The government did not reveal its plans until the parliamentary debate on the State of the Nation in October 1984. Prime Minister Gonzalez then advanced a ten-point programme — the so-called 'decalogue' — which contained the basic principles that the Socialist government had been developing on Spain's defence and security policies. The programme recognized that it was in Spain's interests to remain in NATO, although this should not involve integration into the military command or deployment of nuclear weapons on Spanish territory. The desirability of Western European Union (WEU) membership was evoked and mention was also made of the advisability of reducing the level of the U.S. military presence in Spain. The Prime

Minister stated his belief that a consensus was needed among the various political parties, on which Spanish foreign and security policies should henceforth be based.

The most important point was undoubtedly that concerning NATO. It underscored the fact that following Spain's accession to the Alliance in March 1982, the PSOE had not undertaken Spanish withdrawal. However, the Prime Minister had not so far publicly proclaimed his belief that it would be better for Spain to remain in NATO. The 'decalogue' was submitted to parliament after almost two years of experience in government, during which opinion polls, both private and public, consistently revealed four phenomena:

1) About 40 percent of those interviewed rejected NATO, mostly on account of the arguments put forward by the left, and particularly by the PSOE, in 1981 and 1982.
2) The number of 'don't-knows' was just under 33 percent, which represented a considerable proportion.
3) A similar number of those interviewed were in favour of the Alliance.
4) The vast majority said they did not have sufficient information on NATO.[12]

In short, it was a situation in which popular perceptions seemed to have been shaped by the left but in which the level of information was inadequate. During the second half of 1984 the debate was revived within the PSOE. As the Thirtieth Congress approached, a division was created between those who supported government policy and those who rejected NATO membership. Certain sectors of the PSOE even called for Spain to adopt a neutralist stance. The media gave prominence to this debate, which reached its climax during the Congress in December 1984.

It was only after great personal effort that Felipe Gonzalez succeeded in winning a majority of the delegates over to his position. In its resolutions, the Congress gave the government a blank cheque in respect to the Alliance, although the other two branches of the socialist family, the General Workers' Union (UGT) and the Young Socialists, made it quite clear that their attitude to NATO was one of opposition.

During the winter of 1985, voices close to the government argued that EC and NATO membership were linked, if not formally, at least in the sense that both would symbolize general integration into the Western world. The Deputy Prime Minister, Alfonso Guerra, even went so far as to say that any delay in accession to the EC could lead to a revision of NATO policy. It is evident that the linkage between entry into the EC and NATO membership lay at the root of Socialist policy, although such linkage was, in fact, repeatedly denied for at least four reasons. Legally, Spain fulfilled all the requirements of the Treaty of Rome for accession to the EC. Politically, Spain satisfied all the conditions established by the EC for previous enlargements. Conceptually, the EC and NATO are, of course, distinct organizations, and there are cases of countries which belong to one but not to the other. It was felt that a recognition by Spain of a link between accession to the EC and NATO membership would have been poor tactics, as it could have led to the former being postponed until the government had clarified its position with regard to the latter. Yet it was clear to government officials that in the public eye these issues were linked, and if Spain were not admitted into the EC, it would be difficult for the government to present NATO membership as a necessary act of rapprochement with the rest of Western Europe.

By 29 March 1985, the obstacles which had frustrated EC membership were finally removed and the Treaty of Accession was signed on 12 June. Spain could now align itself with those West European nations which had made it possible for Spain to fulfil a twenty-five-year-old aspiration. However, the referendum posed a problem since large numbers of people saw it as a device to withdraw Spain from NATO and many advanced the idea that it would be prudent not to hold a referendum at all. Government arguments in favour of holding the referendum included:

— Failure to hold the referendum would damage the PSOE's prestige and, consequently, that of any party aspiring to hold office. In a country that had only recently become a parliamentary democracy, non-adherence to a solemn commitment might considerably harm the credibility of the incipient democratic political class.
— Any damage done to the PSOE's prestige would be detrimental to the nation (not just the party) given the PSOE's pledge to undertake a thorough modernization of Spain.

— If the Spanish people, under the proper guidance of the government, were to support the government in the referendum, this would make it possible to develop security policy in the future on a much firmer basis. It would also help to get rid of the NATO issue, thus ending all the strife that it had caused.

Weighty arguments against holding the referendum included:

— No other country had ever had a referendum on NATO membership. (Against this position, it was argued that the referendum was part of the process of Spanish accession, and that in other countries NATO membership had not been so consistently questioned as in Spain.)
— The government might not be able to carry the majority of the nation with it, which would give rise to a politically delicate situation.
— A problematic situation would be even more likely if the right-wing opposition voted 'no' in the referendum, or abstained.
— The referendum campaign and the referendum itself would cause considerable turmoil in Spanish society if the majority parties failed to reestablish a minimal consensus on the basic principles of security policy.

Certainly, it was possible that the Communist Party and other groups of the extra-parliamentary left might become more radical. A 'pacifist' movement had developed in Spain over the previous few years. It was still diffuse but had already influenced large sections of middle-class youth who were completing secondary education or were beginning their university studies.

During the autumn of 1985 the NATO issue became even more embroiled in the turmoil of domestic politics. The referendum commitment split the political parties and polarized all political activity. Felipe Gonzalez vainly tried to reestablish some degree of consensus with the right-wing opposition, whose leader Manuel Fraga refused, after some hesitation, to endorse the government's position. The full reasons for this rejection are unclear but apparently they had largely to do with domestic political factors. Fraga had not been successful in obtaining an absolute majority in the regional elections in Galicia, which were held in October. Since he had placed all his personal prestige at stake in a region where his party held hegemony and had not attained the desired results, Fraga's position within the Popular Coalition had become somewhat shaky.

The conservative Christian Democrats of the PDP, who were firmly against holding the referendum, took advantage of Fraga's situation. They argued that helping the government win the referendum would pave the way for yet another Socialist victory in the impending general election, which would take place before October 1986. However, if the right-wing opposition abstained from participating in the referendum, there was a chance that the Socialists might have difficulties in winning. Eventually the PDP — of which Senator Javier Ruperez (a former ambassador to NATO) was one of the leaders — was able to win Fraga over to its theses. The disagreement between the right-wing coalition and the Socialist government became increasingly bitter, and by the time of the parliamentary debate on peace and security in early February 1986 it had not subsided. After the debate, the Socialist majority in the Lower House, supported by the Communist members and a few others, gave the government the necessary go-ahead to hold the referendum.

The government stated clearly its two principal reasons for holding a popular consultation. The first was the desire to establish a framework for Spain's international relations, after its accession to the EC, which would lay the foundations for a policy of peace and security best serving the national interest. The second reason was to ensure the strength of that policy by receiving the express support of the majority of Spanish citizens.

The proclaimed goals of government policy were essentially three. First, it desired to serve national interests properly, by enabling Spain to make an effective contribution to peace and détente. Second, it wished to complete Spain's incorporation into Western Europe through participation in the Western system of collective security. Third, it aimed to overcome the existing division among Spaniards by establishing a common basis for security policy on which most of the political factions and public opinion could agree.

The government, therefore, deemed it advisable for the national interest that Spain should remain in NATO on the following terms, which formed the essence of the referendum issue:

1) Spain should remain a member of NATO without becoming a part of the integrated military structure;
2) The Government should maintain the prohibition against the deployment, storage or entry into Spain of nuclear weapons;
3) The government would work to reduce progressively the U.S. military presence in Spain.

The referendum campaign was extraordinarily intense and, as was feared, profoundly divided Spanish society. A strong movement against continued NATO membership developed, which was joined by the Communist and regional parties, many well-known intellectuals and a wide gamut of pacifist and ecological organizations. Only the Socialist Party campaigned in favour of a 'yes' vote. The right, both nationally and regionally, recommended abstention and so gave rise to predictions of a government defeat in the final opinion polls taken before the date of the referendum. Those polls published by Spain's most influential newspaper estimated a negative vote of between 52 and 56 percent, a positive vote of between 40 and 46 percent and a 30 to 35 percent abstention.[13] The major effort made by the PSOE and the government, and the fact that Felipe Gonzalez placed his personal prestige in the balance, enabled the government to win the referendum. Out of an electorate of nearly 29 million people, 16 million went to the polls. The abstention figure, therefore, totalled 40 percent. This was certainly a higher figure than in previous referenda. However, given that during the referendum on the constitution in 1978 there had been a 22 percent abstention rate, and that the NATO referendum was clearly more divisive in terms of domestic politics, the effort by the right-wing opposition to obtain abstentions did not have the desired effect. Of the votes cast, about 8.5 million were positive (almost 53 percent) and somewhat more than six million were negative (almost 40 percent), while there were one million blank votes (6.6 percent). The difference between 'yes's' and 'no's' amounted to almost 13 percentage points — somewhat more than 2 million votes. The referendum, thus, marked the end of Spain's intense domestic debate about membership in the Atlantic Alliance.

SPANISH SECURITY PROBLEMS

Spain's involvement in NATO is only one aspect, albeit an important one, of Spanish security policy. This policy is concerned, broadly speaking, with the need to counteract Spain's vulnerability to external developments, to alleviate the tensions with which Spain may be confronted because of geopolitical, strategic or economic factors, as well as to defend against specific threats from abroad whether in a NATO, or some other, context. Since, as Régis Debray has pointed out, security is a condition (not a value in itself) 'which consists of the ability to survive, as a decision-making subject, the attempts of other subjects to adapt us to their own decisions,'[14] it is important to consider security in the widest possible sense. Spain must be able to defend itself against a wide range of economic and military vulnerabilities linked with the nearest security scenarios in the Atlantic and the Mediterranean, as well as those that relate more widely to the East-West conflict as a whole. A precondition of meeting external threats is the ability to strengthen internal structures and eliminate domestic vulnerabilities. Several points can be made in this respect.

First, there is an economic crisis in Spain which reduces its ability to project its influence abroad. It is not possible to carry out an active and enterprising foreign policy without important matériel, organizational and human resources. The austerity policy (involving severe budget cuts for certain programmes) carried out by Spanish policy makers has made it impossible to increase substantially the resources on which foreign policy draws. Fund shortages have, for instance, hindered Spanish efforts to reinforce its traditional Latin American orientation. This situation has also been aggravated by other factors such as disorganization, conflicting jurisdictions and the proliferation of private fiefs which have generated an institutional waste that the Socialist government is determined to stamp out. The small expansion of foreign policy budgets will severely limit the possibilities of more dynamic cultural, political and economic action abroad.

Second, since the 1960s, the Spanish economy has been extraordinarily dependent, technologically and productively, on the Western industrialized countries. This tends to increase Spain's vulnerability vis-à-vis external pressures.

Third, Spain depends heavily on external sources for energy, certain agricultural products and a wide range of raw materials. In an economy such as Spain's, which is medium sized and poor in natural resources, only a high degree of economic interaction with other countries makes it possible to achieve a proper allocation of production factors. It is widely held that in the medium term it is essential to achieve greater agricultural equilibrium. This means increasing the export of products in which Spain holds comparative advantages. It is also important to reduce energy dependence, diversify the sources of production and supply, and make better use of productive inputs. Finally, it is necessary to start closing the technology gap, even though any efforts in this direction can only be effective in the long term.

Fourth, Spain suffers from a higher degree of dependence, than many other European countries, on maritime connections. An extremely high proportion of Spain's foreign trade is carried out by sea — mostly by foreign ships.

Fifth, Spanish security is weakened by geographical vulnerabilities. Spain's national territory is discontinuous and communications between its regions have to be kept permanently open. In the past this need has caused dramatic problems. During World War II, the allies disrupted the lines of communication to the Canary Islands in order to put extra pressure on the Franco regime to remain outside the conflict. Many of these vulnerabilities do not directly affect the purely military aspect of security, but they do have a bearing upon its political, economic and social dimensions. These are very important since they shape people's perceptions of governmental efficiency and ability. In addition to such problems, Spain is exposed to the effects of tensions arising from the geostrategic and geopolitical features of its immediate surroundings, both in the Atlantic and the Mediterranean. The north Atlantic is a stable area in which there are hardly any points of actual friction although it is still an arena of competition. Further south are the Canary Islands which, together with the Portuguese archipelagos, are European outposts. These islands flank essential sea lanes and provide a base for operations on the nearby African continent. They are thus affected by any destabilizing forces or events in neighbouring countries.

The whole Mediterranean area — scene of some of the world's most important conflicts — poses special problems. Spain has an overriding interest in the stability of the region,

173

especially in the western part, and is particularly sensitive to tensions in North Africa. This is not only because of geographical proximity, but also because of the Spanish presence in Ceuta, Melilla and the adjacent islands and rocks. These tensions stem from a wide range of causes: border disputes, diverging processes of national consolidation, ideological and religious differences, patterns of historical behaviour, and aspirations to local hegemony. They are often exacerbated by the projection into the region of superpower antagonisms.

The British position in Gibraltar is naturally a continuing security concern to the Spaniards as is the situation in North Africa. A process of 'Morocconization' is taking place in Ceuta and Melilla, and there are potential sources of friction stemming from the non-delimitation of territorial waters. The Spanish fishing fleet's practice of fishing on the Saharan bank led to pressure by both Morocco and the Polisario movement that had detrimental effects on Spanish interests. However, this situation seems to have improved since the signing of a bilateral agreement with Morocco in 1983.

The countries of North Africa themselves are, of course, not immune to domestic troubles, including the possible spread of Islamic fundamentalism. This latent instability could erupt at any time and pose a threat to Spanish interests. Instability in North Africa could in some cases give rise to action against Spain. In others, it could take the form of an exacerbation of nationalism projected outwards. In Ceuta and Melilla, for example, domestic Moroccan nationalism might be harnessed against Spanish interests.

With respect to the East-West conflict, Spain also shares vulnerabilities with other NATO countries. Difficulties affecting the supply of certain products in the event of an outbreak of conflict outside Europe could be significant. There is also the possibility that Soviet influence will spread to some countries on the southern shores of the Mediterranean. Spanish security policy seeks to take all of these various threats into account and, hence, it is difficult to develop action that is, at once, perfectly consistent with that of other NATO members and suitable to Spain's specific security needs.

DEFENCE STRATEGY

As part of its 1982 electoral platform, the PSOE announced the following three defence policy objectives: to bring the Spanish defence structure into line with patterns already tested in neighbouring Western countries; to make the armed forces more professional, effective, and streamlined; and to create an industrial system that, without being unduly protectionist, might make Spain more independent from foreign suppliers with regard to weapons and equipment.

In the sphere of defence policy, therefore, the priority was the modernization of the defence system, the incorporation of the armed forces into the constitutional order and their reorientation away from the obsession with domestic security. The government carried out a threefold reform: the first part was institutional, the second affected defence planning and programming, and the third concerned the military judiciary.

Institutional Reform

A series of legal measures was passed in connection with the institutional side of the reform. One of the most important of these was the modification of the 1980 law on basic criteria for national defence. Its purpose was to redefine the relationship between the government and the armed forces along the lines of the West European countries. In early 1984, a legal amendment reinforced the role of the Prime Minister who was personally charged with directing defence policy. Command and coordination of the armed forces, and the approval of defence and strategic plans would fall within his sphere of responsibility. The Prime Minister would be advised by the National Defence Board and by the reformed Joint Chiefs of Staff, which ceased to be a command body and became a consultative body. The 1984 amendment also introduced a new formalization of the powers of the Minister of Defence. As a delegate of the Prime Minister he now formulates defence and military policies and proposes economic and financial programmes for equipping the armed forces. In 1985 a new law was passed which radically transformed some of the corporate military bodies. The higher councils of each service — consisting of commanding generals and admirals who previously could decide on senior

175

appointments in the armed forces — became consultative bodies and henceforth decisions on promotions were transferred to the Chief of Staff of each service or to the Minister himself, depending on the circumstances.

Part of the institutional reform consisted also in the creation of a new position, that of Chief of the General Staff (JEMAD), conceived to increase efficiency in military policy. The Chief is the Minister's major collaborator in the planning and implementing of military operational aspects. He is responsible for planning the joint action of the three services and, in wartime, he may conduct military operations if entrusted to do so by the Prime Minister.

Finally, the Ministry of Defence was restructured into three large blocks. The first one deals specifically with military matters and is headed by the Chief of the General Staff. Its major goal is to increase operational effectiveness and make possible joint action by the three services. The second block is under the responsibility of the Secretary of State and deals with all matters pertaining to the management and control of financial resources, weapons and procurement policy, and infrastructure. In the third area, the Undersecretary of Defence is in charge of management and the development of personnel policy and military education. The Minister of Defence is, therefore, responsible for ensuring that the real powers of decision making (hitherto the domain of the military commands) lies with the government.

Once institutional reform had been carried out, the Minister of Defence — Professor Narcis Serra — could proceed with a thorough overhaul of defence planning and programming procedures.

Revision of Defence Planning and Programming Procedures

The first instrument created was the National Defence Plan (NDP), which did not exist until 1985 because of coordination difficulties among the three services and the different ministries. Felipe Gonzalez had previously approved the National Defence Directive (NDD) in July 1984. This outlines defence goals, the action needed in order to achieve them, their assignment to different ministries, and the necessary resources. It consists of twenty different types of basic action. The NDD initiated a defence policy cycle which has been developed in three main stages. The first is the planning stage, in which a set of long-term goals is fixed which culminate in the NDP. The second is the programming stage, in which schedules are established in each ministry for the tasks assigned. As far as the Defence Ministry is concerned, this implies converting the joint force goal into programmes relative to personnel and matériel, in accordance with the priorities determined and the resources actually available. The third stage is that of budgeting, in which decisions are taken regarding the maximum amounts available to the different sections of the Defence Ministry in order to meet the expenditure incurred by the implementation of the aforementioned programmes (see Table 4.1).

Perhaps one of the most important tasks undertaken during the last few years has been the redirection of military personnel policy. Here the government had to act with caution. The goal of transforming the armed forces into a really effective instrument to meet challenges from abroad undoubtedly required that the optimum ratio between equipment and investment costs on the one hand, and personnel costs on the other, be determined. In early 1983, this ratio was about 48 to 52, whereas the goal set by Minister Serra was 60 to 40. Therefore, an adjustment of the number of men to real needs was undertaken. The cutting down involved army, navy and air force officers and men. A 16 percent decrease in the number of army officers was initiated and will be completed over a six-year period. In the navy and air force, the reductions predicted will amount to 8 percent.

Table 4.1: Distribution of Spanish defence budget 1982–1986 (figures are in 1985 Pesetas millions)

Organizations	1982	1983	1984	1985	1986
Central organizations	69,473	57,582	76,468	84,332	106,309
	13%	10%	13%	14%	17%
Army	245,132	264,504	250,201	262,827	258,524
	46%	48%	42%	42%	41%
Navy	126,289	130,073	155,556	154,269	150,488
	23%	23%	26%	25%	24%
Air Force	94,448	105,577	144,835	117,203	115,662
	18%	19%	19%	19%	18%
Total	535,342	557,735	597,061	618,631	630,984

Source: Spanish Ministry of Defence, *Memoria de al Legislatura, 1982-1986* (Madrid, 1986), 302.

177

The numbers of service men were also made explicit. For the army, this meant a reduction from 275,000 to 195,000. The number of officers estimated for the 1990s will be about 58,000: 35,000 for the army, 12,000 for the air force, and 10,897 for the navy. The armed forces will then total 300,000 men for a population of 39 million. These reductions are a complex undertaking since they have an important bearing on personal interests and careers. The government, therefore, has established a new military status called the 'interim reserve,' very similar to that of retirement, in which the financial situation of the officers concerned is identical to that which they would enjoy if they were still in active service.

Reform of the Military Judiciary

The guiding principle for the government in its efforts in this area has been to confine military jurisdiction to the strictly military sphere and to define carefully the limits between jurisdiction and command. Military justice has been brought closer to the guiding principles of ordinary justice. Previous regulation of the former dated back to 1945 and the differentiation between the two was very obscure. The reform was first introduced with the passing of a new military criminal code, which only refers to military offences. Many other cases previously covered by the military criminal code under the Francoist system, were transferred to the system of ordinary criminal justice. Among them was a wide range of offences allegedly against national sovereignty, in which the defendants were charged with such crimes as destroying property of the armed forces. New laws now regulate the disciplinary system of the armed forces. The administration of justice is carried out by courts staffed by professional jurists who are independent and whose decisions may be appealed before the Supreme Court.[15]

Joint Strategic Plan

On 31 July 1985, the government adopted the NDP, which states four priorities:[16] the defence of the constitutional order and guarantee of the unity, sovereignty, and independence of Spain and its full territorial integrity; the protection of the population against the risk of direct aggression or the threat of war, catastrophe or disaster; a tenacious commitment to the preservation of international peace and a contribution to the security and defence of the Western world; and the development of an adequate deterrent capacity against foreseeable threats, as well as effective control of the Straits of Gibraltar and its approaches.

The military instrument for implementing this plan is the so-called Joint Strategic Plan (JSP). In military terms, the JSP pursues the following goals: guaranteeing the defence of Spanish territory and the protection of Spain's interests; achieving an adequate level of effective deterrence against, and developing the capability for reaction to, those countries that may threaten Spanish territorial integrity; cooperating with allied countries in the defence of common values; and maintaining an effective presence on the Balearic Islands-Canary Islands axis, the area of confluence of Spain's Atlantic and Mediterranean strategy.

In order to achieve these goals, the JSP envisages two courses of action. The first concerns strategic objectives and the action necessary to ensure their fulfilment. The second, which is embodied in the so-called 'joint-force goal,' establishes the integrated system of command and control, the organization of each service, the deployment and equipment of the armed forces, the purchases planned to meet the priorities fixed for the purpose of facing foreseeable threats (in accordance with the means currently available), matériel renewal needs, and the availability of financial resources.

The JSP will cover the 1986–1994 period. It defines an area of national interest which stretches as far north as Brest, including the whole of the Bay of Biscay. To the south, it reaches as far as 900 kilometres south of the Canary Islands, encompassing the continental shelf off the Saharan coast. To the east, it goes as far as the southernmost part of Italy, and to the west, as far as the Azores Islands — a distance deemed to protect the shipping routes and the supply of Spanish territory by sea.

In terms of the JSP's major goals, Spanish military strategy can be broken down into two basic tasks. First, the reinforcement of the southern part of the peninsula in order to face possible conflicts with Morocco, acting either alone or in conjunction with some other North African country.[17] Second, the command over the Balearic Islands-Peninsula-Canary

Islands axis, which involves sea and air control of the strategic Atlantic (Azores-Canaries-Gibraltar Straits) and western Mediterranean (Gibraltar Straits-Sicily-Golfe de Lion) triangles. The strengthening of the Canary Islands is not only connected with their direct defence, but also with the need to assert Spain's presence in the Atlantic and contribute to the control and possible blockade of western North Africa. Both tasks highlight the centrality to Spain of the Straits of Gibraltar area.

Actions have already been taken towards the strengthening of Spain's southern regions. Among them are:

— The unification of the second and ninth military commands within the army modernization plan. The establishment of a new military region to the south has entailed several changes in the deployment of the armed forces.[18]
— The purchase of low-flying anti-aircraft missiles, capable of hitting objects at an altitude lower than one hundred metres. The first system will be deployed in the Straits area.
— The purchase of low-altitude missiles for defending the air bases and the military telecommunications centres using static batteries.
— The purchase of anti-tank missiles for the defence of Ceuta and Melilla.
— The reinforcement of the 'Guzman el Bueno' Mechanized Division — the only division with three brigades instead of two.
— The strengthening of the aeronaval combat group, consisting of the aircraft carrier Dedalo (which will be replaced by the Principe de Asturias), the naval air units, and the escort units allocated to them. The group will have three frigates and planes equipped with anti-submarine warfare systems.
— The strategic projection southwards of two of the three air bases, from which the new F18-A aircraft will take off.
— The upgrading of the air bases at Manises (Valencia), Los Llanos (Albacete) and Moron (Seville). The strengthening of the aircraft shelters at some of these bases has already begun, as control of the airspace in the event of possible conflict in North Africa is deemed absolutely vital.
— The implementation of the third stage of the 'Combat Grande' alert and control programme, which will allow for complete monitoring of the eastern and southern area as far as the Canary Islands.

- The concentration of submarines and corvettes at Cartagena (on the southern Mediterranean coast).
- The modernization of the Legion and the enhancing of its readiness for operations in North Africa.[19]
- The reinforcement and strengthening of crack units which may eventually signify a change in Spanish military doctrine vis-à-vis North Africa.

In the past, security policy concerning North Africa was based on merely defensive considerations that are now deemed outdated in view of the new technologies available; there is no better defence, it is asserted, than effective deterrence. The JSP argued for the adoption of a counterstrike strategy for the purpose of counteracting any possible aggression against Ceuta and Melilla. The idea would be to create 'a hostage situation' which could eventually be used for finding a political solution in the event of a military conflict. Another priority is centred on the Canary Islands, with a view to repelling any armed aggression and preventing the Islands from being threatened by hostile forces from the so-called Saharan corridor, which is open to possible occupation. The area is of the utmost strategic importance for Spain. About 24,000 vessels sail in the vicinity of the Canary Islands annually, transporting nearly 70 percent of the energy products needed by Europe. Moreover, 44 percent of Spanish foreign trade is carried out along these routes.

Spain and NATO have a common interest in ensuring the defence of the destination points of the sea lines of communication (SLOC) from the United States to central and southern Europe as well as of the oil route and the sea routes that go through the Straits of Gibraltar. Consequently, it could be argued, Spain's greatest contribution to *collective* defence lies in securing its own area of national interest; but it is also widely accepted that Spain might perform logistical and reinforcement functions within NATO's overall strategy of European defence. There are additional areas in which Spain could be useful, particularly in providing access to aeronaval bases and infrastructure and logistical systems. The exact role Spain will play in NATO is naturally conditioned by the precise terms of the referendum.

SPANISH NATO POLICY AFTER THE REFERENDUM

On 21 March 1986, nine days after the referendum, Spain signed NATO's Nuclear Planning Group communiqué for the first time, having until then only been present as an observer. It was the beginning of the end of the situation in which the Socialist government had kept Spain's exact position in NATO in abeyance. On 22 May 1986, Spain signed the final communiqué of the NATO Defence Planning Committee, also for the first time. By then, the Socialist government had submitted a memorandum to the NATO authorities listing the major desiderata according to which Spain's future participation in NATO was conceived. This memorandum contained the following points:

1) Spain would participate fully in the Atlantic Council and its subordinate bodies.
2) Spain's position in respect to nuclear weapons would not prevent its participation in the Nuclear Planning Group.
3) The Spanish contribution to collective defence would take place outside the integrated military structure.
4) In order to achieve the desired coordination in terms of planning and strategy, Spain would continue to be present at the Defence Planning Committee. To this end, Spanish military representatives ought to be appointed who would be responsible for liaison with the major NATO commands.
5) Spain would participate in the planning cycle, run by the Defence Planning Committee.
6) Spain would take part in logistical coordination, the development of equipment and supplies and in civil defence measures, leaving open its form of participation in the integrated communications system.
7) Spain would negotiate its contribution to the infrastructure and military budgets.
8) Spain would nominate candidates for posts on the International Staff, in proportion to its level of contribution, and for the International Military Staff to an extent compatible with its non-participation in the integrated military structure.
9) Finally, and in accordance with the foregoing principles, Spain would start formulating concrete proposals for debate by the appropriate bodies.

This memorandum was equivalent to accepting a high level of participation in the Alliance without joining the integrated command structure. Therefore, on 30 May, Spain also signed the final communiqué of the Atlantic Council for the first time, following the meeting at Halifax in Canada. The Minister of Foreign Affairs, Francisco Fernandez Ordonez, then informed the Council that, in accordance with the will of the Spanish people as expressed in the referendum of 12 March, Spain had put an end to the provisional situation with regard to Alliance membership.

The singularity of Spain's position consists of maintaining the three conditions of the referendum, while taking steps to mitigate the effects of remaining outside the military structure. In particular, participation in the NATO defence planning cycle will help to coordinate and harmonize Spanish and Alliance operational plans. Under the desired arrangements, Spain will keep control and command over its armed forces that participate in the common defence. However, the formula for NATO participation chosen by the Socialist government is potentially capable of eventually bringing about a greater degree of involvement in the Alliance than that of France.

The Spanish armed forces have been assigned five strategic missions which are relevant to NATO needs:

1) To guarantee, in so far as possible, the security of the Iberian peninsula.
2) To contribute to the strengthening of the defence of the western Mediterranean flank.
3) To participate in the task of keeping the Atlantic routes open and, if necessary, guarantee the aeronaval passage between the United States and Spain in the event of conflict.
4) To monitor and control the two approaches to the Straits of Gibraltar.
5) The integration of the Spanish air-warning network into NADGE, which will significantly enhance its monitoring capacity.[20]

The operational implementation of these points and the exact relationship of Spain to NATO will take some time to iron out. At the end of October 1986, once the PSOE had been returned to office for another four-year term following the general election of 22 June, formal conversations with NATO officials started.

PROCUREMENT STRATEGY

The guiding principles of current Spanish procurement policies have evolved over the course of the past few years. There are two major motives for improving national capacities for procurement. First, there is a belief that Spain's large dependence on foreign suppliers must be reduced, and, second, the level of Spain's own technology must be raised. In order to accomplish this, the government's view is that it is necessary to enhance international military cooperation.

The first principle does not imply a return to what would be unrealistic autarchy, but merely reflects the will to develop policies that, while meeting demand, tend to give preference to activities that generate added value in Spain. To this end, procurement is being redirected to systems that can be obtained economically in the domestic market, with imports mostly limited to those which cannot be manufactured in Spain or produced domestically as a result of international cooperation. The preference for the purchase of domestic products has been implemented through mechanisms of manufacture under licence, coproduction, and industrial compensations. Important organizational reforms in the Ministry of Defence have paved the way for considerable improvement in the procurement planning machinery. A fundamental factor in this connection has been that the Ministry itself has assumed executive and management responsibilities in procurement policy, which until not long ago were in the hands of the three services. The government believes that the reduction of direct purchases abroad of weapons systems and the preference for formulas of cooperation or coproduction will enable the introduction into the defence industry of new and advanced technologies. Spain bought the Franco-German Roland missile, on condition that half the amount spent will eventually accrue to Spanish industry.

It is true that few Spanish firms can compete with foreign firms in very advanced technology products. Nevertheless, significant progress has been made over the past few years. Circuits are now manufactured in Spain for the Aspide missile, the F-18A fighter-bomber radar, and the Exocet missile. An air-cushioned amphibious vehicle will soon be marketed. The aircraft carrier Principe de Asturias, the F-18A flight simulators, and the laser-guided flying bombs are other projects now under way which will allow for a qualitative leap forward by the Spanish defence industry. Weapons systems of an intermediate technological level are moving in the same direction. Among them are the AX tactical aircraft, the sea-patrol early-warning plane, and new design minesweepers. The preference for domestic production is disciplined by two essential restraints which prevent production costs from getting out of hand and new lines being created that would not be competitive internationally: the concern for obtaining competitive-quality products, and promotion of export capacity. International cooperation with a view to formulating a modern procurement policy has been developed both multilaterally and bilaterally. The first sphere is related to NATO: Spain participates in the Independent European Programme Group (IEPG), the Conference of National Armaments Directors (CNAD) and the NATO Industrial Advisory Group (NIAG). Under the Socialist government, Spain also started working in the NATO Maintenance and Supply Organisation (NAMSO).

Among the major projects in which Spain's participation is already confirmed, the case of the European frigate of the 1990s is noteworthy. The feasibility study was directed by a Spanish naval officer. Halfway through 1984, an agreement in principle was reached, and later reinforced, with a view to participating in the European Fighter Aircraft (EFA) programme, which involves the largest ever investment in a weapon system made by Spain. At the beginning of the coming century, European combat planes will replace the French Mirage F-ls in Spain. The Spanish air force combat group will then consist of F-18A planes, those which are developed under the EFA programme, and the AX tactical aircraft. Within the IEPG, Spain takes part in more than a dozen weapons programmes. Among them are, apart from the future European medium-sized transport plane, the tank of the 1990s, the medium-range surface-to-air missile, and various light weapons. With respect to less sophisticated weapons systems, the present procurement policy consists of entering into bilateral agreements with other countries that will enable development costs to be reduced and ensure a share of the market for Spain.

U.S.-Spanish cooperation in the defence industry has improved and Spain has been a good customer of the United States — at times, its best in Western Europe. Nevertheless, this cooperation has led only to very limited coproduction of advanced technology systems. While the attitudes of other European countries towards Spanish coproduction have been quite positive, the United States has not been interested in Spain developing its own technological capacity, and frequently the disequilibrium in the bilateral defence balance of payments has been immense. At the beginning of 1984, the U.S. refusal to purchase the Spanish Aviocar plane for the U.S. air force European Distribution System Aircraft (EDSA) programme made it clear that the 1982 agreements still in force were not sufficient to ensure a minimal two-way street interchange between the two countries. The Socialist government has diversified bilateral cooperation in the defence industry and has signed agreements in this area with other NATO members including France, Italy, the German Federal Republic, Greece, the United Kingdom and Norway, as well as with neutral Sweden. Another agreement with Portugal is being prepared.[21]

FUTURE TRENDS

On 22 June 1986, the date of the third parliamentary elections that had taken place in the country since the approval of the constitution, the Spanish people were able to pass judgement on the results of the first socialist legislature in Spanish history (see Table 4.2).

A new political coalition, the United Left, grouped around the Communist Party, based a large part of the electoral platform on foreign policy considerations. The group criticized the conditions of the NATO referendum and called for the renouncement of the military agreement with the United States. It was clear that the coalition sought an alternative defence policy that would lead to the departure of Spain from the Alliance and the pursuit of a neutralist policy. The electoral results of the United Left were disastrous: the group received sightly more than 930,000 votes as against the 865,000 received by the Communist Party alone in 1982. This translated into a victory of three additional seats since the Communist Party had gained four in 1982.

186

Table 4.2: Spain's 1986 election results

Voters: 20,492,052 (70.77%). Abstentions: 8,464,635 (29.23%). Null Votes: 319,456 (1.56%). Blank Votes: 114,856 (0.56%).

Parties	Votes	% Votes	Votes 1982	% Votes 1982	Congress Seats	Congress seats 1982	Senate Senators	Senate Senators 1982
Partido Socialista Obrero Espanol (PSOE)	8,887,345	44.06	10,127,392	48.40	184	202	124	134
Coalicion Popular	5,245,396	26.00	5,478,533	26.18	105	106	63	54
Centro Democratico y Social	1,862,856	9.23	604,309	2.89	19	2	3	
Partido Reformista Democratico	193,694	0.96						
Izquierda Unida (PCE)	930,223	4.61	865,267	4.13	7	4		
Unidad Comunista	225,571	1.12						
Convergencia i Unio	1,012,054	5.02	772,726	3.69	18	12	8	7
Esquerra Republicana de Catalunya	84,103	0.42	138,116	0.86		1		
Partido Nacionalista Vasco	308,991	1.53	395,656	1.89	6	8	7	7
Herri Batasuna	231,558	1.15	210,601	1.01	5	2	1	
Euskadiko Ezkerra	106,937	0.53	100,326	0.48	2	1		
Partido Andalucista	94,126	0.47						
Coalicion Galega	80,800	0.40			1			
Partido Socialista de los Trabajadores	78,860	0.39						
Partido Aragones Regionalista	72,889	0.36			1			
Agrupacion Independ. de Canarias	66,153	0.33			1			
Union Valenciana	64,462	0.32			1			
Partit dels Comunistes de Catalunya	58,356	0.29						
Unificacion Comunista de Espana	45,897	0.23						
Partido Soc. Galego-Esq. Galega	45,843	0.23						

Source: *El País*, 24 June 1986.

The other political parties accepted Spain's membership in the Atlantic Alliance. Nevertheless, the right-wing opposition grouped in the Popular Coalition, stressed that membership in NATO should not take the form of second-class citizenship. They argued that if Spain is required to undertake all the tasks that Alliance membership implies, the country should also be the beneficiary of all the advantages that NATO can provide. The right's electoral results were slightly lower than in 1982 — 5,245,000 as against 5,478,000 — with a loss of one seat in the Lower House (from 106 to 105). Following the elections the right suffered from a process of disintegration due to its difficulty in offering a credible alternative to the PSOE.

The conservative Christian Democrats left the coalition and following the regional elections in the Basque country in November 1986, the small Liberal Party also withdrew. A few weeks later the leader of the conservative opposition, Professor Manuel Fraga resigned, thus raising a number of questions about the future of the Spanish right. It is difficult to assess whether the election of his successor, Antonio Hernandez-Mancha, in the extraordinary party congress of February 1987, will mark the end to the tribulations of the conservative opposition. As a member of a different generation, Hernandez-Mancha is not tainted with links to the Francoist legacy. The extent to which he will be able to mould the Spanish right remains a matter of speculation.

The elections signalled the comeback of Adolfo Suarez, whose party, the Democratic and Social Centre (CDS), gained seventeen seats in the Lower House, thus holding a total of nineteen. With 1,863,000 votes it became the third largest political party in the country. His electoral platform called for the immediate denunciation of the agreement with the United States and for the reduction of the period of military service to a maximum of three months — one quarter of the present requirements.

The PSOE maintained its absolute majority in both houses of parliament, although with fewer votes and seats than in 1982. This meant that foreign and security policies developed by the party during the first legislature could continue.

In the PSOE's platform for the June 1986 general election, it was stated that, based on the terms of the referendum, Spain's presence in the Atlantic Alliance would not entail participation in the military structure and would not be detrimental to the general interests of the other allied countries. However, the progressive reduction of the U.S. military presence in Spain would be initiated immediately, also in compliance with the terms of the referendum. The overall policy design for future Spanish security policy under the renewed Socialist mandate would proceed in accordance with the following guidelines:

1) Spain would work to strengthen the European security pillar, by contributing to the development of mechanisms for the improved defence of European interests and specific needs. Spain would initiate the process of accession to the Western European Union and would make every effort to progress, within the context of political cooperation, towards a common West European security policy.·

2) Spain would contribute to the reactivation of the process of détente and the fostering of a climate of trust that might facilitate weapon reductions.

3) Spain would contribute to the development of European unity in successive stages.

Between 1982 and 1985 Spain entered into a number of international obligations (entry into the EC, and reconfirmation by referendum of the decision to join NATO) that symbolized the Spanish role in the European 'project.' Spain's capacity to impose itself in the international system increased. Spanish interests, objectives and traditions in foreign policy will therefore be affected by the various fora in which most other European democracies also participate. This may lead to a reduced Spanish dependence on the United States.

In the years following the 1986 elections, the most important Spanish challenge will be to elaborate better Spain's contribution to the construction of Europe, and to absorb the economic and structural effects of Spanish membership in the Community. This double task will naturally have important repercussions on organizational and management structures. There is some concern that with the increased Spanish involvement with Western Europe certain Spanish interests may be lost, and political leaders will need continually to reassure Spaniards of the relevance of West European institutions to their needs.

The second large challenge for Spanish foreign policy will be to create proper relations with Latin America that take into account the conditions created by Spanish entry into the

European Community. During the first Socialist legislature, the government made clear its intention to increase the Spanish presence in Latin America and to defend, on behalf of Spain, the process of democratization in the Western hemisphere. The Socialist government believes that this process constitutes an historical opportunity for the strengthening of links with Latin America which the rest of Western Europe should not forego.

It stands to reason that policies directed towards Europe and Latin America need not be in conflict with each other, and that likewise, there is no need to establish either as being a priority of Spanish external policy. Both are natural and essential dimensions of Spanish activity. Nevertheless, integration into the Community will have highly important economic effects and is likely to attract considerable government attention in the next few years. Unless there is some basic increase in Spanish foreign policy capacities, it is likely that Spain's ability to exert influence in Latin America will be constrained. Nevertheless, Spain will attempt to hold an open dialogue with Latin America, both directly and through the mechanisms of the Community.

In recent years the government has been profoundly pre-occupied with changes in Central America. It continues to support the efforts of the Contadora Group as a genuine regional attempt by interested parties to contain the conflict without the interference of outside powers. It has helped countries of the Isthmus and has attempted to support moderate elements in Nicaragua. This effort has largely been in conflict with the interpretations and actions of the United States. However, Spain's relations with the Western superpower are suffering from other important changes.

In the view of the Socialist government, Spain's 'anchorage' to the Community and NATO has created a qualitatively new situation which requires an adaptation in the bilateral agreement with the United States. During the course of 1986 exploratory talks and negotiations were undertaken to reduce the level of the U.S. military presence, as has been stipulated in the NATO referendum. The Foreign Minister Francisco Fernandez-Ordoñez explicitly declared in December 1986 that Spain would not sign any new accord with the United States unless there were agreements on troops reductions. The most important demand was the withdrawal from Torrejon of the seventy-nine aircraft and the majority of American soldiers stationed there. The Spanish also requested that the United States leave its base in Zaragoza. Missions that would be undertaken by such forces, within a coordinated Western defence strategy, could be taken up by Spanish elements.

In the early months of 1987, the negotiations reached a stalemate although signs were increasing that U.S. political and military decision makers had come to the conclusion that the Spanish demands were indeed to be taken seriously. Meanwhile, in the course of the State of the Nation debate in February 1987, Prime Minister Felipe Gonzalez stated solemnly that the Spanish government would shortly sign the Non-Proliferation Treaty. This announcement represented a final break with Francoist policies in this particular field.

While politicians have concentrated on changes in Spain's international security policy required by Spain's new obligations, defence modernization has proceeded at a rapid pace. In 1986, important reforms included the reorganization of the Joint Chiefs of Staff, the establishment of direct operative control by the Minister of Defence over political and strategic issues, and the nomination of a civilian, for the first time in history, as the head of the Civil Guard.

These three measures confirm that under the Socialist government basic changes have taken place in traditional civil-military relations. In November 1986, this was clearly demonstrated when the parliament approved a bill that pardoned those military personnel who had been punished for the expression of democratic views — they would be reintegrated into the armed forces with the rank which they would normally have reached. Civil-military relations in Spain are therefore becoming closer to those in other European countries. Having previously been an essential balancing element in the domestic political debate, the armed forces have now become a simple pressure group with considerably less political weight.

The Ministry of Defence is now a full political department whose leadership is virtually entirely made up of civilians, a factor which means there is now considerably less tension than in the past between Defence and other government departments. Spain's capacity to formulate security policy has therefore been enhanced as the bureaucracies of the Ministries of Defence and Foreign Affairs have learned to work closely together, putting aside their past rivalries. It can be expected that in the period 1986–1990 numerous detailed adjustments in

191

defence and security policy (such as reforms in military education) will take place.

It is likely that in the immediate future the execution of Spanish security and foreign policy will create fewer debates than during the first legislature. The most important decisions have already been taken and the government seems to have come out of each major debate reinforced rather than weakened. The right, unable to take power away from the Socialists, is now in disarray and is forced to concentrate on internal reorganization. There is a generally accepted view that there are no alternatives to the PSOE. On the left, the Communists have been extremely critical of the government, and especially of its policy on the Atlantic Alliance. The right also has concentrated on this aspect of government policy, arguing that Spain should be much more closely integrated into NATO. Between these two, the centre, led by Suarez, has still not been able to establish coherent and identifiable positions.

The 1982–1986 period has been extremely important for developing a new Spanish attitude towards the problems of peace, security and relations with the outside world. The referendum aligned a solid majority of the Spanish people behind the government, demonstrating their approval of Spain's presence in NATO. This change would not have been possible if other changes had not previously taken place within the government and the Socialist Party. The domestic debate on NATO, which for so many years had led to profound dissension among the Spanish body politic, was closed. It was not revived after the renewed Socialist victory in the 1986 parliamentary elections.

In the future, it does not seem likely that government policy will be hindered for domestic reasons. The PSOE has been able to survive its traumas over defence policy and NATO. It is now united and believes firmly in the need to strengthen the European pillar of the Alliance and to reinforce a European identity in international politics. It hopes that Spain, for too long separated from Western Europe, can now contribute positively to its growth. These will be major objectives of foreign policy for a government that commands a comfortable majority and is confident of its capacity to carry out major designs.

Naturally, the internal debate will not end. The Communist Party, stronger in the trade unions than in parliament, has ideas that are totally opposed to those of the government and the rightist opposition. Resistance from the right to the government's NATO policy and negotiations with the United States will continue to be important. Some decisions taken by the government have been totally uncontroversial. The establishment of full diplomatic relations with Israel and Albania, for example, has inspired no criticism. The news in December 1986 that Spain would deliver military equipment to Morocco was considered by most as a positive sign that relations with the great neighbour to the south were improving and no one took a negative view of this.

Spanish public opinion and opinion makers in Spain have learnt over the last few years that the world of defence and international relations is not drawn in black and white but is sketched in grey tones. The arrival of the Socialists to power and the solution of the NATO problem created a new situation in which Spain has ceased to be at the margin of European affairs. Increased Spanish involvement in Europe's economic and security institutions will continue to be seen as part of Spain's necessary modernization, and is likely to enjoy considerable domestic support.

NOTES

1. The end of British occupation is desired by all Spanish political parties.

2. To compress several centuries of Spanish history into a few pages would be an impossible task. Among the very extensive bibliographies in existence, the most up-to-date analysis is to be found in the collective *Historia de España* (Madrid: Historia 16, 1986).

3. Douglas Little, *Malevolent Neutrality: The United States, Great Britain, and the Origins of the Spanish Civil War* (Ithaca and London: Cornell University Press, 1985).

4. For a very modern account, see Manuel Tunon de Lara, et al., *La guerra civil española cincuenta años después* (Barcelona: Labor, 1985).

5. The best-documented analysis of Spanish foreign economic policy is Angel Viñas, et al., *Politica comercial exterior en España (1931–1975)* (Madrid: Banco Exterior de España, 1979), three volumes.

6. Angel Viñas, *Los pactos secretos de Franco con Estados Unidos* (Barcelona: Grijalbo, 1981).

7. Archivo de la Presidencia del Gobierno, Madrid. Admiral Carrero Blanco's files.

8. Francisco Villar, *El proceso de autodeterminacion del Sahara Occidental* (Valencia: Fernando Torres Editor, 1982).

9. The best account so far is by Paul Preston, *The Triumph of Democracy in Spain* (London and New York: Methuen, 1986).

10. Julio Busquets, *El militar de carrera en España* (Barcelona: Ariel,

1985) (updated edition). This is the most thorough sociological analysis of the military profession during Francoism.

11. 'La opinion publica espanola ante la OTAN,' *Revista Española de Investigaciones Sociologicas*, no. 22 (April-June 1983): 187-262.

12. Ibid.

13. *El Pais,* 6 March 1986.

14. Régis Debray, *La Puissance et les Rêves* (Paris: Gallimard, 1984), 128 and 132.

15. This section draws heavily on an unpublished lecture by the Minister of Defence, Narcis Serra, at St. Antony's College, Oxford, 31 January 1986; and on Ministry of Defence, *Memoria de la Legislatura (1982–1986)* (Madrid, 1986).

16. The NDP and JSP are classified documents. However, many references to them are to be found in newspapers. The following is based on *ABC, Ya* and *Diario 16,* 24 October; *La Vanguardia,* 26 October; and *Diario 16,* 13 November 1985.

17. This has been stressed repeatedly by many analysts. See, for instance, Alberto Santos, 'Le basculement vers le Sud de la politique de défense de l'Espagne,' *Revista CIDOB d'Afers Internacionals* (Barcelona, Autumn-Winter 1985): 23-46.

18. Alberto Pozas, 'Asi se defiende el Sur,' *Interviu,* 23 April 1986, and Carlos Yarnoz, 'La situacion estrategica de España,' *El Pais,* 20-25 February 1986.

19. Vicenc Fisas i Armengol, *Una alternativa a la politica de defensa de España* (Barcelona: Fontamara, 1985), 169-188.

20. See, for example, *ABC, El Pais* and *Diario 16,* 23 May; *La Vanguardia,* 24 May; and *Ya,* 30 May 1986.

21. This section draws heavily on Angel Viñas, 'La politica industrial española de defensa,' *Leviatan* (Madrid), no. 20 (Summer 1985): 53-63. A thorough analysis of the Spanish defence industry is to be found in the report prepared for the Prime Minister's office by Manuel Castells, et al., *Nuevas tecnologias, economia y sociedad en España,* vol. 2 (Madrid: Alianza Editorial, 1986), 717-819.

5

Italy: A New Role in the Mediterranean?

Maurizio Cremasco

INTRODUCTION

Italy, because of its geographic location, military commitments in NATO, and political and economic relations with the riparian nations, is 'by necessity' a Mediterranean country. From a geostrategic point of view, Italy's Mediterranean character is evident. The peninsula juts into the Sea towards the African coast and this projection is accentuated by the position of Sicily and the smaller islands, Lampedusa and Pantelleria. The central position occupied by Sardinia in the western Mediterranean also gives Italy an important role in the area. The peninsula's shape and the position of the islands make an ideal platform for extensive radar coverage of NATO's Southern Region, for air coverage of the entire Mediterranean and for control and screening of maritime traffic through the important choke point of the Straits of Sicily.

Militarily, Italian commitments in NATO require Italy to concentrate considerable efforts in the Mediterranean and Southern Region generally. Essentially, these commitments call for advanced defence of the northeastern border in coordination with NATO's central European forces, protection of mercantile traffic, control of maritime areas of interest, support of allied naval forces and participation in NATO's aeronaval operations in the Mediterranean, integration of the Italian national air defence system with that of the Alliance for the defence of the Southern Flank, and participation in NATO's nuclear and conventional counterair and interdiction campaigns.

On a political and economic plane, Italy's Mediterranean role is partly determined by its colonial past, but also by new trading and other relations entered into with countries in the region. A fundamental aspect is Italian dependence on oil imports. This has often conditioned Italy's international policy stance and especially political relations with Arab countries. Italian oil imports and Italian exports — including arms — force the country to be cautious in its dealings with states in North Africa and the Near East. Some of these attachments may be broken in time but at present they do not overly impinge on Italy's freedom of action in the Mediterranean.

Political and military commitments assumed by Italy since mid-1979, and the higher profile of its foreign policy, contribute to its Mediterranean dimension. Three examples can be singled out. First, since July 1979, an army helicopter unit is part of the United Nations Interim Force for Lebanon (UNIFIL). Second, in September 1980, Italy signed a treaty for economic, technical and military assistance with Malta, in which it agreed to safeguard the island's neutrality. This agreement was renewed in November 1986. Third, in March 1982, an Italian naval force formed part of the Multinational Force and Observers (MFO) and was specifically tasked to guarantee free navigation in the Strait of Tiran and the Gulf of Aqaba. Italy's participation in the Multinational Force (MNF) in Lebanon (1982–1984) and in the minehunting operations in the Gulf of Suez (1984) as well as in the Persian Gulf (1987) were other major examples of the higher profile Italy has recently taken in the Mediterranean.

These Mediterranean roles do not detract from the fact that in geostrategic, political and economic terms, Italy is also, again 'by necessity,' a European country. In fact, the firmest and most irrevocable points of reference for Italian foreign policy — NATO and the European Community — are centred outside the Mediterranean region.

Since war in the Mediterranean between NATO and the Warsaw Pact is credible only in the context of a wider conflict involving all of Europe, the military links between NATO's Central Front and Southern Flank are very close. Italian foreign and military policy reflect an understanding of these links. Italy's close political and economic ties with the Community, and the country's policy to push for full European political integration, link Italy closely to the principal forces in Europe. But there is a sense in which Italy's Mediterranean 'vocation' can sometimes appear to take preeminence over strictly European concerns.

The coexistence of a Mediterranean 'vocation' (implying close relations with a number of Arab countries) and a Euro-Atlantic role (full loyalty to the Alliance and to the European Community) is fully understandable, given Italy's diverse interests, but can sometimes lead to important ambiguities in the formation of policy and misinterpretations by those who seek to understand it. A tendency to vacillate between a Mediterranean and a Euro-Atlantic policy inevitably causes confusion and it is important, therefore, to understand the new security challenges to which Italy seeks to find original and sometimes individual responses.

Italian official interest in a Mediterranean policy is conditioned by the fact of geography and by politico-military choices related to Italy's position as a leading NATO country in the Mediterranean. External events from the mid-1960s have gradually forced the Italian elite to develop policies that have important Mediterranean elements, especially since many of the areas of potential crisis are outside NATO's area of responsibility. Parts of the Italian political spectrum, notably the Socialist Party, have always advocated the importance of appealing to the Mediterranean political environment — to help conduct, for example, a North-South dialogue — while recognizing the enduring importance of continental European issues. Because of the geostrategic transformation of the Mediterranean and its growing instability, however, many sections of the Italian elite have argued that Italy cannot remain passive in the face of such changes. A general recognition has emerged, therefore, that Italy must develop policies that can affect the Mediterranean environment in which the country finds itself.

This recognition of a need for a Mediterranean policy is tempered by the instinctive understanding of the constraints under which leaders operate. The armed forces, for example, have an important role to play in giving military expression to Mediterranean commitments or undertakings and yet they do not have the capacity to act autonomously in the region. Italian foreign policy makers, equally, are theoretically in a position to play an important 'brokerage' role in the area, mediating between competing powers. But this potential ambition of Italian policy is constrained by the need to obtain a sound consensus amongst political parties on all aspects of policy. Finally, to the extent that a consensus can emerge, the vision and the actions of the Italian political elite may confront a public unsupportive of the choices of the political leadership; especially when these choices emphasize the possibility of deploying military force outside the NATO area. These tensions very much shape the substance and the form of Italian foreign and defence policy and make new initiatives, however much desired by elements of the political elite or by foreigners, extremely difficult.

In the late 1980s, given Italy's desire to develop a foreign policy that is more 'decisive' and 'visible' in the Mediterranean, certain long-standing questions still need to be asked. Has Italy really opted for a new role in the Mediterranean and will it eventually be able to manage such a choice? What concrete form would such a role take in terms of foreign policy? Could this also mean a greater willingness to broaden Italy's role outside the Mediterranean area from diplomatic and economic relations to politico-military initiatives? Is there a relationship between the objective of more active foreign and military policy and the programmes of the armed forces themselves? Lastly, to what extent will the chronic instability and fragmentation of Italy's political system affect this line in the future?

To answer some of these questions, this chapter examines the evolution of Italian foreign and defence policies, including the influence that parliament, political parties and senior government officials have had on their formation. It looks at recent Italian security initiatives and their impact on domestic opinion as well as the most recent international factors that have forced Italian leaders to consider whether a new security role, particularly in the Mediterranean, would be sustainable and credible both to Italy and to the outside world. It concludes with an assessment of the limitations on a truly independent Italian policy in the Mediterranean.

FOREIGN POLICY

The political elite in Italy has never really taken an interest in security problems and has only sporadically laid down basic guidelines for the country's military policy. Even a clear definition of the concept of security seems to be lacking in Italian political culture.[1] Questions of military policy — and, to a certain degree, of foreign policy — have never really influenced the vote of the Italian people and so it is perhaps logical that political parties concentrate their attention on matters of economic and social policy that are more central to popular concerns.

The decision to enter NATO and participate in the integrated military structure of the Alliance was naturally decisive for Italy's future international position, and was seen at the time as the only rational solution to its defence problems. The NATO choice was not, therefore, merely a 'choice of civilization,' it was an explicit expression of faith in NATO's ability to supply security assurances which no other alternative could offer.

Italy's participation in NATO (which had to be fought for both at home and abroad) quickly became a concrete element of Italy's international legitimacy and, as a consequence, led to a close connection between Atlantic and national military policy as a means of preserving and strengthening that legitimacy. Italy has traditionally recognized the preeminence and validity of NATO defence requirements and their equally substantial contribution to national needs. Italy has adopted NATO strategic doctrine, criteria for use and deployment of forces, infrastructure construction plans and arms acquisition programmes. Italian governments have accepted NATO requirements automatically, but have done so not because these necessarily corresponded to national defence requirements — although very often they did correspond — but because of a perceived need to 'choose camp' for domestic political motivations. Presenting a decision as based on NATO requirements made easier the development of a domestic consensus on security policy. It is even arguable that up until about 1979, Italy did not really have its own military policy but merely copied that of NATO; this drew criticism only from leftist parties which maintained that defence decisions were being imposed on Italy by the United States. It is true that the apparent unconditional acceptance of NATO policy was often more formal than concrete and often commitments taken on within the political framework of the Alliance were not carried out in the manner and time called for, either owing to lack of funds or to organizational deficiencies. But the broad acceptance of NATO policy, nevertheless, corresponded to a general consensus on the military situation in NATO's Southern Flank, and to the role that the Italian armed forces were to play in the region in the event of an East-West conflict.

In the 1950s, the Mediterranean was considered an 'American lake.' The 'threat from the south' had not yet entered NATO's terminology and Yugoslavia's withdrawal from the Soviet sphere of influence freed the northeastern front from the spectre of Belgrade's certain support of Warsaw Pact forces in the event of war between the two blocs. In this situation, NATO was the only plausible point of reference for Italian military policy. No military requirements other than those deriving from the Alliance's operational planning were envisaged. The only defence against a threat from the east was through integrated action and no scenarios of bilateral crisis outside the Atlantic context were imaginable. Progressive changes in the military situation of the Southern Flank initially led to a rise rather than a fall in the element of consistency between Italian and NATO military policy, since these changes were determined by the growing Soviet military and political presence in the Mediterranean region which started in 1964. The threat from the south was made concrete by several factors: the qualitative and quantitative increase of the Soviet fleet in the Mediterranean, reaching a peak, in 1973, of 21,000 ship days and a daily average of 58 vessels;[2] Moscow's direct involvement in the Middle East (especially with Egypt); the signing of a Soviet friendship and cooperation treaty with Syria; the supply of armaments to Libya from 1970;[3] and the close relations between the Soviet Union and Algeria. All these factors justified a coherent policy within the Alliance. This threat was seen not only in terms of increased Soviet military capabilities in the Mediterranean, but also arose from the possibility of a North African country siding with Moscow during an East-West crisis and offering the Soviet armed forces the use of its air and naval bases as well as its arms supplies.

Logically, the new strategic equation in the Mediterranean was bound to be evaluated by Italy from a NATO perspective; thus, Italian and NATO military policy coincided. In fact, since the threat from the south was fundamentally Soviet or pro-Soviet, in the context of a conflict between the two alliances, it could still only be dealt with through NATO. Inevitably, Italy's strategic position gained importance in the 1970s as did the specific role of the air force and the navy within the Italian armed forces.

The signing of the Treaty of Osimo between Italy and Yugoslavia in 1975 and the agreement — already reached before the

Helsinki conference — for reciprocal information on military exercises and important troop transfers, totally stabilized Italian-Yugoslavian relations, reducing the operational priority of the northeastern front. In 1973, when the Yom Kippur War almost led to a military confrontation between the United States and the Soviet Union, and the Arab countries began to use oil as an instrument of political blackmail, it became obvious that a new evaluation of the political and military situation in the Mediterranean was needed. The fact that the Mediterranean region had become a potential theatre of out-of-area crisis and of U.S.-Soviet military confrontation made it necessary to reconsider the security problem in a more multi faceted and subtle perspective, rather than simply in a NATO context.

Italian foreign policy was modified to establish more diffuse contacts with the Arab countries and a more explicit independence from U.S. Middle Eastern policy, even though this revision took place within the framework of the European Community. It affected military policy mainly in so far as it allowed the speedier approval of special laws — the so-called 'promotional laws' (concerning the navy in 1975, the army and the air force in 1977) which provided for funds outside the defence budget — for the acquisition of new weapons aimed at satisfying the most pressing needs for modernization of Italian military power. Further changes of emphasis followed the events of the late 1970s and early 1980s, especially the Islamic revolution in Iran, the Soviet invasion of Afghanistan and the war between Iraq and Iran. These events emphasized the strategic importance of the Persian Gulf and the Indian Ocean and created a geostrategic link between these areas and the Mediterranean region. Owing to these crises, the out-of-area problem became an issue of debate. Should Italy be prepared to participate — and if so, with what instruments — in the defence of the stability of the Gulf, and in political and possibly military initiatives aimed at preventing Soviet control of the oil flow from the region? Would it be better for Italy to confine itself to a strictly Mediterranean role, not using its armed forces outside the Sea, while demonstrating its willingness to act on a diplomatic level and to supply technical and logistical support to the American Rapid Deployment Force?

This debate spurred a further review of the elements of change in the Mediterranean area and a more thorough analysis of how, and to what extent, national security policies, including arms procurement programmes, would be affected. A perception emerged that total acceptance of NATO decisions was no longer sufficient for national security needs and that the complexity of the Mediterranean situation called for a more diversified foreign and military policy.

Finally, the growing saliency of international terrorism in Europe, often evidently supported by some Arab states, and the varying responses to this threat by different Alliance partners and especially the United States, brought new elements of instability and concern into Italy's security picture forcing new adjustments in its foreign policy. These changes will be examined below, but to understand their form, it is necessary to analyse the method by which the debate proceeds within Italy.

The Role of the Political Parties and Security Choices

As a rule, Italy is certainly capable of being a reliable partner, but it does not seem able to come up with initiatives in the field of Western military and arms control policy. The basic attitude, similar to that of other European countries, is to react to American initiatives. Generally, Italy is willing to participate in projects that clearly have wide, common approval but often the tendency is to 'wait and see' what others have chosen to do, or to seek to play a 'mediating role' that does not require taking a fixed stance. These tendencies of foreign policy are also reflected in the military domain, given that Italy's contribution to Europe's basic defence problems is rarely central.

Confrontation between Italian political parties on foreign and defence policy issues takes place less as a result of differing analysis of the value of certain policies but more because of the power games and basic requirements of Italian domestic political battles. Since membership in NATO was not originally considered negotiable and the parties of the coalition government considered that belonging to the Alliance helped bring international legitimation and domestic stability, it was logical that there was not much to debate regarding foreign and military policy: being a member of the Alliance necessitated certain basic and generally acceptable responsibilities. Thus, it was just as logical that unorthodox choices in respect of the U.S.-Italian relationship (the only foreign connection considered by elites to help 'legitimize' Italy within the Western political system) had to be avoided, as this would have had negative repercussions on the already unstable equilibrium of the Italian political system. Basic questions regarding foreign and military policies were thus rarely raised. Governments manoeuvred carefully to avoid supplying leftist parties with domestic policy topics that could be used for propagandistic or electoral purposes. Adoption of more active foreign and security policies, which could be attacked for being too openly pro-American or for being politically damaging to Italy's international relations in the Mediterranean would only help the Communists. Since the Communist Party (PCI) often used foreign and military policy as an instrument to create problems for the government and to mobilize public opinion, this reinforced a government tendency to keep a low profile. Even a less 'Atlantic' policy might be harmful if, as a result, it received support from the Communists, thus creating rifts and crises within the Italian political system.

The image of *immobilisme* that has often characterized the Italian presence on the international scene has been largely produced by the governments' fear that active diplomacy would necessarily lead to domestic instability and, in the case of initiatives taken outside the Atlantic framework, international 'delegitimation.' However, when requested, Italian governments have assumed controversial international responsibilities, in particular with respect to NATO military policy and arms deployment, even in the face of communist opposition. The drafting of a truly autonomous foreign policy has tended to create problems in a political system that depends on a delicate internal balance.

At the end of the 1950s, the political scene was polarized, with anti-Atlantic left-wing parties on one side and pro-Atlantic parties on the other. It was only in 1963, with the election of Italy's first centre-left government, that the range of political options began to widen. The Socialist Party (PSI) had gradually given up anti-Atlantic attitudes and its traditional neutralistic approach to security problems and was therefore accepted as part of the government led by Aldo Moro and the Christian Democrats. The development of the Socialist Party implied that for any party to be considered a government party, it would have to accept, without reserve, Italy's fundamental foreign and defence policies. The centre-left coalition was, therefore, important because it marked a significant moment in the evolution of Italian political life. It also allowed the Socialist Party to use its support of Italian military and foreign policy to gain external legitimacy and, indirectly, greater bargaining power within the Italian political system. The PCI also eventually had to adapt itself to these changes.

In 1977 the Communist Party approved the government's foreign policy line. PCI recognition of the need for Italian membership in NATO was said to be based on an analysis of the international situation; party officials denied that this was done to gain a passport to government. That recognition was both a clarification and a complication for Italian politics. The clarification was evident. All major parties now accepted the core of Italian foreign policy. The complication arose from the fact that other 'government' parties were not willing to consider the PCI's evolution as a sufficient condition for possible entry into government. This complicated the tactics of the PCI within the Italian political system. It had to adjust carefully the nature of its opposition to the security and defence policies of the government — in particular those stemming from NATO decisions — in order to retain its new image of a truly 'Western' communist party and any hope of eventually sharing power.

Today the PCI feels itself to be an integral part of the European left. Since the mid-1970s contacts with the British Labour Party and the West German Social Democratic Party have increased, even though the PCI has retained a more explicit anti-American (and specifically anti-Reagan stance) than these other parties. The PCI naturally approved the Craxi government's negative reactions to the American military operations against Libya in March and April 1986; and it 'agreed' with Secretary Gorbachev's reformist efforts and arms control proposals. Nevertheless, the PCI is keen to underline the political differences which separate the 'new' approach of the Italian Communists to international affairs from that of the 'old' pro-Soviet Communist Party. The PCI has accepted Italian military commitments in NATO, but not to the point of accepting NATO's nuclear modernization programme, endorsing the American Strategic Defense Initiative (SDI), or the Reagan administration's arms control policy. The PCI's security position emphasizes the need for a European defence organization — more independent from American defence policies — and for a European policy in the areas of arms procurement and arms control. The shift in position of the PCI allowed the PSI, within the context of its explicit but not unconditional pro-Atlantic stance, to distinguish itself from other parties of the centre as well as from the Communists. This made the PSI more attractive to that part of the electorate which, while wanting Italy to stay in NATO, desired greater independence, but yet was afraid of too radical initiatives if the PCI were to achieve power.

The Role of Parliament and the Security Debates

Serious political debate on security questions has been rare, and often obscured by intentionally vague pronouncements. Most politicians, who take for granted the broad lines of NATO's military policy, are indifferent to strategic questions and in any case have traditionally never thought that the Italian position carried much weight. In the early years discussion of military policy centred largely on the deliberations of the Defence Commission during presentation of the military budget by the Minister of Defence. These discussions focused mainly on the sum to be allocated, not as a function of actual defence needs, but as a percentage of GNP. No real effort was made by parliament to check whether declared military needs were real or whether armaments proposed for procurement could carry out tasks required by NATO or by government military policy. Not until the mid-1970s, beginning with the process of evaluation and approval of military promotional laws, were members of parliament actively involved in the choice of structure and development of the Italian armed forces.

Budget analysis also took place along ideological lines with the left always arguing that the budget was too high and the government parties maintaining that within the country's economic constraints the budget was acceptable but still insufficient given real defence requirements. Parliamentary debates rarely concentrated on the essentials of defence policy or larger Alliance strategic issues.

Not much more attention has been paid, in parliament, to the general lines of foreign policy. In a twenty-five page speech to parliament, as head of his first centre-left government, Prime Minister Aldo Moro dedicated only one page and a half to foreign policy.[4] After the fierce political and parliamentary battle in 1949 over Italy's entry into the Atlantic Alliance, only one other topic, the question of deployment of Euromissiles in 1979, aroused as much interest and an equally wide-ranging, even if less heated, debate. Earlier parliamentary debates were either short or inconclusive. The debate in 1959 about the decision to deploy American intermediate-range Jupiter missiles in Italy ended without a final vote. The government refused to reveal where the missiles would be deployed, and turned down a request to provide the Senate with the text on the U.S.-Italian agreement concerning the dual-key system. At that time, the deployment decision was presented by the government as part of those 'forms of cooperation' provided for by Article 3 of the NATO treaty and, thus, as a routine measure in the framework of NATO defence strategy. Presenting the question in this manner automatically relegated political forces to a marginal role in the debate which was, in any case, polarized along the traditional pro-NATO and anti-NATO line. Furthermore, the Jupiter missile deployment did not arouse any widespread public opposition.

In 1979, in connection with Italy's decision to participate in NATO's Euromissile deployment, a new security debate took place in the country.The principal feature of this debate was the important interest shown by public opinion and the rebirth of anti-nuclear and pacifist movements which forced political parties to deal with the issue seriously. In 1979, Italy felt the need to regain the role among Western countries and in the Alliance which it had lost because of its exclusion from the Guadeloupe summit in January of that year. Italian participation in the NATO theatre nuclear forces modernization programme was determined by several factors: the conditions set by the Federal Republic of Germany[5] meant that Italy was the key country in the implementation of the programme; the value, on a European level, of Italy's close link with the German position; and a tradition of thirty years of loyalty to the Alliance and its military choices. The position of political parties with regard to Italy's approval of the NATO decision of 12 December 1979, is interesting and symbolic of the use made of international questions for domestic purposes.[6]

The Christian Democratic Party (DC) was in favour of the decision, as were the minor parties forming the government. The Communist Party was obviously against, but its opposition was not unyielding and there were even points of agreement with the theses of the governing parties, such as the necessity and the significance of maintaining a military balance in Europe. The Communist Party's efforts to avoid an explicitly pro-Soviet attitude were evident, as it was essential not to provide PCI adversaries with a new excuse for isolating it politically. The PCI called on the Italian government to move in three directions: to suspend or delay for a period of at least six months any decisions to install the Euromissiles; to invite the Soviet Union to suspend production and deployment of the SS-20s; and to propose the immediate opening of negotiations between the two alliances in an attempt to establish a nuclear balance in Europe at the lowest level possible to guarantee reciprocal security.[7] Although the PCI could not accept that its political maturity as a possible government party be evaluated on the basis of its compliance with NATO military decisions, nevertheless, it could not underestimate the importance of the effect of its attitude towards Euromissiles on its position in the Italian political system and on the possible growth of ties already created with certain sectors of the Christian Democratic Party during the period of 'national solidarity.'[8] The Socialist Party was equally attentive to domestic policy implications. Even if there were some in the party who held views close to those of the Communists, awareness of the influence on the government of the Socialist stance, of the opportunity to hold a position similar to that of the Social Democratic Party in power in Germany, and of the usefulness of creating a distinction from the PCI capable of politically relaunching the party, induced the Socialist Party Secretary, Bettino Craxi, to support the government decision. The domestic and international importance of the Euromissile question could help build the image of an Italian left-wing party able to take on responsibility in the field of defence without being ideologically conditioned.

It is obvious that the American administration was sensitive to the novelty of the PSI's position and thankful for the PSI's parliamentary stance which played a fundamental role in the final approval of the NATO missile programme. The Socialists' support of the government's Atlantic policy isolated the PCI, reduced the Communists' room for manoeuvre and the prospects of a possible recovery of the 'national solidarity' formula. It also underlined the PCI's incapacity to take decisions truly independent of Moscow and opened up new avenues of collaboration between the PSI and DC.

In retrospect, the Socialist decision in 1979 may be taken as the point of departure of that long political road which was to carry Secretary Bettino Craxi through the five-party coalition

and the first Italian 'lay' government, with Republican Giovanni
Spadolini as Prime Minister and Socialist Lelio Lagorio as
Minister of Defence, to the leadership of the new coalition
government formed in 1983.

Political Parties, Parliament and Mediterranean Policy

Italy's foreign policy in the Mediterranean, and in particular its
position with regard to the Middle East problem, represented
the second field of interaction between international objectives
and domestic ends. In the Mediterranean, Italy has had a high
profile mainly because of its peacekeeping and crisis stabilization policies in the region.

While Italy's traditional Mediterranean 'vocation' was always
upheld by right-wing nationalistic forces and some sectors in the
centre, the majority of politicians as well as the industrial and
the business world — at least up until the beginning of the 1980s
— felt that foreign policy should address to a greater extent the
problems of the Third World and that Italy should concentrate
on mediating between European and Arab countries. This line
of policy was eagerly supported by left-wing parties, progressive
Catholic movements, trade union movements and leftist
factions of the Christian Democratic Party. Some division on
the issue of Italian relations with the Arab world was created by
different views on the Palestinian question.

Perhaps the most important influencing factor was Italy's
heavy dependence on oil from OPEC countries and the various
economic and commercial ties with Arab countries which
affected Italy's foreign policy in the region. Furthermore, there
was the feeling that being 'everybody's friend,' ready to
promote and participate in mediation initatives, was the best
way to defend national interests and avoid domestic political
crises. In fact, during the Arab-Israeli conflict in 1967, the
Italian government's stance was so uncertain and cautious that
many observers considered it ambiguous. In 1973, the government sided with those European countries that formally refused
the United States permission to use their bases to support Israel.
In January 1974, Foreign Minister Moro declared to the Senate
that the Italian position was founded on the preservation of the
state of Israel in its entirety, but also on Israel's withdrawal from
all occupied territories, emphasizing that this was in keeping

with the decisions adopted by the European Community in November 1973. Later, Moro's visit to Cairo as the first European foreign minister to go to Egypt after the Yom Kippur War, confirmed Italy's inclusion among countries 'friendly' to the Arab cause. Progress towards a political solution between Israel and the Arab countries between 1974 and 1975 reassured those parties which, like the DC, considered equidistance not a merely convenient or weak policy, but an appropriately balanced approach.

In 1982, there was substantial agreement by all government parties on the participation of an Italian military contingent in the MFO called for by the Camp David agreements. Communist Party opposition, though, was rigid: participation was considered contrary to the line of the European Community, an implicit extension of NATO's area of action and the symbol of a unilateral and partial 'pax americana.' The 1982–1984 Lebanese mission, analysed in detail below, influenced the decision taken a year later to participate in the mineclearing operations in the Gulf of Suez. The reserve expressed by the Italian government in dealing with the mine problem, and the positions taken by the political parties (PCI: opposition, DC: prudence) were a clear sign of how important the Lebanese experience had been in shaping Italy's out-of-area attitudes.

Italy underlined both the strict bilateral nature of the agreement with Egypt and the 'technical' aspects of the minehunting operation which lacked any political significance. The government stressed the fact that this operation was not a repetition of the Lebanese MNF, so as to avoid having its participation seen as an alignment with another 'Western' initiative 'led' by the United States, or as indirect support of American Middle East policy. This distinction was meant to confirm Italy's autonomous Mediterranean policy, and the fact that it was so explicitly underlined was indicative of the post-Lebanon political climate and the government's difficulty in deciding on the participation of Italian military contingents in operations outside the NATO area and the UN framework.

Finally, the increase of international terrorism — the hijacking of the Achille Lauro liner (October 1985), the massacre at Rome Fiumicino airport (December 1985), and the bombing attack at the 'La Belle' nightclub in West Berlin (March 1986) — brought up the difficult problem of how relations with the United States and the Arab world could be kept in balance. It also showed clearly how foreign policy was used by the parties in Italy's domestic political struggles. The Achille Lauro hijacking, followed by the U.S. interception and the forced landing in the Sigonella air base in Sicily of the Egyptian aircraft carrying the Arab terrorists,[9] and the subsequent release of Abu Abbas provoked high tension in the relationship between Rome and Washington, on the one hand, and, on the other, cast serious doubts about the pursuit of a Mediterranean policy which did not save Italy from Arab terrorism and which seemed ever less rewarding. On this question the four major parties — DC, PSI, PC and the Italian Republican Party (PRI) — held different positions.

The Christian Democratic Party, although there was considerable perplexity among its ranks, was generally in support of the line expressed by Foreign Minister Guilio Andreotti: dialogue had to be maintained with all countries in the Mediterranean; Italy had no 'enemies' in the region, and its policy could not be identified with American policy; and the Middle Eastern question had to be solved through the diplomatic action of all countries in the Mediterranean. For the Socialist Party, Mediterranean policy meant a growing Italian presence and role in the region which required taking clear stances and, like the DC, it looked to Yasser Arafat's Palestinian Liberation Organization (PLO) as an indispensable element in the peacemaking process. However, after the Achille Lauro terrorist action and the Christmas massacre at Rome's airport, the PSI also started to have some doubts as to Arafat's real representativeness and the prudence of Andreotti's policy. The Republican Party, always opposed to a too openly pro-Arab Italian foreign policy, less inclined to recognize the function of the PLO in the peace process and more willing to follow the United States' tough line against terrorism and its presumed supporters, saw no alternative to an American role in the Middle East and called for a 'vast international agreement' which should also include the Soviet Union. Republican Defence Minister Spadolini clearly felt that recent Italian foreign policy on this question had been opportunistic and vacillating. The Communist Party, which was in favour of an Italian 'equidistant' policy and approved of the Craxi government's conduct during and after the Achille Lauro hijacking, also believed the key to Middle Eastern policy to depend on the recognition of the PLO and on support of Arafat's line within the Palestinian organization. Therefore, the problem facing the five-party coalition at the beginning of 1986 was to decide which direction Italy's Mediterranean policy should take.

In an editorial printed on 30 December 1985, three days after the Fiumicino airport terrorist attack, and while a heated inter-party debate raged on Italian foreign policy, Eugenio Scalfari, editor of the daily newspaper, *La Repubblica*, wrote that Italy's Mediterranean policy 'had preferred to wink at Syria, flatter Gadaffi and attribute a presumed status to Arafat, mixing foreign policy strategies with petty domestic policy squabbles with the result that Italy finds itself inside the theatre of conflict rather than at a strict and effective arbitral distance.' In describing the failure of this policy and the fact that the problem should have been discussed at the time of the political crisis following the Achille Lauro hijacking, Scalfari concluded the article with the statement: 'But nothing came of it at the time other than confused messages and hidden manoeuvres for local power. Nor is there hope that the questions that were not brought up, not to say deliberately suppressed, will come to light today. Will Craxi last at Palazzo Chigi? Will De Mita and Natta win their party conventions? That's all that interests our 'politique politicienne.'

The events of March and April 1986 opened up a new debate in Italy and forced the Italian government to take explicit and difficult positions. In March, during a naval exercise conducted by the U.S. Sixth Fleet in the Central Mediterranean, outside and inside the Gulf of Sirte, carrier-based American aircraft, responding to Libyan missile attacks, bombed radar and missile sites in Libya and sank threatening Libyan missile fast attack craft. The American military intervention, and the allegations that the American navy had utilized the logistic support of Italian facilities in Sicily, forced the Italian government to take a position and, at the same time, reopened the question about American use of so-called 'NATO bases.' The Italian government, while recognizing the international character of the Gulf of Sirte waters and the legitimacy of the American naval exercise, stated that to repeat military manoeuvres in an area full of tension was 'inappropriate,' and contained elements of high risk which raised 'the utmost concern.' In the words of Italian Premier Bettino Craxi: 'Italy does not want wars in its frontyard.'[10] Furthermore, the Italian government reiterated that 'NATO' bases on Italian territory could not

211

constitute 'the starting point for military operations outside NATO's framework.'

The American air raid on Libya, on 15 April 1986, and the subsequent Libyan missile attack against the island of Lampedusa, where a long-range aids to navigation (LORAN) station manned by American Coast Guard personnel is located, was another example of the volatility of the Mediterranean situation and highlighted both Italy's peculiar geostrategic location and Italian vulnerability to Mediterranean international developments over which Italy has no control. Italy's negative reaction to the American military intervention against Libya was the least nuanced among those of key European allies. Speaking to parliament on 15 April 1986, the Italian Premier Bettino Craxi said that 'notwithstanding the concern expressed by the Italian government and by all governments of the Atlantic Alliance and the European Community, the U.S. government has maintained and realized its plan to attack Libya.' Making reference to the common position taken by the EC and to convergent views with Madrid, Paris and Bonn, Craxi stated that the Italian government disagreed with the American action and insisted that responsibility for it must be assumed by the United States. Furthermore, Premier Craxi said that military actions 'far from weakening international terrorism, run the risk of provoking a further explosion of fanaticism, extremism, and criminal and suicidal actions.' Finally, he regretted that the position taken by the European governments had been ignored by the United States, and argued that this was 'a decision which did not take appropriately into account the value of the Euro-American partnership in confronting of important issues.'[11] The Libyan missile attack against Lampedusa put Italy in the forefront of the U.S.-Libyan 'war.' It raised public fears about the situation in the Mediterranean, while at the same time highlighting the presence of a threat to which Italy also might have to respond.

The Post-Sigonella Foreign Policy

The release of Abu Abbas sent U.S.-Italian relations to the lowest level since 1947. However, they soon emerged from the cold, even though the scar provoked by the Italian attitude during and after the Sigonella affair is bound to last some time in the memory of the American administration. Over the following few months, various efforts were made to patch over the differences that had emerged between the two countries. The effect of these exchanges was perhaps indicated by the tenor of an important speech made by Foreign Minister Andreotti on 3 June 1986, in which he forcefully stated the continuing importance of Italy's Atlantic and European choices.[12] However, he added that this did not mean a 'flattening' (*appiattimento*) of the Italian foreign policy, whereby Italy denied itself any initiative outside the Euro-Atlantic framework. Andreotti's speech underlined the fact that Italy has a role to play in furthering European political union and in helping build a European pillar of the Alliance within an Atlantic context. Italy has also a role to play in the Mediterranean, but its Mediterranean policy integrates itself in, and is not in contradiction to, the Atlantic and European policies. He emphasized Italy's steadfast opposition to terrorism and — with an explicit reference to Libya — warned that no country can count on Italy's presumed weakness or acquiescence. He noted, finally, that the government was negotiating with the U.S. government 'the general conditions and the technical modality of participation of Italian industries in the research phase of the SDI.'[13]

MILITARY POLICY

Evolution of Defence and Security Requirements

Italian defence policy is centred on certain basic principles: good military relations with the United States both inside and outside the NATO framework; faith in the deterrence ensured by American nuclear forces; full agreement with NATO's flexible and graduated response doctrine; and strict acceptance of NATO's military planning and commitments, and traditional threat assessments.[14]

Nonetheless, in the last ten years, there has been a gradual but evident transformation in Italian military policy. This transformation has not changed the basis on which this policy has rested since 1949, but has extended its boundaries and created new prospects. These developments imply that Italy has passed from having a mere 'defence policy' to a full 'security policy.'[15]

NATO continues to be the essential and decisive reference

point in military planning. The strengthening of Soviet nuclear and conventional forces continues to constitute a concrete element of concern. The necessity of responding to this threat was the main reason behind the acceptance of the NATO decision, of December 1979, on deployment of Euromissiles in Italy. Even if the probability of a conflict between NATO and the Warsaw Pact is considered rather remote at the moment, the threat from the east continues to be seen as the most overwhelming and the most difficult to counter. The Soviet naval presence in the Mediterranean continues to be an element warranting careful evaluation within the framework of national defence requirements. The quantitative and qualitative growth of the Soviet fleet, as well as its operational readiness are closely monitored. After the Soviet submarine intrusions in the Gulf of Taranto in February 1982 and August 1985, particular emphasis in Italy has been placed on the improvement of ASW capabilities.

Nevertheless, threat perception has broadened beyond the traditional hypothesis of an attack on national territory from the east in the context of a NATO-Warsaw Pact conflict. Today, it includes the possibility of a bilateral military confrontation between Italy and a Mediterranean country over a controversy affecting important national interests, and the possibility of Italian involvement in a Mediterranean crisis precipitated by other actors (such as a repetition of the aftermath of the April 1986 U.S.-Libyan confrontation). Futhermore, the prospect of indirect threats to the country's political and economic systems, of hit-and-run military actions conducted by foreign small-scale military units, and blackmail by terrorist groups are also considered forms of threat with which Italy must deal.

The evolution of the Mediterranean situation is being followed with great attention. The strengthening of the riparian countries' air and naval forces (which are now almost all equipped with high-performance combat aircraft and warships armed with sophisticated anti-ship missiles) grants them a greater sea-denial capacity. This is bound to have an effect on the employment of Italian naval forces as a foreign policy instrument and as a means for diplomatic pressure and coercion.[16]

These developments mean that new military requirements and operating strategies have arisen. There is a need for surgical use of military force against terrorism and for the extension and increase of rapid deployment capabilities — including the creation of a rapid intervention force (Forza di Intervento Rapido — FIR).[17] Italy must also have the ability to participate in multinational forces for peacekeeping missions, both in hostile environments (interposition roles, military police operations, territorial defence and protection of the population), such as the MNF in Lebanon, or within the framework of peace agreements such as the MFO in the Sinai.

Defence policy is no longer centred exclusively on hypotheses of East-West conflict and NATO operational planning. It has turned into security policy with an attentive eye to the North-South and South-South dimensions of possible crises in the Mediterranean area and to the 'national' aspects of a threat which has become more complex and ambiguous than that coming from the east. This evolution is characterized by a number of elements.

First, it has not affected NATO's importance as a reference point. Italy's adhesion to the Alliance, to its principles and its decisions, is still complete. There have been no symptoms of detachment or even vague signs of neutrality. Italian deployment of cruise missiles at Comiso confirms the fact that Italy's attitude towards NATO has not changed. Similarly, Italy's relations with the United States have remained unchanged, despite momentary tensions caused by the Achille Lauro hijacking episode and by the explicit disapproval expressed by the Italian government on the American air raid against Libya.

Second, although there is an awareness that a crisis in the Persian Gulf could involve Italian vital interests, there seems to be no intention of going beyond the Mediterranean region in military missions, even for peace enforcing or peacekeeping, unless as part of multinational initiatives under the aegis of the United Nations. It therefore seems quite unlikely that Italy would agree to undertake military intervention outside the Mediterranean as part of an operation conducted by the U.S. Rapid Deployment Force or by a Western multinational force (either U.S.-European or solely European). Willingness to offer the technical and logistical support of Italian infrastructures to American units transferring to the crisis area, nevertheless remains, even if decisions will be taken on a case by case basis. This policy avoids any automatic commitment and reserves the right for Italy to evaluate politically the meaning of a too evident identification with American policy, which in some

215

cases could lead to a refusal of support, as occurred during the Arab-Israeli conflict in 1973. The repeated statements by Italian high officials, following the U.S. military operations against Libya, that Italian bases can be utilized for NATO contingencies only, indicate that the issue has become especially sensitive and that the United States may have difficulty in the future receiving Italian infrastructural support for out-of-area activities.

Third, there is a new political and social awareness of the strategic transformation of the Mediterranean area and the implications this may have for Italian policy. This does not mean to say that Italy will play a role in the Mediterranean in which its military policy — and therefore the possible use of force — has more weight within the traditional sphere of its foreign policy. In fact, there is also an awareness of the political and military constraints which will influence and limit the Italian attitude and response to any Mediterranean crisis.

Fourth, the strategic transformation of the Mediterranean has pushed the Italian navy to intensify its cooperation on a bilateral level with the Spanish and, in particular, the French navies. The French-Italian naval entente encompasses joint military exercises (such as the 'Olive Noir' and the 'Tridente' series), and exchanges and cooperation in the fields of amphibious warfare and undersea research and rescue.

Fifth, the change in Italian military policy has been brought about by a second catalyst: a foreign policy which has achieved a higher profile because of the use of military force. Military policy has had to take into consideration missions other than the classic ones of defence of national territory in the case of East-West conflict. It is true that the mission carried out by Italian military contingents as part of UNIFIL and MFO, and the mineclearing operation in 1984 in the Gulf of Suez, were typical tasks for the army and the navy and did not represent anything new other than their political context. However, participation in the second multinational force in Lebanon raised other problems, due to a combination of political, humanitarian and military aspects.

Defence Minister Lelio Lagorio's Years: 1980–1983.

The beginning of the 1980s saw an important evolution in Italian military policy, not only because of the impact of international events, but also because of the policies pursued by Lelio Lagorio, the first Socialist Defence Minister in the history of the Italian republic.

In June 1980, only two months after taking office, Lagorio appeared before the Defence Commission of parliament with an extensive and detailed report on military policy problems and trends, thus breaking with traditional practice wherein Italy's military policy was discussed only during analysis and approval of the defence budget. Once again, NATO was seen as the 'cardinal point' of Italian military policy. The novelty lay in the fact that, for the first time, a Defence Minister felt the need to outline NATO's characteristics as a geographically limited and defensive-oriented alliance. Lagorio's report recognized that the Alliance must still take into account out-of-area problems, but it underlined that this did not mean that certain automatic military mechanisms and bonds of political solidarity could be extended beyond the NATO area. He defined Italian defence priorities as being characterized by four Ds — deterrence and defence, détente and disarmament — and argued that special emphasis should be placed on the need to pursue East-West dialogue.

Lagorio argued that the Italian voice had to become more authoritative and added (in answer to questions) that military policy should be the means to realize a more prominent Italian international position. He stated, however, that the aim of military policy should not be the use of force, but rather techni-cal assistance of third countries in the Mediterranean region. Arguing that a threat from the south was emerging that had to be met with imaginative political initiatives and not with a 'rumble of weapons,' Lagorio pushed for a greater national commitment to a Mediterranean policy especially since, in his view, conceptions of military threat that focused on the Goriz-ian Gap were clearly dated.[18]

In the following two years, Lagorio's stance became even more definite and explicit, in parallel with the growing Italian role in the Mediterranean. A national dimension to Italy's military policy emerged alongside the steadfast ties to NATO and Atlantic strategy. It was recognized that the Italian contrib-ution to stability and détente in the Mediterranean could be credible only if based on concrete military capability. Thus, the link between the possibility of carrying out a diplomatic action and the capability of the military forces to assist in this was emphasized at the very time when Italy was involved in the MNF in Lebanon. In 1982, Lagorio expanded on these themes by pointing out that Italy had its own policy which, although it coincided to a large extent with that of NATO, did not correspond to it in all respects and, above all, was independent and autonomous as far as areas not covered by the North Atlantic Treaty were concerned. Furthermore, he stated that, as opposed to the situation in the mid-1970s, the Alliance no longer totally guaranteed Italy's defence.[19]

Table 5.1: Italian Military Budgets (in billion Lira)

Year	Budget approved
1980	5780
1981	7501
1982	9918
1983	11649
1984	13820
1985	16380
1986	17585
1987	19188

Note: Actual expenditures vary slightly but not significantly from the approved budget.
Source: For years up to 1984, *Libro Bianco della Difesa 1985* (Rome, 1984), 66. For years 1985–1987, Official Budget Documentation.

On the whole, Lagorio's term as Minister of Defence constituted a real revolution in Italian military policy for a number of reasons. He asserted, for the first time, the role of military policy in the context of Mediterranean policy; he recognized the priority of the southern front with respect to the northeastern one; he strengthened the Italian military instrument in the southern regions; he gave a strong boost to increase defence spending (see Table 5.1); he introduced the development of a new defence model characterized by greater harmony among its components, greater efficiency and operational readiness; and, finally, he opened the question of a rapid intervention force for use throughout the country not only in an operational situation, but also during national calamities.

The Spadolini Adjustments: 1983–1987

Nomination of the Republican Giovanni Spadolini to the position of Minister of Defence of the Craxi government, which emerged out of the 1983 elections, came at a difficult moment in the management of the Lebanese mission. At home, opposition to the Italian military contingent's stay in Beirut was growing. In Lebanon, risks were increasing, posing new problems for military and foreign policy.

In November 1983, Spadolini presented the policy line of his ministry. There were no real changes with respect to traditional Italian military policy. The fundamental points of reference were unchanged and Spadolini confirmed the need for Italy to modernize its armed forces, especially given the possibility that Italy would play a stabilizing role in areas where 'for historical and geographic reasons, Italy is at an advantage compared to other countries. Lebanon is one example, the Mediterranean another.'[20] However, there were adjustments in tone, in emphasis, and in priorities. Emphasis was no longer put on the defensive nature and the geographical limits of the Alliance. East-West mediation and a contribution to the stability of the Mediterranean area were considered feasible and desirable only 'in close connection to the Western strategic plan.' While Spadolini reconfirmed his concern about potential crises in the Mediterranean area, he de-emphasized the existence of national defence requirements not covered by NATO. Spadolini's declarations were cast in a tone intended to reestablish the 'Atlantic' centrality of Italian military policy, and to dispel illusions about an independent and autonomous role for Italy in the Mediterranean. The essential link between Italy's Atlantic and Mediterranean policies was stated again in the Italian 1985 White Paper on Defence.[21]

The 1985 White Paper, the first of its kind since 1977, was not a product of the Italian policy in Lebanon, although the Lebanese experience was clearly reflected in the paper's content. It arose from a precise commitment given to parliament by the Craxi government to provide an overall picture of the problems of the armed forces and also from the need to define the situation after several years of official silence (only interrupted by two wide-ranging reports given by Minister Lagorio in 1980 and Minister Spadolini in 1983). Such a document, giving a complete and official version of Italian military policy, was also necessary because of the debate being carried on in Italy at that time. The fundamental lines of the Italian military policy were defined in the White Paper: first, the renunciation of the use of force as a means to resolve international controversies; second, NATO membership; third, the European dimension of the policy; fourth, Italy's Mediterranean 'specificity.' Furthermore, it indicated the four principles on which the defence model should be based as deterrence, forward defence, integration of forces, and technological efficiency.

The White Paper also contained, however, important innovations as far as the structure of the armed forces was concerned. It argued for the enlargement of the competences of the Chief of General Defence Staff, of the Defence General Secretary and of the National Director of Armaments. It provided the option for equipping the ASW through-deck cruiser Garibaldi with V/STOL aircraft, thus opening the door to the deployment of naval aviation. But, above all, it updated the defence model through the definition of five main 'interforces operational missions': defence of the northeast border; defence of the south and of the sea lines of communication; defence of air space; operational defence of national territory; peace, security and civil defence actions.

The paper sought to define military tasks better in order to rationalize the modernization process of the armed forces, and to establish, through greater integration, a better cost/benefit ratio, thus avoiding duplication and reducing competition and rivalry among the services. The proposals to broaden the areas of responsibility of the top military positions and the possibility given to the navy to adopt V/STOL aircraft were later set down in two bills approved by the Council of Ministers in August 1985.[22] These reforms will probably not stir up much opposition. Allowing the navy to create its own air arm is more controversial.

On the whole, the 1985 White Paper can be considered positively, as an attempt to link the defence model to operational missions in a more coherent way than in the past, and to overcome, through greater integration, the operational inconsistencies and waste of resources caused by sectorial employment of the armed forces and independent arms acquisition programmes.

Furthermore, the conceptual defence approach to interforces missions made long-term planning more convincing, and, in this sense, was in keeping with studies which NATO was carrying out at the same period on the criteria to adopt in strengthening the Alliance's conventional deterrent. However, there was perplexity and concern about a rigid application of the inter-forces criteria leading to a revolution in the command and control structure, or to the creation of new operational components. In other words, the danger was perceived that the innovations contained in the White Paper could be interpreted as a possibility for every service to equip itself with all means needed to carry out 'its' mission, while integration would take place only at a command level and in very specific cases.

Only after some time will it be possible to ascertain the direction which the Italian armed forces have actually taken. For now, it can only be stated that there is opposition within the armed forces to a rigid application of interforces concepts. The traditional tendency to evaluate new arms acquisition requirements in a narrow service optic remains, despite the common awareness that limits imposed by inadequate military budgets can only be overcome by greater military integration.

ITALIAN MILITARY POLICY IN LEBANON

It is impossible to analyse the nature of current political and military reforms being considered or undertaken by Italy without reference to the country's participation in the two multinational forces in Lebanon in 1982–1984. This experience can be considered as a turning point in Italy's postwar politico-military history. The Lebanese mission was the logical outcome of a process of greater Italian involvement in Mediterranean affairs which started in 1979 with UNIFIL, continued in 1980 with the signing of the treaty for economic, technical and military assistance with Malta, and with participation in the MFO in the Sinai in March 1982. This process further developed with Italian participation in the multinational minehunting operation in the Gulf of Suez in 1984.

The Italian contingent arrived in Beirut for the first time on 26 August 1982, to facilitate evacuation of the city by Palestinian guerrillas. After leaving on 12 September 1982, it returned almost immediately on 23 September, following the massacres in the Palestinian camps of Sabra and Chatila. The first contingent (approximately 500 men) was composed mainly of *bersaglieri* (light mechanized infantry). The second consisted of motorized infantry, paratroopers, marines, navy special forces units and *carabinieri*, as well as technical and logistic staff and

221

field hospital personnel (in total around 2,200 men, and 500 wheeled, tracked and armoured vehicles). It was the most complex and risky military operation involving Italian armed forces since the end of World War II. The mission was political (to ease reestablishment of the sovereignty and authority of the Lebanese government in Beirut), humanitarian (to guarantee the safety of people in the area and put an end to violence), and military (possible combat actions in support of the Lebanese armed forces or in self-defence). The contingent's size and its deployment some 2,000 kilometres from national territory called for considerable technical and logistical effort on the part of the armed forces. Because the mission involved draftees who were put at considerable risk, this required the government to maintain constant contact with the mass media to inform public opinion properly about the nature of Italy's peacekeeping role in the country.

The Beirut mission was a success from the point of view of Italy's international image and a very significant experience for the armed forces. But it was also an operation which left its mark both politically and militarily. Militarily, the repercussions of the Lebanese experience were felt at two levels.

The first was the legitimation of the armed forces as an efficient and important element in Italian society. The Lebanese mission uplifted the pride of the armed forces, gave them new motivation and provided them with an opportunity to demonstrate their professionalism in the face of the scepticism and indifference of a considerable part of the public. It gave them a chance to show the politicians the importance of having ready and efficient armed forces as an instrument of foreign policy and as a means of projecting Italy's image abroad. Furthermore, by confirming that there were numerous occasions for the use of military force for 'peaceful' purposes in the Mediterranean, the mission gave the military reason to demand greater attention from political parties for its needs. If the government wanted to implement a more high-profile Mediterranean policy, it had to understand the military implications and, consequently, the need for allocation of enough funds to allow the armed forces to increase their capability and operational readiness. Lebanon was a very positive military experience in that it provided an opportunity to test operational and organizational concepts as well as technical and logistic support structures. The experience was seen as an example of the role which the armed forces could play in Italian foreign policy. The then Army Chief of Staff General Umberto Cappuzzo went so far as to state: 'without designating [for ourselves] a role as peacekeepers, it can nevertheless be affirmed that international commitments are technically and humanly congenial to our armed forces.'[23]

The second military repercussion of the Lebanese experience was that it gave rise to the formulation of new potential missions and requirements for the armed forces, and a further understanding of possible crisis scenarios outside the NATO-Warsaw Pact context. This led to special and competing demands from the armed forces. The navy, for example, began again to make its case for naval aviation. Earlier, in 1973, the navy had included among the objectives of the Italian strategic concept that of readying the armed forces for autonomous intervention in the Mediterranean. The navy argued that operations like that of Lebanon now clearly demonstrated the need for an aeronaval component able to provide support fire at a range and an intensity greater than that of ships' guns. The requirement was not only operational, but also political, in that it would free Italian forces from dependence on foreign forces for support. Furthermore, according to the navy, aircraft carriers were also needed for those typical sea-control missions required in the Mediterranean in the event of an East-West conflict. The air force, drawing on the specific experience of Lebanon, insisted that air support had not been vital to the Italian contingent's operations in Beirut and, in any case, argued that it could provide any necessary air cover for the defence of naval vessels operating in the Mediterranean. The open and harsh controversy between the navy and the air force was not merely a traditional conflict in defence of specific service interests but reflected deep differences about the role of Italian military power.

The navy saw a role for Italian armed intervention forces in crisis-cooling and peacekeeping operations and felt that it was necessary to prepare the armed forces for international tasks required of Italy as a leading partner in the Mediterranean region. The army did not argue forcefully in favour of these positions but did not really object to them. The air force, however, felt that Italian military policy and the development of the armed forces should remain closely bound to NATO defence objectives. The strategic transformation of the

223

Mediterranean was seen mainly in terms of the military balance between East and West and the Mediterranean region was considered a secondary theatre of operation in a NATO-Warsaw Pact conflict.

The feeling of disagreement among the services on the fundamental aspects of the tasks and structure of the armed forces — in particular the harsh controversy between the navy and the air force on the creation of naval aviation by equipping the Garibaldi helicopter carrier with the Sea Harrier V/STOL aircraft[24] — had given the impression that each of the services was preparing to fight a different war. In the opinion of General Lamberto Bartolucci, the then Chief of General Defence Staff, it was time to 'review the defence model and adapt the military instrument to enable it to fulfil NATO obligations and carry out an important stabilizing function in the Mediterranean.'[25] He argued that one should not speak of a change in Italy's role in the Mediterranean, but rather of a strengthening of it. It was necessary that Italy 'participate in all initiatives, including those of a military character, that can contribute to the active search for a settlement to crises by means of peace operations that favour the progressive extinction of destabilizing aspects.' In this framework, the Italian armed forces must 'be ready to provide a valid contribution to stabilizing and peace operations, as has already occurred in the past.'[26]

Whereas the military regarded the Lebanese mission as an invaluable experience and an operation from which advantages could be gained on both a political and social plane, the political parties were forced to evaluate their support of Italian participation taking into consideration the particular political and humanitarian elements of the mission. Most parties stated a general preference for such matters to be handled by the United Nations, but also elaborated reasons to defend an active Italian policy in the region. These reasons included the opportunity for Italy to participate in attempts to stabilize the Middle Eastern situation, the need to show a consistent Italian Middle Eastern policy that included support for the PLO (whose recognition the PCI demanded), and the need, after the massacres of Sabra and Chatila, to protect the Palestinian population and to restore the sovereignty of the Lebanese government.

The attitude of the five parties composing the government coalition was partly humanitarian (particularly in the Socialist Party) and partly political (most evident in the Republican

Party). There was substantial agreement within the coalition, as well as with the Communist Party, in condemning the Israeli invasion and in backing the government's decision to participate in the second multinational force. This political solidarity did not last long, however. The PCI gradually retreated and, in September 1983, already considered withdrawal of the Italian contingent as necessary unless the multinational force was expanded to come under the aegis of the United Nations. It insistently demanded independence from the American line. The greater the U.S. military role, the stronger its dissent. Finally, in October, the Communists presented a formal request for withdrawal in a motion to the Chamber of Deputies' Defense Commission. After having criticized the government for pulling the first Italian contingent out of Beirut too soon, the PCI now felt that the very reasons behind the multinational force's presence no longer existed, not only because it had lost its buffer function — having become party to the conflict — but also because the United States had entrusted to the MNF the preservation of its interests in the Middle East. The American decision to recall the marines to the ships of the Sixth Fleet off the coast of Lebanon, took both the government and other parties by surprise and elicited remarks about a 'vacillating American policy' and 'Washington's unilateral decisions' from even the most pro-American component of the government, namely the PRI.[27]

After the U.S. withdrawal, the Italian government decided to recall the Italian contingent to Italy. This took place between the 26 February and 4 April 1984. The tendency of most parties was to forget the whole experience, without going into a political or strategic analysis of events. The PRI spoke of success with respect to the official objectives set. The PSI preferred to put the emphasis on the achievement of humanitarian goals, while acknowledging the errors made by the West: having intervened too late, and not having recognized the demands and the role of Syria. The DC was occupied with preparations for its national convention and did not go into the results of the mission, other than to exalt the humanitarian work carried out by Italian soldiers. In any case, the Lebanese experience certainly affected the way in which Italy participated in the mineclearing operations in the Gulf of Suez. And undoubtedly, it will be kept in mind should the Italian government decide to participate in other politico-military initiatives outside the UN institutional framework.

225

Although not overjoyed, the public at first accepted the intervention of an Italian contingent in Beirut as part of a peace operation aimed at safe-guarding and protecting the Palestinian and Lebanese populations, victims of the massacres in the camps and years of war between opposing factions. The human-itarian aspect seemed a sufficiently valid reason to participate. There were risks, certainly, but they were thought to be limited and, in any case, it was considered that the whole matter would be taken care of in a short time. The continuation of the crisis and its aggravation, clearly exemplified by the murderous attacks against American marines and French paratroopers, as well as the extension of the mission beyond the deadline initially set, and the ever greater employment of draftees were all elements which gradually led to a change in public opinion. This was stimulated by reports in the press about dangerous trends in the Lebanese situation and the consequent risks for Italian soldiers. The PCI's position that only U.S. and Israeli interests were being served by the Italian presence in the region began to be more widely accepted.

The popular enthusiasm with which the Italian soldiers were welcomed home following their withdrawal was a sign of a contingent new-found unity between the people and the armed forces, returning proudly after having received international acknowledgement of their capabilities and humanity. But there was also a sense of relief for an operation brought successfully to completion with minor losses (one death and seventy-five wounded). Pressure exerted by public opinion during the Lebanese experience was felt politically, however. The reluct-ance of the Italian people to accept and support high-risk inter-national military commitments outside the national territory, calling for the employment of non-volunteer draftees, will be a factor conditioning future choices in Mediterranean policy. All the more so, if the initiatives are opposed by the PCI, a political party still capable of effectively mobilizing and affecting public opinion.

THE 1986 MEDITERRANEAN CRISES AND THEIR MILITARY REPERCUSSIONS

The Libyan missile attack against the small Italian island of Lampedusa, following the 15 April 1986 American air raid on

Tripoli and Benghazi, reinforced the Italian armed forces' trend
to consider the Mediterranean region as preeminent in terms of
military posture and tasks. Colonel Gadaffi's threats about
possibly increasing military pressure on Italy were taken
seriously. Naval radar picketing and warships deployment were
increased. Improvements were made in the area of air defence
system readiness and interceptor capacities. MB-339 light
fighter bombers were redeployed to the island of Pantelleria,
while paratroopers were sent to Lampedusa to protect the
American Coast Guard LORAN station and confront any
terrorist attempts to attack civilian targets on the island.
Furthermore, in the opinion of the Italian military, international
terrorism had become a truly military threat against NATO
countries, a type of undeclared war, and an integral part of an
indirect strategy of destabilization.[28]

The rise in tension in the Mediterranean in 1986 reinforced
the perception both that the Mediterranean was becoming the
centre of the more important international crises and that Italy
might be alone in the forefront of this situation.

Following these events in the Mediterranean, the Italian
Chief of Defence Staff, General Riccardo Bisognero spoke
about the possibility of military attacks coming from the south
which, while incapable of threatening Italy's territorial integrity,
could play on public opinion and create a disturbing sense of
insecurity. This required the armed forces to be prepared to
take immediate action in response to unforeseeable events, and
in order to do this improvements had to be made to Italy's
capacity to detect the incoming threats with precision and in
real time. A programme of progressive improvements of the air
defence system is being implemented, and the acquisition of a
space reconnaissance capability is being evaluated.

Many of the modernization programmes already underway
will provide additional capacity to meet this emerging threat.
For the land forces, improvements will concentrate on battle
management, C3, force mobility, and rapid intervention
capability, including the achievement of full operational status
for the FIR. For the naval forces, modernization involves the
completion of the present acquisition programmes with the
construction of the new Audace-class destroyers and of the
Minerva-class corvettes. The Garibaldi-class helicopter carrier is
expected to become operational by autumn 1987. For the air
force, the most significant improvements will take place in the

medium- and low-level air defence sectors with the adoption of the Patriot surface-to-air missile, to be added to the already operational Spada systems, and with the eventual acquisition of Stinger and Mistral missiles. Furthermore, Italy is participating, together with the United Kingdom, West Germany and Spain, in the development of the high-technology European Fighter Aircraft (EFA).

Envisioned first when Lagorio was Minister of Defence, as a force with a dual civilian and military role, the Italian FIR was subsequently separated from the force designated to intervene in cases of natural disasters, the so-called 'Forza di Pronto Intervento'(FOPI). The FIR (about 10,000 men) is made up of three components (land, sea, and air) with their own logistical and technical support, and it has been put under the command of an army general (General Giorgio Malorgio), who is directly responsible to the Chief of Defence Staff. Apart from the permanent command and staff structure, the army, navy and air force units of the FIR are, in peacetime, earmarked for assignment and are called upon to join together in case of emergency in the *mode* most suitable for the given contingency.

The FIR is also assembled for periodic training exercises to improve the operational integration of the units and to test tactics and procedures. The land component of the FIR is composed of six battalions: two motorized, one mechanized, one airborne, two engineering, with logistic support and communication, and two helicopter squadrons of the First Army aviation Antares regiment with CH-47C and AB-212 helicopters. The sea component is made up of one amphibious group. The air component is composed of an air transport squadron with G-222 and C-130 aircraft. Obviously, if and when needed, the FIR will be supported by the combat aircraft of the Italian air force and by the warships of the Italian navy.

The land component of the FIR first exercised in December 1985 at the range of Monte Romano. A further exercise that simulated the parachute landing of small groups of terrorists, was conducted in Sicily in July 1986 with the participation of all three components. The Italian FIR, according to the Army Chief of Staff General Luigi Poli, should not be considered analogous to the American Delta Force, or as an anti-terrorist unit, but as a highly mobile interservice force capable of intervening in any part of the Italian territory and in the Mediterranean region as an operationally autonomous complex or in support of standing forces.

The FIR's problems, though, are far from being all solved. The most important one is the lack of air transport, in particular over long distances, owing to the limited operational radius of action of the G-222 and, to a lesser degree, the C-130 aircraft, and the lack of specialized armaments and logistic sustainability. Another problem is that draftees still constitute a significant percentage of the land component personnel. This poses an evident constraint in all cases where the FIR may be employed in high-risk out-of-area operations, entailing the possibility of casualties.

There is little doubt that the rationale behind the creation of the Italian FIR is related more to the perceived need to improve the defence of national territory, than to a desire to perform out-of-area missions. This latter capability exists, but is severely limited. At the moment, the hope is that the existence of a rapid action force may have a deterrent effect. As it improves and becomes more sophisticated, the FIR would be the sort of unit to be integrated in a possible 'European' rapid intervention force to be employed for the defence of vital European interests, or for stabilization and peacekeeping missions, should such a force be created. Yet such eventual integration can for the moment only be theoretical. Integration of national military units in international forces is simplified when they have similar characteristics in terms of organization, equipment and training.

However, the need to maintain tight political control, and the difficulty in deciding who will command the force in the field, will likely lead to the employment of those forces on a strictly national basis. As the MNF in Lebanon has clearly demonstrated, even simple *coordination* among national forces involved in a complex and risky out-of-area mission is a difficult and politically biased task.

CONCLUSION

Membership in the Atlantic Alliance will continue to be a fundamental element of Italian foreign and military policy; and the European Community will continue to be a constant point of reference for its diplomacy. Although Italy will continue to be a loyal ally, NATO decisions will be examined more closely in the context of Italy's specific national and international interests, and Italy's specific military requirements will be given more weight.

Atlantic loyalty and the special relationship with the United States will remain an element of international legitimation and international status for Italy, and will continue to play a significant role in inter-party relations. Since the Mediterranean is an area of particular importance for both its economy and its security, it can be expected that Italy will carry out an intense and multifaceted Mediterranean policy. In both its Atlantic and Mediterranean 'dimensions,' Italy will keep close and preferential ties with the United States. However, specific national interests (oil, trade, arms sales, political relations with Middle Eastern and North African countries) will affect this Mediterranean policy, and, thus, differences in opinion with Washington may arise again, as may differences in ways and means to deal with regional problems and crises.

Inevitably, should disagreement arise, Italy will try to soften U.S.-Italian divergences and possible domestic political instabilities by placing government positions in the broader context of the policy lines adopted by the European Community. Italy's Mediterranean policy in the future may differ from the attitudes and actions undertaken in the early 1980s, partly because the limits to Italy's mediating role and capacity have become more evident, and due also to growing opposition by some political forces to the tendency to give too much saliency to Italy's so-called 'Mediterranean vocation.'

This does not mean that Italian foreign policy in Europe and in the Mediterranean area will lose its high profile, but the utility of military intervention, the difficulties and risks involved in crisis-cooling or peacekeeping operations and the fragility of agreements among allies, will be important considerations in any Italian government's decisions. The Lebanese experience will provide the reference point for all further discussion about out-of-area operations.

The rise of international terrorism since the end of 1985 confirmed the inadequacy of Italy's Mediterranean policy. Since it has become possible for Italy to be either directly or indirectly involved in a Mediterranean conflict, adjustments both in foreign policy and military deployments have naturally been necessary. Hence, Italy must be especially vigilant about the wider implications of its Middle Eastern policy and the decision to deploy forces more substantially in the south. Relations with the United States will have to be carefully managed, especially since Italy is not likely to support all aspects of U.S. Middle Eastern policy at a time when U.S. bases in Italy make Italy more vulnerable to acts of violence and reprisal from terrorist groups or radical states. Even though there have been many public declarations to the effect that the bases can be used by American armed forces only for contingencies connected with East-West crises, specific agreements have been signed by which, on a case by case basis, Italy may provide logistic and technical support to American armed forces in the event of out-of-area crises. This policy is bound to continue, but Italian governments will become increasingly concerned about the wider implications of supporting U.S. policies in the Mediterranean and there may be cases when the use of these bases will be denied. In all of this, the tendency of Italian political parties to exploit international events for domestic political purposes will be important.

While the strictly Mediterranean aspect of Italian foreign policy was perhaps toned down after Lampedusa and the stalling of the Middle Eastern peace initiatives, practical steps have been taken — notably Italy's bilateral accords on terrorism with the United States, Egypt, Morocco, Turkey, Israel and Tunisia — to combat the terrorism. These sorts of pragmatic arrangements may become increasingly important. Even if many of the more general lines of Italy's policy in the Mediterranean (notably in support of a negotiated peace process in the Middle East) will remain the same, Italian leaders are likely to be more discriminating than in the past in their dealings with Arab countries.

The political requirement to be more cautious in dealing with sensitive Mediterranean issues has its military complement in the emerging need to develop more national capacities of response: the intended modernization of the Italian armed forces to deal with threats in the Mediterranean. Financial constraints are likely to make progress slow and not all proposed acquisitions will be made within the expected timeframe.

Generally, Italy will continue to be committed to the 'Europeanization' of defence not as an alternative to the Atlantic Alliance and the strategic and nuclear tie with the United States, but in order to strengthen overall Western capacities. But as Italy assesses its individual needs in the Mediterranean, it may be required to make procurement decisions that are more relevant to its perceived need to defend itself against specifically Mediterranean contingencies than to its commitment to play a role in European continental defence.

The reaction of the armed forces to the strategic transformation in the Mediterranean has been a combination of new perceptions, new expectations and old concerns. On the one hand, the Soviet military presence in the Mediterranean has extended Italy's NATO commitments and made them more demanding; on the other, greater regional instability has enlarged the perceptions of threat — including the terrorist threat — and therefore increased the possibilities of military confrontation.

Expectations were raised among the military that greater resources would be devoted to the modernization and strengthening of the armed forces and their adaption to possible missions in the Mediterranean. Against this, many in the military consider that Italy should concentrate its resources to meet purely 'Atlantic' commitments. Others argue that if the armed forces are put in a position to confront the most challenging threats (that is, from the USSR), then they will be capable of dealing with national contingencies of other types.

However, the post-Lebanon expectations have rapidly faded and the military are again suffering from the belief that they are underpaid in comparison to managers and technicians of the civilian sector of society. Despite the fact that the armed forces continue to benefit from technological developments and general policies of military modernization, their status within Italian society remains low. This anxiety was reflected in several protests led by the lower ranks of the armed forces in early 1987.

On the whole, particularly after the American attack against Libya in 1986 and Gadaffi's attempted reprisal against Italy, Italians are now more deeply aware of instability in the Mediterranean and of the possibility of Italy being involved in a new Mediterranean crisis. There seems also to be a new recognition of the consequent need to possess efficient armed forces. A new spirit of nationalism has emerged,[29] although accompanied by the perception that Italy's role in the Mediterranean will be limited, even if it requires important military expenditures. But because domestic problems are so important, any Italian role in Mediterranean affairs will be conditioned by the endemic instability of its political system. It may well be that the persistent need to build consensus on every foreign policy issue will prevent Italy from developing the leading Mediterranean role many individuals desire.

NOTES

1. See, Virgilio Ilari, 'Concetto Difensivo e Dottrina Militare Italiana nel Dopoguerra,' in *Lo Strumento Militare Italiano. Problemi e Prospettive* ed. Maurizio Cremasco (Milan: Franco Angeli, 1986).

2. On the growth of the Soviet naval presence in the Mediterranean see, Michael MccGwire, ed., *Soviet Naval Developments* (New York: Praeger, 1973), 325-388. See also, Maurizio Cremasco, *Il Fianco Sud della NATO* (Milan: Feltrinelli, 1980), 79-100.

3. On early Soviet military assistance to Libya see, Harold D. Nelson, ed., *Libya: a Country Study* Foreign Area Study (Washington, DC: The American University, 1979), 259-271.

4. See, Roy F. Willis, *Italy Chooses Europe* (New York: 1971), 278-279.

5. The Federal Republic of Germany had declared that it would accept the deployment of Pershing II and cruise missiles on its territory only if another European 'continental' country would install them. Excluding Great Britain which is not a continental country, and considering the reserves of Belgium and Holland, Italy automatically became the key country upon whose decision the viability of the deployment depended.

6. On this subject see, Maurizio Cremasco, 'The Political Debate on the Deployment of the Euromissiles: the Italian Case,' *International Spectator,* no. 2 (April-June 1984): 115-121.

7. See the speech by Communist Party Secretary Enrico Berlinguer, House Parliamentary Records, no. 71 (5 December 1979), 5178-5188.

8. In the late 1970s, at the height of Red Brigade terrorism and economic crisis, the Communist Party collaborated with the governments in power. In 1978, a Christian Democratic government was established with formal Communist parliamentary support. This collaboration ended early in 1979. This was known as the period of 'national solidarity.'

9. An American C-141 aircraft with on board elements of the Delta Force touched down in Sigonella, without authorization, soon after the forced landing of the Egyptian jet carrying the Achille Lauro hijackers. The Delta Force surrounded the Italian military air police and *carabinieri* which had taken the aircraft into custody and the American general in command tried to force the Italian base commander to hand over the Arab terrorists. Moments of high tension followed, with the American and the Italian military on the brink of an armed confrontation. When the Egyptian jet moved from Sigonella to the Rome airport of Ciampino, American F-14 aircraft tried to interfere with the flight and the escorting Italian F-104 fighters. Finally, an American EW T-39

aircraft landed at Ciampino, again without any authorization, soon after the landing of the Egyptian jet.

10. See Premier Bettino Craxi's statement, Italian Senate Parliamentary Records, no. 431 (25 March 1986), 5-7, and House Parliamentary Records, no. 465 (25 March 1986), 28-30.

11. This and the preceding quotations are from Premier Bettino Craxi's statement, House Parliamentary Records, no. 471 (15 April 1986), 31-33.

12. This and the following quotations are from Andreotti's intervention as published by the Christian Democratic Party's paper, *Il Popolo* (5 June 1986).

13. Eventually, a 'memorandum of understanding' on the technical aspects of Italian industries' participation in the SDI research was signed in Washington in September 1986. As in the case of Germany, the agreement did not mean the Italian government's political and strategic endorsement of the American space shield. Andreotti's presentation, with its strong pro-Atlantic and pro-American stance, was a clear attempt to correct the course and image of Italian foreign policy, without renouncing the elements which had characterized it in previous years.

14. During the preparatory phase of the *Libro Bianco della Difesa 1985* the Defence Intelligence Community responsible for the threat evaluation asserted that threats came 'solely' from the east.

15. See, Stefano Silvestri, 'Il Quadro Generale e i Problemi della Difesa Italiana,' in *Lo Strumento Militare Italiano. Problemi e Prospettive,* ed. Cremasco.

16. On the militarization of the Mediterranean riparian states see, Maurizio Cremasco, 'The Military Presence of the Riparian Countries,' in *The Mediterranean Region,* ed. Giacomo Luciani (London: Croom Helm, 1984), 206-227.

17. On the Italian Rapid Intervention Force see, Maurizio Cremasco 'An Italian Rapid Intervention Force: the Geopolitical Context,' *The International Spectator,* no. 2 (April-June 1985): 51-60; and Luigi Caligaris, 'Possible Scenarios for an Italian Rapid Deployment Force,' *The International Spectator,* no. 3/4 (July-December 1985): 64-87.

18. See, Lelio Lagorio, 'Gli Indirizzi di Politica Militare,' Servizio Pubblica Informazione della Difesa — SPID (Defence Department Public Information Service, Rome) (June-July 1980).

19. See, Lelio Lagorio, 'Relazione alla Commissione difesa della Camera dei Deputati,' SPID (13 October 1982): 1.

20. See, Giovanni Spadolini, 'Indirizzi di Politica Militare,' SPID (8 November 1983): 9.

21. See *Libro Bianco della Difesa 1985* (Rome, 1984).

22. In early 1987, the two bills had not yet been approved by Parliament.

23. See, Umberto Cappuzzo, 'L'Esperienza del Contingente Militare Italiano in Libano,' Centro Studi Strategici (Rome: Luiss, April 1985), 8.

24. The navy-air force controversy was formally settled in November 1986 in an encounter between the two newly appointed Chiefs of Staff,

Admiral Giasone Piccioni and General Franco Pisano. The meeting took place in the office of the Minister of Defence with the participation of the Chief of Defence Staff, General Riccardo Bisognero. The cautious words of the official communiqué released at the end of the meeting were interpreted to imply that the air force had finally accepted the possibility for the navy to acquire its own air arm. It is likely that parliament will approve the acquisition of Sea Harrier aircraft, thus allowing the navy to fulfill its 50-year old aspiration.

25. See the speech of General L. Bartolucci during the closing ceremony of the 35th session of the Centro Alti Studi della Difesa (CASD), SPID (19 June 1984): 9.

26. See, Alfonso Sterpellone's interview with General Bartolucci, *Il Messagero*, 10 September 1984.

27. See, *La Voce Repubblicana*, 9 February 1984.

28. See the speech of General Bisognero at the closing ceremony of the 37th Session of the CASD, SPID (25 June 1986).

29. This new surge of 'neo-nationalistic' feeling was evident after the Achille Lauro hijacking and the Sigonella affair and after the April 1986 attempted Libyan reprisal against Lampedusa.

6

Greece and Nato: Continuity and Change

Thanos Veremis

INTRODUCTION

Greece is a small country of ten million inhabitants strategically located in the centre of the Mediterranean Sea — a position which has made it the proverbial crossroad of civilization as well as of invading forces. In modern times Greece's involvement in international conflagrations has been considerable and the cost that this has entailed has been disproportionate to Greece's size and resources. Shattered by two world wars and civil strife, the country recovered economically but was faced with difficulties in reestablishing the basis of its parliamentary politics. A maverick among NATO allies since 1981, Greece is still attempting to recover a lost consensus in a society marked by past political cleavages.

It is impossible to speak of the Greek state as though it were an immutable entity. At least since the Civil War of 1946–1949 Greece has persistently suffered from deep political and social divisions that have prevented the formation of a coherent and broadly supported foreign policy. Ruling majorities have advocated official policy without considering substantial minority opinion, or, as in the case of the military dictatorship of 1967–1974, a small minority has taken power by force and instituted an authoritarian regime little inclined to invoke popular support in matters of foreign policy.

The nature of Greek domestic tensions since World War II has naturally altered Greek security perceptions which tend to confuse internal and external sources of threat. Opposing factions have viewed foreign powers supporting their adversaries as indirectly threatening the realization of their own ideals as well as the interests of the Greek nation as a whole. Since 1974, however, factions have slowly come to terms with each other. The rise of the Greek Socialist Party (PASOK) has been symbolic of a wider disappointment with the United States and NATO, but the PASOK government has also helped to redress certain social and political imbalances inherited from the Civil War period.

Greece's present security preoccupations are with external threat, both from the north and the east. The northern problem stems from Greece's long-standing rivalry with Bulgaria (and more recently with Yugoslavia) over Macedonia and Thrace — a situation exacerbated in the postwar era by an incompatibility of social and political systems. The Soviet Union, which backed the claims of Balkan communist states against Greece, was perceived as the major threat to Greek security during the Cold War period. At present, Turkish hostility (originating in the Cyprus dispute and intensifying after 1974 over the Aegean Sea quarrel) constitutes the eastern threat which is now considered of primary importance. Since NATO provides no effective mechanism for the resolution of conflict among its members, Greece is left to manage the eastern problem alone.

This chapter will present the historical background of Greece's major security considerations, the domestic tensions that marked postwar defence priorities, the impact of international factors on internal politics, Greece's present policy of defence and its relations with the West. A division of Greek defence policy in the postwar era into three main periods of development, may help to elucidate certain themes of internal perceptions and external constraints:

— 1946–1949: during the Greek Civil War the Greek government's sole security concern was to avoid domination by the communist forces supported by Greece's northern neighbours.
— 1949–1974: the one thousand kilometres of shared borders with three communist states (Albania, Yugoslavia, and Bulgaria) heightened domestic awareness of the 'northern danger.' A link between national and Western security priorities was established upon Greece's entry into NATO (1952) and with the installation of four military bases and communication stations by U.S. forces, although Greek loyalty to the United States and NATO began to waver

during the period of military dictatorship (1967–1974).
— 1974 to the present: after the fall of the military regime,
caused by the Cyprus crisis (1974), a reorientation of
national defence priorities occurred. Greece's defence
policy has increasingly focused on the threat from Turkey
during the last twelve years and has enjoyed wider domestic
public consensus than at any other moment in its history.

HISTORICAL CONTINUITIES

Greece, like most emerging states in the nineteenth century
(such as Serbia, Rumania or Italy) rose out of a disintegrating
empire.[1] Unification of its territories did not grow out of a swift
series of victories, as was the case with Germany, but from a
long, spasmodic process of irredentist rebellions from within the
Ottoman realm. The irredentist aims of Greece, Bulgaria and
Serbia often clashed, and after their successful joint assault on
the Ottoman Empire in 1912, the countries became entangled
in internecine war among themselves.

The wars in the Balkans (1912–1922) found Greece,
Bulgaria and Turkey rotating in different alliances — two of
them always pitted against the third.[2] The Treaty of Lausanne,
signed in 1923 after the expulsion of the Greek forces in Asia
Minor, concluded the era of irredentism and heralded a period
during which Greece sought to maintain the status quo in its
relations with its neighbours. In 1930, the Greek statesman
Eleftherios Vanizelos and Kemal Atatürk (founder of modern
Turkey) signed an accord settling all pending matters between
their two countries, thus establishing a relationship which
outlasted any other treaty concluded in the Balkan region.

Bulgaria, discontented with its failure to achieve its irredentist goals and isolated, in the interwar period, from Balkan
bilateral and multilateral treaties, became a permanent source of
irritation for Greece. Whereas Turkey had ceased since 1930 to
pose a security problem, a series of hostile incidents with a
disgruntled Bulgaria led Greece to fortify its northern borders in
the late 1930s. At the heart of Greek-Bulgarian differences was
the ethnic makeup of the part of Macedonia annexed by Greece
in 1913. Although the issue of sizeable minorities in this area
was largely resolved with the population exchanges following
World War I and the settlement of about 700,000 Greek

refugees from Turkey, Bulgaria continued to press claims concerning the slavophones of Greece. Furthermore, the Comintern, in its Sixth Balkan Communist Conference in 1924, endorsed the Bulgarian Communist Party's plea for a 'united and independent Macedonia and Thrace.' This policy, which would have amounted to ceding Greek Macedonia to an independent state under Bulgarian tutelage, was naturally abhorrent even to left-wing Greeks. The Greek Communist Party, badly split over the issue, was forced by its unswerving loyalty to the Comintern to underwrite the decision and suffer constant embarrassment until 1935, when the slogan was repudiated. The right-wing regime of Bulgaria and its outlawed Communist Party were both, although from different angles, laying claims on a territory that had been incorporated into Greece.

Greece's attachment to Great Britain, a leading power in the eastern Mediterranean since the mid-nineteenth century, reflected a need to align with an important naval force in the region. Similarly, Greek entry into both world wars on the side of the major sea powers was largely determined by geopolitical vulnerabilities. Yet, on both these occasions the price of wartime commitment was extremely high. During World War I, the decision to enter on the side of the Triple Entente was carried out after an internal schism had damaged national unity. Although Greece's response to the unprovoked fascist attack of World War II was unanimous and heroic, the subsequent hardships of German occupation culminated in a civil war of unprecedented violence. Communist and other members of the left-wing resistance clashed with nationalists, right-wingers and, between 1946–1949, with the regular forces of the official Greek government. No doubt this second and bloodier national schism also reflected the contours of global politics. By the end of this process the Americans had replaced the British as the major foreign influence in Greece, and the country became the first battleground for the Cold War.[3]

The nature of the divisions which culminated in civil conflict is difficult to describe but it is possible to point to some of its causes: the role of the prewar dictatorship (under the throne's tutelage) in diminishing the prestige of parliamentary politics; the emergence of the Communist Party during the occupation as a major force of the resistance; the relative ineffectiveness and apathy of most prominent politicians during the same period; the unpopularity of the King who was widely associated with foreign power domination; and, finally, the complete destruction of the economy by the occupation forces and the extreme privation suffered by large sectors of the population which served to radicalize the masses. If resistance fighters seeking to establish social justice constituted the moral backbone of the leftist camp, narrow-minded devotees to Stalinist orthodoxy were its leaders. The nationalist camp included smaller resistance groups, a number of credible liberal politicians of the prewar period and a multitude of conservatives who rallied around the King and his foreign support. Collaborationists, seeking absolution, joined the ranks of the anti-communist forces. It was the Soviet threat, however, which inadvertently nurtured cohesion and resolution in the nationalist camp. Stalin, who had honoured his agreement with Churchill to allow Britain a free hand in Greece in 1944, demanded a withdrawal of foreign troops in 1947 and made claims on the Dodecanese islands ceded to Greece by Italy that year. Finally, the existence of a communist Yugoslavia and Bulgaria with claims on Greek territory, provided the nationalists with their overriding cause.

The urgency of Civil-War-related problems and the inability of a divided and paralysed government to handle the domestic situation effectively disposed Greek politicians to allow the United States an implied role in Greek internal affairs even if this was a natural affront to national sovereignty. Committed Greek anti-communists exploited this situation, and pressed for American involvement because they saw it as the only guarantee of a quick victory against left-wing rebels. It was at this time that American aid agencies began to function in Greece. The American administration, faced with an isolationist Congress, took pains to convince its public of an imminent Soviet threat which was not limited to Greece but would have serious implications for Turkish and indeed West European security. The Truman Doctrine, officially announced on 12 March 1947, inaugurated an era of U.S. involvement in Europe and an overt American role in running Greek affairs. The Marshall Plan was proclaimed in June 1947. Greece's total share of the Plan was 1.7 billion dollars in economic aid (loans and grants) and 1.3 billion dollars in military aid between 1947 and the 1960s.[4]

The fratricidal struggle that raged for four years aggravated the conditions in the already ravaged country. To the 550,000 (8 percent of Greece's population) who died during 1940–1944 were added another 158,000 dead between 1946–49.[5] Caught in the middle of a war between the government army and the communist-leftist forces, Greek peasants and townspeople paid the highest price of this civil strife. Ultimately, their politicization — to the right or left — was determined arbitrarily depending on whether they had been victims of a right- or left-wing 'tyrant.'

American policy towards Greece, although dictated primarily by defence considerations, was initially guided by liberal principles. The Department of State had discouraged admirers of authoritarian methods and viewed King George of the Hellenes as an obstacle to the reconstruction of liberal democracy in Greece. Yet, as the rift between the Soviet Union and the United States widened, the American administration's willingness to soft-pedal its influence and to treat the Greek opposition with understanding, diminished commensurately. As Cold War tensions heightened, Greece was increasingly viewed as a bulwark against communist expansion and its administrative, military, economic and political institutions were shaped to serve that purpose. Efficiency and modernization acquired priority over sorely needed democratic ideals. American missions favoured politicians eager to cooperate but lacking in stature and principles. John Nuveen, head of the Economic Cooperation Administration (ECA) was an outspoken advocate of strong-armed efficiency. The head of the military mission, General James van Fleet expressed his preference for an authoritarian regime in Greece.[6] Representatives of the American Mission to Aid Greece (AMAG) participated in most important Greek committees and boards and Americans were employed in top administrative positions in Greek ministries and other government agencies. Members of the AMAG were granted extra-territoriality, inviolability of property and exemption from taxes, custom duties and currency controls.[7]

Greek governments usually had to bear Washington's stamp of approval and in March 1950, Prime Minister Sophocles Venizelos was compelled to resign in favour of Nikolaos Plasteras following an open request by the American Ambassador. In June of the same year, the departing van Fleet communicated to King Paul his preference for a strong government under Marshal Alexander Papagos. Three months later, the new American Ambassador, John Peurifoy, stated that 'while before the Korean conflict a centre-left government had been

appropriate for Greece, a centre-right government is now necessary.'[8] Internecine strife among the Greeks invited not only
suffering and destruction but also foreign penetration. The
nationalist victory over the communist forces was made possible
through U.S. military aid, advice and diplomatic backing. However, as Argyris Favouros points out, a high degree of control by
one country over another should entail the assumption of an
equally high degree of responsibility towards it.[9] The control exercised by the American armed forces which was not always astute,
became a crucial issue in the shaping of Greek politics.

The operations of the Greek army were coordinated and
supervised by the Joint United States Military Advisory and
Planning Group (JUSMAPG). By 1949, the U.S. mission
exerted virtual control over the Greek armed forces and often
expressed its disdain for politicians and impatience with parliamentary politics. Given the anomalous circumstances of the
Civil War the JUSMAPG advised that the military be isolated
from the rest of society and protected from the ideological
contagion which would destroy the unity of the forces. Many
Greek officers shared this view and, furthermore, believed that
for the sake of operational effectiveness the army should
become an autonomous body answering only to its foreign
advisors. Such ideas were not abandoned with the termination
of the war and American influence in the Greek forces persisted
through Military Assistance Programs (MAPs) even after interference in Greek politics had ceased.[10]

Greece's accession to NATO was initially obstructed by
Britain's own concept of Western defence in the Near East and
the opposition of certain Scandinavian countries to an overex-
tension and therefore dilution of NATO's primary aims. When
Greece and Turkey dispatched combat forces to South Korea in
1950, they were acting as members of the United Nations but
their motive was in fact to override objections to their entry into
NATO. As far as the United States was concerned, Greek and
Turkish participation would link its allies in NATO, the Central
Treaty Organization (CENTO), the Southeast Asian Treaty
Organization (SEATO), and the security treaty of Australia,
New Zealand and the United States (ANZUS). For Greek politi-
cians of the liberal coalition government which pressed for
Greek membership, NATO not only provided an additional
guarantee against Balkan communism, it also constituted a door
to a community of democratic European states and a partial

emancipation from exclusive American control. In September 1951, NATO foreign ministers in Ottawa approved Greek and Turkish entry.[11] Two years later, American military presence in Greece was consolidated by the signing of a bilateral base agreement which provided the United States with the right to establish and supply its bases and the use of Greek airspace. It also set out the legal status of U.S. forces in Greece. In the following years some liberals who had worked for Greece's accession came to regret their original position but in 1951–1953 the difference between conservatives and liberals on security issues and NATO was one of degree rather than kind. Although the latter preferred closer ties with Europe and less American control, they agreed that the country's main security concern was with its northern borders.

Relations between Greece and the communist Balkan states remained troubled throughout the 1950s and 1960s. During German occupation, Bulgaria incorporated the eastern part of Macedonia and most of western Thrace and subjected its Greek inhabitants to a regime of terror. Bulgaria's subsequent supervised transformation into a communist state initially implied that its position in the community of Socialist Republics could not match that of a self-liberated Yugoslavia with its partisan resistance record.[12] The Yugoslav policy of an autonomous Macedonia which would include Skopje as well as the Greek and Bulgarian Macedonias, provoked a strong general reaction but initially failed to stir the Bulgarians. Since Yugoslavia had more influence with the Soviets, the Bulgarians had to wait until Tito's break with Stalin before they could exercise their own foreign policy over Macedonia. After Tito broke with the Cominform in 1948, the Bulgarians repudiated the existence of a separate Macedonian nation proclaiming instead their own historical destiny in the area. As long as the issue between the two communist neighbours remains unresolved Greece may risk entanglement in their periodic flareups.[13]

The fluctuations in Yugoslav-Soviet-Bulgarian relations usually has had an impact on Greece. The clash between Tito and Stalin terminated Yugoslav support for the Greek communist forces and contributed to their defeat. In 1953 Greece, Turkey and Yugoslavia signed a treaty of friendship and cooperation followed by a formal alliance. The pact might have served as an indirect link between Yugoslavia and NATO had it not been for the former's rapprochement with Moscow in

1955 which effectively ended the treaty. Since the end of World War II, Greece has sought to secure the status quo in Macedonia making it clear that Greece has no claims against its neighbours and will tolerate none in return.

Since its emergence in the 1950s, the Cyprus issue has become the main problem in Greece's relations with Turkey. Occupied by Britain in 1878 and a British colony after 1925, Cyprus was no exception to the rule of anti-colonial struggles that rocked the British empire after the war. Greek Cypriots, who represented 80 percent of the island's population repeatedly appealed to Greek governments for support and hoped for unification with Greece. Although Greek liberal politicians discouraged such pleas it was the conservative government of Papagos that, in 1954, embraced the cause of the Greek Cypriots. When Archbishop Makarios, political and spiritual leader of the Greek Cypriot community, introduced the issue to the forum of the United Nations, Britain responded by bringing the previously neutral Turkish Cypriots and Turkey into the conflict.[14] The foundations of future intercommunal conflict were thus laid and what began as a struggle for independence gradually deteriorated into a confrontation between Greeks and Turks.

External factors have had an important role in shaping Greek security perceptions. The processes of Greek nationalism and irredentism have been heavily affected by Western influence in the region. The unification of Greek-inhabited territories under Ottoman rule created an ideological link between the citizens of a dependent and impoverished kingdom involved in the difficult task of state building. Dependence on Britain largely determined Greece's foreign and irredentist policies, and Greece's alliance with the Triple Entente, as well as its misconceived Asia Minor campaign, must be examined in the context of European alignments and strategic objectives in the eastern Mediterranean and the Near East. The two recurring security considerations of Greece have been Bulgaria and Turkey, and although relations with the latter improved during the interwar period (acquiring an institutional base after entry of both countries into NATO), Bulgaria, throughout the same period, remained a source of problems for Greece. War, occupation, civil conflict and subsequent dependence on the United States, are the dominating features in the public perception of Greece's postwar affiliation with the West.

244

DOMESTIC TENSIONS AND SECURITY PERCEPTIONS

The Greek Civil War is the single most important factor in the political development of Greece since its liberation from Axis occupation. It is impossible to understand past and current tensions between different sectors of Greek society without appreciating the significance of this catalytic event and its enduring heritage. Although the elections of 1985 demonstrated that the divisions of the past were receding to the background of party politics,[15] most of the preceding period was affected by the Civil War legacy. Thus, the transition from coalition governments in the 1940s to single-party conservative governments in the 1950s, followed by the return to power of the liberal centre after eleven years of right-wing monopoly (1952–1963) and the brief interlude of liberalization (1964–1965), the clash of a popular prime minister with the throne and royal intervention in parliamentary politics (1965), the military regime of 1967 and its collapse seven years later due to the Cyprus disaster, the return and establishment of perhaps the most orderly parliamentary regime in Greek history, and, finally, PASOK's accession to power in the elections of 1981, were directly or indirectly influenced by the deep civil cleavage brought about by the war which raged between 1946–1949.

The Greek Civil War, like others of its kind, had the effect of polarizing politics, ideology, and institutions in a way that affected the whole of society. This situation did not arise from dictatorial rule but in a state which, in spite of various constitutional irregularities and extraordinary measures, observed the essential rules of parliamentary democracy.[16] The Communist Party that abstained from the 1946 elections and called upon its followers to defy the outcome, was outlawed with the outbreak of hostilities, but most of the Greek parties continued to operate, undeterred by the Civil War and equally unresponsive to the new political and social challenges confronting postwar Europe. Ideological polarization left little margin for middle-class leaders and the intelligentsia to deal with issues other than those of Greece's national identity and its place in Western Europe. The left wing was either muffled or fled the country after its defeat. Consequently, Greece completely missed out on the constructive dialogue between liberal and socialist principles which was occurring elsewhere at this time.

The nation state 'presented itself both as a concrete agent of the professional and social integration of a large number of people and as the obvious highly valued symbolic entity of a collective identification.'[17] The role of the state grew considerably in the postwar era: having assumed the entire burden of reconstruction, the allocation of massive foreign aid and the promotion of a nationalist orthodoxy, its impact on society became much greater. High unemployment and a wrecked economy (which only reached its prewar level in the 1950s) turned the state into the chief employer which remained a social patron even after the completion of reconstruction and the advent of the economic boom. From 1940 to 1970 the population increased by 19 percent while the number of civil servants increased by 140 percent.[18] Public planning, which consisted of currency controls, price and exchange rate regulation, investment, and the extension of credit to the private sector, further enhanced the state's importance in propelling economic growth.

State ideology (legitimized by democracy and transmitted through the channels of education and state-controlled radio stations) presented an image of Greece as an integral nation fighting enemies, namely socialist or communist adversaries who threatened to destroy it, and did not invoke principled liberal arguments. In state rhetoric, the term 'civil war' was replaced by the derogatory 'bandit war,' which years after the events continued to denote the baseness of the rebels' motives. This term was also convenient as a linguistic symbol whose use or non-use by persons would reveal their political affiliation. There emerged in this way a nationalist form of fundamentalism which, unlike nineteenth century irredentist movements, was defensive, exclusive and parochial.[19] Within the state apparatus, a cluster of agencies developed, filled with functionaries (policemen, military personnel and other guarantors of public order and state creed) who enjoyed relative freedom from parliamentary scrutiny. Liberal attempts during 1964–1965 to dislodge these functionaries from power provoked the wrath of the crown. Yet, the state's scrupulous attachment to legalism, which often served to protect individual rights of citizens, deserves credit.

No other institution had a greater stake in the prolongation of the Civil War heritage and its attendant anomalies than the crown. In this respect the King often referred to the communist insurrection and continued to invoke the 'threat from within' years after it had ceased to have any real substance. Throughout the war years, the future of the crown remained an outstanding issue of contention between the Greeks and their allies, and the royal family returned to Greece in 1946 only after a plebiscite had decided the monarchy's fate. King George's death in 1947 brought his brother Paul to the throne. The interventions of his dynamic wife, Queen Frederica, in the affairs of state became a permanent feature of his reign. Rather than play down the royalty's role, Frederica brazenly exercised the extra-constitutional powers that accrued to the throne due to the political anomalies of the time. Both she, and later her son Constantine (who succeeded his father in 1964) failed to understand that the power invested in the throne after the Civil War was a transitory anachronism. Although the monarchy initially secured the unity of the victorious camp, in time it became a cause of dispute even among its former allies. Frederica's rivalry with Marshal Papagos, head of the government forces during the Civil War, split the officer corps into two camps. The Queen's fear that the prestigious general would wield an influence in the army rivalling that of the King was confirmed. Long after Papagos' death, his military admirers harboured hostility against the throne until they removed its power in 1967 and abolished it altogether in 1973.

Since socialist parties were isolated from central political discourse (albeit not from parliament), the only political force that could instill vitality into the ossified system, intent on growth but not modernization, was the Centre Union Party (EK) under George Papandreou. The general objectives of the forces of the centre were to end political polarization, reform the educational system, defend civil liberties and further the democratization of the political process. The Centre Union Party, which won a resounding electoral victory in 1964, was a merger of forces ranging from moderate right to socialist, and found support in the growing urban centres where the anonymity of large populations weakened the power of patronage and collective grievances were freely and loudly expressed. Communists and socialists formed the United Democratic Left (EDA) which became the second party in parliament (with over 25 percent of the vote) in the elections of 1958, nurturing discontent against Constantine Karamanlis' ruling National Radical Union (ERE).

Determined to challenge the crown's influence in the armed forces, Papandreou came into conflict with Constantine II soon after taking power. In the summer of 1965 the popular Prime Minister was forced to resign in the midst of his followers' outcry. At the same time forty deputies defected from his party and became supporters of a government formed by the King and designed to prevent the holding of elections that would bring the Centre Union Party back to power. The clash between the heads of state and government caused a major political crisis and a power gap which the military filled nearly two years later. The failure of the Centre Party, despite its popularity, to consolidate itself while in power and survive the clash with the monarch betrayed the precariousness of postwar democracy in Greece. It also showed that established extra-parliamentary forces such as the crown and the military were resistant to change and reform.

In no other profession than in the armed forces was allegiance to the crown or to conservative members of government more vital for personal advancement. Paradoxically, this very dependence of the officers on royalty or political patrons became a source of resentment even among those who were most eager to profit from it. Officers formed clandestine organizations in order to purge the army of leftist elements, while simultaneously promoting their own corporate interests and waiting for the opportunity to assert their autonomy. The weakening of parliamentary institutions between 1965 and 1967 encouraged certain officers, who had come of age during the period of civil strife, to intervene in politics and challenge the authority of the politicians. The officers' sense of isolation was partly due to their 'total institutional life'[20] but also to the widening gap between their own social importance and that of prominent civilian professionals, technocrats and businessmen in the 1960s.

The 1967 coup was to a large extent the reaction of 'praetorian' officers against the impact of détente at home. Refusing to accept the end of the Civil War polarization and to give up their role as guardians of a repressive state ideology, the officers invented a threat to internal order — a possible communist uprising — to justify their armed intervention. The takeover succeeded in preventing George Papandreou from winning the upcoming elections. Moreover, it freed a certain military clique from the restraints of a conservative political camp which had failed to remain in power. Many of these officers, in fact, supported the coup knowing that their chances for promotion would increase given the numerous dismissals that would inevitably follow. The coup also served to separate large elements of the military from the monarch, who had been unable to slow the political advances of George Papandreou.

In January 1967, King Constantine finally made his move against the rebellious colonels but his countercoup failed and he had to flee the country with his family. In 1973, following another abortive coup against its authority, the ruling junta formally deposed the exiled monarch and presented the people with a republican constitution, approved by a fraudulent referendum. Although brutal and unprofessional in administering the state, the regime had the good fortune to ride the crest of a sustained economic boom and thus secured the prolonged acquiesence of the populace.[21]

The Turkish invasion of Cyprus triggered off the disintegration of the military regime in Greece. On 23 July 1974 members of the junta handed power over to politicians who summoned Constantine Karamanlis (self-exiled in France since 1963) to assume leadership of a civilian government and hold elections. The conservative electoral outcome of 1974 was an endorsement of Karamanlis' effort to secure an orderly transfer of power without provoking the stunned but still dangerous forces of the fallen military regime. The outcome of the referendum deciding the future of the monarchy was more in keeping with the public desire for change. Karamanlis did not take a clear position on the referendum but his silence was widely interpreted as a condemnation of the institution which had destabilized Greek politics on several crucial occasions. The referendum of December 1974 sealed the fate of the monarchy: 69 percent of the vote was against it.

With 220 out of 300 seats in parliament, Karamanlis' New Democracy Party (ND) firmly dominated the opposition consisting of the Centre Union with sixty seats, Andreas Papandreou's PASOK with twelve, and the United Left with eight. The outcome of the 1977 elections — relatively unthreatened by the possibility of a military reversal — betrayed a growing shift of voters leftward, as illustrated by PASOK's rise from 13.6 percent of the vote in 1974 to 25.3 percent in 1977 and the parallel decline of New Democracy from 54.5 percent to 41.8 percent.[22] After almost five years as head of government, Karamanlis was elected President of the Republic by parliament in 1980. During his term in office, a cautious 'de-juntification'

of the state mechanism was carried out along with the recognition and legalization of the Communist Party (KKE), the
removal of Greece from NATO's integrated military command
(a response to its 'passive' stance during the Cyprus affair), the
liberalization of the state, and the negotiations that led to
Greece's entry into the European Community in 1981.
Karamanlis' own political transformation after he left politics in
1963 reflected the change of mood of the general public and his
new party's liberal position deprived the Centre Party of its
powerful platform of the 1960s. The demise of the Centre
Union, however, swelled the ranks of support for PASOK
allowing it to take power in 1981.[23]

Economic and Social Developments

The rapid urbanization of the 1950s and 1960s eroded the
traditional rural structures of Greek society and led to the
integration of former peasants into the emerging modern urban
environment. Horizontal organizations based on class interests
have been gradually replacing vertical patron-client networks
and the power of kinship. The economic boom of the 1960s and
1970s relieved the country of underdevelopment and altered
the life-style of its population. The Greek socioeconomic system
did not cease to emulate Western pluralistic prototypes, even
during the period of military dictatorship. Social and political
emancipation became significant options in the 1970s, once the
old spectre of the Civil War faded. The rising expectations of
the Greek public, stifled by the reversal of 1967, surfaced after
the collapse of the dictatorship and gained momentum in the
late 1970s. Likewise, the unprecedented political freedom
enjoyed by the Greeks since 1974 has created a more stable
climate for pragmatic and interest-oriented politics that have
partly replaced fanatic pre-junta quarrels between left and right.
The victory of the socialists in the elections of 1981 reflected
the disappointment of the middle and lower-middle classes who
felt that they had missed out on the boom of the 1960s and the
1970s.

Between 1962 and 1978 the average yearly growth rate of
the economy was 6.6 percent and per capita income rose to
3,000 dollars. Foreign capital inflows represented a decreasing
percentage of total investment and some have argued that in

financial terms Greece became less dependent on foreign capital. Economic growth based on imports, however, has widened the foreign trade deficit gap. This deficit, covered by immigrant and merchant marine remittances, tourism and foreign loans, has gotten out of hand during the last years. From the late 1970s and early 1980s inflation rose steadily to 20–26 percent during a period of economic stagnation. The public sector, whatever the government in power, added an increasing burden to the strained economy. The PASOK government became deeply involved with the losses of the private sector. Firms indebted to state banks were kept afloat because the government wished to prevent the growth of unemployment. In certain cases the state converted loans to big businesses into equity and then took over the concerns. The administration of nationalized industries proved unsatisfactory. Since PASOK's victory in the June 1985 elections, businessmen have been unresponsive to Papandreou's attempts to encourage private investment.

In the beginning of his second term the Prime Minister launched an anti-inflationary policy which reduced the rate of inflation to 18 percent and devaluated the drachma by 15 percent, but productivity has remained at low levels. Unemployment (11 percent at the end of 1985) has risen because of austerity measures, and industrial production, after a 2.3 percent increase in 1984, remained stable in 1985. The austerity policies which PASOK was obliged to pursue created discontent even among the party's supporters who bore the burden with great difficulty. The stabilization measures introduced in October 1985, designed to bring the public sector and current account deficits under control, included a two-year wage and salary freeze which met with trade union anger. The party's left wing, composed mostly of trade unionists and exponents of a 'third way to socialism,' see PASOK's policy as a drift away from socialist ideals.

PASOK's constituency is made up of inherited Centre Union support[24] and the generation which came of age during the junta years. PASOK has also capitalized on the left wing's desire for legitimacy and on the guilt feelings of certain conservatives who have ideological affiliations with preceding right-wing governments. The reconciliation of conservative democrats with liberals and leftists, merging in a united front against the military dictatorship, was the most positive, albeit

251

unintended, product of the dictatorship, as it broadened the consensual basis of post-1974 parliamentary politics. PASOK was also able to draw on a younger and more radical constituency to recreate the socialist promise that the pre-junta Centre Union had been unable to fulfil.

After the late 1940s and early 1950s Greek security policy was almost entirely in line with American regional defence priorities and the Greek forces remained under the supervision and influence of the American military missions long after U.S. involvement in Greek politics ceased to be so overt. Furthermore, the number of Greek officers trained in the United States under the Military Assistance Programs between 1950 and 1969, exceeded 11,000.[25] For a number of years, the defence orientation of the Greek armed forces was directed by the U.S. doctrine that Greece should have a 'military establishment capable of maintaining internal security in order to avoid communist domination ... .'[26] The Greek army was, therefore, primarily supplied and organized to confront internal threat though also expected 'through limited accessories to cause some delay to Soviet and satellite forces in case of global war.'[27] International détente in the 1960s decreased the threat from the north but Greek-Turkish disputes over Cyprus demanded a reappraisal of Greece's eastern defences. Totally dependent on the United States for arms and spare parts, the Greek government was faced, in 1964, with pressure to reduce its air force and naval hardware.

The instigators of the 1967 coup spread rumours of American backing among their wavering colleagues in order to secure wider support. Officers who looked to the United States for guidance could not fail to notice that American officials were not displeased with the takeover. An embargo on heavy weapons, initially imposed on Greece, was suspended shortly thereafter and then lifted altogether, while state visits to Greece of high-ranking Americans — including the Vice President of the United States — lent sorely needed legitimacy to the military regime.[28] The colonels expressed their gratitude by making Greek airspace available to American flights during the June 1967 Middle East war and the September 1970 crisis in Jordan, and by granting home-porting privileges to the Sixth Fleet in Elefsis. When Brigadier Ioannides sought to eliminate the neutralist President of Cyprus, Archbishop Makarios, he believed that he was doing the United States a service as well as ridding himself of an 'upstart' who undermined the authority of Athens. His attempt against Makarios' life triggered the Turkish invasion and ultimately the collapse of the Athens junta. The American Secretary of State, Henry Kissinger, remained conspicuously inactive during the invasion and failed to obstruct Turkish violations of the cease-fire (while discussions were underway in Geneva) which led to the occupation of 40 percent of the island by the Turkish army. Two consecutive American administrations worked diligently to lift the arms embargo imposed by Congress on Turkey for having used U.S. military aid against Cyprus and eventually succeeded.

Official American backing for the junta and the subsequent U.S. role (or lack thereof) in the Cyprus issue, created a deep rift in U.S.-Greek relations which transcended party lines. It was, in fact, the politically conservative public which had always considered the United States a guarantor of Greek rights that experienced the greatest disillusionment. Reflecting the changes that transpired in the mentality of the conservative public, New Democracy has revised the traditional right-wing position of total identification with the West and chosen a more pragmatic relationship based on mutual interests rather than ideological ties.

Although PASOK's theories of dependence are leftist, as are its appeals to the victims of the Civil War, its nationalist slogans have deprived the traditional right wing of its most effective rallying standard of the past. Papandreou evokes a patriotism which is associated with Greek sacrifices during World War II and derives its moral authority from resistance against attack and occupation by the Axis powers. His nationalism is defensive rather offensive. Greek resentment against dependence on great powers has inspired PASOK's Third World and non-aligned inclinations. According to some party luminaries, Greece belongs to the Third World periphery which is exploited by the capitalist metropoles of the West. The Soviet Union has been criticized less sharply for sharing world domination with the United States. Yet, although state visits have been exchanged between Greek and Soviet high officials, no substantial change in Greece's Western orientation has occurred. Relations with the United States did, nevertheless, reach an all-time low after 1981. Papandreou fuelled anti-American sentiments at home with occasional rhetorical outbursts which distracted his public from his otherwise pragmatic policies of continued affiliation with the European Community and NATO and alignment with the United States through a new agreement to maintain U.S. basing facilities at least until the end of 1988.

Since 1974, the Turkish factor has largely determined the course of U.S.-Greek relations and has become the top priority in Greek security policy. New Democracy governments have pursued a much more independent course than any of their conservative predecessors who were ultimately limited by their declared attachment to the West. Since U.S. and NATO concern over Cyprus and the Greek-Turkish dispute were inspired by the need to stabilize the southeastern flank, it became evident to the Greeks that the Western powers were not neutral mediators. PASOK has appeared determined not to make concessions over Greek rights and has promised to defend the status quo in the Aegean at all costs. Nevertheless, Papandreou proclaimed a 'moratorium' in 1982 in order to create a favourable climate for negotiations. The 'moratorium' was suspended in November 1982 following the cancellation of a NATO exercise which excluded the island of Lemnos and the violation of Greek airspace by Turkish aircraft.[29] Although New Democracy leader Constantine Mitsotakis declared his willingness to repeat bilateral discussions with Turkey over outstanding matters, the two larger parties differ only marginally on issues concerning relations between Greece and Turkey.

The election of June 1985 gave PASOK a comfortable margin (45.82 percent of the vote and 172 deputies in parliament) and hence it continued to pursue its program unhindered by leftist or rightist opposition. Papandreou's success was reinforced by Communist losses and consequently his decision not to back Karamanlis for a renewal of his Presidential term, for fear of alienating left wing voters, was unexpectedly vindicated. PASOK's egalitarian wage-price indexation permitted people of low and medium incomes to beat the rate of inflation. Price controls and the protection of workers' job security had a negative effect on business but won the support of a large section of the population. There was, therefore, a clearer correlation of income level and electoral behaviour in 1985 than in 1981. Businessmen, managers and certain professional groups opted for New Democracy, as have legal and medical associations which showed much support in the early 1980s. New Democracy, with 40.85 percent (126 deputies) of the vote, added 4.98 percent to its 1981 percentage while the KKE with

9.89 percent (12 deputies) lost 1.4 percent. Finally, the small but influential Eurocommunists with 1.84 percent managed to elect one deputy (see Table 6.1).

The entire campaign concentrated on internal rather than external issues and in spite of invectives exchanged by partisan newspapers and an enormous mobilization of followers, there was none of the pre-junta fanaticism to undermine the outcome. No doubt the long-standing feud between Papandreou and Mitsotakis added a personal element to their rhetorical battle but both parties ultimately remained within civilized boundaries of confrontation. Probably the best assessment of the nature of contemporary Greek democracy which gives a flavour of the 1985 election is as follows:

> Democracy is a question of rule by the people, as the Greek word clearly states. Of course there are rights entrenched in the Constitution and in a variety of laws, but though Greeks will gladly make use of the legal system, there is not the implicit respect for 'the law' as an institution summing up the whole tradition of a people .... Since the popular exercise of power is central to the concept of democracy in Greece, and since the country has a friendly climate and an extroverted people, it is not surprising that an air of festivity should surround an election.[30]

Greece's domestic tensions reflect the postwar identification of external with internal threat perceptions. The phenomenon is by no means confined to the right wing in Greek politics but became the creed of the left as well. If the conservatives believed that the Soviets constantly conspired with the Greek communists to subvert the system, the leftists saw the hand of the United States in every act of the Greek state. The internal developments discussed here have been largely responsible for shaping, and (as of 1974) revising security perceptions in Greece. Left-wing suspicion of the United States which emerged during the Civil War resurfaced after 1974 and was more widely supported. The rise of PASOK is due largely to this very development. The long and intermittent process of rebuilding democratic institutions, from the debris left by the Civil War and its protracted aftermath, is now at the centre of Greek politics.

Table 6.1: Greek national elections, European parliament elections and parties in parliament

Parties	1974 Votes %	1974 Seats	1977 Votes %	1977 Seats	1981 Votes %	1981 Seats	1981(a) Votes %	1981(a) Seats	1984(b) Votes %	1984(b) Seats	1985 Votes %	1985 Seats
New Democracy	54.4	220	41.8	171	35.87	115	31.34	8	38.05	9	40.85	126
PASOK	13.6	12	25.3	93	48.07	172	40.12	10	41.58	10	45.82	172
KKE	9.5	5	9.4	11	10.93	13	12.84	3	11.64	3	9.89	12
KKE-Interior	(c)	3	–	–	1.34	–	5.29	1	3.42	1	1.84	1
Symmachia(d)	–	–	2.7	2	–	–	–	–	–	–	–	–
Kodeso(e)	–	–	–	–	0.7	–	4.25	1	0.80	–	–	–
Centre Union-EDIK	20.4	60	11.9	16	0.4	–	1.12	–	0.28	–	–	–

Notes: (a) European Parliament elections; (b) European Parliament elections; (c) The two communist parties collaborated in the elections of 1974; (d) The KKE-Interior (Eurocommunist) along with four other smaller parties collaborated in the elections of 1977; (e) Kodeso was formed by a splinter group of the Centre Union and appeared in the elections of 1981. During the elections of 1985, it collaborated with New Democracy. During the same elections, what remained of the original EDIK collaborated with PASOK.

The most prominent of the extreme right-wing parties in national elections were the following: National Alignment secured 6.8% of the vote in the elections of 1977 and 5 seats in parliament. Progressive Party secured 1.68% in the elections of 1981 and 1 seat in parliament; it also secured 1.95% in the European Parliament elections of 1981 and 1 seat in the European Parliament. EPEN secured 2.29% in the European Parliament elections of 1984 and 1 seat. It secured 0.60% in the national elections of 1985. The three parties alternated in elections.

THE INTERNATIONAL FACTOR IN DOMESTIC DEVELOP-MENTS

The legacy of certain outstanding political questions of the past that still persist in the confrontations between the leaders of PASOK and New Democracy having been described, it is necessary to turn to contemporary problems and trends that link Greece with international developments.

The elections of 1985 were dominated by the verbal exchanges between Papandreou and Mitsotakis but the main concern of all parties was the economy and its uncertain future. New Democracy adopted a liberal prescription promising to decrease the role of the state and provide incentives for a revival of the private sector. Mitsotakis' constant references to the country's ever increasing dependence on foreign loans in order to finance a cumbersome and expensive state, underlined the most sensitive issue of the contest. PASOK's own platform, focusing on decentralization and redistribution of income, made fewer promises than New Democracy of handouts and post-electoral bliss and stressed the need for improvement in productivity. Although both parties realized that the economy was ailing, they lacked the courage to promise the public 'blood and tears.' The absence of new investment even before 1981, and the current pressure on business have led to an increase in unemployment which mainly affects the young. According to an influential editor of an economic journal[31], the KKE's failure, marked by its electoral losses, to convince its constituency that the destruction of the private sector would benefit the people, constitutes a clear message to PASOK. The public must fully understand the reasons for economic policy and not be given illusions about domestic prospects for rapid improvement.

Adverse conditions of the international economy have had a direct impact on Greece. The balance-of-payments deficit has traditionally been offset by emigrant workers' remittances, shipping receipts and tourism. Of these three, only tourism has fared well in the period since 1981. High unemployment in Europe has reduced remittances and added the repatriated workers to the ranks of the domestic unemployed. Shipping receipts have declined by 726 million dollars between 1981 and 1984 because the merchant marine has been hard hit by the slump in the international shipping market. Foreign borrowing which artificially sustains the life-style of the Greeks has

257

increased the external debt from 4.5 billion dollars in 1978 to 12.4 billion dollars in 1984.[32] The most pressing need facing the Greek government in the near future is for foreign resources to finance its deficit and arrest the declining growth rate of the economy. The inflow of revenue from Western governments has increased with Greece's entry into the European Community, while U.S. military aid remains a necessity for a country whose defence budget between 1975 and 1982 averaged over 20 percent of total public budget (see Table 6.2).[33]

The effect of the Western recession amplified by PASOK's own errors, obliged the Papandreou government to impose austerity measures after a spree of pay rises and benefits. Official statements supportive of Soviet policy secured the passivity of communist-controlled trade unions, while every move to improve relations with the West was promptly followed by a commensurate official pronouncement against the United States and NATO. The signing of the Defense and Economic Cooperation Agreement (DECA) between Greece and the United States in the autumn of 1983, was preceded by mass mobilizations of PASOK and KKE followers demanding the expulsion of U.S. bases from Greek territory. The Soviets considered PASOK's reluctance to join the West's condemnations of Soviet involvement in Poland and the destruction of the Korean jumbo as friendly acts and were quick to adopt Papandreou's line on the extension of the U.S. bases' tenure as the beginning of a process for removal. The opposition of the KKE was predictably frustrated.

The KKE remains loyal to the main tenets of communism and must now grapple, on the one hand, with Moscow's unwillingness to antagonize PASOK for fear of a right wing alternative in power, and, on the other, with the growing unrest and disappointment of its own members with the socialist movement's failure to keep its promises. The prolonged austerity measures of the government and the gradual easing of control over activities of the private sector have outraged the KKE which has not, however, made a strong stand for fear of deviating from Soviet guidance to the contrary.

In his May 1985 interview with a New York Times correspondent, Papandreou predicted that Greece's relations with the United States and NATO would enter 'calmer seas' if his party won the elections. By pointing out the diminished interest of the public in foreign affairs and the focus of his campaign on

Table 6.2: Greek defence expenditure

	1976	1977	1978	1979	1980	1981	1982	1983	1984	1985	Estimated 1986
Def. Ex. as % annual real growth	7.5	5.3	1.8	−2.8	−8.2	22.8	−1.1	−7.9	17.1	1.0	−5.9
Def. Exp. as % of GDP	6.9	7.0	6.7	6.3	5.7	7.0	6.9	6.3	7.2	7.1	6.7
GDP per capita	3,051	3,107	3,273	3,352	3,377	3,336	3,310	3,303	3,378	3,404	3,354
Def. Exp. per capita	210	218	219	210	191	232	228	209	244	243	226
Def. Exp. as % of total budget	26.6	25.1	24.2	23.0	21.1	20.4	20.1	17.3	19.3	17.5	16.6
Military personnel (a)	186,341	186,543	186,437	186,484	186,222	187,558	187,658	176,610	197,082	201,274	205,261
Civilian personnel (b)	28,485	28,944	29,226	29,415	24,521	25,101	25,635	24,838	35,488	34,460	34,940

Note: Figures in US dollars; (a) Figures in thousand U.S. dollars.
Source: The Hellenic Institute for Defense and Foreign Policy Studies — Calculations based on NATO figures

domestic problems, he was in fact implying that his public would grant him a free hand in conducting his foreign policy. Greek membership in the European Community and NATO were not questioned, but the leader of PASOK implied that his objections to Western policies towards the Greek-Turkish dispute, which have limited Greek participation in NATO exercises, still stand. He welcomed foreign investment, denied allegations of further state control of the private sector and considered the increase of productivity his highest priority.[34] Two years after his victory Papandreou has remained true to his prediction of improving relations with the United States. Surprisingly no strong statements against President Reagan were uttered after the latter called for an embargo on the use of Greek airports following the hijacking by Shiite Muslims of an American passenger plane in the Athens airport. The Greek Prime Minister's new attitude is no doubt partly motivated by the country's economic problems which dictate friendlier relations with the West but also by Greek concern over Turkey. Official reactions to PASOK's anti-American rhetoric were amplified by the State Department in order to convince Congress that the seven to ten ratio of American military aid between Greece and Turkey, which has secured a tentative balance in the Aegean since 1978, should be abolished. In 1985–1986 there was concern that the Reagan administration would increase military aid to Turkey to 785 million dollars while keeping assistance to Greece unchanged at 502 million dollars. Furthermore, the Turkish package of aid has always been considered by Greeks as superior in quality since much of it is an outright grant, a large portion is a loan at below market rates, and only a small part a loan at market rates. Present aid to Greece is totally commercial rate credit[35] and will go towards the purchase of forty F-16s and forty Mirage 2000s ordered in 1985 at a projected cost of 2 billion dollars to match Turkey's order in 1983 of 160 F-16s.[36]

The U.S. administration's efforts to do away with the seven to ten ratio and simultaneously improve relations in NATO's Southern Flank, have stumbled on the chronic problem of Cyprus. Following the failure of the initiative by Javier Pérez de Cuéllar, in December 1984–January 1985, the United States backed another effort by the Secretary General of the United Nations to bring the two communities of the divided island to the negotiation table.

A new proposal submitted in April 1985 was accepted by the Greek Cypriots but rejected by the Turkish Cypriots. At the end of March 1986 de Cuéllar presented the two sides with his final 'draft framework agreement' which sanctioned the island's division into two zones. President Kyprianou and the political parties in parliament agreed that this draft was disproportionately favourable to the Turkish side and pointed out the outstanding problems involved:

1) Regardless of the course of negotiations the plan would be binding on both sides and thus would preclude a return to the present state of affairs in the case of a breakdown of discussions.
2) It would give the federal states the right to sign treaties with other states without the consent of the central authority.
3) The defence of Cyprus would be examined in conjunction with the Treaty of Guarantee and Alliance which provides for the retention of Turkish forces on the island. No assurance is given that foreign troops would leave Cyprus before the installation of a provisional government.
4) The Turkish Cypriot veto would extend to all matters.
5) International guarantees and the withdrawal of foreign troops, which are the most important issues for the Greek Cypriots, are referred to working parties and postponed for future discussion.
6) Turkey's unilateral right of intervention promises no peace of mind to the Greek Cypriots.

Kyprianou's counterproposals included most of the points stated above and it seems that a solution is now further away from sight that ever.[37]

Greece's attitude towards the United States since 1981 has been more defiant than that of other West European countries but reflects a wider trend that began in the 1970s. The post-oil crisis period was marked by Greek and West European efforts to profit from détente and to build bridges with Warsaw Pact and COMECON members. This policy was widely shared by Greek political parties. In 1982, following the banning of the Solidarity trade union and the imposition of martial law in Poland, the United States imposed economic sanctions on Poland and the Soviet Union, and called a reluctant European

Community to follow suit. Such measures at a time of recession were unpopular with some Europeans who were hoping to do business with communist neighbours and to maintain avenues of communication with the Soviet Union. Western Europe's military disadvantage and vulnerability in a nuclear exchange between the superpowers had dictated for some a far more cautious stance towards the eastern half of the continent than the Reagan administration was prepared to accept. The INF deployment controversy, the SDI programme and the U.S. President's decision to scrap the SALT II Treaty, accentuated European fears and underlined the differences of security perceptions among the allies.

PASOK called for a six-month postponement of the deployment of cruise and Pershing II missiles in Western Europe, although in December 1981, it approved of the NATO foreign ministers' declaration in support of President Reagan's 'zero-option' proposal. Papandreou's efforts to promote détente, and his participation in the group of six government leaders who met in Mexico in September 1986 to propose solutions to disarmament, reflect the internationalist aspect of his party's socialist vocation as well as his predilection for a 'third way' in the solution of international problems. Furthermore, PASOK appeals to a concerned domestic public by proposing the establishment of nuclear-free zones in the Balkans. The concept has, however, been undermined by a lack of unanimity among Balkan states.

Greece's relations with Warsaw Pact countries have been cordial since the mid-1970s after almost two decades of intermittent hostility. The rapprochement was initiated by Karamanlis who exchanged official visits with Rumania, Bulgaria and the Soviet Union and was pursued actively by Papandreou. Such efforts, however, failed to proceed further than certain commercial agreements and declarations of good intent. The Declaration of Friendship, Neighbourly Relations and Cooperation between Greece and Bulgaria on 11 September 1986, includes promises of mutual consultation in the event of a local or international crisis. It is no more than a statement of friendly intentions and not a formal treaty since it has not been ratified by the Greek parliament. The document is typical of a long line of intra-Balkan efforts at improved relations between states of the two blocs, and in the Greek view has no more impact on Greece's position in NATO than the Soviet-Turkish agreement of 1978 (The Principles of Good Neighbourly and Friendly Relations) had on Turkey's role in the Atlantic Alliance. High NATO officials have argued that the treaty is welcome to the extent that it may contribute to an easing of tension between the Warsaw Pact and NATO countries.

Relations with Yugoslavia, traditionally closer than with other communist states, have been strained by occasional disputes over the Macedonian issue. Greece's primary concern over Macedonia is to maintain the territorial status quo and to avoid entanglement in the chronic conflict between the (Yugoslav) Skopjean Republic and Bulgaria over alleged Macedonian slavophone minorities in the Balkans. Although PASOK has been less outspoken against Skopjean propaganda than New Democracy, both Papandreou and the President of the Republic have made public statements disavowing the existence of a Macedonian nation.

The Middle East is a source of divergent views between the Western allies. Since the years of the oil crisis, the Americans have been more active than the Europeans against Islamic fundamentalism and Arab nationalism and are more committed to the support of Israel. The Greek government after 1981 pursued a policy based on the principle that it should side with the underdog, but soon found itself caught in the crossfire of inter-Arab and inter-Muslim disputes. Ongoing strife between Muslims has obscured Greek attempts at mediation and confused PASOK's Middle Eastern priorities. Relations with the Palestinian leader Yasser Arafat were clearly affected by Syrian President Assad's May 1986 visit to Athens. In PASOK's calculations, Syria is the key to Middle Eastern affairs and could facilitate Greece's role as a bridge between the Arabs and the West. A symbol of this ambition was Mrs. Papandreou's visit to Damascus in July 1986 to mediate for the release of an American priest held captive in Lebanon.

The American action against Libya in mid-April 1986, caused a stir among many NATO members. Although supporting a broad campaign against international terrorism, some thought the United States had gone too far with an operation that might consolidate the forces of Islam against the West and escalate random violence in the region. Greece, Italy and Spain voiced their concern. PASOK was faced with the delicate task of appeasing its own Third World supporters without provoking American reaction. The forceful interruption by the police of a midnight press conference in Athens held by Libya's Under-secretary of State, indicated that the Greek government eventually decided not to allow the Libyans an unrestricted right to speak out in ways that might be provocative. A few months later a large section of the Libyan mission was quietly removed from Greece.

Papandreou's initial opposition to Greek accession to the European Community and his subsequent promise to hold a referendum to decide the issue, were quietly dropped after 1982, when about 800 million dollars a year from EC funds were directed to Greece's rural areas. After Karamanlis' unqualified attachment to the European ideal as the panacea of all Greek problems, a more pragmatic outlook has developed towards the EC which in many ways is more in keeping with the attitudes of other European members. In the Milan Summit conference of June 1985, Great Britain, Denmark and Greece joined forces to oppose a decision of the founding EC states to reduce the right of members to veto majority decisions. As it happened, West Germany, the strongest advocate of abolishing the veto, made use of precisely that prerogative in order to support its own interests in a controversy over cereals.[38] On other occasions, as in late 1986, when Britain sought to promote a strong anti-terrorist policy within the Community, the Greek government stuck carefully to the sidelines and refused to sign a document that might have compromised some of its Third World links.

The most significant action of Greece within the EC was the Greek Memorandum which set conditions to future enlargement demanding the implementation of the 'Integrated Mediterranean Programmes,' designed to finance and assist Mediterranean areas of the EC with structural impediments to development. In October 1985, Greece asked for a loan of 1.75 billion ECUs and the permission to impose trade restrictions in order to alleviate the effect of a deteriorating balance of payments. The 'Memorandum' constituted an attempt to secure a smoother transitional period by relaxing the pressure of competition on Greek industrial products. Although the Community partly satisfied Greek demands by retarding full abolition of protective import taxes and duties, it refused to accept measures that would encourage infant industries and industrial projects. At the Summit meeting of December 1985 in Luxembourg, Papandreou withdrew his reservation for the amendment of the Rome Treaty which would facilitate the decision-making process in the EC by limiting the use of the veto. The measure clearly favoured the larger members of the Community but Papandreou's cooperativeness was rewarded with the formal recognition of the 'convergence' between the economic structures of member countries — a principle which will tend to benefit the weaker states.[39]

Papandreou's foreign policies (particularly with regard to the West) stripped of their more flamboyant declaratory aspects, are not as different from those of many other West European states as is widely believed. Yet Papandreou insists on creating the impression of being a far greater maverick than his actions would seem to imply.[40] There is no doubt that his public, thrilled with the prospect of attracting European attention after years of docile agreement, has supported his 'proud' policy. Ultimately, however, these tactics are inspired by Papandreou's efforts to create a common ideological denominator which will bind his followers and indeed all Greeks together.[41]

Greece's economy which has always been sensitive to international turbulence has now become even more dependent on foreign capital.[42] PASOK's foreign policy is a balancing act between economic and security priorities, on the one hand, and domestic public opinion which has acquired a greater say in policy making than in the past, on the other. Having failed to manage both fronts simultaneously, the Greek Prime Minister appears to have turned his efforts to improving relations with the West.[43]

Given Papandreou's undiminished control over his own party mechanism, his flexibility in questions of political doctrine cannot be contested effectively from within the movement. Furthermore, his ability to perform volte-face in foreign policy issues owes much to the internal problems that plague the opposition. Leading members of New Democracy have been unable to direct their criticism effectively and have concentrated their attacks on PASOK's contradictions even when its policy resembles their own. PASOK's current tilt towards closer relations with the West has taken New Democracy by surprise. Since he cannot disagree with policies which are not dissimilar to his own, Mitsotakis has harangued the government and especially its leader for deceiving the people and has pointed out that PASOK — at least in foreign policy issues — is now following New Democracy's lead.

265

New Democracy's foreign policy tends towards more open support of the West and more outright criticism of communism both at home and abroad. It is generally presumed, however, that in power, New Democracy's policy would differ only in degree, not in kind, from that pursued by PASOK. The party would make Greece appear less of a maverick in the EC and NATO decisions that are based on consensus. It would still, however, be confronted with the same series of Greek-Turkish problems and might adopt similar tactics, such as refusing to participate in NATO's Aegean exercises, in order to register protest. Mitsotakis has declared his willingness to engage in bilateral discussions with Turkey, but when Foreign Minister he made little progress at solutions via discussions. It is probable that a New Democracy government would continue to seek to improve relations with the Soviet Union and Greece's Balkan neighbours, but would probably insist on better treatment of the Greek minority in Albania and be more censorious of Skopjean claims in Macedonia.

The simplicity of the basic rivalry between the two principal parties gives an indication of how few forces have an effect on the process of decision making in Greece. Until 1974, the decision-making process was shared by the government and other influential groups such as the crown and the military. After the fall of the dictatorship, the basic trends in policy making were drawn by Karamanlis and then by Papandreou. The former was assisted by senior diplomats, while Papandreou relies on personal advisors rather than members of the Foreign Ministry. Diplomats and ministers implement decisions dictated from above and exercise their discretion at the technical level rather than on the substantive aspect of most issues. Parliament serves as the forum in which the administration presents and defends its policy against the criticism of the opposition. Televised screenings of parliamentary debates on foreign policy attract the public's interest which is further stimulated by the press. The sensationalist newspapers thrive on foreign policy issues and capitalize on the various statements of the leading political leaders. With the exception of *Kathimerini, To Vima, Avgi* and, to some degree, *Eleftherotypia*, which tend to be the opinion makers of the more educated readers, most of the newspapers address the emotions of a wide public that retains a strong interest in foreign affairs.[44] Given this atmosphere, it is inevitable that the nature of political debate within Greece, and therefore its presentation to the outside world, often takes extreme forms.

THE ELEMENTS OF GREECE'S DEFENCE POLICY*

There is no significant difference between the process of Greek foreign and defence policy making. Although defence appears relatively constant, while foreign policy more evidently reflects the ideological inclinations of the party in power, the source is identical in both instances. As was the case under Karamanlis, Papandreou as Premier is the major initiator of defence policy, aided by his minister, the Chief of the Defence Staff and certain personal advisors.

Unlike the case in Portugal, the transfer of power in Greece from the military to politicians was immediate and total rather than gradual and piecemeal. Since 1974, the armed forces have promoted government policy without ever questioning civilian supremacy. To the degree that Papandreou's defence policy is still more conservative than his foreign policy, this can be explained by the fact that most Greek political leaders consider that security considerations do not lend themselves to experiments and statements that serve exclusively political goals, while in foreign policy a degree of flamboyancy is tactically useful. This general attitude is reflected in public opinion, which expresses itself more dramatically in foreign rather than in defence issues.

Superpower politics determine the margins within which middle and small powers exercise their foreign and defence policies. At a time of international détente, therefore, such states may drift into regional conflicts which often supersede the defence priorities of power blocs. Thus, Greece's differences with Turkey, rather than the considerations of the Atlantic Alliance of which it is part, have since 1974 become the focal point of Greece's security concerns. What was perceived as a threat from within the Alliance became the initial cause for Greek reconsideration of its relations with the United States and NATO; this problem constitutes the most serious constraint on Greek foreign and defence policy. As already mentioned,

*Note: The author wishes to acknowledge that this section of the chapter was written in collaboration with George Tsitsopoulos.

the Greek economy is heavily burdened by the cost of the arms race with Turkey, and Greek defence policy has been largely determined since 1974 by Turkish initiatives.

PASOK's move towards the West for solutions to Greece's most urgent problems, although not in keeping with its original non-aligned and Third World orientation, also reflects a wider consensus in the Greek public towards Western Europe. Most Greeks feel that their country is an integral part of Europe whether its political leadership recognizes the fact or disputes it. Greek culture and history testify to this contention but the ongoing debate on the composite elements of the national identity often rekindles old xenophobic reactions associated with the West rather than with the less familiar East. After 1974, anti-American and anti-NATO sentiments were generated by a widespread perception among the Greeks of a double injustice inflicted upon them through American support of the Greek military dictatorship and the mishandling of the Cyprus crisis. This basic perception has been shared by conservatives, liberals and left-wingers and formed a consensus on which Greece's defence policy was based.

Karamanlis' Defence Policy

Only one day after the second Turkish offensive in Cyprus, Greece under the leadership of Karamanlis withdrew from the integrated military structure of NATO headquarters in Izmir. This move constituted a protest against the Alliance's lack of active concern over the Turkish invasion. A further consequence was the termination of the 1973 home-porting agreement with the United States.

According to Greek government evaluations, Turkish diplomacy, by extending the dispute over the Aegean, skilfully diverted international attention from the maintenance of its forces on Cyprus to a 'composite of directly and indirectly related and mutually reinforcing issues.'[45] Another more serious consequence was that Turkish claims over a portion of the Aegean territorial waters, seabed and airspace, extending well to the west of the major east Aegean islands, convinced the Greek public that Turkey would attempt to realize these claims by using its powerful Aegean army.[46] A broad consensus was thus formed among Greeks of all political tendencies that the immediate security threat was no longer directed from Greece's northern neighbours but from Turkey.[47] The Karamanlis' government took immediate measures leading to the fortification and the militarization of the east Aegean islands, which (according to American military estimates of 1980[48)] involved between 20,000 and 30,000 men mainly concentrated on the most exposed islands of Lemnos, Lesvos, Chios and Samos.

Greece's withdrawal from NATO's military structure was more of a trial separation than a divorce as the country remained in the political arm of the Alliance. Karamanlis repeatedly rejected the non-alignment option and emphatically stated that Greece 'belongs to the West.' As early as August 1975, and after the rapid normalization of the internal situation, the Greek government expressed its willingness to reenter the military structure of NATO. This decision was based on the argument that reintegration would serve Greece's national interests.

Greece's reintegration attempts were vetoed by Turkey, which having raised a claim over the reallocation of the Athens FIR, was, in effect, also demanding a reallocation of the operational control zones of the Aegean airspace. According to the pre-1974 arrangements, NATO had ceded the military control over the Aegean airspace (Greek and international) as well as the Aegean Sea (Greek and international sea waters) to Greek command.[49] Furthermore, it must be stressed that any other arrangement would result in an unprecedented situation where defence responsibilities over Greek territories (east Aegean islands) would be placed under Turkish protection.[50] Negotiations of the country's reentry have proven long and arduous. Three reintegration plans by the Supreme Commander Allied Forces Europe (SACEUR) General Haig (1978–1979) and a fourth one by his successor General Rogers (1980) with settlement proposals on the reallocation issue were rejected. A solution was offered in October 1980, by another plan of General Rogers, with a provision for the reintegration problem allowing the reallocation question to be settled later within the Alliance.[51] According to this settlement package a new allied air force command (7th ATAF) — similar to that of Izmir (6th ATAF) — was to be established in Larissa. Both 7th ATAF and 6th ATAF would be subordinate to the NATO headquarters in Naples (AFSOUTH). The Greek government maintains that decisions on the delimitation of the operational control zones of the two headquarters, should precede the establishment of 7th

ATAF, and the whole issue still remains pending within the Alliance.

Papandreou's Defence Policy

While in opposition (1974–1981), Andreas Papandreou declared that once in power his government would withdraw Greece from NATO and remove the U.S. bases from Greek soil. However, his defence policy since his October 1981 electoral victory has not deviated substantially from that of his predecessors. Nonetheless, although the country maintained its membership in both the military and the political structures of NATO, its relations with the Alliance have been strained. Shortly after taking office, Papandreou asked NATO to guarantee Greece's borders 'from every threat, from whatever side it emanates,' implying that a guarantee from eastern threats was potentially desired. His administration partly froze the Rogers' agreement (December 1981) but did not withdraw from the military structure of the Alliance. Greece has repeatedly cancelled its participation in Aegean NATO exercises, refusing to accept the exclusion of the Lemnos airfield from NATO scenarios. Lemnos is an island situated at the mouth of the Turkish Straits and therefore of vital strategic significance. According to a North Atlantic Assembly sub-committee on the Southern Flank, Lemnos 'in an East-West context could be crucial for the security of the Aegean and the entire Mediterranean because of its dominant position vis-à-vis the Dardanelles.'[52] In his effort to overcome the Lemnos deadlock Papandreou attempted another approach by the end of 1984. Greece officially notified the presence of its forces on the island in the Defence Planning Questionnaire (DPQ) and asked that they be placed under NATO command but failed to override Turkey's veto.[53]

Papandreou's government completed the negotiations initiated by Karamanlis in 1975 on the future of the U.S. installations in Greece. In September 1983 a DECA was signed which updated and replaced the 1953 U.S.-Greek Defense Agreement and other bilateral security arrangements.[54] The new agreement limited some of the privileges U.S. forces had enjoyed in Greece over the previous thirty years. Greek and American officials have disagreed over the interpretation of its final article which

270

states that the agreement expires on 30 December 1988. Papan-dreou emphasized for some time that the DECA was 'an agree-ment for the removal of the U.S. bases,' while American officials maintained that it was not clear from the treaty text whether after five years the treaty is terminated or terminable. U.S. Secretary of Defense Caspar Weinberger visited Athens in April 1984 hoping to gain some clarification from Papandreou on the expiration date of the base agreement, but apparently left without assurances. In the spring of 1986, U.S. Secretary of State George Shultz came to Athens in an attempt to build a climate of improved relations between the two countries. Shultz did not put pressure on the Greek government for an immediate answer on the future of the bases and the Greek Premier's state-ments implied that the issue was still pending. On 10 November 1986 a new Defense and Industrial Cooperation Agreement (DICA) was signed between Greece and the United States that would last for five years but be subject to renewal. The DICA is indirectly linked to the DECA and its signature was widely interpreted as an indication that a new DECA would also be signed.

Negotiations of this kind between the United States and Greece are necessarily complex because of the important politi-cal and symbolic role played by U.S. military aid. Military assistance is a central element of U.S.-Greek relations, particu-larly since the maintenance of a seven to ten ratio in military aid between Greece and Turkey is considered by Athens as proof of American resolve to maintain a regional balance of power between both countries. Article 8 of the 1983 DECA provides that aid and regional balance be clearly linked with the overall goals of the agreement.[55] Washington remains flexible on the question, pointing out that the ratio has never been legislated but is merely a Congressional tradition since 1980.[56] For the Greeks, this arrangement safeguards the balance of forces between the two allies, and therefore serves as a stabilizing factor in NATO's Southern Flank.

An Assessment of the New Defence Doctrine

The notion that the primary threat to Greek security does not come from NATO's main adversary, has led to a gradual recon-sideration of Greek defence policy, especially in the first years

271

after the 1974 crisis. This change has been formalized by the 'New Defence Doctrine' publicized by the Greek government in January 1985. Greece, like Turkey, has sought to institutional-ize changes that have already taken place in its defensive stance. These changes reflect a national-regional perspective on defence rather than considerations directly related to the frame-work.[57]

Today, eleven years after the reorientation in Greek defence policy, Greek forces are organized and deployed roughly as follows:

a) *Air force:* Besides the major airfields on the mainland (Thessaloniki, Larissa, Anchialos/Volos, Tanagra, Araxos, Andravida) and on Crete (Souda, Heraklion), new ones were constructed and became operational in the 1970s and 1980s located on a north-south line crossing the central Aegean (Chryssoupolis/Kavala, Skyros, Thera and Karpathos).

b) *Navy:* The arrangement of forces has remained unchanged. The modernization of the fleet through acquisition of modern submarines as well as small ships and patrol boats has improved the operational capabilities and flexibility of the Greek fleet vis-à-vis the larger units of the Soviet Black Sea Fleet.

c) *Army:* Forces, since 1974, have been concentrated mainly in Thrace-Macedonia and on the Aegean islands.

The inherent flexibility of air and naval forces minimizes the necessity of a special peacetime deployment. Greece's limited land border with Turkey to the east and the much more exten-sive one with its neighbours to the north continue to be the main determinants of the deployment and defensive doctrines of the Greek army.

In the annual Greek report to NATO on its allocation of forces in response to the DPQ, there is no evidence of a signifi-cant movement of troops away from Greece's northern borders. This assertion has been confirmed by Admiral Lee Baggett Jr. (CINSOUTH and then SACLANT) in an interview with the Turkish daily *Cumhurriyet* on 17 June 1985. Greece's borders of 1000 kilometres with Albania, Yugoslavia and Bulgaria are being covered by the First Army Corps for Albania, the Second and half of the Third for Yugoslavia, the other half of the Third with the entire Fourth for Bulgaria. The Third and Fourth Corps have the highest level of manning in peacetime and flexible mobilization plans in case of emergency. The most likely routes of attack against Greece would naturally follow the Vardar-Axios river through Yugoslavia and the Nestos and Evros rivers from Bulgaria and therefore Greek armed forces are concentrated in these regions.

The lack of strategic depth in northern Greece has been a central problem for NATO strategy against a Warsaw Pact threat. The distance between the Bulgarian borders and the Aegean coastline is very short — in Thrace it ranges from twenty-six to sixty-five kilometres. The fortification of the western and eastern Aegean islands provides some strategic depth to a geographically weak northern defence. In the same *Cumhurriyet* interview cited above, CINSOUTH Chief of Staff General Blaint pointed out the value of the Greek islands in a 'defence in depth' against a Warsaw Pact attack. His argument could be summarized as follows:

a) The Lemnos airfield could provide full air support to the land operations in Thrace, and that island along with Samothrace and Lesvos form the first of a succession of choke points to hinder the passage of the Soviet fleet in the area. If the Eskadra, circulating in the Aegean or eastern Mediterranean, attempted to aid Warsaw Pact forces in their Thracian land operations, these islands could form the last choke point which would deny the Soviets access to their destination.

b) The islands of Chios, Samos and Ikaria together with the Cyclades and Euboea form a compact complex in the middle of the Aegean archipelago and the most dense of successive choke points.

c) Further to the south, the Dodecanese islands are situated along the passage to the southeast while Karpathos and Crete control the southern route to North Africa.

The militarization of the islands would make it easier to resist, in the case of war, a Soviet attempt to occupy and transform them into naval bases. Karpathos, in particular, might be a likely objective of Soviet strategy.

While the Greek navy continues to operate largely as it did before 1974, the air force's role, given the fortification of the

273

Aegean islands, has been considerably widened. The new airfields on the various islands (including Lemnos) are in a circular arrangement offering Greek pilots full control over the Aegean Sea. The Skyros airfield is in an especially dominant position, fully controlling the central and northern Aegean. Furthermore, in the case of an East-West confrontation, the success of Soviet vessels operating in the Mediterranean largely depends on the support received by Backfires taking off from Crimean airfields. A partial defence against their effectiveness might be the network of Greek radars located on various strategically located Aegean islands.

The 3,000 islands of the Aegean archipelago canalize the maritime traffic in lanes going through at least three main island complexes. Greek forces operating from these islands can impede the passage of any ship through the Aegean archipelago. Thus, the successive choke points form a narrow corridor for the Soviet fleet that extends from the Bosporus and ends at the Rhodes-Karpathos-Crete-Kithira-Peloponnese line, which can block not only the exit of Soviet vessels from the Black Sea but also their effort either to return from the Mediterranean to their bases or to blockade Turkish ports and thus disrupt the lines of communication between Turkey and the West.[58] General Rogers was well aware of the strategic value of such a corridor when he stated to the Turkish journalist Ali Birand, that 'it is important not only to keep the Aegean vis-à-vis the Soviet forces which pass through the Straits, but also to impede the Soviet forces of the Mediterranean to enter the Aegean in order to regain the Black Sea going through the Straits. I am interested in all measures taken to deter these two possibilities.'[59]

The Causes for Reconsideration and Present Policy

The Cyprus crisis was the catalyst for all changes in Greek foreign and defence policy after July 1974. A threat from the Warsaw Pact was no longer perceived as the primary security consideration and disillusionment with the United States and NATO contributed to a reconsideration of Greece's defence orientation.

The Greek government felt that Ankara rapidly escalated the 1974 crisis by challenging the status quo in the Aegean and, thus, turning the original dispute into a complex, multifaceted problem. The following issues between Greece and Turkey have been added to the Cyprus problem.[60]

a) *The width of the territorial sea:* the Third United Nations Conference on the Law of the Sea (UNCLOS III) almost unanimously accepted the option of the twelve-mile territorial limit. Ankara had already in 1964, long before the convocation of this conference, extended the sea limits to twelve miles along its southeastern Mediterranean and Black Sea coastline. Turkey opposes Greece's right also to extend the territorial waters around its mainland and the islands from the present six to twelve miles and Turkish officials have declared that such a move would be regarded as a *casus belli* because it would effectively block Turkey's passage to and from the Straits.[61] The Greek side has stressed that the sole purpose of exercising this right stems from economic considerations, notably the desire to exploit fishing resources.[62] In the event of Greece extending its territorial waters, it would seek to ensure that other countries would retain an unobstructed right of traffic through the waters. For the foreseeable future, an extension of Greek territorial waters appears to be unlikely, yet Greece is not prepared to relinquish its right to exercise this option.

b) *The delimitation of the Aegean continental shelf:* the Turkish position is that much of the Aegean continental shelf is a geological prolongation of the Anatolian mainland and hence its rights extend west of the major Greek islands. Greece, stressing the principle that islands have a continental shelf — as indicated in the Geneva Convention of 1958 — maintains that Turkish rights to exploit the Aegean seabed reach the median line between the east Aegean islands and the Anatolian peninsula. Furthermore, the fact that Turkey can exploit the vast lands of the Anatolian peninsula and the extended seabed of the southeastern Mediterranean and Black Sea makes the Turkish claim to explore the limited space between the Greek east Aegean islands appear extravagant to Athens.[63]

c) *Control of airspace:* International Civil Aviation Organization (ICAO) regulations of 1952 and 1958 designated the Athens Flight Information Region (FIR) to coincide with the sea and air boundaries separating Greece from Turkey. This resulted in Greek control of air traffic over most of the Aegean Sea. Although Turkey had worked with this arrangement for over twenty years, on the day of the Cyprus invasion, it unilaterally extended the Istanbul and Ankara FIRs to the middle of the Aegean (NOTAM 714). Greece protested and closed all corridors for international commercial flights over the Aegean (NOTAM 1157). The Aegean airspace was reopened in 1980 when Turkey and subsequently Greece withdrew the NOTAMs.

d) *Fortification of the east Aegean islands:* Turkey, by invoking the relevant provisions of the Lausanne Treaty and Convention (1923) as well as the Paris Treaty (1947), protests against the fortification and militarization of the east Aegean islands. Greece has argued[64] that Lemnos and Samothrace were relieved of their demilitarized status when Turkey was able to revise the regime governing the entire Straits region through the Montreux Convention of 1936.[65] The islands of Chios, Lesvos and Samos have been fortified by Greece in response to Turkish threats and especially after the establishment of the Turkish Fourth Army (also known as the Aegean Army) in 1975 based in Izmir. According to American estimates,[66] the Fourth Army has a peacetime force of 35,000 combat personnel, and is equipped with landing craft and an amphibious capability which is the second largest among NATO members.[67] The Aegean Army has been placed outside the command structure of NATO and because of its amphibious capacities Greece believes that it has an aggressive rather than defensive mission.

e) *Exercises and arms procurements:* Greek exercises can be divided into the following categories:

1) Technical exercises take place without scenarios and are centred on methods and tactics of electronic warfare which include NATO member countries. An example is the Niriis exercise of 10–17 November 1986 in the Aegean between Greece, Italy and France. From time to time so-called PASSEX exercises are conducted between Greece and NATO member fleets.

2) National joint exercises are conducted five times a year. Three include live manoeuvres and two are Command Post

Exercises (CPX) for the testing of operational contingency plans for possible threats to Greek security from any direction.

3) NATO joint exercises which are based on NATO plans approved by its Military Committee have recently been largely boycotted by Greece as part of the government's protest over unresolved aspects of the Aegean dispute. Nevertheless, in May 1986, Greek naval units took part in a NATO-wide exercise under the code name Sea Supply-Med Supply, which concentrated on capacities to protect merchant shipping.

Greek arms procurements have recently been relatively modest and correspond to long-established priorities. An order for forty Mirage 2000 and between forty and sixty fighters from the United States was concluded after considerable delays. Ten Corsair A-7 aircraft will be converted and modernized by the Hellenic aerospace industry. The latter will also develop a remote pilotless vehicle (RPV) in collaboration with a U.S. firm. A number of air-to-air missiles are on order and the navy plans to put six frigates under joint construction soon. The army is purchasing second-hand M-48 1A tanks which will be upgraded on receipt.

Continuity and Limits

Greek defence policy from Karamanlis to Papandreou appears continuous and coherent even though their foreign policies differed. Although Karamanlis initiated an important opening towards the communist Balkan states and the Soviet Union, his preference was unmistakably for the West. His dogged effort to bring Greece into the European Community was based on the premise that entry would be useful for Greek economic modernization but would also serve Greek national security ends. Papandreou took an entirely new tack in Greek foreign policy by adopting, at least in theory, the arguments of the non-aligned, professing solidarity with Third World demands and castigating the superpowers for threatening the world with extinction. His statements against U.S. policy often provoked the wrath of the American administration and quickly established his reputation as the maverick of the Western world.

277

Yet, although his declaratory policy was radical, he in fact shirked from decisions that would compromise Greek security. Thus, he did not withdraw from NATO and in 1983 he renewed the tenure of American bases in Greece. On major security issues, the Socialist Prime Minister appears to agree with his conservative predecessors on the following lines of argument. First, by remaining in NATO, Greece can better mobilize Western support on the key Aegean issues. Second, given the unanimity principle, Greece can prevent the adoption of collective NATO decisions that would prejudice command and control arrangements in the Aegean and undermine the Greek position there.[68] Third, relations with Turkey must be kept below the level of armed confrontation. Both countries have abstained from action that could precipitate an armed clash. Greece has not extended its territorial waters to twelve miles while Turkey, for the time being, has not pursued the question of the continental shelf (both reserve their rights on the above issues).

Unlike Papandreou, Karamanlis conducted bilateral discussions with Turkish officials but with no success. In 1980, Karamanlis expressed his frustration with the continuing impasse over Cyprus, the Aegean and NATO, to a Senate delegation.[69] His failure to make headway despite his conciliatory intent created a precedent which Papandreou invoked to counter criticism of his own unwillingness to negotiate and contributed to PASOK's meteoric rise to power. It appears that Papandreou's initial invective against NATO reflected not only the predictable position of the left but also the frustration of the right.

Both PASOK and New Democracy would summarize Greece's strategic importance for the West in the following terms: Greece shares a common border with Albania, Yugoslavia and Bulgaria; it provides an avenue of support for the Yugoslavs; it guards the approaches to the Adriatic Sea; it lends strategic depth in the Aegean; it controls the sea lanes in the eastern Mediterranean and off northeastern Africa through the island of Crete; and, finally, along with Turkey, Greece helps to control an area that is of vital importance to the West.

New Democracy is more willing to recognize the limits of Greece's independent security stance but PASOK has also come to terms with harsh realities. During 1986 the Greek government seemed to accept the fact that a small state cannot depend only on principles of justice and its own resolution to fight but must also be able to mobilize support from its allies.[70]

CONCLUSIONS AND PROSPECTS

As has been already noted, the intermittent process of rebuilding democracy in Greece after the Civil War appears to have established a steady course since 1974. The most significant factor in this process was the peaceful settlement of outstanding issues between right and left which also facilitated Greece's belated transition into the era of détente. While in power New Democracy, under Karamanlis, shifted from total identification with the West to a more independent and pragmatic relationship which was in keeping with the practice of most European democracies. The rise of PASOK as the inevitable alternative and the orderly change of political guard in 1981 confirmed the end of the Civil War heritage, it also signified the reorientation of Greek foreign policy into new areas.

The political preoccupations of the two figures who have most dominated Greek politics since 1974 have been fuelled by what may appear as anachronistic hopes and fears. The insecurity and polarization of the postwar period of reconstruction and the Cold War are things of the past, but both Karamanlis and Papandreou each took his own lesson from this period in orienting his foreign policy and giving it a special stamp. The former's single-minded dedication to Greece's entry into the EC and the latter's unyielding opposition to American influence, were motivated by past realities even if both, in turn, have naturally profoundly affected current events and attitudes.

Six years of PASOK in power have precipitated certain social and economic changes in Greece. The public sector has predictably become more cumbersome than before and the private sector has shrunk from new investments for lack of confidence in a government which (in spite of current retractions) widely publicized its hostility against big business. Modernization has recently followed the path of legal reform. Civil marriages were allowed, divorces simplified and the institution of the dowry abolished. The spirit of defiance in foreign policy may have purged the Greeks from feelings of past subservience but it ran out of steam as the economy increasingly required foreign loans to fill the financial gaps caused by overconsumption and low

279

productivity. The antagonism between Papandreou and Mitsotakis over which party represents best the principles of democracy is losing its relevance to the average citizen who is mainly preoccupied with his dwindling income and the state's failure to deliver higher rates of growth and employment. It was precisely public discontent with the state of the economy which resulted in New Democracy's success in the October 1986 municipal elections. Benefitting from a significant abstention of KKE voters, New Democracy candidates became mayors of Athens, Piraeus and Thessaloniki, positions previously held by PASOK.

An important element in the post-1974 developments is that Greece's European vocation was reinforced by the upgrading of its democratic institutions and its full membership in the European Community. PASOK's Third World affiliations notwithstanding, Greece is now more entrenched in the Western camp than before 1974. Mutual interest rather than doctrine has also proved a convincing basis of its relationship with the United States.[71]

PASOK's preoccupation with activities that promote peace and international détente reflects the deep-seated fear among the Greek left of a Cold War resurgence.[72] PASOK also realizes that the polarization of the international climate could easily drive its supporters to the extreme ends of the political spectrum. Papandreou's pleas for an all-out East-West détente and a denuclearized zone in the Balkans have provoked criticism ranging from irritation to outrage from the conservative camp. But the two large parties in parliament tend to agree on the major issues affecting Greek security:

a) Withdrawal of the Turkish forces from Cyprus would facilitate a rapprochement between Athens and Ankara.
b) Settlement of the allocation of operational control responsibilities in the Aegean must precede the establishment of the 7th ATAF allied headquarters in Larissa.
c) Inclusion of Lemnos in NATO's exercises will lead to Greece's renewed participation in Aegean exercises.
d) Maintenance of the seven to ten aid ratio and of the regional balance will contribute to good relations with the United States and to the prospects for a lasting peace in the region.
e) A settlement of the disputes between Greece and Turkey would lessen the burden of arms purchases on the two

economies and would diminish the dependence of both states on foreign creditors. Despite the obvious incentives, the prospects of a solution are still remote as the crisis of 27 March 1987 proved only too clearly.[73]

Although in the past the EC remained aloof from the Greek-Turkish conflict, Turkey's interest in reviving its special relationship with the Community and filing a formal application for membership may increase European willingness to mediate between the two states. Greece would stand to gain if Turkey became officially part of an organization which requires friendly relations among its members, but Turkish membership in the Community is still very much a future prospect and the EC cannot therefore be expected to play an important role in mediating Greek-Turkish differences.

If international détente prevails and there is no successful diplomatic solution of Greek-Turkish problems, Greece will feel compelled to maintain its present state of vigilance while performing its part in the NATO alliance as best as it can. If tension in East-West relations dramatically increases, the United States and other NATO allies would naturally expect Greece to play its part in collective defence. Any increase in Greek commitments would require wide support at home. Such support, however, would only exist once Greek-Turkish tensions in the Aegean had been lowered. Currently, the burden for improving relations and therefore strengthening regional security in the Western interest remains with the two principals in the dispute. For the foreseeable future Greek security policy will be driven by a cold assessment of the nature of the threats from the north and the east and foreign policy will be inspired by a broad view of what Greece can contribute to the improvement of both East-West and North-South relations.

NOTES

1. John Petropulos, *Politics and Statecraft in the Kingdom of Greece 1833-43* (Princeton: Princeton University Press, 1968).

2. Thanos Veremis, *Greek Security Considerations — An Historical Perspective* (Athens: Papazissis Publishers, 1980), 15-21. (Hereafter cited as: *Greek Security Considerations*).

3. Ibid., 21-35.

4. Theodore Couloumbis, *The United States, Greece and Turkey:*

The Troubled Triangle (New York: Praeger, 1983), 13-14. (Hereafter cited as: *The United States, Greece and Turkey*).

5. T. Couloumbis, J. Petropulos and H.J. Psomiades, *Foreign Interference in Greek Politics* (New York: Pella, 1976), 117.

6. John Iatrides, 'American Attitudes toward the Political System of Postwar Greece,' in *Greek American Relations*, ed. T. Coulumbis and John Iatrides (New York: Pella, 1980), 60-64.

7. A.A. Fatouros, 'Building Formal Structures of Penetration: the United States in Greece, 1947-1948,' in *Greece in the 1940s: a Nation in Crisis*, ed. John Iatrides (London: University Press of New England, 1981), 252-253. (Hereafter cited as: *Greece in the 1940s*).

8. Iatrides, in *Greek-American Relations*, 65.

9. Fatouros, in *Greece in the 1940s*, ed. Iatrides, 254.

10. T. Couloumbis, 'The Greek Junta Phenomenon,' *Polity*, VI, no. 3 (Spring 1974): 353.

11. Couloumbis, *The United States, Greece and Turkey*, 13-16.

12. E. Kofos, *Nationalism and Communism in Macedonia* (Thessaloniki: Institute for Balkan Studies, 1964), 188.

13. T. Veremis, *Greek Security: Issues and Politics*, Adelphi Paper, no. 179 (London: The International Institute for Strategic Studies, 1982), 6-9.

14. C.M. Woodhouse, *Something Ventured* (London: Granada, 1982), 133.

15. With the exception of PASOK; other parties disavowed the evocation of past divisive experiences as being in any way relevant to Greek problems of today.

16. Constantine Tsoucalas, 'The Ideological Impact of the Civil War,' in *Greece in the 1940s*, ed. Iatrides, 319.

17. Ibid., 328.

18. Kostas Vergopoulos, 'The Emergence of the New Bourgeoisie, 1944-52,' in *Greece in the 1940s*, 313.

19. Tsoucalas, in *Greece in the 1940s*, 329, 331.

20. Keith Legg, *Politics in Modern Greece* (Stanford: Stanford University Press, 1969), 191-92.

21. For a concise account of the Greek military dictatorship see, Richard Clogg, *A Short History of Modern Greece* (Cambridge: Cambridge University Press, 1979), 185-200.

22. For details on the elections of 1974 and 1977 see the collective volume on Greek elections edited by Howard Penniman, *Greece at the Polls: The National Elections of 1974 and 1977* (Washington, DC: The American Enterprise Institute, 1981).

23. For more details on the rise of PASOK see, Christos Lyrintzis, 'Political Parties in Post-Junta Greece: A Case of 'Bureaucratic Clientelism'?,' *West European Politics*, 7, no. 2 (April 1984): 109-114.

24. George Mavrogordatos, *Rise of the Green Sun, the Greek Elections of 1981* (Athens, 1983), 3.

25. Couloumbis, 'The Greek Junta Phenomenon': 353-354.

26. Yannis Roubatis, 'The United States and the Operational Responsibilities of the Greek Armed Forces, 1047-1987,' *Journal of the Hellenic Diaspora*, VI, no. 1 (Spring 1979): 46.

27. Ibid., 47.

28. Maurice Goldbloom, 'United States Policy in Post-War Greece,' in *Greece under Military Rule,* ed. R. Clogg and G. Yannopoulos (London: Secker and Warburg, 1972), 220-257.

29. Van Coufoudakis, 'Greek-Turkish Relations, 1973-1983,' *International Security,* 9, no. 4 (Spring 1985): 212.

30. The excerpt and some of the evaluations of the election were communicated to the author by Mr. Costas Carras.

31. Yannis Marinos, 'The Prime Minister Must Teach the Public and Some of His Own People a Few Lessons in Political Economy,' *Oikonomikos Tachydromos,* 13 June 1985.

32. Robert MacDonald, 'Greece after PASOK's Victory,' *The World Today,* 41, no. 7 (July 1985): 134-135. For a systematic treatment of the Greek trade union movement see Beate Kohler, *Political Forces in Spain, Greece and Portugal* (London: Butterworth, 1982), 136-142.

33. See also Statistical Yearbook of Greece, volumes 1975-1982 (Athens: Greek Bureau of Statistics).

34. Henry Kamm, 'Papandreou Foresees "Calmer Seas" if he Wins,' *International Herald Tribune,* 29 May 1985.

35. Edouardo Lachica, 'U.S. Troubles with Greece Prompt Closer Turkish Ties,' *The Wall Street Journal,* 27 February 1985. See also James Brown, 'The South-Eastern Flank: Political Dilemmas and Strategic Considerations,' in *Defence Yearbook* (London: Royal United Services Institute/Brassey's, 1985), 6.

36. MacDonald, 'Greece after PASOK's Victory': 135.

37. 'Still in the Tunnel?' *Athena* (May 1986): 122-123.

38. André Fontaine, 'Europe without Faith' (in Greek), *To Vima,* 14 July 1985.

39. T. Veremis and Tassos Yannitsis, 'Herorientatie in Griekenland: Grenzen vat het Economisch Draagvlak,' *Internationale Spectator* (May 1986): 338-339.

40. ' ... in broad economic and military terms, Greece in 1984, is even more entrenched in the Western camp than she was in 1974,' Constantine Melakopides, 'Greece: from Compliance to Self-Assertion,' in *Semialignment and Western Security,* ed. Nils Orvik (London: Croom Helm, 1986), 97.

41. For a critical account of PASOK's policy and tactics see, Roy Macridis, *Greek Politics at a Crossroad* (Stanford: Hoover Institution Press, 1984).

42. Professor Nancy Bermeo of Princeton University has offered the author valuable insight on the subject of dependent economies.

43. John Loulis, 'Papandreou's Foreign Policy,' *Foreign Affairs,* 63, no. 2 (Winter 1984-85): 383.

44. T. Couloumbis, 'The Structure of Greek Foreign Policy,' in *Greece in the 1980s,* ed. R. Clogg (London: Macmillan, 1983), 95-122.

45. Van Coufoudakis, 'Greco-Turkish relations and the Greek Socialists: Ideology, Nationalism and Pragmatism,' *Journal of Modern Greek Studies,* I, no. 2 (October 1983): 375.

46. Statements by Turkish officials consolidated and confirmed this

fear. 'The defence of the Aegean Islands should be jointly undertaken by Greece and Turkey as allies within Nato' said the Turkish Prime Minister on 30.7.1974, while his Foreign Minister stated half a year later (4.4.75): 'neither the government nor Turkish public opinion can accept that the Aegean belongs exclusively to Greece. Half the Aegean belongs to Turkey and the other half belongs to Greece. This has always been the official view.'

47. This threat perception is still vivid in Greece. An opinion poll taken in 1984 showed that 91 percent of the persons asked acknowledged that the main threat comes from Turkey's side. Ton Frinking, *Interim Report of the Sub-Committee on the Southern Region* (Brussels: North Atlantic Assembly, October 1985), 9.

48. U.S. Senate, *Turkey, Greece and NATO: The Strained Alliance*, A Staff Report to the Committee on Foreign Relations, 96th Congress, 2nd Session (Washington DC, March 1980), 57. It should be also noted that few elementary defensive precautions had been already adopted after the 1964 Cyprus crisis and the Turkish threats formulated during that year (see Ronald Meinardus, 'Griechenlands gestörtes Verhältnis zur NATO,' *Europa Archiv* (4/1982): 43-44.

49. The sea command was ceded to Greece in 1957 and the air command in 1964. *To VIMA*, 10 September 1978.

50. A division of the operational control of the Aegean would make the coordination in times of war in such a restricted area difficult to achieve without violating national airspace or sea waters. This would be against a basic Military Committee principle (36/2) which provides that 'countries retain their sovereignty and are, therefore, ultimately responsible for the defense and security of their own territories and space.'

51. Meinardus, 'Griechenlands gestörtes Verhältnis zur NATO': 108-111.

52. Ton Frinking, *Draft Interim Report of the Sub-Committee on the Southern Region* (Brussels: North Atlantic Assembly, November 1984), 24.

53. Although the Lemnos forces were not included in the DPQ, its airfield and radar are contained in the contingency plans of the SACEUR.

54. The United States and Turkey signed a Defense and Economic Cooperation Agreement on 29 March 1980 and renewed this agreement in December 1986.

55. See Athens press of September and October 1983.

56. Ellen Laipson, *The Seven-Ten Ratio in Military Aid to Greece and Turkey: A Congressional Tradition*, Congressional Research Service (CRS) Report (Washington DC: 15 June 1983 and revised 10 April 1985), 1-11.

57. Bulent Ecevit, 'Turkey's Security Policies,' in *Greece and Turkey (Adversity in Alliance)*, ed. Jonathan Alford, Adelphi Library, 12 (London: IISS, 1984), 136-141; and Michel M. Boll, 'Turkey's New National Security Concept: What it means for NATO,' *Orbis* (Fall 1979): 609-631.

58. Lt. Gen. (ret.) N. Lazarides, *Indirect Strategy in the East Mediterranean and the Role of Greece* (in Greek), Special Study no. 1

(Athens: The Hellenic Institute for Defense and Foreign Policy Studies, 1986), 15-18. See also Tim Lister and Bruce George, 'Troubles on NATO's Southern Flank,' *Jane's Defence Weekly*, 5, no. 16 (26 April 1986): 750. 'Today 3,000 Greek islands in the Aegean extend the choke-point of the Turkish Straits several hundred kilometres southwest to the islands of Crete, Karpathos, and Rhodes.'

59. Printed in *Milliyet* and reprinted in *To VIMA*, 19 July 1984.

60. For more details on the legal as well as the security aspects of the Greek-Turkish dispute over the Aegean, see Andrew Wilson, *The Aegean Dispute*, Adelphi Paper, no. 155 (London: IISS, 1979/80), 4-29; Veremis, *Greek Security: Issues and Politics*, 9-15, and Duygu Bazouglu Sezer, *Turkey's Security Policies*, Adelphi Paper, no. 164 (London: IISS, 1981), 16-17.

61. See statements made by the Turkish Prime Minister S. Demirel to *Hurrieyet*, 15 April 1975; and *Le Monde*, 20 May 1975. Also Sezer, *Turkey's Security Policies*, 17.

62. See Christos Z. Sazanides, *The Greek-Turkish Relations in the Five Years of 1973-1978* (in Greek) (Thessaloniki, 1979), 184-190.

63. Ibid., 129-131.

64. Yannis G. Valinakis, 'La Grèce et L'Alliance Atlantique,' to be published in *Arès*, 1986, 5-9. See also, C.P. Economides, 'La prétendue obligation de démilitarisation de l'île de Lemnos,' *Revue Hellénique de Droit International* (1981): 7 ff. and by the same author, 'Nouveaux éléments concernant l'île de Lemnos: un problème totalement artificiel,' *Revue Hellénique de Droit International* (1984): 4-10.

65. For the legal right of Greece to fortify her other east Aegean islands, see Philip Drakidis, 'Le statut de démilitarisation de certaines îles grecques,' *Défense Nationale* (1984): 74-82; and by the same author, 'La démilitarisation de Dodécanése,' *Défense Nationale* (April 1983): 124-136. Ronald Meinardus, 'Der greichisch-turkische Konflikt über den Militärischen status der ostägäischen Inseln,' *Europa-Archiv* (2/1985): 41-46.

66. U.S. Senate *Turkey, Greece and NATO*, 57; and U.S. Senate, *Perspectives on NATO's Southern Flank*, a Report to the Committee on Foreign Relations, 96th Congress, 2nd session, (Washington DC, 1980), 13.

67. Veremis, *Greek Security Considerations*, 61.

68. See Prime Minister George Rallis' statements at the time of Greece's reintegration: 'We have retained the option of using our veto to block efforts at modification of the pre-1974 status quo that may prove damaging to Greek interests,' in *Kathimerini* (13-14 December 1981).

69. U.S. Senate *Perspectives on NATO's Southern Flank*, 22.

70. Hélène da Costa, 'La Diplomatie Grecque: Endiguer la Turquie,' *Défense Nationale* (August-September 1986): 103-118.

71. Bruce Kuniholm, 'Rhetoric and Reality in the Aegean: U.S. Policy Options Towards Greece and Turkey,' *SAIS Review*, 6, no. 1 (Winter/Spring 1986): 149.

72. Christos Rozakis, 'La Politique étrangère Grecque 1974-85: Modernisation et rôle international d'un petit état,' *Les Temps*

Modernes, no. 473 (December 1985), 878-879.

73. On 27 March 1987, Greece and Turkey came as close to an armed confrontation as they have been for years. The cause of the crisis was Turkey's decision to send a research vessel escorted by warships to explore for oil in the disputed continental shelf around Lesbos, Lemnos and Samothrace. *New York Times,* 28 March 1987. This author had been to Turkey and Greece a few days before and discovered that the Turks were misreading Papandreou's threat to nationalize the North Aegean Petroleum Corporation (NAPC) consortium of oil companies operating in Greek waters. As the former leader of the New Democracy Party, Evangelos Averoff, pointed out to this author, Papandreou was clearly trying to prevent NAPC from drilling in a disputed area of the north Aegean Sea in order to avoid trouble with Turkey. The Turks made their own interpretation of that move and decided to beat him in what they believed to be his game. Although the crisis was diffused, it is indicative of the delicate situation in the Aegean.

7

Turkey and the Southern Flank: Domestic and External Contexts

Ali Karaosmanoglu

INTRODUCTION

Turkey's geopolitical characteristics make the country strategically important for the defence of Western security interests. Turkey's own security has been successfully maintained within the Atlantic Alliance for thirty-five years. Despite very close cooperation in defence and other fields, however, it has not always been easy for Westerners to discern Turkey's real motivations and to understand its problems and policies. What are the forces which have induced Turkey to seek greater autonomy in its national security affairs? Why have Turkey's relations with Warsaw Pact countries remained purely economic in character without ever yielding substantial results at the politico-military level? What is the significance of Turkey's new Middle Eastern policies?

The lack of understanding is not entirely unjustifiable. Turkey does indeed have ambivalent characteristics and finds itself in a complex position within the Western Alliance. Ideologically and politically it is a part of the Western community of nations. It is not only a NATO ally but also a member of the Council of Europe and of the OECD, and hopes to join the European Community in the future. It is, however, set apart from the West by many features such as geographic location, socio-political evolution and level of economic development. It is also predominantly a Muslim, albeit secular, country with a special democratic tradition.

Turkey defines its security options within the framework of three interacting strategic contexts: the global system, which is dominated by relations with the Soviet Union and the United

States; its bilateral relations with Greece, involving mainly Cyprus and the Aegean; and its position within the Middle Eastern subsystem. Turkey's security objectives are determined not only by the global interests of the Alliance but also by regional and national conditions. Turkey's fundamental problem has thus been to overcome a number of security dilemmas stemming from the need to accommodate competing security interests in the three environments mentioned above. These dilemmas may be summarized as follows: playing an active and constructive role within the Alliance and contributing to the strengthening of allied deterrence capacity without challenging vital Soviet security interests and without reawakening suspicions in Moscow; improving relations with the Soviet Union without raising American and West European fears of a neutralist foreign policy shift; playing a more effective role in the Middle East without becoming entangled in regional conflicts or provoking Western anxieties about Islamic resurgence; and, finally, defending its vital interests in Cyprus and the Aegean without antagonizing an ally and complicating its own position within the Alliance. Turkey's struggle against drastically increasing terrorism, a factor which at one point pushed the country to the threshold of civil war, has provoked West European criticism citing alleged human rights violations. This, in turn, has undoubtedly created a new security dilemma.

Geographical and historical circumstances have always affected security perceptions in Turkey. The most elusive aspect in the formation of Turkey's security policy, however, is certainly the domestic environment of the country. In this respect, some specific internal factors such as religion, civil and military bureaucracy, political parties, and public opinion are of special interest. In addition, Turkey's security policy and behaviour have been affected by specific events in the international system and by the evolution of its bilateral relations with other states. None of these factors, however, has played a determining role in itself.

Turkey's security dilemmas, the compatibilities and incompatibilities between its security options and the policies of its allies, can be understood only through an analysis of all these factors and their interaction with each other.

GEOGRAPHY AND HISTORY

The Turkish people has been able to transform a cosmopolitan empire into a nation state, and a traditional Muslim society into a modern secular polity in one of the most strategically critical areas of the world. The Turkish nation state, however, has never been able to dissociate itself entirely, in either internal or external respects, from its Ottoman heritage. Turkey's contemporary security policy presents itself as a requirement dictated largely by long-term geopolitical and historical factors. The shadows of history are particularly discernible in Turkey's relations with the Soviet Union and Greece. Turkey's historical quest for security through alliances and its circumspect foreign policy have been a function of its geopolitical environment.

Geopolitics

Turkey is situated in a very critical and perilous environment. Paradoxically, its location increases its strategic value, and constitutes a vital contribution to Western security. Turkey occupies a crucial area at the intersection of Asia, Europe and Africa, and, together with Germany, the Arabian Peninsula, the Persian Gulf, India and China, it is situated on the geopolitical belt that Halford Mackinder called the 'Inner Crescent.' The contemporary superpower rivalry may be characterized as a struggle between what is substantially a land power (the Soviet Union), in control of the 'Heartland,' and an insular power (the United States), primarily maritime-dependent, for the control or denial of control of the 'Inner Crescent.'[1] Control of those regions and of the marginal seas by the insular power means the denial of eventual global hegemony to the 'Heartland' power. The emergence of the Middle East as the world's main source of petroleum and natural gas has added a new and overwhelming dimension to the strategic importance of this part of the 'Inner Crescent.'

All the natural routes (land, sea and air) from the Black Sea to the Mediterranean and from the Balkans to the Persian Gulf lead across Turkey and through the Bosporus Straits. Precisely because of its location, Turkey has always protected and is still protecting the Middle East and the Persian Gulf area against threats coming from the north. 'Any operations in or towards this area will certainly have implications for Turkey and the operations will be vitally affected by Turkish behaviour.'[2] Furthermore, Turkey is in a position potentially to play a very significant role in the defence of the eastern Mediterranean and Greece.

The considerable distances separating Turkey from Western Europe and the United States (both sources of military resupply and reinforcement in case of war) are a serious defence problem for Turkey. Another difficulty stems from the country's jagged topography which forces defence planners to consider various separate theatres of operations, each having specific terrain features and requiring different types of operational units, tactics and logistic arrangements.[3]

Experience with Russia

Turkey's past experience with Russia has greatly influenced its present approach to security matters. The hostility between Turks and Russians has a long history. When it was at the zenith of its power, the Ottoman Empire extended into southern Russia, Hungary and the Caucasus, as well as into the Arab lands and northern Africa. The emergence of Russia as a great power in the eighteenth century brought about a significant change in the European balance of power to the detriment of the Ottoman Empire. For several centuries, successive Tsars expanded their territory at the expense of the enfeebled Ottoman Empire and of the Turkic populations of Crimea and Central Asia. It is only natural that this violent history, punctuated by thirteen wars between the Russian and Ottoman Empires, created an atmosphere of traditional enmity between the two nations. In the mind of the average Turk, Russia is a hereditary enemy.

The survival of the Ottoman Empire during its years of decline, depended on its ability to balance successfully the European rivalries created by the question of the partition of the Ottoman lands. Exploitation of these rivalries in order to neutralize the most threatening power of the day was the essence of Turkish diplomacy. Nonetheless, this continuous effort of adaptation to changing circumstances through alliances never prevented Turkish statesmen from regarding the Tsarist Empire as the most immediate and ominous danger. This image softened somewhat after the Bolshevik Revolution and during the Turkish War of Independence. At that point, Soviets and Turks shared a commitment to anti-imperialism and a common objective to fight Western powers which were intervening in both countries. This rapprochement led, in 1921, to the conclusion of a Treaty of Friendship, stipulating Moscow's restitution of the provinces of Kars and Ardahan, which had been annexed from Turkey in 1878. Both countries delineated their frontiers in the Caucasus, and all former treaties between the Tsarist and Ottoman Empires were annulled.

Despite the common interests that brought about this rapprochement between Turkey and the Soviet Union, their policies differed in some fundamental respects. First, the Turkish revolution was nationalistic while the Soviet one was internationalist. The new Turkish leaders pursued Western-oriented reformist policies and they had no intention of adopting a Marxist-Leninist socio-economic system. Moreover, Kemal Atatürk never ceased to show his distrust of communism, and despite his friendship with Moscow, he pursued an anti-communist policy within Turkey. In 1932, he expressed his suspicion of the Soviets as follows: 'We Turks, being a close neighbour to Russia and a nation who has fought numerous wars against her, are following the events that are taking place there and watching the real danger as a bare truth. Bolsheviks have become a principal power threatening not only Europe but also the continent of Asia.'[4]

Tsarist Russia and the Soviet Union have been interested not only in extending their territories and projecting their power beyond their borders, but, naturally, also in protecting their frontiers from invaders. Russians have always perceived the Northern Tier, in general, and Turkey, in particular, not only as a gateway to the marginal seas and to the 'Outer Crescent,' but also as a possible invasion route to Russia. Threats to the Russian homeland have historically come from all directions, with the possible exception, for obvious geographical reasons, of the north. To a great extent, the Soviet Union was able to secure its western, eastern and southern borders by creating buffer zones. One area that remains vulnerable, however, is its southwest territory. Within this context, Turkish membership in NATO complicates Soviet defences and strategy by exposing some large, important and industrial regions in the USSR to Western monitoring in times of peace, and to Western arms in times of war. It should be noted that the importance of Turkey in the Soviet perspective stems also from its demographic and economic potential, its democratic aspirations, and its ethnic, linguistic and religious bonds with the rapidly increasing Turkish population in the USSR.

Given this traditional fear of encirclement, the Russians have always been acutely aware that the Black Sea and the Caucasus are very important strategic approaches to their homeland, and to their important industrial areas and energy resources. In other words, the Black Sea area is regarded as the 'soft under-belly' of the Russian homeland. In so far as the Western Alliance is able to exert influence in the Black Sea, it has the means of checking the advance of the Red Army westward into central and Western Europe. Therefore, the Turkish Straits are important to the Soviet Union not only for the deployment of its Black Sea Fleet into the Mediterranean, but also, and prob-ably more vitally, for its own security.

Experience with Greece

The influence of history has also left its mark in the area of Greek-Turkish relations. 'For more than nine centuries the Turks and Greeks have found themselves interlocked in war and peace.'[5] Under the Ottoman Empire they lived together in Asia Minor, in the Balkans, in the Aegean islands and Cyprus. Although to a certain extent they adopted each other's manners and habits of life and spoke one another's language, profound religious and cultural differences prevented broader or total integration.

The Greek War of Independence which began in 1821 led to the establishment of an independent Greek state. After gaining independence, Greece pursued an irredentist Panhellenic policy, known as the 'Megali Idea,' which aimed at the unifica-tion of all Greeks and the resurrection of the former Byzantine Empire. The Greek kingdom gradually increased its territories at the expense of the Ottoman Empire and this process of expansion continued until the failure of the Greek invasion of Asia Minor between 1919 and 1922. In the nineteenth and twentieth centuries regional affairs were alternately affected by the politics of empire building and those of national self-deter-mination.

According to Arnold Toynbee, the modern history of the Near East is characterized by a *reductio ad absurdum* of the principle of nationalities.[6] This ideology has had a particularly disastrous impact on ethnic groups in the Balkans. A product of Western civilization, it was introduced into a region where non-territorial and economically interdependent ethnic groups coexisted peacefully. As a result, the establishment of nation states in this part of the world required the massive reallocations of peoples and an increasingly extreme use of force became common practice between different ethnic groups. The political development of the Turks and Greeks in the nineteenth and twentieth centuries, and of relations between them, were enormously affected by the implications of this Balkan version of nationalism. This phenomenon, which Toynbee calls 'the Western Question,' constitutes the background of the Cyprus and Aegean problems, and it continues to reinforce mutual distrust between the two nations.

After the defeat of the Ottoman Empire in World War I and the invasion of Asia Minor by the victorious powers including Greece, the Turkish people were faced with the danger of losing their homeland. On 28 February 1920, the Ottoman parliament adopted a 'National Pact' which acknowledged the Arabs' right to self-determination and limited Turkish claims to the portion of the former Empire in which the Turks themselves constituted a decisive majority of the population. Following the successful War of Independence against the invaders, Turkey concluded the Treaty of Lausanne, on 24 July 1923, with the allied powers. The terms of the treaty stipulated that Greece and the other allied powers renounce all claims to Asia Minor and to eastern Thrace beyond the Maritza river. Thus, the Turks secured frontiers consistent with the 'National Pact,' and relieved themselves of the bulk of their 'Ottoman burden.' By so doing, they provided themselves with the necessary ground to focus their energies on developing the economy and initiating a domestic programme of Westernizing reforms.

Republican Foreign Policy

In foreign policy, the principle formulated by Kemal Atatürk: 'Peace at home, peace abroad,' became the cornerstone of Turkey's conduct in external relations. This implied a policy

293

based on the maintenance of the status quo and on the survival of a relatively homogeneous national state with a clear Turkish identity. For this reason, the Turks have always been very sensitive about the Treaty of Lausanne, and have vehemently opposed any development which might disrupt the 'balances' established by that treaty. In line with this thinking, Turkish leaders considered security as a whole, and were concerned not only with regional problems but also with security matters beyond their immediate environment. Nevertheless, Atatürk decided to cut his country's intimate political ties with the Arab world, and republican Turkey distanced itself from Middle Eastern politics. During the period 1923-1941, Turkey's main foreign policy preoccupation was to balance cautiously the measures taken by the revisionist powers and to consolidate its security by a series of friendship treaties and non-aggression pacts concluded with its neighbours and some European states, such as the United Kingdom, France and Germany. To this end, Turkey signed a Treaty of Friendship and Non-aggression with the Soviet Union in 1925. In 1930, it initiated a successful process of reconciliation with Greece; and in 1934, in response to the Italian threat, it concluded the Balkan Pact with Greece, Yugoslavia and Rumania. In 1937, it entered into the Saadabat Pact with Afghanistan, Iran and Iraq. Moreover, in the face of the increasing threat to European security, Turkey requested the revision of the Lausanne Straits Convention which it deemed inadequate for the protection of its security in the event of war. In 1936, the Lausanne Straits Convention was replaced by the Montreux Convention which gave Turkey control over the Straits. In terms of the new Convention, Turkey was authorized to militarize the Straits area, and, by a unilateral decision, to close the Straits to warships when it deemed that there was an imminent peril of war likely to jeopardize its safety.

During World War II, Turkey was able to pursue a policy of neutrality. It was only upon the insistence of the Allied Powers that it joined forces with them against Germany in the last days of the war. This enabled it to participate in the United Nations Conference on International Organization in San Francisco. After the War of Independence, Turkey's foreign policy had been characterized by a certain flexibility, seeking friendly relations in every direction, including Moscow. But this flexibility had been achieved without sacrificing the long-term goal of Westernization, and ideologically, Turkey remained clearly

Western-oriented. In the post-World War II era, new circumstances forced Turkey to adopt an exclusively Western-oriented policy, not only in terms of its ideological stance but also in security and defence matters.

After World War II, Turkey and Greece adopted similar foreign policies. Both countries were directly threatened by the Soviet communist expansion; both turned to the West for protection and received American aid under the Truman Doctrine; they became NATO members on the same day; they concluded the Balkan Defence Pact with Yugoslavia in 1954; and both countries obtained an associate status in the European Community.[7] A cooperative process continued to characterize Greek-Turkish relations until the revival of the traditional feud, triggered by the Cyprus affair in the 1950s. Even in that decade, both nations proved capable of overcoming their mutual distrust and in 1959 they concluded the London and Zurich Agreements establishing the Republic of Cyprus. Cooperation between the two Cypriot communities, however, was only ephemeral. They would soon fall into disagreement over many substantive issues and the new constitutional order would break down after violent incidents, leading to even bloodier conflicts in the following years, thus complicating the positions of Greece and Turkey within the Atlantic Alliance.

Conditions of Turkey's Alignment with NATO

Emboldened by its new position of strength after World War II, the Soviet Union attempted to obtain control over the Straits and claimed Turkey's northeastern provinces (Kars and Ardahan). At the same time, Moscow and Sofia launched an aggressive propaganda campaign against Turkey and massed troops along the frontier areas. As it had already done in the nineteenth century, Turkey, confronted with the Russian threat, turned to the West for protection. The United States took a series of measures to safeguard Turkey and Greece. First, it sent a naval force to the eastern Mediterranean to demonstrate its will to contain Soviet expansion in the area. Second, on 12 March 1946, it proclaimed the Truman Doctrine which committed Washington 'to support free peoples who are resisting attempted subjugation by armed minorities or by outside pressure.' Then, on 12 July 1947, the United States and Turkey concluded a military assistance agreement.

Turkey's final objective was membership in NATO. When the North Atlantic Treaty was concluded on 4 April 1948, Turkey was denied membership, as was Greece. In the following years, Ankara experienced considerable difficulties in obtaining admission to NATO. Although there was a general feeling that the defence of the Southern Flank was important for the security of the Alliance, most members demonstrated considerable reluctance towards extending security commitments to the Causasian border of the Soviet Union. They argued that the inclusion of Turkey (and Greece) would increase the danger of war, would add to the rearmament burden, and would spread NATO too thin. The British government was more interested in the establishment of a separate Middle Eastern defence alliance built around Turkey, than directly supporting its NATO application.

Ankara, however, showed no interest in any substitute to full membership in NATO, and continued its efforts to convince the member states. The Turks argued that the policy of containment was weakened by the gap in the Southern Flank, and that Soviet expansion in the area would not only endanger the security of Turkey and the Middle East, but would also threaten the security of Western Europe. The Korean War provided Turkey with an excellent opportunity to show its solidarity with the West. It sent the third largest contingent (a brigade of 4,500 men) after the American and South Korean forces, to participate in the conflict. Turkey showed its allegiance to the West and to the Western political system by initiating a process of democratization of its political regime. The first free elections in Turkey took place in May 1950, and brought the Democratic Party to power with an overwhelming majority. These developments, combined with the worsening security situation in the Middle East, finally moderated the allied views on Turkey's membership in NATO, and on 18 February 1952, Turkey was formally admitted to the Alliance as a full member at the same time as Greece. Turkey's adhesion to NATO was approved by the Turkish Grand National Assembly by a vote of 404 to zero.

Beyond the Soviet threat, Turkey's enthusiastic attachment to the Atlantic Alliance was prompted by a yearning towards Westernization that had become a tradition since the time of Atatürk. Turkey's entry into NATO was considered as a success by the elite and by the two major political parties — the

Democratic Party and the Republican People's Party (RPP) of Ismet Inönü — because it constituted not only a security guarantee against the Soviet threat but also an acceptance into the Western community of nations. This conception of Westernization, implying cooperation with the West, became the leading philosophical principle of Turkey's foreign policy and has survived to the present day.[8]

Consensus and Change

During the late 1940s and the 1950s, Turkey established very close ties with the United States, and considered its security policy simply within the framework of U.S.-Turkish relations; NATO was generally viewed as an extension of the United States. The containment of Soviet expansion was the major preoccupation. Relations with the Middle East and other Third World countries were approached from this unidimensional perspective of East-West tension. In this period, although there occurred long discussions in parliament on the Cyprus affair and Turkey's attitude towards the Middle Eastern countries, the basic orientation of Turkish security policy was not contested. This policy rested on a broad consensus based on the need for a common defence with the United States and other Western allies. This state of affairs did not change immediately after the military takeover of 1960 since its leaders made clear that they were neither against Turkey's alliances, such as NATO and CENTO, nor against the United States. The unconditional Turkish support of Washington during the Cuban missile crisis of October 1962 was clear evidence of continuity along these lines.

The developments that took place after 1960 in the domestic as well as in the international environment of Turkey began to undermine the national consensus on security policy. On the domestic level, Turkey's economic potential, industrial power and population had grown considerably since the 1950s. In the period 1950–1978, Turkey enjoyed fairly rapid economic development. Economic growth rates exceeded an annual 7 percent in the 1970s. Per capita income rose from about 300 to over 1,000 dollars. Between 1950 and 1985, the Turkish population grew from 20 million to about 50 million. Industrialization brought about trade unionism and the right to collective

bargaining. It led, however, to rapid urbanization, rising expectations and psychological insecurities as well. The growing
business, managerial and technical groups began to be more
assertive in politics. The highly liberal constitution of 1961 had,
however, allowed for the expression and organization of all
kinds of ideas and ideologies.[9]

In the mid-1960s, the Turkish people became involved in a
prolonged debate on security affairs. The major issues discussed
in parliament and the press, included: the degree of credibility
of American commitments; bilateral agreements concluded with
the United States concerning the U.S. bases and the status of
American military personnel in Turkey; security implications of
the flexible response strategy and of the deployment of tactical
nuclear weapons on Turkish soil; the appropriateness of
Turkey's NATO membership; and relations with Greece,
especially with reference to the Cyprus problem. These discussions were not ignored by governments or the policy-making
elite. A series of attempts were made to pursue a more autonomous foreign policy and to normalize relations with the Soviet
bloc and Middle Eastern countries. Turkey refrained, in 1965,
from participating in the Multilateral Force. The perceived
abuse of bilateral agreements by American personnel, and the
resulting anti-American feelings among the public, led the
Turkish government to propose, in 1966, the revision of the
Military Facilities Agreement of 1954 and of the thirteen secret
bilateral agreements stemming from it. After almost three years
of negotiations, the two governments concluded the Defense
Cooperation Agreement in 1969 which brought about a considerable reduction in the number of American military personnel
in Turkey. Likewise, the Cigli air base and the radar installations at Trabzon and Samsun were transferred to the Turkish
armed forces, while the status of the other bases and installations were adjusted to the new agreement. In spite of these
modifications, however, the question of bilateral agreements
remained a critical issue in Turkish public opinion.[10]

In July 1975, when the U.S. Congress decided not to lift the
existing arms embargo on Turkey, the Turkish government
declared that the Defence Cooperation Agreement of 1969 and
all other related agreements had lost their legal validity and put
all installations in Turkey used by the United States under the
'full control and custody of the Turkish Armed Forces' with the
exception of the Incirlik air base which was to be utilized only

for NATO purposes.[11] After the lifting of the arms embargo on 26 September 1978, the Turkish government allowed the United States to resume operations at the military installations where activities had been suspended since the summer of 1975. New negotiations which started in 1979 resulted in the conclusion of the Defense and Economic Cooperation Agreement on 29 March 1980. This agreement is still in force today.

While relations with the United States were being critically scrutinized by public opinion, changing circumstances induced Turkish policy makers to attempt to normalize relations with the Soviet Union and the Middle Eastern countries. The policy of rapprochement initiated by Ankara and Moscow led to a visit to Moscow by Turkish Prime Minister Süleyman Demirel in October 1967. After that visit, relations between the two countries steadily improved, particularly in the economic field, and the Soviets became the major supplier of project credit to Turkey. Turkey's relations with the Soviet Union and other Warsaw Pact countries, however, have never culminated in a politico-military rapprochement which would have been incompatible with Turkey's NATO membership. The political document on 'The Principles of Good-Neighbourly and Friendly Cooperation,' signed in June 1978, during Premier Bülent Ecevit's visit to Moscow, largely recapitulated the terms of a similar declaration signed by the two countries when President Podgorny had visited Ankara in April 1972. It was clearly far from being a non-aggression pact. It confined itself to reiterating the principles of the Final Act of the 1975 Helsinki Conference on Security and Cooperation in Europe, and concluded by stating that it did not affect the rights and obligations of the parties under other agreements.

In the 1970s, Turkey began to increase its economic cooperation with Iraq, Libya, Saudi Arabia and the Gulf states. The Turks recognized the Palestine Liberation Organization (PLO) in 1976, and allowed it to open an Ankara office in August 1979. Although Turkey was cooling its relations with Israel, it did so without completely severing diplomatic ties. In 1980, the Demirel government finally decided to withdraw all its embassy staff from Tel Aviv, except for a Second Secretary acting as a Chargé d'Affaires, and asked the Israeli government to lower its diplomatic representation in Ankara to the same level. The Turkish-Arab rapprochement also had significant politico-military ramifications. During the Arab-Israeli war of 1973,

Soviet overflights of Turkish airspace were tolerated. During the same Middle Eastern conflict, Ankara refused to grant the United States refuelling and reconnaissance facilities for airlift to Israel — in obvious contrast with Turkish policies in the 1950s, when Turkey allowed the United States to use the bases on its soil to carry out the landings in Lebanon during the civil war of 1958.

The efforts of attaining greater autonomy in security policy eventually led Ecevit's government, in 1978, to attempt the elaboration of a 'New Defence Concept' which seemed to include the following major elements.[12] First, Turkey's security should not be confined to defence and armaments; it should be strengthened by the establishment of friendly relations in the region. Second, historically and geographically, Turkey is primarily a Balkan, Middle Eastern and east Mediterranean country. Third, in order to decrease its dependence on one source for its military equipment, Turkey should develop its own defence industries. Fourth, the new defence system and structure of Turkey should be compatible with its continued membership in NATO, but Turkey's contribution to the Western Alliance should not expose it to serious risks by rendering it provocative in the region where it is situated.

The operational (military) aspects of the New Defence Concept were never made clear. Throughout Premier Ecevit's tenure of office (which ended as a result of the October 1979 election) official explanations of the concept were confined to its political aspects. Questions relating to the size and mission of the armed forces, and to a flexible deployment plan, remained unanswered.[13] The project was essentially, therefore, an *ex post facto* formulation of the security policy orientation that had been pragmatically developed since the mid-1960s.

THE DOMESTIC CONTEXT

Institutionally, the executive, including the civil and military bureaucracies, acts as the primary policy-making authority in foreign and security affairs. The social and structural changes that occurred in the 1950s and 1960s produced several significant results, however, and somewhat increased the weight of domestic restraints imposed upon the executive. First, they brought about an acute ideological polarization and political fragmentation. The infiltration of Marxism, fascism and Islamic fundamentalism into Turkey, made Turkish politics more pluralistic, a development which has led to political violence and terrorism. Second, religion began to play a greater role in society; the reassertion of Islamic values has had implications at the political level. Third, the political fragmentation of the public bureaucracy, combined with the growing importance of managerial elites, has decreased the political role of the civil bureaucratic elite. Fourth, these developments have increased the regulatory role of the military in internal politics.

The Institutional Framework of Decision Making

Under the constitution of 1921 and during the years of national struggle against the occupying powers after World War I, parliament in Ankara (the Grand National Assembly) played a determining role in foreign affairs and defence. But the subsequent constitutions of 1924, 1961 and 1982 considerably reduced the role of the legislative in foreign and defence policies. At present the Council of Ministers, presided over by the Prime Minister and advised by the National Security Council, appears to be the main decision-making organ. In cases of vital national interest, the cabinet may be chaired by the President of the Republic, and the Chief of the General Staff also attends the meeting. The reports of the Minister of Foreign Affairs and the advice of the Chief of the General Staff usually play a considerable part in governmental decisions on security policy. The Ministry of National Defence seems more to execute policies than to make strategic decisions. It deals with the political, legal, social, and financial aspects of national defence. The Ministry of National Defence is responsible, within the framework of the principles and priorities decided on by the General Staff, for the recruitment of the armed forces, weapons procurement, the defence industry, infrastructure, military health services, and financial matters.

The National Security Council has been playing a growing role in security affairs. It is composed of the Prime Minister, the Chief of the General Staff, the Ministers of National Defence, Internal Affairs and Foreign Affairs, the Commanders of the Army, Navy and the Air Force, and the General Commander of the Gendarmerie. The National Security Council normally functions under the chairmanship of the President of the Republic, and in his absence the Prime Minister presides. Its main function is to advise the Council of Ministers on the formulation and implementation of the national security policy of the state. The constitution of 1982 provides that the Council of Ministers shall give priority consideration to the decisions of the National Security Council concerning the measures that it deems necessary for the preservation of the existence and independence of the state, the integrity and indivisibility of the country, and civil peace.

In the terms of the 1982 constitution, the office of the Commander-in-Chief is inseparable from the 'spiritual' existence of the Grand National Assembly, and is represented by the President of the Republic. In times of war, this duty is exercised by the Chief of the General Staff acting on behalf of the President. The Chief of the General Staff is appointed by the President on the proposal of the Council of Ministers, and he is responsible to the Prime Minister.

Naturally the Council of Ministers is responsible to the Grand National Assembly for foreign affairs, national security, and the organization of the armed forces. The annual parliamentary debate on the budget of the Ministry of Foreign Affairs provides an opportunity to discuss foreign policy questions. These questions, and security matters in general, can at any time be brought before the Grand National Assembly by its members. In practice, however, the legislative branch has little control on defence policy in the strictest sense. Defence is regarded as a question of vital national interest, and is usually kept outside of political conflicts. The strategic choices are made by the General Staff, and are implemented by the Council of Ministers normally without parliamentary restriction. In fact, although the government annually presents the defence budget to the Grand National Assembly, national defence problems and expenditures have never been critically debated in parliament. Each year, therefore, the defence budget receives automatic approval.

Treaties are usually ratified and promulgated by the President of the Republic. Although the ratification of treaties is legally subject to adoption by the Grand National Assembly, agreements in connection with the implementation of a treaty, or administrative agreements concluded on the basis of special legal authorization, do not require parliamentary approval. A parliamentary enactment in 1963 authorized the Council of Ministers to conclude all the international agreements related to NATO without recourse to the legislative. In the 1960s and 1970s, the constitutionality of this law was subject to long discussions in the Turkish legal community. Nevertheless, the Constitutional Court decided on 4 March 1965 in favour of this law and practice. In conformity with the same law, the government concluded, on 18 November 1980, the Agreement for Cooperation on Defense and Economy between Turkey and the United States, and all the supplementary agreements annexed to it.

The government's decision to send troops to the Korean War provoked a long public discussion on the respective powers of the Grand National Assembly and the Council of Ministers. The constitutions of 1961 and 1982, in order to eliminate the ambiguities of the constitution of 1924, unequivocally gave the Grand National Assembly the authority to declare war, to send Turkish armed forces to foreign countries and to allow foreign armed forces to be stationed in Turkey. Notwithstanding this provision, the constitution of 1982 authorizes the President of the Republic to decide, while the parliament is in recess, on the use of the armed forces if the country is subjected to armed aggression.

Party Politics and Public Opinion

Although a multi-party system was established in Turkey in the mid-1940s, ideological and social cleavages were not apparent in party politics. Instead, political parties developed as vehicles for conflicts among the elite. The 'centre-periphery' cleavage inherited from the Ottoman Empire,[14] and, to some extent, the factional alliances based on sectarian or community-oriented divisions, acquired new political significance through the system of multi-party politics.[15] The only ideological cleavages were between Westernization, Islamism and 'Turkism,' and this had negligible influence at the foreign and security policy level. Until 1960, political competition existed mainly between the two major parties, the Republican People's Party, representing the bureaucratic intelligentsia with its traditional policy of state-directed reform, and the Democratic Party (succeeded by the Justice Party after 1960), opposed to the domination of the

303

bureaucratic intelligentsia and capitalizing on the grievances of small-town inhabitants and peasants living in the periphery. Nevertheless, both political parties pursued Western-oriented foreign policies. Their economic policies, too, were both based on the notion of a mixed economy — although the Democratic Party displayed rather more liberal tendencies — advocating direct cooperation with Western economic and financial organizations.

In the 1960s, the rise of socio-economic problems in Turkey brought about an increase in the relative significance of functional-ideological cleavages despite persisting cultural divisions. The replacement of the 1924 constitution by a more liberal constitution in 1961 greatly contributed to the relative democratization of foreign policy making. A number of small political parties — ranging from extreme leftist to Islamic fundamentalist — the press, the universities, trade unions, intellectual and professional societies emerged as pressure groups with influence over public opinion on foreign and security policy matters. Although the leftist parties did not maintain an official link with Moscow, they advocated, as did the communist parties in Western Europe, détente at any price, supported the Soviet-launched campaigns on security issues and organized propaganda campaigns against Turkey's NATO membership. The Marxist-oriented trade unions, unified under the Confederation of Revolutionary Workers (DISK), and many other leftist professional organizations persistently attacked Turkey's affiliation with the Western Alliance, arguing that it created economic dependence and insecurity, and was conducive to the exploitation of the country's working class by international capitalism. Even in the RPP there existed some extreme leftist elements favouring similar ideas. Nevertheless, both major parties (the RPP and the Justice Party) continued throughout the 1960s and 1970s to express their support of NATO unequivocally on every possible occasion.

These two major political parties were supported by more than 80 percent of the electorate. The remaining 20 percent was shared by a number of splinter parties. But the significance of the Turkish left has gone beyond the percentage of the votes it has garnered in general elections. It has always been very active politically and successful to a considerable degree in propagating its ideologies among the Turkish elite. While the Turkish electorate (which continued to vote for the political parties that it trusted) seemed only minimally influenced by the anti-NATO propaganda, the foreign policy debate of the 1960s and 1970s certainly had an impact on Turkish intellectuals. Although most of them remained committed to Atatürk's pro-Western outlook in general terms, they began to reconsider Turkey's position in the world. They questioned the necessity of being the staunchest ally of the United States without, however, disputing the appropriateness of Turkey's NATO membership. They argued, nevertheless, that certain Turkish interests might not always be in conformity with those of Turkey's Western allies.

In the 1960s, foreign affairs in general and Turkey's relations with the United States and the Alliance in particular, became the subject of heated debates in parliament. But these discussions never resulted in a clear condemnation of government policies. The emergence of political parties and the increasing influence of ideological cleavages did not, in fact, alter parliament's role as an organ of automatic approval for the decisions of the President and the Council of Ministers in foreign and security policy matters. Rather, it increased the importance of parliament as a political forum where the government-opposition dialogue took place in the form of parliamentary debates and consultations. In this way, the multi-party system helped to establish links between public opinion and foreign policy decision makers.[16] Furthermore, during the same period, it became customary for the government to inform and consult the major opposition party leaders on important foreign policy questions. It appears, however, that this practice has been abandoned since 1980: the present government is content with informing the opposition through public declarations and occasional parliamentary debates on foreign policy.

Finally, the increasing polarization of politics in the 1970s led to domestic violence and to the paralysis of Turkey's political life. Leftist-rightist tensions infected the police, teachers, students, and civil servants. Law and order broke down completely. There were, on average, twenty-eight killings a day. The victims were not only left- or right-wing extremists, political assassinations involved journalists, members of parliament, university professors as well as a former prime minister. The purpose of killing the moderates was apparently to weaken the political centre and to accelerate the process of polarization. The political extremists were also exploiting dormant cleavages of ethnic (Turkish-Kurdish) and sectarian (Sunnite-Alevi)

305

character, inciting bloody communal conflicts. The electoral system, based on proportional representation, did not allow the major parties to have a working majority in the parliament. The large parties remained dependent on the small parties which were pursuing destabilizing policies. Political polarization and cabinet instability led to a deadlock on many critical issues. More importantly, there was no consensus on how to deal with terrorism. In the midst of this chaotic atmosphere, political parties were involved in petty politics, and the parliament seemed to be killing democracy by its own procedures and rhetoric. The silent majority was the victim of raging terrorism, on the one hand, and of the absence of state authority, on the other. Terrorism was about to attain the character of an overt civil war when the military intervened on 12 September 1980.

The elections of 6 November 1983 constituted a significant step forward in the development of Turkish democracy. The Motherland Party (ANAP) of Turgut Ozal, which had been regarded with disfavour by the military regime, won a decisive victory. After the elections, the process of democratization became firmly entrenched, and new parties and leaders emerged. The merger between the Populist Party in parliament and the Social Democratic Party that remained outside it, was an important step in the formation of an effective opposition. The leaders and grassroot supporters of the outlawed political parties today seem to have gained a considerable measure of influence in the new parties that they sponsor, and also of control behind the scenes. This rapid multiplication of political parties reminds many Turks of the pre-1980 period. Despite such misgivings, there exists a growing consensus among the population and the elite that Turkey cannot evolve into a workable and sustainable pluralistic democracy without the representation of all political ideas. It will be necessary to wait for the next general elections in 1988 to consolidate the multi-party system. All political parties, including those which are currently unrepresented in parliament, will stand for the elections, but the system will most likely evolve around a traditional two-major-party structure. The ruling Motherland Party will be competing with the Social Democratic opposition. The elections will also provide a test for the popularity of the old political leaders.

The dramatic shift in parliamentary composition which occurred in mid-1986 was essentially caused by the dissolution

Table 7.1: The changing composition of the Turkish parliament

November 1983	
Motherland party (ANAP)	211
Populist Party	117
Nationalist Democracy Party	71
Vacant	1
May 1986	
Motherland Party (ANAP)	227
Social Democratic Populist Party	84
Free Democratic Party	22
True Path Party	21
Democratic Left Party	4
Citizens' Party	2
Independents	29
Vacant	11
October 1986	
Motherland Party (ANAP)	237
Social Democratic Populist Party	85
True Path Party	29
Free Democratic Party	20
Democratic Left Party	5
Citizens' Party	2
Independents	21
Vacant	1

Note: At present, the only major political party outside parliament is the Welfare Party which advocates an Islamic political line. This party will also stand for elections in 1988.

of two of the political parties represented in the General Assembly (see Table 7.1). First, the disappearance of the Nationalist Democracy Party, which had been established in 1983 under the leadership of a retired General, paved the way for the creation of a new liberal party — the Free Democratic Party — and for the representation in parliament of the True Path Party (DYP), which is a conservative centre-right party actively supported by the former Justice Party leader, Süleyman Demirel. Some of the members of the dissolved Nationalist Democracy Party, however, joined Ozal's ANAP. Second, the Populist Party merged with the Social Democratic Party which was not represented in the General Assembly, and the new party was baptized the Social Democratic Populist Party (SDHP). Only four of the Populist Party parliamentarians preferred to join another social democratic group, namely the Democratic Left Party (DLP) supported by the former Republican Party leader, Ecevit. Despite the rapid revitalization of party politics, it cannot be said that the opposition parties have yet been able to put forward alternative policies. They all try to capitalize on the anti-democratic provisions of the 1982 constitution, on the social cost of the rapid liberalization policies of the ANAP government, and on some cases of alleged corruption.

Another reason for the change in parliamentary composition was the by-elections of 28 September 1986 which took place in eleven constituencies. Results of the by-elections were full of surprises for many people primarily because the Turkish political scene showed an undisputed shift to the right. The True Path Party won four parliamentary seats and 23.7 percent of the votes. The Motherland Party was able to take six of the eleven seats at stake but only 32.2 percent of the total vote. Although this was considered a slight setback for Ozal, the outcome did not affect the parliamentary majority of his party. The result was a shock for the main opposition party, the Social Democratic Populist Party, which lagged behind with a single seat and 22.7 percent of the votes. The Democratic Left Party was able to take only 8.6 percent of the total vote, and this was not enough to earn it a seat in parliament. (Seats already held by the party were due to defections from other political groups in parliament.) All the other small parties were wiped out. For instance, the Welfare Party, which advocates an Islamic political line, suffered a crushing defeat getting only 5.2 percent of the total vote.

Following the by-elections, Turkish political life was revitalized. The Social Democratic Populist Party began to seek new changes in its administration. Political bans became the subject of daily discussion. The True Path Party which had received a high percentage of the vote (not reflected in the total number of seats held) was perceived as the main rival of the Motherland Party, opening a period of tense competition within the right. Meanwhile a number of independent deputies joined the ranks of various political parties. These recent developments have reconfirmed that it will be necessary to wait for the next general elections in 1988 to consolidate the multi-party system.

In Turkey, generally speaking, public opinion and the press are far less preoccupied with international affairs than with domestic politics. Although in the 1960s and 1970s foreign policy discussions became widespread and intensified in the press, at public meetings and in universities, the interest of the average Turkish citizen in such matters remained limited.

Obvious exceptions to this apathy are questions affecting national sentiments, such as Cyprus, the situation of Turkish minorities in the Balkans, U.S.-Turkish relations, and terrorist activities against Turkish nationals — issues which have always provoked deep interest. The recent measures of liberalization and the subsequent increase in the significance of economic affairs have induced leading newspapers to show much greater interest today in international economic relations, the European Community and Middle Eastern affairs, than they did in the 1960s and 1970s. There is a clear preference in the press for analytical criticism of governmental policies and much less partisan editorializing of the sort that was common in the 1960s.

Religion

The ambiguous position of contemporary Turkey in the Islamic world reflects an idiosyncratic religious character that is to be found throughout Turkish history.[17] The idea of a state power independent of religion had always been dominant in the ideology of the Ottoman polity. The state had priority over religion because its viability was regarded as essential for the preservation of religion. This provided the Ottoman official with a pragmatic and relatively secular view of politics.[18] This realism in Ottoman statecraft matured and became more refined through centuries of experience as a major power wavering between conflictual and cooperative relations with West European states and Russia. This development, together with the long process of Westernization which began in the second half of the eighteenth century, has 'injected a strong cultural internationalism' into the approach of the Turkish elite to foreign policy which, in turn, has had a moderating and secularizing influence on Turkish nationalism.[19]

It was this same pragmatic sense which induced Ottoman statesmen to become sponsors of Westernization and to initiate a policy of reform designed to reinforce the institutional foundations of a decaying empire.[20] Herein lay the Ottoman intellectual background of Kemalism. Although during the period of transition from empire to nation state Islam served as a source of national unity against the invading foreign powers, the aim of the Kemalist reformers after the victory was to free the polity entirely from religious considerations. They adopted a purely territorial and linguistic brand of nationalism. Atatürk,

309

unimpaired by a colonial heritage, refrained from placing the moral responsibility for Turkish underdevelopment on Western nations.[21] Thus, unlike nationalism in Arab countries, Turkish nationalism is essentially secular and devoid of any anti-Western component.

In spite of the secularization movement, Islam has always been present in the individual and social life of a great majority of Turkish citizens. The aim of Kemalist reforms was not, in fact, to eradicate religion from individual and social life, but to achieve a complete separation of religion from political life. Between 1945 and 1970, some politicians used religion as a means of political mobilization. There was also an attempt by leftist groupings to politicize the Alevi minority of Turkey. But these initiatives were clearly motivated by reasons of power politics rather than by religious fervour, and there were no politically organized attempts to repudiate the fundamental priniciples of Kemalism. An explicit Islamic element entered Turkish politics only in 1970 through the National Order Party, which was eventually dissolved by the Constitutional Court for violation of the law on political parties and was replaced by the National Salvation Party (NSP). The NSP, founded in 1972, advocated an Islamic policy and favoured Turkey's withdrawal from what it called the 'Western Club.' However, it was never able to muster more than 12 percent of the votes in general elections. Its share of the vote declined from 11.9 percent in the 1973 elections to 8.6 percent in 1977, and it performed rather poorly in the local elections of 1979. In a recent study of the NSP, a Turkish social scientist has made a content analysis of the party chairman's speeches and has found that from 1973 to 1980 day-to-day secular politics gradually pushed religious issues into the background. The analyst concluded that the NSP represented a stagnant socio-political force with a defensive posture.[22]

Despite these observations, a reassertion of Islamic values is clearly taking place and some Turks are becoming more critical of the process of Westernization. But this criticism is having little effect on politics and on the secular legal system which remains unaltered. It will in no way be conducive to radical political change and much less to a mass uprising against central authority like the one witnessed in Iran. First of all, unlike Iran, no organized clergy exists in Turkey. Second, as Serif Mardin put it:

in the last three decades the Turkish Republic has been able to establish institutional channels for the expression of political preferences and social ideals which take the pressure in this matter away from religion ... .It is this pluralistic system that Turkish 'anarchists,' as they are described by Turks, have wanted to upset, and they have been partially successful.[23]

Today, after a transitional period of crisis and consolidation, the system is gradually being reestablished.

Bureaucracy and Entrepreneurial Groups

Despite the increase in attention given to foreign and security policy, these matters have, to a great extent, remained within the purview of the bureaucratic (civil and military) elite. Turkish bureaucracy has not only an 'instrumental' but also a 'patrimonial' aspect, in the sense that it always regards itself as the guardian of state sovereignty and reforms, and as the promoter of national interests. The Ministry of Foreign Affairs, and the military have not been immune to this patrimonial attitude. Ministry officials have a classic conception of international politics that emphasizes the primacy of foreign policy and intergovernmental relations, but overlooks the growing transnationalism in world politics. Turkish politicians have not, as a rule, professed great interest or inclination towards involvement in the complexities of foreign and security policies. They usually take office with very little knowledge about these problems. Thus, in most cases, the advice provided by the members of the General Staff and the officials of the Foreign Ministry plays a determining role. In other words, the traditions, ideology and political notions of this elite play a crucial part in the formulation and execution of foreign and security policies. This bureaucratized foreign policy undoubtedly guarantees stability and predictability. On the other hand, it may also lead to a form of policy rigidification that undermines the need for flexibility and freedom of manoeuvre. Furthermore, the problem of how the executive can control the bureaucracy in foreign and security policy matters adds a new dimension to the overall problem of democratic control.

Recent developments, however, have exerted some moderating

311

influence upon the civil bureaucracy, and minimized its interventionist political role. In the 1970s, the civil bureaucracy
began to lose its homogeneity and cohesiveness. Although the
Foreign Ministry has remained immune to extremist political
infiltrations, the civil bureaucracy in general has been influenced by different socio-political groups. After the takeover of
September 1980, the military took measures to curb the powers
of the civil bureaucracy which had become dangerously polarized.[24] Although these measures do not directly concern the
foreign policy field, they have occasioned a decline in the
overall status of the civil bureaucracy in Turkey. This is particularly noticeable in economic and financial matters. Parallel to
this development, the civil government of Ozal has made
genuine efforts to promote entrepreneurial interests and to
change the state-controlled, protectionist economic structure.
Premier Ozal, a firm believer in economic liberalism, urges the
removal of state control over the economy and views Turkey's
external affairs from the perspective of economic interdependence. Although it could take years to complete the task of liberalization, the policies adopted have already had significant
effects on Turkey's international economic and financial
policies. The rising importance of economic considerations in
internal as well as in external affairs is likely not only to increase
the role of entrepreneurial groups and managerial elites in
foreign policy making, but also to introduce a significant
element of transnationalism into the outlook of the traditional
foreign and security policy elite.

The Military

The regular officer corps of the Turkish armed forces is trained
at the military schools and academies which are open to all
classes, and the candidates are drawn from a broad social base.
Most of the manpower is provided by conscripts normally doing
twenty months of compulsory service. The function of military
service is not only to teach the conscripts how to defend their
country, but also to improve their education and skills. The
army also plays an integrative role by mixing up recruits from
different regions and by increasing their ability to work
together. This educational aspect of military service has,
however, decreased in importance as Turkey has moved, in the

last thirty years, from a predominantly traditional and agricultural society to a progressively more modern and industrial one.

The Turkish armed forces descend directly from the Ottoman army. In the Empire, the military establishment was the vanguard of reform and Westernization. In fact, the military was itself the first institution to undergo drastic reform in the eighteenth century.[25] Turkish democracy came into existence in the 1940s with the consent and support of the armed forces. In the republic, the military has emerged as the custodian of the state and of reforms against anti-secularist, communist, separatist and irredentist-fascist movements, and 'as the defenders of political democracy against the continual failure of the civilian governments to implement or protect it.'[26] The Turkish military's high level of discipline and professionalism does not favour the adoption of extremist ideologies by its officers. Despite this professionalism, however, it shows certain 'praetorian' tendencies.[27] Its 'praetorianism' does not consist of attempts at changing the socio-political system or the main course of Turkey's security policy. On the contrary, its political interventions have been of a moderating and civilian-oriented nature. There have so far been three military interventions in the political process in 1960, 1971, and 1980. Although the socio-political forces motivating each intervention differed, there was no instance where the aim of the military was to establish an authoritarian regime. The military considered these interventions as necessary to preserve, rather than abrogate, the country's democratic institutions. The generals have always disliked the immersion of soldiers in political affairs to the detriment of their military function. Whenever the military intervened in the political process, it did so unwillingly, and for the purpose of consolidating democracy. It is quite natural that this situation would seem paradoxical to Western students of politics who are accustomed to thinking in terms of the usual democratic paradigm which takes democracy as an antidote to militarism and whose prerequisite is the ability to resolve conflicts progressively and smoothly through compromise rather than by regulation from above.[28] The point, however, is that the military has acquired this regulatory function through a socio-political evolution peculiar to Turkish history, and its political role should be evaluated accordingly.

How is the democratic process developing at present? Is there any danger of future intervention by the military in the political system? There are some readily noticeable signs that the democratic system is improving. There is, for instance, a rapid multiplication of political parties. The continuing legal restraints imposed after 1980 are being circumvented with impunity by the old political leaders. Human rights abuses are being criticized by the press and by politicians alike. Turkish newspapers recently reported that the International Press Institute had recognized the restoration of freedom of the press in the country. There seems to be a general consensus that Turkey has recently moved closer to the West European democratic system. All these developments may be taken as evidence of rapid progress in the reestablishment of the democratic system. But such an approach to the regime problem in Turkey would be less than adequate for those who remember that the rapid liberalization of the political regime following the military intervention of 1960 did not bring about a workable and sustained democracy, but led instead to a debilitating pluralism that culminated in the intervention of 1971.

It is important to understand the role of the Turkish military in the light of Turkey's unique historical evolution. Such an historical approach shows that there are at present some deep, even if not easily observable, changes promoting the institution-alization of democracy in Turkey. These changes have been elaborately analysed by Metin Heper.[29]

According to Professor Heper, the Turkish military has proved to be an institution that learns. Studying the recent enactments, declarations and publications issued by the military establishment, he observes that the post-1980 military regime has changed the traditional republican system of ethics by infusing it with new principles. One novelty is undoubtedly the reference to 'Turkish historical and moral values' in the preamble of the 1982 constitution. The emphasis on these values seems to represent a considerable moderation in the attitude of the military towards Islam as a social force and as a valuable source of personal development. The military has also emphasized, in the post-1980 publications on Atatürkism, tolerance of others' opinions as well as the need to defend the integrity of the nation. Another significant change derives from the fact that the military did not insist on étatism, one of the fundamental guidelines set down by the republican reformers. Following the intervention of 1980, they continued to pursue the monetarist economic policy of the Justice Party. They also took measures to reduce the patrimonial character of the civil bureaucracy and to reform it on the basis of a purely instrumental rationale. The changes in the economic and administrative fields can be expected, in the long run, to lead to the advent of solid business and economic middle classes with political influence, to the strengthening of links between political parties and social groups, and towards facilitating the development of intermediary structures necessary for the functioning of a democratic system.

Professor Heper correctly points out that:

> The electorate in Turkey has constituted another category of political actors which has learned fast ... .Neither the politicians nor the intellectuals in Turkey have performed as well ... .In the popular referendum, they endorsed by an overwhelming majority the 1982 constitution, the handywork of the military, and then turned around and voted in the general elections for a political party (the Motherland Party of Turgut Ozal) ... which was considered at the time the most anti-military among the three parties allowed by the military to compete. Many politicians and intellectuals in Turkey were puzzled by the results of the referendum and the elections in question .... [30]

These developments can be read as indicating strongly that the military no longer views civil society as a subordinate entity or itself as possessing a monopoly of wisdom and truth. The post-1980 behaviour of the military, together with the growing maturity of the electorate and changes in the economic system, will lead to a better system of checks and balances which will make 'regulation from above' a less necessary means of moderating political conflict.

INTERPLAY OF FACTORS

This analysis of domestic factors has shown that, despite the rise of some anti-Western forces, the elements of stability are still predominant in Turkey's domestic environment. In spite of the relative erosion of the security policy consensus, Turkey has largely remained a deferential society seeking security mainly through the Atlantic Alliance. While in most of the allied

315

countries consensus on matters of defence and security can no longer be expected to derive simply from trust in political and military institutions,[31] an important majority of the public in Turkey is still willing to trust governments and experts on matters of security policy.

Beyond internal factors, however, Turkey is influenced by its international surroundings. Turkey has mostly reacted to threats, dangers and opportunities without much desire to change its environment or to create more favourable local conditions. Nevertheless, this aspect of Turkey's foreign policy is less conspicuous today than in the past, especially in its relations with the Middle East.

Turkey's security behaviour in the late 1940s and 1950s was shaped by a series of external constraints. The bipolar system and ideological heterogeneity of international life were the two main factors affecting Turkish policy: Turkey was locked in an East-West and ideological struggle. In addition, there were constraints tied to geography — ones simultaneously affecting the Soviet Union — and exemplified by the Soviet-Turkish dispute over the Straits after World War II.

While a strong case for the impact of the international system and geography on the formation of Turkish security policy can thus be made, Turkey's decisions and behaviour cannot be adequately understood without reference to its domestic situation. To a certain degree every state finds itself faced with a certain geopolitical environment, and conducts its policy as a function of the necessities dictated by that setting. Ultimately, however, actual choices are determined by the alternatives proposed by decision makers. A given geopolitical situation may be very important 'but still more important is how to conceive that situation.'[32] Turkey's geopolitical setting and the international system have acquired significance only in relation to Turkey's internal socio-political milieu, and to the Western-oriented ideological perspective held by the policy-making elite. Turkey's resistance to Soviet demands and its alignment with the West have derived mostly from a profound belief in the virtues of Western political systems. The exclusion of the Soviet option, therefore, does not result primarily from the effects of geography or of the international system *per se,* but rather from a combination of the peculiarities proper to the Turkish domestic environment *and* the heterogeneity of the international system.

316

The rigid alliances of the years of containment became more relaxed during the 1960s and 1970s. Rivalry and cooperation between diversified centres of power within the East and the West became more relevant than the conflict itself. The process of détente gave rise to hopes of permanent peace between the two blocs and many Westerners began to overlook the irreconcilable aspects of the two socio-economic systems. The rise of non-military issues as a result of détente, coupled with the feeling of security promoted by the successful functioning of NATO deterrence, encouraged the Western allies, including Turkey, to assert independent interests increasingly and to act autonomously in order to protect these. In the general atmosphere of détente, the revival of the Greek-Turkish feud over Cyprus and the Aegean brought about a relative shift in traditional perceptions of the threat. To certain policy makers, the Soviet threat seemed less immediate and less direct as competitive relations with Greece began to take precedence over East-West tensions.[33] The Turkish perception of Greek-Turkish problems, nevertheless, remains more moderate than the Greek view. This is apparent in the greater attention given by the government to domestic troubles (the struggle against terrorism) and to Turkish diplomatic and economic overtures towards the Middle East than to Greek-Turkish issues. Many Turks continue to view the Greek question more as a nuisance than as a threat.

The Cyprus dispute has been one of the contributing factors in Turkey's rapprochement with the non-aligned nations and the Middle East. In order to secure their support in the international community, Turkey has made great efforts to improve relations with all of these states, although the trend is most visible in Turkey's relations with the Arab countries. Yet, within the context of the Cyprus issue, Turkey has had a frustrating experience with Third World states. The PLO and most Arab countries have continued to vote for the Greek Cypriot-sponsored resolutions condemning Turkey at the non-aligned conferences and at the United Nations General Assembly. The new states have approached the Cyprus question keeping in mind their own problems of decolonization and national integration. Consequently, they have usually regarded Turkish Cypriot resistance as a separatist movement, and the Guarantee Treaty of 1960 as an instrument of neo-colonial intervention. The interests of Turkey and the non-aligned states have proven to be irreconcilable in this respect.

Turkey's orientation towards flexibility in foreign policy was undoubtedly accelerated by economic problems in the second half of the 1970s. Successful economic growth was adversely affected by the dramatic increase in oil prices and the global recession of 1975 and, less significantly, by the U.S. arms embargo. The growth of GNP slowed down considerably, whereas unemployment attained figures of 20 percent. Turkey's foreign exchange reserves were depleted and its external debts grew enormously. This negative economic experience led to the conviction that Turkey would be more secure economically if it found alternative sources of economic cooperation and diversified its economic connections.

Turkey's diplomatic overtures to non-Western regions are further linked to a number of specific events which undermined Turkey's ties with the United States. First, the advent of intercontinental ballistic missiles (ICBMs) in the 1960s and 1970s led to the growing belief, in the United States and Turkey, that the importance of forward defence allies such as Turkey was decreasing.[34] As the interior zone of the Soviet Union became vulnerable to nuclear destruction by missiles launched either from U.S. territory or from submarines in the high seas, the military value of allies for deterrence and war-fighting purposes seemed obsolete. This erroneous assessment of Turkey's geostrategic position affected not only American views of Turkey's importance for the Western Alliance, but also led many Turks to question the credibility of American pledges of protection.[35] The Turkish anxiety was somewhat exacerbated by the withdrawal of intermediate-range ballistic missiles (IRBMs) from Turkey in the aftermath of the Cuban missile crisis. The Jupiter missiles in Turkey and Italy had become obsolescent and their withdrawal had been ordered by the Kennedy administration even before the missile crisis. But Ankara regarded the Jupiters as an important demonstration of Washington's commitment to Turkish security. Widespread public opinion about the Kennedy administration's unilateral decision to remove the IRBMs provoked fears about Turkey's growing vulnerability. This incident allowed Turkish policy makers to consider that the United States might take unilateral decisions without prior consultation with Turkey even in cases where Turkish security was directly involved.[36]

The Cyprus affair played a crucial role in complicating U.S.-

Turkish relations. The first dramatic event was President Lyndon Johnson's blunt letter to Premier Inönü in June 1964 attempting to prevent Turkish troops from landing in Cyprus. In his letter, President Johnson made clear that Turkey did not have permission to use American equipment in a military operation against Cyprus. He also warned that NATO might not feel obliged to defend Turkey in the event of a Soviet retaliatory action against it because of its intervention in Cyprus. It is not difficult to imagine how this letter undermined the credibility of the whole Western Alliance system in the eyes of Turkish leaders and the general public.[37]

The credibility of American security commitments was further eroded by the arms embargo on Turkey (1975–1978), following the Turkish intervention in Cyprus in 1974, an operation instigated by the Sampson coup and based on the 1960 Treaty of Guarantee. The Turkish armed forces suffered badly as a result of this embargo, but the real damage was psychological. By obliterating the distinction between allies and enemies, the embargo greatly reinforced Ankara's suspicions that in the event of a Soviet aggression the United States might leave Turkey to fend for itself. The embargo not only failed to promote a settlement in Cyprus, but also worked against Western security interests by weakening further the defence posture of the Southern Flank. Finally, the embargo affair revealed to the Turks the extent to which the U.S. Congress was beginning to play an increasingly influential role in important foreign policy and security decisions. Domestic political issues and special interest groups in the United States were now essential components of the U.S. foreign policy decision-making process. This caused some anxiety in Turkish political circles: What sort of reliance could be placed on an allied nation where vital decisions were made by a legislative body that enjoyed power without accepting responsibility for it, and which was so vulnerable to pressure from special interest groups?

The Military Situation in NATO's Southeastern Region

These factors militating against Turkey's alignment with the West have been offset by certain other developments in the international system. The Soviet Union considerably increased its military power and potential in the 1960s and 1970s, adhering to its intention of extending its sphere of influence beyond the 'heartland' of Eurasia, and of increasing its freedom of action in 'peripheral' areas such as the Middle East. As a result, the threat facing the Southern Region of NATO generally, and Turkey in particular, has grown steadily in recent years. First, since the 1960s, the Soviet Union has gained strategic nuclear parity with the United States, and has greatly increased the range and strength of its power projection forces. This may well encourage Moscow to be more assertive in a time of crisis. Second, the military balance on the southeastern edge of NATO has tended to change in favour of the Warsaw Pact.[38] The growing strength of the Soviet Mediterranean squadron and of the Black Sea Fleet recently caused NATO to reconsider the mission of STRIKEFORSOUTH. In order to carry out its task of supporting a land battle, it will first have to neutralize the Soviet naval presence in the area. Although the West's naval forces are adequate for this task, it will still be difficult to bring necessary reinforcements into the region quickly. Time will not favour NATO's land forces which could not hold out for very long against the Warsaw Pact forces without tactical and logistic support arriving via the Mediterranean.

Another challenge in the Mediterranean is posed by Soviet submarines and Soviet naval aviation. There are usually about a dozen Soviet submarines in the Mediterranean and their number can be easily augmented to thirty in time of crisis. These are mostly diesel-powered units of low performance which would need reinforcement by nuclear-powered units from the Northern Fleet at such moments. Yet, the diesel submarines, while not effective against NATO carrier task forces, do constitute a serious danger for the Alliance sea lines of communication. The growth of the anti-ship capability of Soviet naval aviation has greatly augmented the threat to NATO carriers and other surface ships, as well as to their logistic support in time of war. It is estimated that there are currently at least seventy Backfires and thirty Badgers and Blinders based in the Crimea. Most of the important targets in the Mediterranean basin are within the combat radius of these aircraft.

NATO's twenty-five divisions in the Thrace/Straits area are largely made up of infantry, and they face approximately thirty-four Soviet, Rumanian and Bulgarian armoured and mechanized divisions. Moreover, the deployment of a new generation of Soviet aircraft, such as the Su-24 Fencer, Su-17 Fitter C/D, and MIG-23 Flogger, has considerably improved the offensive capabilities of the Soviet/Pact frontal aviation forces in the area. The Soviet/Pact electronic-warfare capability has also improved over the past decade. These developments, combined with the weakness of Alliance air defences and early-warning systems in the region, have substantially decreased warning time. The rolling farmland of Turkish Thrace is particularly suited for offensive operations towards the Straits based on a high-speed manoeuvre strategy. Furthermore, the triangular shape of the area, narrowing towards the Bosporus, offers any invader attacking from the northwest the choice of interior lines. Warsaw Pact offensive action towards the Straits might be supported by amphibious operations on suitable beaches on the Black Sea shore not far from the Bosporus. The possibility of this type of operation was confirmed by the Warsaw Pact Shield 82 and 84 exercises undertaken by Bulgarian and Soviet forces, including the Black Sea Fleet, 2,000 combat aircraft and an airborne division of the Odessa military district. These exercises have shown that a Warsaw Pact offensive in the region would involve heavy allocation of air force and naval units.

Eastern Turkey lies at the extreme limit of NATO's long logistic line and is important for Soviet access to the Middle East and the Persian Gulf area. In this region, where NATO shares a 610-kilometre common border with the Soviet Union, the force ratio is even more adverse than in the Thrace/Straits area. The Turkish army's eight divisions face approximately twenty Soviet divisions from the northern Caucasus and Transcaucasus military districts. Although most of these forces are estimated to belong in Category 3 (low state of readiness), the Soviets have been carrying out a military upgrading programme since the mid-1970s, improving the combined-arms capability of their divisions. These forces are equipped with about 4,300 tanks and 4,800 artillery pieces, whereas the Turkish army in eastern Turkey has only 1,000 tanks and 1,800 artillery pieces.

Another complicating factor is that Ankara has to allocate substantial forces in the southeast region of Turkey for the protection of its extensive borders there. The vulnerability of this area has increased mainly because of Soviet-Syrian defence cooperation which was intensified during the war in the Lebanon. In a NATO-Warsaw Pact contingency, Syria's formidable military force could seriously harass the Turkish armed forces operating in northeastern Turkey by attacking

321

their lines of supply. Railroads, seaports and oil pipelines in the area, which are critically important for supplying Turkish forces, are all within easy range of Syrian air and land forces.

Terrorism as an International Threat

In Turkey, terrorism has developed as a multidimensional, international (and transnational) phenomenon. It cannot be satisfactorily explained merely on the basis of sociological or economical analysis.[39] When terrorist activities began in Turkey in 1968, they were led by a mild educational reform movement of university students, but they rapidly changed character, escalating to violent clashes with the police and security forces. University campuses were used for accumulating arms, ammunition and propaganda material. Violent attacks were also directed against U.S. and NATO personnel and installations. Terrorist acts were organized and carried out by extreme Marxist organizations such as the Revolutionary Students Federation (DEVGENC), the Turkish People's Liberation Army and the Turkish People's Liberation Front. All these groups acknowledged having drawn their inspiration from the ideas of revolutionaries such as Che Guevara and Carlos Marighella. They also adopted propaganda themes which were being transmitted in Turkish by Soviet-supported clandestine radio, broadcasting in particular from the Democratic Republic of Germany and Bulgaria.

Terrorism after 1975 became more widespread and destabilizing than it had been during the 1968–1972 period. Separatist Kurdish and extreme leftist organizations proliferated, singling out the erosion of state authority as their main target. The extreme nationalist right also became a major force in political violence, regarding itself as the 'defender of the Turkish state against communism.' In reality its terrorism dangerously undermined state authority. Its methods and tactics seemed less sophisticated, and received far less coordinated international support from abroad than did the leftist terrorist factions.

Parallel to the terrorism in Turkey, acts of violence by Armenian terrorists against Turkish targets abroad escalated. There are still two major Armenian groups. The Armenian Secret Army for the Liberation of Armenia (ASALA) is a Marxist organization, whereas the Justice Commandos of the

1915 Genocide (JCAG) seems to be nationalist rather than Marxist. But both use exactly the same methods and aim primarily at Turkish offices, diplomats and their families. Armenian terror has emerged as the product of one-sided propaganda and of a distorted account of history dating back nearly one hundred years. Armenian terrorists allege that the Ottoman government systematically massacred one and a half million Armenians, and claim that the Republic of Turkey should accept responsibility for this act, apologize, pay compensation and surrender large portions of eastern Anatolia to the Armenians. In August 1980, ASALA declared openly that the territory to be usurped from Turkey should be united with Soviet Armenia. These statements and actions indicate that the primary goal of Armenian terrorists is not to create an independent Armenia, but to remove eastern Turkey, strategically a very important region, from Western influence. ASALA's objective of separating eastern Turkey from the West is also reflected in its willingness to cooperate with radical Kurdish groups, traditional enemies of the Armenian people, who share the same goals.[40]

The total number of various arms (ranging from pistols to anti-tank and anti-aircraft missiles) captured from terrorists after September 1980 amounts to 800,000; the total value of such an arsenal is estimated at approximately 300 million dollars. Almost none of these weapons were manufactured in Turkey. Profits from bank robberies by terrorist organizations can account for only a very small fraction of their cost. Turkish authorities estimate total terrorist spending from 1977 to 1980 at one billion dollars. (This is the equivalent of U.S. and other NATO military aid to Turkey for the same period). This fact constitutes circumstantial evidence that terrorism against Turkey has been financed by external powers with considerable interest in destabilizing the country. There is some suspicion in Turkey that Moscow has acted as a sponsor of terrorist activities. This feeling is confirmed by other evidence such as the interception of arms shipments from Bulgaria and Syria, and the training and logistic support that some terrorist groups received from pro-Soviet elements of the PLO in Lebanon and Syria. The Bulgarian and Syrian roles, moreover, have become quite clear from the confessions of captured terrorists.

Elements of the Iraqi Kurdish Democratic Party and of the Kurdistan Workers Party still receive Syrian support. These separatist terrorists infiltrate Turkey after having trained in Syria, in close cooperation with other terrorist organizations. It is reported that members of ASALA have also obtained refuge in Syria.

Terrorism has complicated Turkey's relations with its allies. Terror inside the country has not only posed a threat to Turkey's democratic stability and internal security, but has also decreased its reliability as an ally. More importantly, it has created indignation and frictions. While some allies have criticized Turkey's efforts to check terrorist activities, they have also tolerated the free movement of Turkish terrorists across international borders and within allied countries. Armenian terror against Turkish diplomats also drives a wedge between the Turks and their allies. Armenian terrorists, murdering civilians in the name of the alleged massacre of Armenians in the terminal phase of the declining Ottoman Empire, try to exploit inherited Western prejudices against the Turks. They have been successful in some allied countries where the Armenian cause and the terrorists themselves are now being viewed with sympathy. This development has generated a suspicion among the Turkish public that Western countries 'looked upon their relationship with Turkey merely as an expedient cooperation with a country of alien culture and religion, carried out for the simple purpose of meeting security needs.'[41]

The unprecedented degree of terrorism from which Turkey has suffered in recent years, on the one hand, and the Soviet invasion of Afghanistan and the destabilized political situation in Iran, on the other, have increased pressure upon Turkey. The Soviet advances took place at a time when Turkey was struggling against a dramatic increase in terrorism. In response to the changes in the strategic environment and to the terrorist threat, Turkish policy makers have returned to their essentially geopolitical policy without, however, resuming the unidimensional approach of the 1950s.

OPTIONS AND PROSPECTS

Today Turkey pursues a much more complicated policy than it did in the 1950s. Its fundamental strategy choices will remain unchanged since they are essentially ideological, and dictated by its socio-political environment and geography. Within the

Atlantic Alliance, Turkey naturally exercises its freedom of action. It can decide the manner in which it should commit itself to its allies and the extent to which this commitment allows development of its relations with third states. These issues, in turn, depend, *inter alia*, on allied attitudes towards Turkey. These broad questions of policy raise more specific issues: To what extent does Turkey have the power of initiative in security matters? What possibilities exist for the improvement of its defence posture? What are its options in the Middle East? How are its relations with the Soviet Union, the United States and Western Europe developing? What are the prospects of a reconciliation with Greece? What compatibilities or incompatibilities exist between Turkey's options and basic Alliance aims, or the aims of other allies?

Modernizing Defence

In order to develop an ability to improve its strategic position rather than simply to react to threats in its region, Turkey must take steps to modernize its defence capacity in concert with its NATO allies. The threats facing the Atlantic Alliance in general and Turkey in particular have diversified in recent years. The major area of conflict has shifted from Europe (and from the lines of direct confrontation between NATO and the Warsaw Pact) to southwest Asia. Parallel to this development, indirect strategies based upon action through surrogate forces, low-intensity operations, economic and ideological techniques of influence, and terrorism have become more prominent. Moreover, the vital character of Soviet and Western interests in the Middle East and in the Persian Gulf area, coupled with the weakness of NATO's defence posture in the Southern Region, invalidate to a considerable extent traditional strategic concepts that give priority to NATO's central region. Instead of confronting NATO directly (in the centre) and so risking a strong conventional, and probably nuclear, response by the Alliance, the Soviets may prefer to take indirect action in the Southern Region, or in the areas adjacent to the region, presenting NATO with a *fait accompli*. Short of being tested by limited attacks, there is also the possibility that the Alliance may be intimidated by a Soviet military buildup that dramatically increased its relative power in the area.[42]

325

For these reasons, the revitalization of NATO's military posture is an urgent necessity. One requirement is to enhance reinforcement and resupply of NATO forces on the southeastern edge of the Alliance. Particularly vital requirements are the improvement of ASW capacities and tactical air power in the eastern Mediterranean. It is also necessary to improve reception facilities in Turkey and to reduce the vulnerability of airfields and ports by improving Turkey's air defence capability. The prestocking of fuel and ammunition and even the prepositioning of some heavy NATO equipment may also be required. A further weakness of NATO is its sparse early warning system in the southeastern region. This deficiency was only partly remedied, in October 1983, by the deployment of NATO E-3A AWACS aircraft at an air base near Konya in central Anatolia.

Possibly the most urgent requirement for the reinvigoration of NATO's defences in the Southern Region is the modernization of Turkey's armed forces which are still suffering an equipment crisis. Their weapon systems are mostly 1950s vintage. There are three principal categories of financial sources available for the improvement of Turkey's military posture: Turkey's own resources and its domestic arms industry; NATO funds; and bilateral cooperation with the United States and some West European allies, especially West Germany, for military assistance and purchases.[43]

In Turkey, there has never been a lack of political resolve concerning defence spending. In spite of tremendous economic difficulties in 1981, Turkey was able to devote 4.5 percent of its GNP to defence, whereas West Germany, the Netherlands, Belgium and Norway allocated respectively 4.3, 3.4, 3.3 and 3.3 percent of their public expenditures to defence. Turkey now allocates about 24 percent of its public expenditure and 5 percent of its GNP to defence. Yet, given the general level of its economic development, this percentage falls short of what Turkey's modernization programme would require. After the United States, Turkey maintains the second largest army in the Alliance, with more than 820,000 active-duty troops. Turkey's soldier/citizen ratio of one/sixty-three is far better than that of most other allies.

A long-term modernization programme should be considered simultaneously with the development of Turkey's arms industry. To some extent Turkey possesses the necessary industrial base and technical skills to create and support a fully fledged weapons industry. Cooperation between the private and public sectors in this field, however, has remained at a very low level. The existing plants are owned and run by the armed forces and the Machinery and Chemicals Industries Institution (MKEK) which is a state enterprise. Factories of the MKEK produce a range of weapons and ammunition, including machine guns, mortars, howitzers and rockets, and an electronics factory has recently become operative. The armed forces also have considerable maintenance and overhaul capabilities. Turkey has recently acquired seventy-seven Leopard 1A3 main battle tanks. In addition, Turkey is upgrading its 3,000 M-48s with new diesel engines, 105mm guns and improved fire-control systems as well as modernizing its anti-armour weapons. On the naval side Turkey has been building its own vessels since the mid-1960s.

A considerable number of Turkey's combat aircraft, with the exception of F-4Es and F-104s, are ageing and need to be replaced. The most important step in modernizing the Turkish air force has been the F-16 coproduction project with the United States which was agreed upon in 1985. This project aims to assemble and ultimately to coproduce 160 F-16 C/Ds in Turkey, in an effort to set up a domestic aircraft industry. Turkey is the first country to produce F-16s under licence. It is expected that Turkey's aircraft industry will attain a satisfactory level of development by the 1990s. Technical staff and trained personnel will be provided to the Turkish air force factories at Eskisheir which have made considerable progress since 1975 in repairs, engine renovation and the manufacture of parts.

Shortage of capital and lack of advanced technology have been the most formidable obstacles for the Turkish defence industry. There has also been a total lack of cooperation between private and public sectors in this respect. Nevertheless, some concrete steps have been taken in recent years to surmount these difficulties. In 1985, the government established a Defence Fund which is expected to generate considerable financial accumulation through a special taxation system. It is estimated that the amount collected in 1986 will reach the equivalent of 600 million dollars. Efforts are underway to make joint investments with Turkish, American and West European firms. The need for the renewal of defence equipment and the acquisition of weapons, in conjunction with export opportunities, is expected to create a demand which will amount to more than 15 billion dollars for a period of seven years. In 1985, the existence of such a suitably sized market and the Turkish government's readiness to cooperate with the private sector led many Turkish and foreign firms to look for possibilities of investment in Turkey. The technological, financial and managerial possibilities of the private sector combined with foreign partnership will certainly accelerate the development of the Turkish defence industry.[44] Its development will not only have positive effects on Turkey's economic expansion and technological development, but will create greater interdependence between Turkey and its allies.

The combined effect of population growth, increasing costs and modernization of the armed forces is likely to pose important questions. Can the system absorb the annually increasing number of conscripts? Is the universal conscription system still useful? Will modernization not require a certain reduction in the size of the army? Although it is difficult to find long-term answers to these questions in the Turkish context, it is clear that in the foreseeable future there will be no fundamental change in the system. Equally, it is most unlikely that a substantial reduction in the size of the army will occur. There are several reasons for this conservatism. First, 'size' is considered an important deterrent factor because a traditional emphasis on size and numbers has always played an important part in Soviet approaches to national defence. Second, the Turkish armed forces should be sizeable enough and ready to cope with a multiple-front offensive which may develop simultaneously on three separate theatres of operations (Thrace/Straits area, northeastern Turkey and southeastern Turkey). Third, although the educative aspect of military service is disappearing, its integrative function is still very important. Finally, because of the traditional nonexistence of parliamentary debates on defence matters, and because the major political parties seem now to be well aware of the above-mentioned aspects of the problem, there will be negligible parliamentary opposition to the allocation of a large share of the government's annual budget to national defence.

Transatlantic Relations and the United States

Until recently, relations between Turkey and the United States have in general developed without major problems. The difficulties experienced during the arms embargo were surmounted. The United States has supported Turkey's struggle against terrorism and the Turkish public has been greatly appreciative. In spite of this general improvement in the U.S.-Turkish relationship, bilateral defence cooperation with the United States suffers from certain defects. The general anti-Turkish bias of the U.S. Congress and its insistence on the application of the seven to ten ratio to its military assistance for Greece and Turkey continues to highlight the precarious nature of bilateral defence cooperation. The Turkish Ambassador in Washington, Dr. Sükrü Elakdag, has criticized the Congressional attitude in the following terms:

> Unfortunately, under the influence of this lobby [the Greek lobby], Congress has created policies establishing a series of linkages which could be called the Turkish-American-Greek triangle. This triangular linkage renders the common interests shared by the United States and Turkey hostage to circumstances that are wholly extraneous to those overarching interests.[45]

Turkey complains that since the amount initially requested by the United States is cut on the basis of the seven to ten ratio in Congress, Turkey cannot expect to get much more than about 700 million dollars in military assistance (including Military Assistance Program grants and Foreign Military Sales credits). Turkish officials argue that this amount is inadequate, because a serious military modernization effort requires at least one billion dollars *per annum* over a period of ten years. They also complain that, due to high interest rates, military assistance procedures, such as the U.S. Foreign Military Sales credit system, become financial burdens for the receiver. The Turkish government feels that the DECA, signed in March 1980, has worked against Turkish interests since the U.S. commitment to the modernization of the Turkish armed forces has not been fully realized. Turkey not only wishes to rid its relationship with the United States of 'extraneous' factors, such as the Greek and Armenian lobbies in Congress, but also wants the United States to adhere to the basic tenets of economic liberalism of which it is the great promoter, and to ensure that the economic aspects of the DECA are implemented in a satisfactory manner. Turkey has been particularly displeased with restrictions imposed on its textile exports to the United States.[46]

Although the DECA was formally extended up to 1990, on 16 March 1987 after eighteen months of tiresome negotiations, the frictions between Ankara and Washington have not ended. The fundamental difficulty stems from U.S. constitutional procedures which do not allow the administration to enter into any commitments in advance. What the Reagan administration was able to do was to sign a 'side-letter' (a declaration of intent) promising to make every effort to get the maximum possible military aid for Turkey each year, in face of Congressional opposition. In Turkey, public opinion, the opposition parties, as well as the Ozal government are becoming increasingly upset with the cuts in aid and the conditions attached to it by Congress. After the Foreign Affairs Committees of both the House of Representatives and the Senate had, in April 1987, proposed cutting aid to Turkey by 300 million dollars, to 569 million dollars, and asked for the prohibition of the use of U.S. arms for Turkish troops in Cyprus, the Ozal government decided to take no action on the approval and official publication of the 'side-letter' which extends the DECA to 1990, until the settlement of the aid question. The opposition parties urge the government to do more than simply suspend the DECA. They emphasize that the DECA will certainly function against Turkey's interests unless it contains concrete guarantees and contractual obligations for both parties. Moreover, they press for the establishment of parliamentary control over international agreements concerning defence installations and bases in Turkey.

Article 5, paragraph 4 of the DECA emphasizes that 'the extent of the defence cooperation envisaged in this Agreement shall be limited to obligations arising out of the North Atlantic Treaty.' Under the agreement, the two governments established a high-level joint military group to improve NATO's military posture in the region and to modernize the Turkish armed forces. The Memorandum of Understanding, concluded within the framework of the Defense Cooperation Agreement of 1980 and providing for the construction, improvement, and joint use of certain airfields mainly in the eastern provinces of Turkey, has, nonetheless, provoked some speculation in the Turkish and American press on the possibility of using these bases in a Persian Gulf contingency, even if the Soviets were not directly involved. Turkish and U.S. officials have declared on many occasions that the construction activities stipulated in the Memorandum have no connection with the U.S. Rapid Deployment Force, and that airfields will be limited to NATO uses during the course of agreed Alliance missions. Moreover, it has been reported that the Memorandum of Understanding contains several provisions linking it to NATO defence plans. Unconditional Turkish approval for use of these bases by the United States to project military power into the Middle East and Persian Gulf area would be incompatible with Turkey's security policy as well as with its self-defined role in the region. Although Turkey is prepared to discuss out-of-area questions within the Alliance, it has no commitments outside the NATO framework and it would not take the risk of participating in an out-of-area operation which was not jointly supported by all members of the Alliance. Furthermore, Turkey's involvement in such an operation would stand in contradiction to its Middle Eastern policy which is based on the principle of non-interference in the internal affairs of regional states and in interstate conflicts in the area.

Any government in Turkey which takes into account the domestic political context and the country's regional interests will have to demonstrate to the public that it is not acting as Washington's 'gendarme' in the Middle East. Any Turkish government will be extremely careful not to make strategic commitments outside the NATO framework. In fact, the strengthening of NATO's Southern Region, and particularly the modernization of the Turkish armed forces would greatly increase deterrence against potential attack and would shift the regional balance in the Middle East and Persian Gulf area in favour of the West, without need for a prior Turkish commitment. The revitalization of NATO's defence posture in the region would also affect the perception of military balance by regional states or non-state entities. In times of acute crisis or war, the behaviour of states such as Syria and Libya would depend a great deal upon their perceptions of the regional balance of forces.

Yet, Turkey's adjacency to the Soviet Union has induced Ankara to act with circumspection. In heightening deterrence, Turkey does not want to become provocative and avoids threatening vital Soviet security interests and internal stability. For example, Turkey is extremely careful not to increase the range of the tactical nuclear weapons deployed in the country. The present modernization programme provides for the improvement of the existing short-range systems without extending their range. Although a member of NATO, Turkey has been interested in maintaining friendly relations with the Soviet Union and other Warsaw Pact countries. During the last three years, there has been a slight increase in the total amount of foreign trade between Turkey and the East European countries. Earnings from exports to these countries were worth 245 million dollars in 1983 and reached 300 million dollars by 1985. The total amount of imports from the same countries was worth 802 million dollars in 1983 but this figure, which increased to 949 million dollars in 1984, is expected to drop in the late 1980s. Nevertheless, there will always be some economic cooperation between the countries. A major joint Soviet-Turkish project today is the natural gas pipeline which will transport 750 million cubic metres of Siberian natural gas to Turkey each year. This amount will increase to more than 6 billion cubic metres per year in the 1990s. An agreement for this joint project was signed in Ankara in February 1986. Both parties accepted to pay through barter: Soviet natural gas in return for Turkish goods exported to the Soviet Union. Turkish economic analysts estimate that this project will considerably increase the total amount of trade between Turkey and the Soviet Union in the 1990s.

The Ozal government believes that development of economic relations between nations, regardless of ideology and other political differences, can lead to mutual political understanding and reconciliation. Reliance on the economic interdependence approach, however, has not been viable in all cases. One example is the case of Turkey's relations with Bulgaria. Since the 1960s, successive Turkish governments have sought to improve economic relations with Sofia. Between the two countries there have been agreements concerning transportation and the importation of Bulgarian electricity into Turkey. The existence of mutual economic interests has not prevented the Bulgarians from persecuting the ethnic Turkish minority in Bulgaria. Nor did the existing economic cooperation between Turkey and the Soviet Union prevent Moscow from putting forward, in January 1986, a proposal concerning the settlement of the Cyprus dispute in a manner contrary to Turkey's interests.

Détente between the superpowers elicits ambivalent feelings in Turkey. On the one hand, détente could decrease the possibility of a general war and provide suitable ground for the development of economic relations. On the other hand, it could enhance the likelihood of indirect and incremental activities of a politico-military nature which are difficult to detect and to deter. Détente may also call forth latent Turkish fears of being abandoned by the United States as a result of a kind of U.S.-Soviet condominium. Would détente or an American desire for a quick rapprochement with Moscow change Washington's view of Turkey? Both Turkish analysts and policy makers were preoccupied with such questions when the Reagan-Gorbachev summit took place in Geneva in November 1985.

The Middle East

Problems in the Middle East are not purely military, but also social, political and even psychological. It would be misleading to emphasize only the military and geopolitical considerations. The interaction of local instabilities, regional conflicts and East-West competition is considered central to the Middle Eastern situation. Turkey's security policy in the Middle East combines a military approach through the strengthening of the Southern Flank and a diplomatic approach that takes into account indigenous social factors and political stakes.

Turkey's growing political and diplomatic concerns in the region have been, to a great extent, a result of intensified economic ties. Like almost all Western countries, Turkey is dependent on Middle Eastern oil for the functioning of its economy. Furthermore, oil plays a key role in achieving a viable conventional defence during international crisis and war. Domestic oil resources satisfy only 16 percent of Turkey's needs.

The proportion of oil imports has risen rapidly. Imported crude oil cost 3.24 billion dollars in 1983 compared with 962 million dollars in 1979. All the oil comes from Iran, Iraq or other Middle Eastern countries. A parallel growth is noticeable in Turkey's exports to the Middle East. Earnings from exports to these countries in 1979 were worth 400 million dollars and were about twice that in 1981. Turkey's exports to the Islamic countries increased to a total of 3 billion dollars in 1984. This figure amounted to 42 percent of total exports. Moreover, there are about 300 Turkish construction firms operating in the Middle East and North Africa. The total value of contracts held by Turks in these regions amounted to 10 billion dollars in 1982. This figure has recently increased to about 17 billion dollars. As Turkish contractors multiply their volume of business, the number of Turkish workers and technicians in these areas has reached 203,000.[47]

The first guiding principle of Turkey's policy towards the Middle East is to refrain from taking sides in local disputes. But this principle does not prevent Turkey from acting as a mediator when invited by all the parties concerned. In fact, Turkey has been an active member of the Islamic Conference mission mediating the Iran-Iraq conflict. Another ruling principle demands that Turkey's cooperation with the West, especially in the field of defence, should not damage the security interests of Arab states. This principle makes virtually impossible the utilization of defence installations in Turkey against Arab interests.[48]

As regards the Arab-Israeli conflict and the Palestinian question, Turkey's position does not appear to differ substantially from that taken by its European allies in the Venice Declaration of 1980. The Turkish government believes that American handling of the Arab-Israeli problem hinders the achievement of a settlement. It also thinks that the Palestinian question, if it is not resolved, will continue to endanger stability in the region and jeopardize Persian Gulf security. Turkey recognizes of course that there are other causes of instability in the region. In order to secure Western interests in the area — the maintenance of the vital flow of commerce and the containment of the Soviet Union — it is necessary to reach a settlement of the Arab-Israeli conflict on terms that moderate Arab states can accept. This would mean the end of the continued Israeli occupation of the West Bank and of the present status of Jerusalem as dictated unilaterally by Israel, as well as the creation of a Palestinian homeland and mutual recognition by Israel and the PLO of the other's legitimacy. Turkey also shares the opinion that asset-seizing strategies based on military intervention in Arab countries would be harmful to vital Western interests in the Middle East and the Persian Gulf area.

The prolonged war of attrition between Iran and Iraq is a cause of anxiety for Turkey. It continues without clear success for either side, and no party seems to have enough strength to mount a decisive offensive. Though the war has not resulted in the participation of extra-regional powers and has not 'escalated horizontally,' it has had direct and immediate implications for Turkey's security. The Gulf War has created a power vacuum in the region. The growing inability of both states to control their own territories effectively is encouraging separatists, militant leftist groups, and other centrifugal forces in Iraq, Iran and the southeastern border regions of Turkey. Turkish villages close to the frontier are being terrorized and roads vital for international transportation are being attacked by armed bands infiltrating from both countries. Apart from the continual operations against these bands in Turkish territory, the Turkish armed forces undertook, in May 1983 and with the consent of the Iraqi government, a police operation against some of these groups based in Iraqi territory. Nevertheless, Turkey is extremely careful to maintain a policy of strict neutrality vis-à-vis the conflicting states, although it has made clear its readiness to make all possible efforts to stop the war and settle the dispute on the basis of mutual consent by both sides. Turkish diplomacy has shown great concern for the preservation of peace and stability in the Middle East, partly for important strategic reasons, but also to facilitate the achievement of Turkey's long-term economic goals in the region. One of Turkey's main purposes in seeking a early negotiated settlement to the Iran-Iraq war is to help prevent the belligerents from fruitlessly depleting their financial resources. Turkey believes that normal economic cooperation with Iran and Iraq could naturally only take place in an atmosphere of peace and security.

Nonetheless, there are indications that Turkey's policy of neutrality is under some strain. On the one hand, Baghdad would like Turkey to make greater efforts to bring an end to the Gulf War, and even to put pressure on Tehran to arrest hostilities; while on the other, Iran wishes Ankara to blame Iraq for initiation of the war. Both countries have, nevertheless, been very cautious about their declarations concerning Turkey's position. Pressures on Ankara to abandon its position of neutrality would certainly become much heavier if the Kerkük-Yumurtalik oil pipeline between Iraq and Turkey were attacked by Iran. Moreover, the continuing existence of terrorist camps on Syrian soil and of infiltrations into Turkey constitute another sensitive question for Ankara. The Turkish government clearly favours a peaceful resolution of differences with Damascus, and both capitals have recently shown initiatives in this direction.

The U.S.-Lybian confrontation in 1986 has shown that Ankara's 'balancing policy' in the Middle East is proving increasingly difficult to maintain. Nevertheless, the Turkish government's approach to the Lybian crisis was not entirely unsuccessful. Ankara refrained from passing judgement on the Gulf of Sirte incident. Indeed, it would be extremely difficult for Turkey to support Colonel Gadaffi's claims to enlarge Libya's maritime area in the Gulf of Sirte without weakening its own position vis-à-vis Greece in the Aegean dispute. The U.S. air raid against Libya in April 1986 embarrassed Ankara even further. Although public opinion and the press were overwhelmingly on the side of Libya, for most Turks, the incident did not generate deep emotions against the United States. After the American raid, the Turkish government issued a statement criticizing the U.S. action in very moderate terms without calling it an 'attack' or an 'aggression.' The statement denounced 'selective' approaches to conflicts of this type, and advocated international cooperation and concerted international measures to cope with terrorism. Moreover, it stressed the necessity to exhaust peaceful means prior to any armed action, and made clear that Turkey was 'unable to reconcile' the air raids against Lybia with the principles of international law. The Turkish statement pleased neither side. Libya, however, found some consolation in the anti-American attitude of the Turkish press. In the eyes of the U.S. administration, the Ozal government's behaviour was ambivalent to say the least. Turkey was able soon after the raid, however, to display its strong anti-terrorist policy when the police apprehended two Lybian terrorists just before their attempt to blow up the U.S. Officers' Club in Ankara in retaliation for the air raid.

Relations with Western Europe

Turkish policy makers do not see the Middle East as an alternative to Western Europe. Both regions are considered complementary to Turkey's economy and security. The Turkish republic's long-term objective has always been to achieve integration in Europe, and Europe has always been the point of reference for the development of modern Turkish society. Leaving aside this ideological consideration, the security factor is becoming more and more salient in discussions on Turkey's membership in the European Community.[49] It is believed that a more lasting identification with the European movement will bridge the psychological gap between Turkey and Western Europe, and thus reinforce allied commitments to Turkey. There is a growing tendency in Turkey to see NATO and the EC as complementary institutions. It is thought wrong that Turkey should be considered as a vital deterring power in the southeastern region of the Alliance while being denied participation in the European integrative process. Ankara feels that it has a great interest in taking an active part in European Political Cooperation (EPC), and in contributing to the development of an independent European strategic identity. In April 1987, Turkey applied to join the Western European Union.

After the southeastern enlargement of the EC, Turkey and Norway are among the few European states that remain outside the EPC framework. Nevertheless, growing Soviet influence in the eastern Mediterranean and southwest Asia, the Gulf War, the European tendency to increase initiatives in the Middle East, and Greek membership in the EC, all tend to increase considerably the importance of the Turkish factor in EPC consultations. Ankara is willing, in principle, to become involved in the EPC process pending its full membership in the Community. But consultations have not yet yielded a satisfactory solution that provides for a special relationship between EPC and Turkey.

As Turkey's membership in the EC would lead to complete and equal participation of Turkey in EPC, it would have important implications for Turkey itself. Turkey would become less dependent on the United States, and would enjoy greater liberty of action in the Middle East. Participation would also provide Turkey with opportunities to give practical substance to its new role as a bridge between the Middle East and Western Europe. Conversely, Turkey's autonomy in foreign policy making would be curtailed. Its low profile and non-interventionist approach to regional affairs may come under new strains because of a growing West European tendency to play a more active peacekeeping role in the Middle East. Turkey would also have to accept the internationalization of the Greek-Turkish conflict within the framework of EPC. The settlement of various issues between Turkey and Greece would probably become easier but Turkey would be subject to more powerful international pressures.

Despite a certain decrease in Turkey's trade with the EC countries in recent years, economic ties between Turkey and the Community remain very strong. Trade with the EC still constitutes one-third of Turkey's total trade. The question of its membership in the EC is clouded, however, by a history of inconsistent positions. Turkey's stance towards integration during the 1960s and 1970s was hesitant, even though full membership had always been official Turkish policy. Ankara participated in the negotiation process with proposals reflecting compromises that resulted from bureaucratic politics and organizational rivalries between the Ministry of Foreign Affairs and the State Planning Organization. Fluctuations in the domestic political context tended to affect the importance Ankara attached to the question of EC membership. These fluctuations have raised doubts about Turkey's real objectives.[50]

Earlier hesitations seem to have dissipated and today there is a much clearer consensus as well as optimism on the issue of EC membership. The withdrawal of the charges against Turkey at the European Commission on Human Rights in 1985 is regarded as a positive sign for future developments. Likewise, Turkey's invitation by Western Europe to participate in the European Research Coordination Agency (EUREKA) project and the decision of the European foreign affairs ministers, on Ankara's request, to agree to a meeting of the EC-Turkey Association Council in autumn 1986 have also been taken as good omens. Despite the persistence of divisive issues and difficulties, such as the free circulation of labour, restrictions imposed on Turkish textile exports, Turkey's own level of economic development, and the Greek tendency to use its veto right as a bargaining chip, the general improvement of relations with Europe encouraged the Turkish government to submit, on 14 April 1987, a formal application for membership in the European Community. There is, however, a general conviction in Turkey, as well as in the EC countries, that the procedure leading to full membership will last more than a decade.

Greek-Turkish Tension

Deteriorating relations between Turkey and Greece are undoubtedly one of the major security problems for Ankara. The tension between these two allied countries undermines Alliance harmony and has a debilitating effect on the security of

338

NATO's Southern Flank. This conflictual relationship detracts the attention of both countries from common security questions confronted by the Western Alliance. Joint training opportunities are wasted because Greece usually declines to take part in joint NATO exercises in the Aegean and eastern Mediterranean. Tension between Greece and Turkey exacerbates command and control problems and creates additional complications for force deployment. Moreover, this uneasy situation complicates not only the defence plans of both nations but also their relationships with other allies.

Disagreements over Cyprus and the Aegean are at the basis of present hostility. Although both parties usually formulate their claims in precise legal terms, the disputes are essentially political and the issues are often dominated by nationalistic perceptions and historically defined attitudes. Leaving aside the legal intricacies of the dispute a few general points are worth making.

Greek-Turkish differences in the Aegean stem partly from the geographical peculiarities of the region, and partly from the respective historical perceptions of the disputants. The Aegean is a semi-closed sea scattered with more than 3,000 Greek islands and islets. The Greek islands in the eastern Aegean are very close to the Turkish mainland (in some cases less than one kilometre away) and more than 150 kilometres distant from the Greek mainland. These facts of geography exacerbate, for the Turks, continual Greek reference to the 'historical rights' of Greece in the Aegean. Turkish officials are, therefore, all the more sensitive to what they call 'the creeping sovereignty policy of Greece' over the last fifty-five years.

In 1919, Greece attempted an invasion of Turkey and its forces came within seventy kilometres of Ankara. After the war, the Lausanne Peace Treaty of 1923 did not merely put an end to the hostilities and draw new boundaries, but also provided for an overall settlement of various outstanding disputes by establishing an equilibrium of interests between Turkey and Greece. The Turks maintain that while they have always remained faithful to this political balance, achieved after long negotiations in 1923, the Greeks have pursued a revisionist policy.[51] Various Greek advances in the Aegean since the 1930s are viewed by the Turks as manifestations of just such a policy. In 1931, Greece extended its airspace to ten miles, without regard for the breadth of its territorial waters which was then three miles and was extended in 1936 to six miles, a breach of the well-established rule of international law, embodied in the 1945 Chicago Convention on International Civil Aviation, whereby the breadth of national airspace must correspond to the breadth of territorial waters. Turkey also argues that the Greeks interpret the Flight Information Region (FIR) not as a technical issue of air traffic services, according to the International Civil Aviation Organization (ICAO) Assembly resolutions, but as a matter of sovereignty over the Aegean airspace. In 1980, Turkey withdrew its NOTAM 714,[52] which had been issued for security reasons during the Cyprus crisis of 1974, and allowed reestablishment of the pre-1974 FIRs whose demarcation line follows Turkish territorial waters, giving to Athens flight control responsibility for all civilian air traffic over almost all the Aegean. Turkish authorities complain that Greece abuses its FIR rights and duties to restrict Turkish military aircraft and air force exercises over the high seas in the Aegean.

In 1960, Greece, claiming the entire continental shelf of the Aegean, began to grant licences for exploration and exploitation on the Aegean continental shelf, and these operations were intensified during the first years of the 1970s. The Turkish government believes bilateral negotiations to be the most appropriate procedure for the delineation of the parties' respective continental shelves. Because many Greek islands are at close proximity to Turkey and on the geological 'natural prolongation' of the Turkish mainland, an equitable solution to the dispute can be found only through negotiations. But Greece rejects this approach and favours the automatic application of the equidistance principle without negotiations, which implies the drawing of a median line between the eastern Aegean islands and the Turkish coast, leaving Turkey with practically no continental shelf at all beyond its territorial waters.

The avowed Greek intention of extending the present territorial waters from six to twelve miles is another major element in Greek-Turkish tension. Due to the same geographical situation, Greece possesses, under the present six-mile limits, approximately 43.68 percent of the Aegean Sea and Turkey 7.46 percent. The remaining 48.85 percent are part of the high seas and the continental shelf that is to be delineated between the two countries. In the case of an extension of territorial waters to twelve miles, the Greek share of the sea would rise to 71.53 percent and that of Turkey to only 8.79 percent. Moreover, the continental shelf problem would be solved automatically in favour of Greece. The Turks also complain that the Greeks view the FIR and NATO command and control problems not as technical questions, but as sovereignty issues.

The question of NATO command and control areas in the Aegean remains unsolved. Until Greece's withdrawal from NATO's integrated military structure after Turkey's military intervention in Cyprus in 1974, the allied command and control arrangements in the southeastern region of the Alliance had existed on a *de facto* basis and were regarded by Turkey as unsatisfactory. After Greece's withdrawal, NATO had to base its operations on new *ad hoc* arrangements. Greece returned, in October 1980, to the NATO integrated command structure as the result of the Rogers Plan. This document, which is a compromise of the views of all concerned, was also accepted by the Greek government in 1980. The Rogers Plan replaced the pre-1974 arrangement by some interim measures pending a final solution of the command and control problems through negotiations within the Alliance's military organization. Greece has accepted by this agreement to return to NATO's military wing, and then to negotiate command and control issues. After the PASOK government came to power, Greece adopted a different interpretation of the Rogers Plan asserting that the command and control responsibility of almost the entire Aegean should rest with Greece because the agreement had restored all of Greece's rights (including command and control in the Aegean) as they had existed before 1974. Since this Greek interpretation is accepted neither by Turkey nor by NATO authorities, Athens declines at present to participate in NATO exercises in the area.

In the 1960s, the Greeks began militarizing some of the islands close to Turkey, among them Lemnos. The Turks declare these militarization activities, which have been proceeding continuously since then, as violations of international treaties, such as the Lausanne Peace Treaty of 1923 and the Paris Peace Treaty of 1947 which seek to reconcile Greek sovereignty over these islands with Turkish security needs. The Greek government initially insisted that its activities on these islands were only civilian. But in 1974, it openly accepted that militarization had taken place. Since then, it has been trying to convince the Alliance to accept the allocation of Greek forces on the island of Lemnos to the NATO command structure. In Turkish eyes this is essentially a ploy to force NATO and Turkey to recognize the militarization of the island as legal.

In response to these Greek moves in the eastern Aegean, Turkey created the Fourth Army, known also as the Aegean Army, which has become the main rhetorical element in Greek 'threat analysis.' The Greek government points to the Turkish Fourth Army as evidence that the 'Turkish threat' is real. Greeks also argue that the remilitarization of the islands is just a defensive measure against the Turkish Fourth Army. Turks refute this Greek view by underscoring the fact that they are under no international obligation to deploy their armed forces only in specific areas within their own territory, and by recalling that this army was established in 1975, long after the militarization of the islands. But this argument, of course, is not sufficient to dissipate suspicions about the Fourth Army's 'real' nature and operational objectives, and certain myths remain that should be elucidated.

First, the western part of Anatolia has been called the 'Aegean Region' by the Turks, and the Aegean Army, therefore, takes its name from its location in that region. Second, the Fourth Army is composed of training units with programmes for artillery, transport and engineering. Air force training bases were deployed near Izmir, where climatic conditions are highly suited to training activities, many years before the establishment of the Fourth Army. Third, the total number of military personnel in the area does not exceed 40,000 cadets and many civilians are included. It should be emphasized that only a small number of troops in the area are ready to fulfil wartime missions. Fourth, although Izmir is not a naval base, naval forces in transit occasionally stop there. One should also note that Turkey has never made military preparations, not even during the crisis of 1974, for offensive action against a Greek island in the eastern Aegean.

Since the early 1950s, the Enosis-oriented (pro-unification with Greece) policies of Athens and of the Greek Cypriots have also worried the Turks. Turkey is involved with Cyprus primarily because Ankara is committed to the survival and safety of the Turkish Cypriot community as a separate ethnic entity. This commitment found its legal expression in the Zurich and London Agreements and in the 1960 constitution of the Republic of Cyprus. A Treaty of Guarantee authorized Ankara to take military action in order to reestablish the state of affairs created in 1959–1960. It was on the basis of this international instrument that Turkey sent an expeditionary force to the island, when Athens staged a *coup d'état*, using Nikos Sampson, a former EOKA[53] terrorist, against the Makarios government. Ankara had every reason to believe that if it did not intervene in Cyprus, the safety of the Turkish community would have been in very grave danger. Even though Cyprus, by virtue of its strategic location, represents an extremely important security question for Turkey as well, Ankara does not regard the conflict as a primarily Turkish versus Greek one. It sees it rather as a dispute which ought to be settled between the Greek and Turkish Cypriot communities and through intercommunal talks.

The fundamental principles of the Turkish Cypriot position can be summarized as follows. First, the new state of Cyprus which is to be established should be a 'bicommunal' and 'bizonal' federation. Second, the withdrawal of Turkish forces from the island should take place after the establishment of a federal government and the settlement of the conflict between the two communities. Third, the status of the new state of Cyprus should be placed under a system of guarantee with Turkish participation. Fourth, a settlement should be negotiated and achieved not in an international conference but between the two communities.

The Turks have always supported all efforts aimed at reviving the intercommunal talks under the auspices of the UN Secretary General. The Greeks, on the other hand, do not seem to have adopted this approach unequivocally and unconditionally. They appear to work for the internationalization of the conflict, especially by drawing in non-aligned nations, the European Community and both superpowers. The Turkish Cypriots complain that the Greek Cypriot leadership, especially since Prime Minister Papandreou took office, has consistently acted with the intention of undermining major points of agreement such as 'bizonality' and so destroyed the only valid framework for a negotiated settlement. The proclamation of the Turkish Republic of Northern Cyprus in 1983 was the result of the Turkish Cypriots' conviction that the Greek Cypriots were not prepared to share power with them within the context of a negotiated federal solution. It was, however, a 'two-track decision,' not only founding a new state in northern Cyprus, but also explicitly leaving the door open for intercommunal talks to seek for the establishment of a new partnership within the framework of a genuine federation.

Differences over the Aegean and Cyprus stem mainly from a deep-rooted Greek conviction that the jurisdiction of Greece extends over the entire Aegean Sea and even over Cyprus, but that of Turkey does not go beyond its territorial waters. This perspective has inevitably led the Greeks to view any Turkish concern beyond that line, such as the seabed delimitation or the rights of Turkish Cypriots, as an 'aggressive' attitude. Turkey has no claims on any Greek territory; a fact which the President of the Turkish Republic has made clear on many occasions. Turkish governments have always maintained the belief that both countries have interests in each other's welfare and security. Accordingly, they welcome any improvement in U.S.-Greek defence cooperation as a contribution to the strengthening of NATO's Southern Region. For the same reason, in 1980, Turkey allowed Greece's return to the military organization of NATO without reciprocal assurance that Ankara's conditions concerning the application of the Rogers Plan and a final solution of the command and control problems should be fulfilled by Athens. What Turkey cannot accept, however, is the establishment of trilateral links between Turkey, Greece and the United States on defence issues that are hostage to the specifics of the Greek-Turkish dispute.

The present Turkish government is cautious about overstressing the disputes between Turkey and Greece. It argues that Turkey should 'freeze' problems with Greece which are not immediately soluble and concentrate, instead, on resolvable issues such as trade and tourism. Premier Ozal believes that the development of economic relations between Turkey and Greece would generate an atmosphere of cooperation which would improve choices for dispute settlement. To this effect, the Turkish government has abolished the visa requirement for Greeks wanting to visit Turkey although this gesture has not thus far been reciprocated by the Greek government. On several occasions the Turks have proposed measures to improve trade relations between the two countries. These too have been rebuffed by the government of Papandreou. The PASOK government has chosen to disrupt the ongoing negotiation process over the Aegean and to increase tension between the two countries. Papandreou's anti-Turkish rhetoric is particularly harmful as it encourages extremist elements in both countries. Its scope of influence is not limited to the promotion of an anti-

Turkish climate in Greece, but extends to Turkey where it mobilizes anti-Greek feelings. The inordinate tone of Papandreou's foreign policy complicates the solution of problems even further by restricting both governments' freedom of action. The opposition in Turkey has begun to criticize the Ozal government for being too mild and tolerant in the face of Papandreou's bitter tone.

At present, all Greek tactics seem to evolve around the objective of isolating Turkey and of convincing the allied governments to exert pressure on Ankara in order to achieve a solution favourable to Greece. In the recent past such tactics have been relatively successful in bringing the United States or other allies to exert pressure on Turkey, as was the case with the U.S. embargo. But they have never been successful in attaining their ultimate aim of forcing Turkey to make concessions. Turkish interests in Cyprus and the Aegean are so great, Turkish public opinion so sensitive, and Turkey such a strategically important ally that no allied pressure would be heavy enough to force Ankara to accept Greek preconditions or to make concessions without negotiations. As a rule such tactics have produced the reverse effect of complicating allied relations even further and hardening public opinion and governmental positions.

At first glance, the Aegean and Cyprus disputes appear as two separate issues. The Aegean dispute directly involves Greece and Turkey and should be solved between these two states, whereas the Cyprus dispute involves the two Cypriot communities (far more directly than it does Turkey and Greece). The intercommunal conflict, however, takes place within the larger framework of Greek-Turkish relations because the two Cypriot communities regard themselves as 'extensions' of their respective peoples in Turkey and Greece. For this reason, an easing of present tensions between Greece and Turkey would inevitably affect positively the attitudes of the Cypriot communities. The resumption of a dialogue between the two states and the conclusion of a positive settlement concerning the Aegean would contribute to the creation of a climate of mutual confidence in Cyprus and facilitate compromises between the two communities.

The Aegean crisis, in March 1987, has highlighted how easily and quickly the persisting tension between Turkey and Greece could lead to war between these two NATO allies. Both nations came to the threshold of armed conflict after Greece declared that it would go ahead in the disputed area with its plans of oil exploration and exploitation beyond its territorial seas. Such activities were considered by Turkey as a violation of the Bern agreement of 1976, in which both parties had committed themselves to refrain from performing exploration and exploitation activities in the disputed waters pending the solution of the continental shelf problem. Turkey retaliated by sending a seismic vessel, Sismik I, to the same area. Both governments ordered their armed forces to be on the alert. Nevertheless, both states having lived through similar experiences in the past were able to act with circumspection and to diffuse the crisis by accepting to remain within their respective territorial waters. Following this agreement Ankara and Athens exchanged a series of diplomatic letters in order to agree on a procedure for peaceful settlement of the dispute.

CONCLUSION

In international affairs, prediction is both a necessary and risky undertaking. Looking at Turkey's domestic socio-political structure and past conduct of foreign policy, it is possible to discern some stable patterns of behaviour and to extrapolate certain new tendencies. Consistency has been one of the remarkable features of Turkish foreign policy.[54] When change came it was slow, deliberate, carefully elaborated and developed gradually by succeeding governments. This has endowed Turkey's foreign and security policies with a high degree of predictability — a feature which appears to be firmly engraved and durable. However, the liberalization of the economy, the demise of the public bureaucracy and the rise of the business elite tend to alter certain aspects of Turkey's classical foreign policy style by introducing into it some elements of transnationalism.

Turkey has remained an active member of the Alliance under different administrations; policies of change have aimed at increasing Turkey's freedom of action without contradicting NATO objectives. These policies, moreover, have been provoked by the oscillations of domestic politics as well as by external events and allied attitudes towards Turkey.

Anti-NATO arguments are still being put forward today in certain newspapers, albeit somewhat mildly and indirectly. There is also a great number of people in the country who are either disinterested in, or inadequately informed about, the Atlantic Alliance and its importance for the defence of their country. Some of these people are likely to be highly susceptible to anti-NATO propaganda. In spite of intense and systematic Marxist propaganda, communism (and any other type of totalitarian ideology) has always been abhorred by an overwhelming majority of the population. Despite terrorism and subversion of an unprecedented degree, the faith of the Turkish people in democracy has remained intact. Existing political parties, unlike some of those in the 1960s and 1970s, do not tend to link economic problems and other grievances with Turkey's membership in NATO. As the democratic process proceeds, the reemergence of extreme leftist and rightist political parties and groups will certainly increase anti-NATO and anti-Western rhetoric. But we know from the experience of the 1960s and 1970s that an increase in the limited electoral influence of such parties in the Turkish political context is highly unlikely. In the foreseeable future it is also unlikely that any substantially serious challenge to Turkey's alignment with the West will arise. The political debate will instead focus on such issues as inflation, income distribution, unemployment, international trade, Middle Eastern politics, Greek-Turkish relations, and on relations with the United States and the European Community.

For the time being it is difficult to gauge the extent of progress in Greek-Turkish relations in part because of Papandreou's hardline policy, but also because of the inherent complexities of the issues involved. On the Turkish side, there is growing pessimism about the prospect of a breakthrough and of a resumption of dialogue with the PASOK government. But it may be expected that Turkey's future entry into the European Community will force both countries to give priority to cooperation in all fields, and thus facilitate the settlement of disputes.

Given the critical geopolitical situation in which Turkey finds itself and the continued relevance of the East-West conflict, it is unlikely that the threats facing Turkey will decrease. New problems are imposing themselves while some of the old ones remain unsolved. Deteriorating relations with Bulgaria are becoming a new factor of insecurity. Turkey views with extreme concern the harsh measures of Bulgarization to which the Muslim Turkish minority in Bulgaria is being subjected. Turkey will also remain a target of destabilization efforts. Within Turkey, subversion and terrorism will continue to pose security problems, even if not at the levels attained in the 1970s. Turkish leaders are well aware of this prospect and they have informed the public on several occasions of the continuing threat of destabilization strategies.

Turkey has had remarkable success in reducing terrorism within the country. But little has been done on the international level. Terrorism and subversion probably pose the most immediate and tangible security threats that the Alliance faces throughout the 1980s. There are no formal allied arrangements for joint efforts to contain the danger. The promotion of allied cooperation to take countermeasures against terrorism is of paramount importance. Given the diversified character of Western democratic societies, however, it is not easy for the allies to reach a common understanding of the terrorist phenomenon. Turkish leaders hope that an increased appreciation of the difficulties of dealing with terrorism will solve the problems resulting from the criticism directed at Turkey for the manner in which it dealt domestically with the terrorist phenomenon, taking, at times, necessarily harsh measures.

Turkey is situated between the Soviet Union and the principal zones of opportunity for Soviet power. As a key element of NATO's Southern Region, Turkey's presence has a deterrent value against direct Soviet military action in the Middle East. Thus, Turkey is beginning to be viewed in the region for its importance as a guarantor of peace and stability, and its security requirements as a member of NATO are now better appreciated at least by the moderate regional states. Turkey's development of a market economy and its reaffirmation of Western democratic values have given it greater international status.

A revitalization of the consensus of the 1950s is not possible, but the conditions for a new consensus are being created. New national interests are being restated and accommodated to general Alliance interests. In Turkey today, there is a general conviction that the country's geographical, historical, and socio-political characteristics not only allow but also require it to pursue a multi-dimensional foreign policy. This trend is particularly evident in Turkey's relations with the Middle Eastern states. Turkey will continue to strengthen its trading ties within the region. The intensification of its relations with Middle Eastern countries, on the one hand, and its role within the Alliance in the area, on the other, may result in Turkey's greater involvement in the region's affairs.[55] This may bring Turkey's neutrality policies under new strains. Turkey's 'bridging role' between the Middle East and Western Europe still needs to be conceptualized at the policy-planning level in order to acquire operational significance. Turkey's principal security concerns, however, are not likely to allow Turkey's regional policy to reach the point where it will no longer be possible to accommodate its regional interests with its fundamental policy line.

NOTES

1. See, Edward B. Atkeson, 'Hemispheric Denial: Geopolitical Imperatives and Soviet Strategy,' *Strategic Review* (Spring 1976): 26-36.

2. Nurettin Ersin, 'Turkey,' *NATO's Fifteen Nations,* no. 1 (1980): 91.

3. Three combat zones are usually distinguished: Turkish Thrace and Straits area, eastern Turkey, and southern Turkey.

4. *Atatürk'ün Söylev ve Demeçleri* (Atatürk's Speeches and Declarations), 93. Cited by Metin Tamkoç, 'Turkey's Quest for Security through Defensive Alliances,' in *The Turkish Yearbook of International Relations* (Ankara University, Faculty of Political Science, 1961), 8.

5. Ferenc A. Vali, *Bridge across the Bosporus: The Foreign Policy of Turkey* (Baltimore and London: The Johns Hopkins Press, 1971), 219. (Hereafter cited as: *Bridge across the Bosporus*)

6. Arnold Toynbee, *The Western Question in Greece and Turkey* (London: Constable, 1922), 18.

7. See, Vali, *Bridge across the Bosporus,* 269.

8. See, Mehmet Gönlübol, 'NATO and Turkey: An Overall Appraisal,' in *The Turkish Yearbook of International Relations* (Ankara University, Faculty of Political Science, 1971), 3, 13; and Tamkoç, 'Turkey's Quest for Security through Defensive Alliances,' 24.

9. For another account of domestic change and its foreign policy implications for Turkey see, Duygu Bazoglu Sezer, *Turkey's Security Policies,* Adelphi Paper, no. 164 (London: IISS, 1981), 2-11.

10. See, Gönlübol, 'NATO and Turkey: An Overall Appraisal,' 24-28.

11. Richard F. Grimmett, *United States Military Installations in Turkey* (Washington, DC: Congressional Research Service, Library of Congress, 1984), 14.

12. See, Bülent Ecevit, 'Turkey's Security Policies,' *Survival* (Sept./Oct. 1978): 203-208.

13. See, *Prime Minister Bülent Ecevit's Speeches* (General Directorate of Press and Information of the Turkish Republic, 1978), 33-34.

14. See, Serif Mardin, 'Center-Periphery Relations: A Key to Turkish Politics,' *Deadalus* (Winter 1973): 169-190.

15. See, Sabri Sayari, 'Some Notes on the Beginnings of Mass Political Participation in Turkey,' in *Political Participation in Turkey: Historical Background and Present Problems*, ed. Engin D. Akarli with Gabriel Ben-Dor (Istanbul: Bogaziçi University Publication, 1975), 123-126.

16. See, Mümtaz Soysal, *Dis Politika ve Parlamento* (Foreign Policy and the Parliament) (Ankara: Faculty of Political Science Publication, 1964), 257-275.

17. John W. Barker, 'Comments on Toynbee's Article,' in *The Ottoman State and its Place in World History*, ed. Kemal Karpat (Leiden: Brill, 1974), 31.

18. See, Serif Mardin, 'Religion and Politics in Modern Turkey,' in *Islam in the Political Process*, ed. James P. Piscatori (London: Cambridge University Press, 1963), 155. See also Halil Inalcik 'Turkey between Europe and the Middle East,' *Foreign Policy* (Ankara), VIII, no. 3-4 (July 1980): 7.

19. See, Dankwart A. Rustow, 'Foreign Policy of the Turkish Republic,' in *Foreign Policy in World Politics*, ed. Roy C. Macridis (Englewood Cliffs, NJ: Prentice-Hall, 1958), 313.

20. Mardin, 'Religion and Politics in Modern Turkey,' 140, 155.

21. See, Metin Heper, 'Islam, Polity and Society in Turkey: A Middle Eastern Perspective,' *The Middle East Journal* (Summer 1981): 350.

22. Türker Alkan, 'The National Salvation Party in Turkey,' in *Islam and Politics in the Modern Middle East*, ed. Metin Heper and Raphael Israeli (London: Croom Helm, 1984), 79-102.

23. Mardin, 'Religion and Politics in Modern Turkey,' 157.

24. See, Metin Heper, 'Bureaucrats, Politicians and Officers in Turkey: Dilemmas of a New Political Paradigm,' in *Modern Turkey: Continuity and Change*, ed. Ahmet Even (Opladen: Leske Verlag, 1984), 66-69.

25. See, Kemal H. Karpat, 'Turkish Democracy at Impasse: Ideology, Party Politics and the Third Military Intervention,' *International Journal of Turkish Studies* (Spring/Summer 1981): 10. (Hereafter cited as: 'Turkish Democracy at Impasse.') For the present functions of the Turkish Army see, Paul B. Henze, 'The Role of the Military in Turkish Society' (paper presented to the Tenth European-American Workshop of the European-American Institute for Security Research, held in Istanbul in September 1979).

26. Karpat, 'Turkish Democracy at Impasse': 7.

27. For different models of military intervention in policies see Amos Perlmutter, *The Military in Modern Times* (New Haven: Yale University Press, 1977), 105.

28. Karpat, 'Turkish Democracy at Impasse': 9-11.

29. Metin Heper, *The State Tradition in Turkey* (Beverley, England: The Eothen Press, 1985), 125-166.

30. Ibid., 152.

31. Kurt Biedenkopf, 'Domestic Consensus, Security and the Western Alliance,' in *Defence and Consensus: The Domestic Aspects of Western Security*, Adelphi Paper, no. 182 (London: IISS, 1983), 8-13.

350

32. Ladis K. D. Kristof, 'The Origins and Evolution of Geopolitics,' *The Journal of Conflict Resolution* (March 1960): 44.

33. See Premier Ecevit's press conference in London on 15 May 1976 in *Prime Minister Bülent Ecevit's Speeches* (General Directorate of Press and Information of the Turkish Republic, 1978), 29. In his talk, Ecevit emphasized détente on the one hand, and the threat from Greece on the other.

34. See, Seyom Brown, *New Forces in World Politics* (Washington, DC: The Brookings Institution, 1974), 10-15; and Oral Sander, 'Turkey: The Staunchest Ally of the United States? Forces of Continuity and Change in the Strategic Relationship,' in *The Turkish Yearbook of International Relations* (Ankara University, Faculty of Political Science, 1975), 10-24.

35. Albert Wohlstetter, 'The Strategic Importance of Turkey and the Arms Embargo,' in *NATO and US Interests* (Washington, DC: American Foreign Policy Institute, 1978), 38-39, who points to the erroneous aspect of this argument and says: 'It simply romanticizes technology to suggest that ICBM or any other sophisticated technology erase the strategic importance of Turkey.'

36. Duygu Sezer, *Kamu Oyu ve Dis Politika* (Public Opinion and Foreign Policy) (Ankara: Faculty of Political Science Publication, 1972), 133; Mehmet Günlübol and Haluk Ulman 'Ikinci Dünya Savasindan sonra Türk Dis Politikasi' (Turkish Foreign Policy after World War II), in *Olaylarla Türk Dis Politikasi* (Ankara: Faculty of Political Science Publication, 1969), 351-352; Oral Sander, *Türk-Amerikan Iliskileri 1947–1964* (Turkish-American Relations 1947–1964) (Ankara: Faculty of Political Science Publication, 1979), 223-224. Although some writers, including Oral Sander, argue that there were some talks prior to actual missile removal between Turkey and the United States, it seems that these talks were either the *ex post facto* rationalization efforts by the United States, or related to the details of the dismantling operations, but not to the decision on the substance of the matter itself. It is, however, clear that there were no negotiations preceding the initial decision of the Kennedy administration.

37. Sezer, *Turkey's Security Policies,* 24; and George S. Harris, 'Turkey and the United States,' in *Turkey's Foreign Policy in Transition,* ed. Kemal H. Karpat (Leiden: Brill, 1975), 59-60.

38. For the recent changes in the strategic environment, see Ali L. Karaosmanoglu, 'NATO's South-Eastern Region between Central Europe and the Middle East,' *International Defence Review*, no. 10 (1985): 1569-1576.

39. For the internal and external aspects of terrorism concerning Turkey's security see, Paul B. Henze, *Goal: Destabilization, Soviet Agitational Propaganda, Instability and Terrorism in NATO South* (Marina del Rey, CA: European American Institute for Security Research, 1981), 15-47.

40. See Albert Wohlstetter and Nancy Virts, 'Armenian Terror as a Special Case of International Terror,' in *International Terrorism and the Drug Connection* (Ankara: Ankara University Press, 1984), 272.

41. 'The Future of Turkish-American Relations,' remarks by His Excellency Dr. Sükrü Elekdag at the Conference on U.S.-Turkish Views of the Middle East, cosponsored by the Heritage Foundation and the Foreign Policy Institute, Ankara, held in Washington, DC, 4 October 1984, p. 29.

42. See interview with SACEUR, General Bernard W. Rogers, *International Defense Review*, no. 2 (1986): 150-151.

43. For Turkey's arms procurement efforts see, Bruce George and Colin McInnes, 'Turkish Security Policy,' *Jane's Defence Weekly* (12 May 1984): 742-744; and Sezer, *Turkey's Security Policies*, 25-28.

44. See 'The Defence Industry and the Development of the Defence Industry in Turkey,' *Middle East Business and Banking* (February 1986): 6-12.

45. 'The Future of Turkish-American Relations,' remarks by His Excellency Dr. Sükrü Elekdag, p. 25.

46. In September 1985, the Turkish government requested the negotiation and conclusion of a new DECA, rather than an extention of the existing agreement, which should have expired in December, but will remain in force with the consent of Turkey pending the conclusion of a new agreement.

47. Erol Manisali, 'Turkey's Economic Relations with the Middle Eastern countries and their Impact on Turkish-European Community Relations,' in *Turkey: An Active Partner in Western-Middle Eastern Economic Relations* (Istanbul: Garanti Bankasi, 1985), 13-17.

48. Ali L. Karaosmanoglu, 'Turkey's Security and the Middle East,' *Foreign Affairs* (Fall 1983): 166.

49. M. Cremasco, 'The Strategic Importance of Relations between Turkey and the European Community,' *The International Spectator* (January-June 1983): 47-61.

50. See Selim Ilkin, 'A Short History of Turkey's Association with the European Community 1962-1983' (a paper prepared for a research project on Turkey and the European Community, carried out by Deutsches Orient-Institut, Federal Trust for Education, Turkish Foreign Policy Institute, Institüt für Europaische Politik and Istituto Affari Internazionali).

51. For a detailed explanation of the Turkish perspective see, 'Views on the Questions between Turkey and Greece,' *Foreign Policy* (Ankara) X, no. 3 & 4 (1983): 5-22.

52. In 1952, Turkey had recognized Greece's responsibility to control all civilian air traffic across the Aegean. So the line dividing the Athens and Istanbul FIRs had been drawn just outside the Turkish coast and parallel to the outer limit of Turkish territorial waters. In 1974, with NOTAM 714, Ankara demanded that all aircraft flying east and crossing the median line of the Aegean Sea inform Turkish authorities about their flight plans.

53. EOKA (National Organization for the Cyprus Struggle) was a Greek Cypriot terrorist organization. It was established in 1953 by General George Grivas, a former career officer in the Greek army. EOKA's aim was to realize the union of the island with Greece. Hundreds of Turkish Cypriots and Britons were killed by EOKA terror-

ists during its campaign from 1955 to 1958. In 1971, the organization was reactivated by General Grivas as EOKAB.

54. Dankwart A. Rustow, 'Turkey's Liberal Revolution,' *Middle East Review* (Spring 1985): 9.

55. Seyfi Tashan, 'Contemporary Turkish Policies in the Middle East: Prospects and Constraints,' *Middle East Review* (Spring 1985): 19-20.

8

NATO's Southern Region: National versus Alliance Priorities

John Chipman

INTRODUCTION

In assessing the influence of domestic politics on foreign and defence policy, it is extremely important not to be deceived by appearances. Apparently strong regimes can be affected by persistent and internal divisions that make the creation of a clear foreign policy extremely difficult. Conversely, coalitions that appear to rest on shaky political foundations may have been able to establish a minimum agreement which permits and even requires a consistent approach to foreign policy. Most Western states have some domestic constraints on foreign policy that affect the style and content of external activities and commitments. Few can afford, as did the England of Lord Russell, simply to 'meddle and to muddle'; most must seek acceptable alignments with others and maintain a clear course that encounters limited domestic opposition.

In countries where there is fragmentation or major rivalries between important groups, the leadership will need both to avoid controversy and to build consensus. Avoiding controversy requires developing policies that do not alienate important support groups, or that at least inspire nothing more dramatic than indifference. Building consensus, on the other hand, involves resolving differences and making concessions before establishing a major foreign policy direction that has wide and lasting approval. Regimes which must deal with considerable domestic opposition may still be strong in their capacity to resist external pressures of a military or economic kind, but they exhibit a marked weakness in the formation of policy. A need to deal carefully with various domestic actors makes the development of dynamic or innovative policies very difficult. This is true of all democracies, but it tends to be all the more evident in states where democracy is a new phenomenon, or where there is a minority government. It can also be true of authoritarian regimes whose leaders must cater to certain support groups. Regimes that are caught between the negative aim of avoiding controversy and the more positive one of building consensus inevitably indulge in ambiguous behaviour, seem incapable of making meaningful commitments and adopt a style of diplomacy that does not allow for the taking of initiatives but may lead to occasional hostility with the outside world.[1]

The ability of states to develop coherent policies, judging by these criteria, is not necessarily dependent on the nature of the political system by which they are governed. Both multi-party regimes and military dicatorships have to make shifts and compromises. In both cases, moreover, the external environment is as important a conditioning factor as is the nature of domestic politics. Few states have any capacity to mould the international environment in their image or exclusively in their favour, but the domestic consequences of different attempts to garner outside support are important considerations for policy makers. Regimes that have been able to establish a domestic consensus on foreign policy, and which are satisfied with their place both within the international system generally and within the specific alliances of which they form part, are relatively strong, at least in the sense of being able to manage their international position. They are able to establish consistent lines of foreign policy, defend a traditional stance, seek returns from allies for their continued loyalty and offer the occasional diplomatic lead. Their relative weakness to outside powers may be exposed when pressured by external actors, but it is not evident in the formation of their policies under normal circumstances.

States which have carefully forged a consensus can deal effectively with the outside world. Those whose tactics to ensure domestic peace have concentrated on avoiding controversy are less equipped to deal with unanticipated outside pressures. These latter powers are perhaps more susceptible to foreign influence and the domestic effects of this influence may be quite disruptive. States which have quelled domestic disputes by building a positive policy with a wide consensus can more easily refer to that consensus when dealing with outside pressure, while those states that have merely avoided controversy in developing their external relations can usually only plead the fear of domestic turmoil in their resistance to demands from outside powers seeking to change a course of action. Known domestic divisions within a given state are often exploited by other powers, even friendly ones, that wish to change a foreign policy with which they have difficulties. The fact, on the other hand, that leaders often seek to rely on particular internal divisions to explain away unwelcome foreign policies, and thus help to protect themselves from outside pressures, indicates also that domestic disputes can frequently be useful to the foreign policy maker who has avoided controversy without building consensus.

Understanding the relationship between domestic debate and foreign policy is necessary to determine whether foreign policy in a given country is likely to become stronger and more challenging to the outside world, or whether the tendency will be in the other direction, towards obfuscation and renunciation. It also helps to explain whether outside powers can pretend to have any influence on internal debates, and, from the point of view of these powers, whether that influence is likely to have positive or negative effects.

The countries that are the subject of this book have had many different sorts of regimes in the past forty years: both relatively strong and weak, relatively democratic and dictatorial. Italy is an exception in this respect. Having ridded itself of the fascist dictatorship at the end of World War II, Italy established a democratic system that has stood the tests of time and of intense political rivalries. While there are persistent changes in government, the political system itself is eminently stable. Avoiding controversy and building consensus are both central political necessities in Italy which clearly affect the country's capacity to play the leading role within the Mediterranean that many would wish it to accept. But the negotiation and bargaining that are such important features of Italian domestic politics pose no pressing problems for any of Italy's NATO allies. Despite many changes in government, Italy has been able to direct consistent and understandable defence and foreign policies. The problem of maintaining government consensus is always present, but the management of external policy is traditionally handled in such a way as not to upset any of Italy's outside commitments or alignments. The formation of Italian policy is a highly complex process, but the outcome of this process does not create frictions for the Alliance.

There are opportunities which Italy will not take up for fear of not being able to sustain domestic support (as is the case in most Alliance countries), but this question is not new for Italy. The countries of the Southern Periphery, on which analysis is concentrated in this conclusion, are, however, confronting a new requirement to decide issues of foreign and defence policies at a time when the domestic political system is still changing or learning to adjust to major institutional reforms. This poses profound problems both for these states and their allies.

What Portugal, Spain, Greece and Turkey have in common is that they have only in the recent past divested themselves (Turkey not yet entirely) of varying forms of authoritarian rule. In the case of defence policy, both Turkey and Portugal have succeeded, for better or for worse, in maintaining an elite consensus and this may reflect the still important (if quite different) influence the military holds in the decision-making process. Defence policies in these two countries are largely perceived as a bureaucratic matter. Consensus in a wider sense may be said to exist, but in Turkey it remains the case that the public is largely insulated from whatever debate on security policy takes place, while in Portugal there is a general indifference (if favourable) which the government has no incentive to change. In Spain and Greece, charismatic leaders have sought openly to make security a matter of public concern. Throughout the early and mid-1980s, Papandreou in Greece often raised both the threat from Turkey and the question of U.S. bases in ways intended to rally public support for his policy. Gonzalez in Spain, without significant government-inspired debate, nevertheless put his country through a most democratic process by calling a referendum on defence policy, the results of which defined the limits of possible government action. In Portugal and Turkey, governments have generally sought simply to execute defence policies quietly, usually justifiably confident that these would not be opposed dramatically by public opinion. Recently, in Greece and Spain, governments have taken a different tack, virtually inciting the public to agree to a consensus that they have drafted, while still retaining the management of defence issues in the hands of a small elite.

These brief examples of the differences (and similarities) in defence and foreign policy formation and presentation show both the importance of analysing domestic influences on external policy and the difficulties of comparative analysis. Along the southern shores of Europe the questions of internal stability, economic growth, democratization, Westernization and modernization will be central domestic priorities in the near and mid-term. As these essentially political goals are advanced, each country will have to measure carefully its relations with the United States and with the major West European powers. While the countries of the Southern Periphery are not in a position to advance the Alliance's defensive military aims rapidly by streamlining and upgrading their military forces, they see membership in NATO in wider terms than do the more developed Alliance members. NATO membership offers proof of 'modernity,' and if these states' loyalty to the Alliance is to be ensured, NATO must continue to appear worth the costs of membership. It must be able to provide something that these countries cannot provide for themselves. In creating national perspectives on security and on the value of NATO membership, the role of political parties, the military and public opinion will be strikingly powerful. Each of these domestic actors is involved in important struggles for influence in the countries studied here. A stable balance of power between them has not been finally established and leaders will be taking decisions in foreign and defence policy that will affect the roles which these actors will play in the future.

Since national leaders in these countries will be moving towards long-term national development and modernization, while the leaders of other NATO powers will be expecting from them more immediate signs of political and military solidarity, there are bound to be problems arising. Military decisions relating to NATO force improvements, arms control questions and the Alliance's political stance towards the East will be taken in the context of considerable domestic institutional flux. When incorporating the countries of NATO's Southern Periphery into Alliance-wide goals it will be important to do so in a way that does not disturb domestic agreements and compromises in these countries that are bound to remain fragile. Alliance leaders will therefore have to be able to distinguish between long-term priorities and short-term benefits and know that aiming for the latter may sometimes mean sacrificing the former.

NATIONAL PERSPECTIVES ON SECURITY

The idea that national security can have international sources still has not been entirely accepted (at least psychologically) by the countries of the Southern Periphery despite their membership of NATO. None of them has a recent experience of fighting in a wartime coalition and this fact, among others, contributes to the suspicions still present in large sectors of the elite and among the wider public about the virtues of alignment, in peace, with other states.

Since these countries tend to see the international environment as one over which their influence is minimal, they feel a regular need to emphasize national policies of independence, rather than a general need for solidarity. Alignment may be quite useful in combatting the most pernicious effects of a hostile environment, but the dependence it creates is especially difficult for leaders of small states who need to prove to an increasingly inquisitive public that their policies are not beholden to the desires of others. This requirement becomes strongest in respect of the United States, so that essentially good relations can be soured by the politics of emancipation pursued from time to time by leaders wishing to show that they can defend national interests within the Alliance. Domestic struggles for power between political parties and the realignment of influence between civilian and military leaders require internal compromises that have wider ramifications. The form, though not the fact, of Alliance commitment is still being tacitly negotiated in these countries as they pursue national reorganization and modernization. Outside powers may have an influence on this process, but only if they understand the roots and complexity of the domestic debate.

The Political Parties

The move towards democratic governments in these countries was in each case quite different, since the duration and form of previous authoritarian rule also varied dramatically. The role played by political parties in increasing the participation of the public in politics has also depended on the nature of the agreements that have had to be struck with forces still retaining power in periods of transition. Where the goal of achieving political legitimacy domestically could be facilitated by promising increased modernization, the search for further international and particularly Western legitimacy naturally followed and had its effects on foreign policy choices. Where domestic strength could be gained by cutting outside links created by former repressive regimes this also has been pursued with results that may sometimes appear counterproductive. A policy aimed at ensuring domestic stability could, therefore, create an impression of foreign policy incoherence. The search for a new solidarity with the states of the West may sometimes appear compromised by open hostility towards the United States. The politics of integration and the rhetoric of independence have often been awkwardly combined; when this has occurred external policy has been incoherent. The problem of this political situation for outside powers is that attempts to intervene in the foreign policy pursued by the government can sometimes serve to upset internal domestic support for broad foreign policy choices of which the outside power approves.

Post-Franco Spain offers many examples of these dilemmas. The transition to democracy in Spain took place in an orderly fashion with strict observance of the rules laid down by Franco.[2] The transition was aided by the fact that the first party to win office in parliamentary elections — the Democratic Centre Union (UCD) — was centre right, and therefore tolerable to important representatives of the old regime. But because the first government of Adolfo Suarez did not have a majority in parliament, and the Union itself was a collection of rival factions, it was forced to negotiate with all parties in government from the left to the right. This established, at the beginning of the new democracy, the need for consensus politics in Spain. The so-called 'Moncloa Pact' of October 1977, signed by the leaders of all major Spanish parties and comprising both a common economic plan and a general political agreement, symbolized the requirement for immediate stabilization of the economy and the political system.[3] From 1977 to 1982, parties and coalitions of the centre and centre right, which had to negotiate carefully with each other to reach a consensus, dominated politics. The left-wing Workers' Socialist Party (PSOE) had an important parliamentary presence, but most of the relevant political manoeuvring was done on the centre and the right.

With the elections of 1982 much of this changed: since the

PSOE won an outstanding majority, the right-wing Popular Alliance (AP) picked up a considerable amount of votes and the UCD (as well as the Eurocommunists or PCE) collapsed totally. The decline of the far left and of the centre, turned Spanish politics into a struggle between the moderate left and the right. Though the centre made a small recovery in 1986, the political system became dominated by PSOE opposed by a still important right wing, but not one with any foreseeable chance to take power. The 1986 campaign, however, was not a vicious one and most observers concluded that there would be no serious danger of the polarization of Spanish politics, though the strong position of the PSOE meant that the types of compromises made within the Spanish political system in the late 1970s and early 1980s would no longer be essential. The PSOE could rule with the confidence and independence of any majority government in an established democracy.

These developments mean that Spanish political leaders are in a position to establish a direction in foreign policy on the basis of a general consensus. This consensus was able to be forged, in part, because there had been a period of consensus building during the Suarez government (perhaps less so during the Calvo Sotelo period) but also because the PSOE was successful in proving that it too could be a responsible party of government, able skilfully to develop support for its policies. Even if the PSOE still has quite an empassioned opposition on the centre right and right, its domestic economic policies and broad programme for modernization command general support. The PSOE and the Spanish political system have been fortunate in that the two great political forces that have long symbolized polarization within the Spanish body politic — the Church and the Communist Party — each made enough small steps towards the centre to make consensus building possible. The Communist leader Santiago Carillo accepted the path towards parliamentary government, while the Church did not provide a protective cover for the enemies of democracy.[4] In conjunction with the fact that the Francoist bureaucracy and the armed forces could still be brought into the new democracy, even with some unfortunate tremors of rebellion, these developments made it possible to think of taking bold steps in foreign policy.

The choice of entry into the European Community was never a cause for serious political dispute. Entry into NATO, however, was initially effected by the Calvo Sotelo government despite considerable opposition. Prime Minister Gonzalez's move to create a stronger consensus on defence policy by offering a decalogue of ten points to the parliament, in October 1984, on which Spanish defence policy would be based and his decision to hold the referendum on NATO helped to create support for his policies. Yet these two efforts and the various political activities which were necessary to make them successful have created constraints, some of them useful, some perhaps less desirable, on the formation of security policy.

Despite the government's majority it does not have absolute autonomy in the development of defence policy. Even though the Spanish Prime Minister has enormous *de facto* and *de jure* powers in the formation of external policy, the carefully constructed lines of the decalogue and the referendum, and the importance attached to them, mean that it would be quite difficult to depart from the principles they contain. This has some advantages and some limitations. In negotiating with the United States over bases in Spain, the Spanish government has no choice but to proceed on the basis of the consensus already acquired; this can add to Spanish negotiating power. On the other hand, should the government decide not to be so insistent on the removal of U.S. bases in Spain, or on the application of other defence principles already publicly accepted, it is likely to encounter significant opposition at home; this puts certain constraints on government action. The very public way in which this consensus was created may even make it difficult for future governments to make significant changes, unless these are clearly proposed in an election campaign. The political elites, all too aware of the detailed open bargaining that has taken place on defence issues, remain vigilant. Forces on the left have criticized the government for not pressing harder on the bases issue, while critics on the right have taken the government to task for organizing an inefficient system of cooperation with NATO. The political challenge of developing a consensus having been surmounted, Spanish governments will have to show that they can manage the public presentation of defence policy.

The political problems confronting Portugal since the fall of the Salazar government have been quite different. From the 1974 coup to the elections in July 1987 there have been sixteen governments. The election of Prime Minister Anibal Cavaco Silva in 1987 marked the first time since the coup that a leader has taken power with an outright majority to govern. Building stable governments, not consensus for foreign policy, has been the main political challenge in post-Salazar Portugal. The transition to democracy in Portugal was not as smooth as in Spain largely because the left-wing forces which contributed to the 1974 coup were not able to negotiate effectively with groups on the centre and the right. Rather than consensus being built into the system, as in Spain, the post-coup order was established on the basis of a constitution which reflected the victories of the left over conservative forces.[5] This guaranteed that there would be quite intense political rivalry between the democratic groups struggling for power in the ensuing years.

During the early development of what has become a liberal democratic system in Portugal, foreign powers played an important role in supporting some of the emerging political parties. The Soviet Union helped the Portuguese Communist Party, while the United States sought to influence, partly through its embassy in Lisbon, the appointments of key individuals and, through the multilateral organizations of which it was a member, tried generally to encourage democratic development. The Federal Republic of Germany took a special interest in Portuguese developments and had excellent relations with the Portuguese embassy in Bonn. West German political parties also developed close links with nascent sister organizations in Portugal. The preponderance of Western interests in Portugal's future and the intensity of the direct and indirect pressure put on the regime meant that potential Portuguese leaders were made acutely aware that a Marxist regime would not be tolerated by the West. This clearly influenced the framers of the new constitution, even if, in the end, it did contain much left-wing language.[6] Ten of the 312 articles of the constitution deal with the transition to socialism and cover such topics as the transformation of Portuguese society into one without classes, and the need to socialize the means of production.[7] The stable political system that will evolve if an appropriate balance of power can be developed between the Socialists and the Social Democratic Party is likely to result in both constitutional reform and accelerated economic modernization.

The tensions and struggles for power that have existed between the opposing political parties in Portugal since 1974 have not dramatically affected either the style or the content of defence policy. The need to avoid controversy in order to have a minimum agreement for the implementation of policy has been easier in external matters than for internal policy. The withdrawal from Africa and the reorientation of Portuguese policy towards Euro-Atlantic questions, marked by entry into the European Community and the reaffirmation of continued loyalty to NATO, while opposed in some extreme sectors, had wide support. Membership of the EC would be particularly important to symbolize the acquisition of a new legitimacy in the Western order, and its pursuit gave purpose to a political elite eager to establish its own legitimacy as the proper leader of the post-Salazar era. The strictly political rivalries of the contenders for power after 1974 have not had a great impact on foreign policy; it is more the continued influence of the military on Portuguese politics, reviewed further below, which has served to affect Portugal's capacity to exert itself effectively in the international arena.

In Greece, the transition to democracy after the reign of the colonels was marked principally by a dramatic event — the Turkish invasion of Cyprus in July 1974 — which precipitated the surrender of power to civilian leadership. Since it was an external crisis that created the conditions by which civilian authority was restored, that authority was able to benefit not only from the support it could expect from those who disapproved of the colonels' regime (though in fact many Greeks approved of the stabilizing role the colonels had played), but also from the universal support naturally given to leaders confronting the imminent possibility of war.[8] National solidarity did not have to be created by the incoming civilian leaders, it was inherent in the domestic and international conditions that had made their arrival to power possible.

In transferring power to the civilians, the Greek military hoped to be able to ensure that the return to democratic politics would not entail a dramatic change in the political system as established by the colonels. But the political factions invited to negotiate with the colonels were committed to the reintroduction of competitive politics in Greece. When Karamanlis took power, he gradually tried to move the internal political centre of gravity from the right to the centre, and legalized all political parties to ensure that a wide range of political forces be accommodated in the new system. He set a high priority on national reconciliation to end the Civil War divisions still evident in Greek politics and worked to create new political institutions that would allow for the running of a smooth political system.

His creation of the New Democracy Party and the establishment of PASOK by Andreas Papandreou ensured that post-1974 politics, while drawing on traditions deep in the Greek postwar order, would be based on new structures and new visions for the future.[9]

The idea that Greece had to 'adhere to the West' was central to New Democracy's political principles as they were developed in 1974. Membership of the EC was seen as essential to guarantee the consolidation of Greek democracy. Integration with the other democracies of Western Europe would assist Greek leaders in maintaining internal political stability. EC membership was also considered important to help distance the new government from the United States which had collaborated with the military junta.[10] The political programme of PASOK, also established in 1974, accorded great importance to foreign policy. Basic goals like the establishment of national independence and freedom from the influence of 'economic oligarchies' translated themselves into the call for withdrawal from NATO and reversal of the decision to join the EC.[11] If New Democracy initially wished Greek political life to be positively influenced by the democratic impulses of other West European states, PASOK argued that true independence could only come from a national effort aimed at national liberation. These general principles served as unifying factors within the party and allowed PASOK to appeal to Greeks who saw themselves badly served by those who demanded too much integration by Greece in the projects of others.

The two main political groupings which emerged in Greece after the departure of the junta felt that foreign policy, properly constructed and intelligently pursued, could hold the key to increased democratization of Greek society and the maintenance of social order. That these foreign policies had, at least superficially, quite different orientations, assured that internal rivalries would have an effect on the presentation of national images and external policy. While Karamanlis would argue that 'Greece belongs to the West,' Papandreou would insist that 'Greece belongs to the Greeks.'[12] Papandreou's need to avoid too much controversy with the Communist Party, while distancing himself from it, made the separation between political oratory and actual practice wider than usual. Equally, the need for New Democracy to oppose Papandreou's policies made the gulf between its ideas and those of PASOK appear wider than was actually the case.

The pursuit of a particular foreign policy also implied the adoption of an idea about Greek identity and Greek defence to a public easily divided by the polemics of nationalism. In a society that had experienced great divisions in the past it was inevitable that foreign policy choices which were intertwined with definitions of national identity would inspire controversy. A broad consensus still exists but this is strongest on the one issue that made it possible for the new democratic government to come to power in 1974: relations with Turkey.

Turkey's political system has suffered numerous changes since the establishment of the Republic of Turkey in 1923 by Kemal Atatürk. The breakdown of civilian government in Turkey on 12 September 1980 was not a new phenomenon for the republic, although the form of the handover to civilians in November 1983 was devised in the hope that a more stable democratic order could be established. The place of the military as the guardians of Turkish democracy is still firmly entrenched, but without the existence of some political parties, that role could not honestly be proclaimed. The gradual process of re-democratization that has taken place in Turkey since November 1983, has been initiated by the military and controlled by it, against rising internal and external pressures for a more rapid return to a fully democratic polity. The careful management of government by Prime Minister Turgut Ozal's Motherland Party (initially not the military favourite) has resulted in increasing though still restricted debate on the full range of political issues.

Foreign policy, however, has not been particularly affected by the reemerging debate between political parties any more than it was in the past. Foreign policy, perceived as a matter of national policy, has always been a subject on which there has existed a national consensus led and developed from the top. Despite regime changes, there have been essential constants in foreign policy, and the existence of authoritarian or democratic governments, responsible and responsive parties, or inadequate and paralysed parliaments has not resulted in major differences in foreign policy direction.[13] Under these various regimes Turkey has naturally been treated differently by outside actors, but despite this, leaders of the Turkish state have attempted to continue a coherent foreign policy. This has been made possible by the fact that foreign policy bureaucrats have been able to command influence. Even weak coalition governments, such as those which were in power during the 1970s, tried to ensure that the Foreign Minister was a widely accepted and uncontroversial figure of Turkish political life who himself would entrust the details of foreign policy to the bureaucracy.[14]

National security, in terms both of internal stability and defence policy, has long been accepted as the preserve of the head of state acting closely with the bureaucracy, and, given the domestic situation, this became all the more evident with the arrival to power of the military in 1980. President Evren has maintained close control over security issues and has sought to ensure that the most important questions of foreign policy are overseen by himself and his closest advisors, though the Prime Minister has pushed for an increasingly important role both in the development and execution of external policy.

This has meant that the major lines of foreign and defence policy are determined as a result of tacit and sometimes open negotiation between the head of state and the Prime Minister. These relations serve more as testimony to the need to establish a balance of political power between the military and civilian leadership (which everyone admits must eventually tilt fully in favour of the civilians), than as an example of the weight that political parties themselves exert on external policy. In any case most political parties, with the exception of those on the extreme left or right, accept the broad orientation towards Europe and NATO taken by Evren. As political parties become freer to express divergent opinions and propose new lines of policy, they will tend to do so on domestic issues rather than on defence or foreign policy questions. No Turkish political leader likely to inspire public confidence and support will feel that his position would be enhanced by the presentation of an innovative foreign policy to a public inevitably more concerned about internal stability, social justice and economic growth. However, as Turkish democracy is strengthened over time, and as civilians regain control of the political debate, politicians will know that Turkey's appeal to the democratic West will be commensurately higher. This will make it easier for Turkish leaders to make compelling demands on Western partners, no longer able to turn down Turkish requests (for increased trade or greater political integration) on the grounds that these fruits could only be delivered to an entirely democratic regime. The understanding that the route to a more effective foreign policy (at least in respect of the West) lies with a more widely acceptable domestic

367

regime, may itself be a modest factor which could help to accelerate the return to a fully democratic system in Turkey.

Civil-Military Relations

The relationship between civilians and the military in each of the Southern Periphery countries has varying effects on the state's capacity to determine effective foreign and defence policies. One major issue, in these states where the military has been able to wield considerable political power, is the residual control retained by the military over the minutae of defence policy which may make it difficult for other forces to contribute effectively to the policy-making process. Another factor is the influence that the armed forces may still hold over the general political process that may force politicians to make certain concessions to them in order to be assured of support, or at least to take into account the military's possible reaction before embarking on new policies. A third element is the general position and prestige of the military in the society as a whole that may affect the spirit in which both defence and foreign policies are made, as well as the image which outsiders have of the state and its institutions.

To return briefly to the case of Turkey, it is clear that the military retains some importance in all three of these senses. Since 1983, Turgut Ozal has made attempts to increase the pace of civilian control over the whole range of political choices. This has been most difficult in the area of defence where the secrecy of the General Staff makes it difficult for the civilians to be in full possession of the information necessary to make appropriate decisions. Ozal's frustrations reached a peak in the summer of 1987, when he claimed to have learned only through the press of army conflicts with Kurdish rebels in Anatolia. His refusal to accept the recommendation of President Evren for the new Chief of the General Staff and his nomination of another candidate was linked to this specific concern for increased control over the facts of internal security, but also symbolized a general challenge, even if modest, to the military. It is unlikely that the General Staff will cease, in the short or medium term, to make the broad strategic decisions related to defence policy, but it is clear that the view of the Prime Minister within the National Security Council will be expressed with greater firmness. Certainly, the relationship between the largely Western-oriented General Staff and the Motherland Party, whose Islamic links are held against it by some army officers, will remain testy.

The military in Turkey does wish to withdraw eventually from politics but there are some strictly military issues over which it will try to maintain control. Certainly questions of internal stability, particularly problems associated with the threat of terrorism or of Islamic fundamentalism, will remain a priority for the military. The management of the armed forces, at present overseen by the Ministry of Defence which is staffed largely by army officers, will also be seen as a duty that the military will wish to retain for itself. The positive social effects of the conscript system which inculcates the values of Kemalism into large sections of the Turkish youth are certainly strongly defended by military officers and appreciated as important by most civilian leaders. This, in itself, is an important enough factor to ensure that the military will be given considerable freedom to manage its own affairs. Finally, the military would only very reluctantly wish to give up policy-making control over the question of Cyprus, and particularly over the deployment of forces on the island. Civilians naturally have a political role to play in eventually negotiating a settlement to the Cyprus dispute but on any military issues raised they will take their cue from the armed forces.

Military control over the general political process is being steadily relaxed (though not entirely eliminated) as the restrictions placed on individual politicians have been perceived to be largely ineffective.[15] The military leadership will, nevertheless, be extremely cautious before allowing the near total freedom of political activity that existed before 1980, although that anarchy was produced by an electoral system which allowed so many groups into parliament that the legislature became effectively paralysed. Future electoral battles are likely to be fought largely between the Motherland Party, the True Path Party and the Social Democrats. If national elections produce a staightforward contest between these parties there will be less justification for the military to keep close control over the political system and a greater need for military and civilian leaders to negotiate a new power-sharing agreement.[16] Despite the fact that the military in Turkey is widely regarded as the protector of democracy, other Western states will tend to give greater credence to a democracy without substantial military involvement. The perception held by outsiders of civil-military relations in Turkey is likely, therefore, to have an effect on the evolution of the situation. This will be less the case in the other countries of the Southern Periphery where the basic problem of military involvement in politics has been solved even if in all cases numerous anomalies remain.

When the civilians took over power in Greece in 1974, efforts were made not to punish the armed forces as a whole for the seven years of military rule and specifically for the important failure of the Cyprus policy that had precipitated the downfall of the colonels' regime. President Karamanlis was careful not to institute an outright purge of the military, though after a coup attempt in February 1975, 500 officers were punished.[17] Steps were taken to reassert civilian control over military affairs as well as the general primacy of the civilians in the political system. The armed forces retained appropriate control over institutional questions, such as promotion and their internal budget, and also broadly benefitted from increases in the defence funds allocated to them by the civilian government, which were considered necessary because of the increased threat from the east. The 1975 constitution contained important provisions which placed questions of national security squarely back into the hands of the civilians, though certain articles of the constitution, as well as subsequent accompanying legislation give the military extraordinary powers in times of emergency.[18]

The civilian governments in power in Greece since the coup have been relatively cautious in their dealings with the military and have clearly attempted to construct their policies in ways which do not incite too much concern in the ranks of the armed forces. This approach has been aided by the fact that there is a basic parliamentary consensus on defence matters and few politicians believe that there are benefits to be gained from overt criticism of the military. Given the consensus about the Turkish threat, the armed forces still are perceived to have an important mission in the defence of national interests. Since the arrival of PASOK to power, attempts have been made to reform the curriculums of military academies so as to inculcate democratic values better in military officers, and it is accepted that many of the officers who received early retirement or were pushed into different positions were those who did not approve of Papandreou's policies.[19]

The military in Greece has therefore lost a good deal of

public respect and political influence while retaining an important role in the defence of national security. Tension between the civilian and military leaderships, however, is sufficiently high for civilians to seek strict control of the military's activities. Papandreou's decision to hold the position of Minister of Defence himself until 1986 is symbolic of the perceived need to supervise the armed forces and to ensure that they follow closely the political lead.

This concern has been, until very recently, all the greater in Spain. While the army did not directly oppose the transition to democracy as it was taking place, many military men were suspicious of some of the political reforms made during this period, notably the legalization of the Communist Party, and were held in check largely because of the considerable authority of the King.[20] At the time of the clumsy coup d'état attempt in February 1981 by some Civil Guards and army officers, virtually all of the Spanish military displayed their loyalty to the constitution and to the democratic system, but it was really only by the mid-1980s that the public stopped considering the armed forces as a potential threat to democracy. The government of Adolfo Suarez followed by that of Calvo Sotelo both instituted important military reforms that included changes in the code of military justice, and redefinitions of the responsibilities and jurisdictions of military authorities.[21] With the coming to power of the PSOE the policy of army reorganization and modernization was accelerated.

Working in close collaboration with his Defence Minister, Narcis Serra, Felipe Gonzalez passed further laws which guaranteed the political control of the armed forces. The Socialist government also proceeded quickly to rejuvenate the officer corps (largely by forcing numerous early retirements) and to reorganize the forces, manning them at much lower levels. The various plans for the modernization of the army and the restructuring of Spanish military districts were put into place without much opposition. The defence budget was expanded mainly to make possible the procurement of more modern military equipment, badly needed given the obsolete matériel that had been maintained by the Franco regime. The thrust of these many changes, which basically continued along the same lines as those pursued by previous governments, was to make the armed forces accountable to the political leadership, as well as more modern and professional. If there was dissent expressed during

371

these changes, it was not politically charged. Certainly a manifestation of the now firm control that the government maintains over the military must be the very low profile the military took during the highly controversial debates surrounding the form of Spanish participation in NATO.

Defence policy making in Spain is well within the hands of the political leadership. As better roles are developed for the Spanish armed forces in the defence of Spanish interests and within the context of European defence needs, it can be expected that the prestige of the armed services will be able to reestablish itself on professional grounds without posing a challenge to democracy or to social order. The difficulty for outside powers and organizations, particularly the United States and the NATO headquarters in Brussels, is that the strength of Spain's political control over defence policy rests on a political consensus that has been carefully crafted but not yet entrenched, and on only a recently acceptable state of civil-military relations. Spanish leaders will therefore claim with increasing confidence that the role they have devised for Spain is non-negotiable by outsiders. An initially stiff and cautious policy is thus inevitable; whether it will change as a result of increased military collaboration within NATO or with the experience of Spanish diplomats operating in the Alliance and through the system of European political cooperation will depend a great deal on the behaviour of other allies.

Some, but not all of these problems, are evident in Portugal. The role played by the army both in the politics of transition and in reorganizing a democratic system could not have been more different from the Spanish case. These differences are, quite naturally, reflected in the form and substance of Portuguese defence and foreign policy. The army in Portugal played the central part in returning Portugal to democracy. As a force of the left, the Portuguese army had also a different domestic agenda than the right-wing Spanish army. But as the force that had brought democracy, it was able, most importantly, to assure for itself bureaucratic power in the Portuguese administration as well as more broadly within the political system. The leader of the revolution, Colonel Antonio Ramalho Eanes, became (as General) the first President of the second Portuguese republic and has retained an important political vehicle for himself for over a decade in the form of the Democratic Renewal Party (PRD).[22]

If in Spain it was generally agreed that it would be necessary to find an external role for the armed forces, or at least one not so obviously focused on internal security, in Portugal the challenge was to discover what missions an army, whose principal recent experience had been in Africa, could perform within the Euro-Atlantic region. The return of the armed forces from Africa and the establishment of a democratic system in Portugal made it easier to normalize certain relations with NATO that had been strained during the colonial wars. This took some time and, in fact, in 1974 and 1975 concern about the influence of the left in Portugal made for rather awkward relations with other NATO allies, particularly the United States. The Ford administration even questioned whether it was still appropriate for Portugal to be a NATO member. Portugal was excluded from the Nuclear Planning Group in NATO and only returned to it in 1976.[23] By this time, outside powers were satisfied that the transition in Portugal was not dangerous, and relations were improved quickly, but the task to establish a proper role for the army within Portugal was still great.

That role had also to be separated from politics. After the coup, the Movement of the Armed Forces (MFA), annoyed at the disputes between the political parties and fearful that the direction which many of the members had hoped for post-Salazar Portugal was not being followed, expanded its own political powers and formed the Revolutionary Council. In the 1976 constitution, the Revolutionary Council and the armed forces as a whole were charged with many essentially political tasks, including ensuring the proper working of democratic organizations.[24]

Despite the provisions of the constitution which gave it considerable powers, the Revolutionary Council did not play as great a role as some military men wished. Military influence, however, was guaranteed through the office of the President, at least until Mário Soares took the position in 1986. Only in 1982 were the armed forces formally put under the control of the government, but a thorough normalization of the military and of its place in civilian society has still not taken place. Direct political influence has clearly waned, but the armed forces still have practical control over many procurement and defence policy decisions. It is still largely owing to external influence (notably the defence agreement with the United States) that something approaching a clear line on defence policy can be pursued.

Much of Portuguese defence policy remains a function of the special links with the United States.

All this means that while there is no profound concern in Portugal about the state of civil-military relations, it will still take some time for civilian and military leaders to develop a clear balance of power and influence between themselves and to resolve the question of how foreign and defence policy issues are to be decided. For the Alliance, this is not necessarily a bad thing as Portuguese external activity can be expected to be both cautious and predictable. There are also few broad policies that at present would be changed in the event of a shift in the decision-making process which more evidently favoured the civilian leadership. But the bureaucratic nature of Portuguese external policy making does prevent the leadership from taking strong stands or developing new ideas. Once the apparatus of decision making is more firmly dominated by politicians and civilians, it is likely that Portuguese external policy will become both more assertive and more demanding.

As the countries of the Southern Periphery further modernize their armed forces, reassert stronger civilian control over policy making, and establish a deeper consensus within public opinion on defence and foreign policy matters, they are likely to become more strong-willed partners within the Alliance. Their demands on the central powers within NATO for more attention or more funds will in all likelihood be coupled with declaratory policies of semi-alignment or independence. Continued loyalty to the Alliance may, *in extremis,* be the barter offered for greater help from other allies; rather than being taken for granted, these states may choose to extract a price for their Alliance membership, even when that membership is accepted as virtually indispensable and satisfies a general security and political need.

Security Threats and the Politics of Emancipation

Such attitudes, as those outlined above, will be possible because of a widespread belief within the countries of the Southern Periphery that they are needed by NATO and, more specifically, by the United States. They have something to sell, in the form of base rights, and there will be a tendency to market these in a way that may inspire resentment on the part of the United

States. These countries, for various political reasons, feel themselves not entirely implicated by all Alliance goals, and to the extent that they are estranged, diplomacy within the Alliance will have in some part to focus on managing the alienation between the countries of the Southern Periphery and the other member states.

As the authors in this book have pointed out, there are important sources of estrangement. Certainly in Greece, many of those who remember the depth of American involvement in the country after World War II are wary of the American presence. In the 1940s, U.S. Undersecretary of State Dean Acheson told senators that it would be necessary 'to put Americans into the essential key [Greek] Ministries which are necessary to be able to control the basic factors.'[25] The policy that ensued from this desire has left its mark on the Greek political conscience. Turkish recollections of the Johnson letter and of the American arms embargo; Spanish memories about the legitimacy implicitly given Franco by the U.S.-Spanish bilateral agreement; and Portuguese remembrance of difficult times during the colonial wars and immediately after the revolution, all offer similar sources for current dismay or diffidence. These feelings are of markedly different intensity in the countries studied in this book. But the concern about what has variously been interpreted locally as American dominance or unwelcome assistance, does have, or could have, an effect on current policy makers, no matter how essentially pro-Western and pro-American they may be.

If the ghost of America past may haunt some policy makers in the Southern Periphery and produce disagreeable rhetoric or action, the ghost of Europe future tends also to concern them, and offer some compensation. In applying to become members of the EC, Greece, Spain, and Portugal all cited, implicitly or explicitly, their contribution to Western defence as justification for entry. Turkey did the same when it applied in 1987 and President Evren, frustrated following a European Parliament resolution claiming that Armenians had been genocide victims, threatened in June 1987 to review Turkey's NATO membership. Though this was not to be taken too seriously it was an example of the mental tradeoffs that can be made between the fact of NATO membership and the strength of relations with other NATO allies: when these are bad, much of the *raison d'être* of NATO membership — closer affiliation to the West —

seems to be less relevant.

Such tendencies can be reinforced by the fact that for both reasons of geography and politics, these countries have foreign policies that engage them quite considerably outside the NATO area: Spain and Portugal in North Africa, Greece with numerous countries in the Arab world, and Turkey more specifically with those of the Near East. While none of these national policies can lead to basic options that are fundamentally non-Western, they help to emphasize to national leaders that stability and security in the Mediterranean area are dependent on numerous variables, many of which do not involve the Soviet Union. These countries are therefore more than usually resistant to defence hypotheses that are centred on the problem of the Soviet Union. All recognize the Soviet threat (Turkey more than the others for evident reasons of geography and history) but that recognition tends to be formal and (again with the exception of Turkey) less driven by a profoundly felt perception of insecurity fomented by the USSR.

The basis for a defence policy in these countries is, therefore, not exclusively focused on NATO requirements or on NATO threat perceptions. Defence policies are individual, and are largely supported by the public — to the extent that the policies are known — precisely because they are regarded as national policies. As outside powers look on and seek to understand these national policies they must also realize how these policies were created. Very broadly, leaders in Greece and Spain, as their democracies have been strengthened and as the balance between civil and military influence has evolved, have sought to build consensus for the policies they now pursue. This has sometimes entailed difficult relations with the United States and NATO, as a whole, but this effort can be justified internally by the fact that it has resulted in a firmer foundation for policy making. In the formation of policy these two states exhibit certain strengths, and for outside powers to change the direction of policies in these countries it will be necessary to do so in a way which permits leaders to defend shifts within the framework of the consensus already built, or in a way which allows, without danger of rupture, for a new consensus to be created. By contrast, the two allies, Portugal and Turkey, that many would view as having been more 'loyal' to NATO and having caused fewer problems within NATO councils or in their relations with the United States, have benefitted from a relatively passive public opinion on defence issues. Leaders have successfully avoided controversy, yet it is uncertain how invulnerable the general direction of defence policy would be to better organized internal opposition. Outside powers that may wish for more from these countries will have to seek to extract a greater national contribution to Alliance defence without inciting opponents who, though lying dormant, may be difficult to deal with once they emerge. The relationship between the United States and these countries will be especially testy, but the Alliance will not be able to afford drawn-out or petty disputes. The United States, like other NATO states, must appreciate the difficult positions of the national leaderships in Southern Periphery countries, but the latter must not play the card of domestic vulnerability so often that the essential U.S. contribution to the Alliance defences in the south is trumped.

PERSPECTIVES FROM THE ALLIANCE

If there is now a widespread view that the Alliance's military weaknesses in the Southern Region have to be addressed, there is still an incomplete understanding of the various historical, political, economic and cultural factors that make the broader management of Alliance security interests more difficult in the south than in other areas. For a coherent defence policy to be established and carried through in the south, at least three conditions must be fulfilled. First, individual states in the region having initial responsibilities for local defence must be able to cooperate with both regional and extra-regional NATO allies. This depends in part on the resolution of bilateral disputes between NATO allies in the region — notably Greece and Turkey — and also on an increased interest on the part of the United States and other allies in the area's economic and military modernization. Second, it is important that the Soviet Union's perception of the place of the Southern Region in its own strategy be understood and that Western policies are elaborated that take full account of the scope of this perception. This requires that the Alliance improve its capacity to react militarily to possible threats throughout the region, but more broadly that a political effort be made to ensure that the security of the south is firmly coupled with the security of the central region. Third, the Alliance as a whole must be fully aware of the nature of the other threats that may destabilize the area. To deal with these emerging dangers, the allies will have to share information and viewpoints, yet also tolerate divergent opinions and approaches.

The dilemma that runs through these considerations is how to strengthen individual capacities and initiative in the south without sapping the means of collaboration and the sense of 'collectivity' required to run an alliance. This dilemma is especially acute given four factors that govern the geopolitical situation in the Mediterranean from the perspective of the Atlantic Alliance. First, most of the countries in the Southern Region see their membership in the Alliance in the light of their special relationship with the United States. Little distinction is generally made between the state's NATO policy and policy towards the United States, so that public debate often confuses the validity of NATO membership with the state of relations with the United States. Second, the states of the Southern Region which would like to make their security relationship with the United States less exclusive are not yet in a position to take leading roles as European decision makers on European defence ideas. Thus, these states are bound to find themselves negotiating for attention from other powers in a way that may, from time to time, encourage the rise of nationalist sentiments that make the management of collective defence more difficult. Third, the Soviet Union is not uniformly considered the principal or most important source of threat; other threats (in the Middle East or in the Maghreb) are widely thought to be relevant. Fourth, regional security in what is termed the 'Southern Region' of NATO is difficult because it is not truly a 'region,' or at least does not present a unified theatre of potential war for which a single strategy can be elaborated. This, at once, raises the need for increased cooperation and also ensures that it is bound to be less efficient than elsewhere in the Alliance.

If these factors are to be partially resolved, it will be necessary for the United States and its allies in the Southern Region (in collaboration with other NATO partners) to establish a fresh basis for their partnership. Too much of recent Alliance history in the Mediterranean has been characterized by the politics of resentment: by the Southern Region allies concerned that they have either been ignored or treated as proxies; by the United States irritated that it has been drawn in as a subject of domestic politics while being threatened with near expulsion from the region. These stereotypical images of a domineering superpower dealing with recalcitrant allies risk becoming entrenched unless more is done to build a minimal interallied consensus on how to cooperate in the Mediterranean. No less than in domestic politics, the attempt merely to avoid controversy is bound to lead to temporary and, in the long run, unsatisfactory results.

The relations between the United States and its Southern Region allies raise in stark fashion all of the classic burden-sharing questions that have affected the Alliance in recent years. The time when the United States can effectively serve as 'federator' of the Southern Region is certainly running out. For some time still, the United States will provide absolutely essential economic and military aid to these countries, and will pledge itself to their general modernization. But it will become increasingly difficult for the United States and other outside powers to influence the policies of these countries whose control over domestic and foreign policy management is likely to strengthen. Tensions with the United States will be all the more acute because of the Southern Region states' reliance on U.S. assistance coupled with a wish for greater independence within the Alliance's structures. Yet their basic desire for more influence over their own destinies, and for eased integration into whatever West European designs may exist or be drafted, cannot be satisfied on demand. Abstract requests for further assistance or increased attention to regional concerns are unlikely to be heeded. This is so because in security terms the principal powers of Europe are bound still to focus on the Central Front and, moreover, only so much can be expected from the central alliance powers in terms of initiatives for improved European regional security.

This places the onus firmly on the Southern Region states for greater cooperation amongst themselves. At the military level this would mean exchanging more information about force modernization programmes and national defence plans. Such exchange of information would be necessary to discover areas where activity can be complementary rather than competitive or counterproductive. Improvements in cooperation are hostage to the problems associated with the Greek-Turkish dispute, but the other Southern Region states can, without sacrificing their independence, make useful advances along this path. At a political level, it will become increasingly important for these states to identify regional problems and propose prospective

379

solutions for them. To do this, they will have to engage the interest and ultimately the responsibility of other Alliance states. It is here that Italy may begin to play an important role in serving as a broker not only between certain Southern Region states, but also between these countries and some of the more powerful members of the Alliance.

National and Alliance perspectives on stability and security in the Southern Region of NATO will only become more compatible if the local states make an effort within Alliance councils to show that their willingness to cooperate with each other justifies the efforts of outside powers to engage themselves more fully in the concerns of the Southern Region. Once these states are able to define more effectively those national security problems that can be attenuated through international cooperation within the Alliance, then they will be in a better position to have their voices heard by the central powers in NATO. The basic challenge that these states will confront in pursuing this aim will be largely domestic: to convince internal actors that stability and security must have important international sources. Having established a firm basis for developing foreign and defence policies, the states of the Southern Periphery will then have to begin to deal with the domestic consequences of more active external policies. Greater assertiveness within the Alliance may have its rewards, but it may also have its costs, and these will have to be judged against the primacy of maintaining internal order in societies where the establishment of domestic consensus is a recent or still evolving phenomenon.

NOTES

1. These features of politically weak regimes are described in the chapter by Joe. D. Hagen, 'Regimes, Political Oppositions, and the Comparative Analysis of Foreign Policy,' in *New Directions in the Study of Foreign Policy*, ed. Charles F. Hermann, Charles W. Kegley Jr. and James N. Rosenau (Boston: Allen and Unwin, 1987), 349.

2. Beate Kohler, *Political Forces in Spain, Greece and Portugal* (London: Butterworth Scientific, 1982), 6.

3. Ibid., 20-22.

4. Kenneth Maxwell, 'Spain and Portugal: A Comparative Perspective,' in *The Politics of Democratic Spain*, ed. Stanley G. Payne (Chicago: Chicago Council of Foreign Relations, 1986), 264.

5. Ibid., 262.

6. Thomas C. Bruneau, 'Portugal after the Revolution: Decoloniza-

tion and Democracy,' contribution in 'Southern Europe and the Mediterranean,' ed. Howard J. Wiarda, *AEI Foreign Policy and Defence Review*, 6, no. 2 (1986): 24.

7. Thomas C. Bruneau, 'Continuity and Change in Portuguese Politics: Ten Years After the Revolution of 25 April 1974,' in *The New Mediterranean Democracies: Regime Transition in Spain, Greece and Portugal*, ed. Geoffrey Pridham (London: Frank Cass, 1984), 74.

8. P. Nikiforos Diamandouros, 'Transition to, and Consolidation of, Democratic Politics in Greece, 1974-1983: A Tentative Assessment,' in *The New Mediterranean Democracies*, ed. Pridham, 54.

9. See the description in Ibid., 54-63.

10. Kohler, *Political Forces in Spain, Greece and Portugal*, 119.

11. Ibid., 128.

12. Theodore E. Couloumbis, 'The Structures of Greek Foreign Policy,' in *Greece in the 1980s*, ed. Richard Clogg (London: Macmillan, 1983), 95-96.

13. Dankwart A. Rustow, *Turkey: America's Forgotten Ally* (New York: Council of Foreign Relations, 1987), 84.

14. Ibid., 85.

15. Kenneth Mackenzie, 'Turkey in Transition,' in *The World Today* (June 1986): 103.

16. Rustow, *Turkey: America's Forgotten Ally*, 118.

17. Constantine P. Danopoulos, 'From Military to Civilian Rule in Contemporary Greece,' *Armed Forces and Society*, 10, no. 2 (Winter 1984): 247.

18. Thanos Veremis, 'Security Considerations and Civil-Military Relations in Post-War Greece,' in *Greece in the 1980s*, ed. Clogg, 180.

19. James Brown, 'From Military to Civilian Rule: A Comparative Study of Greece and Turkey,' in *Defense Analysis*, 2. no. 3 (1986): 179.

20. Maxwell, in *The Politics of Democratic Spain*, ed. Payne, 265.

21. Stanley G. Payne, 'Modernization of the Armed Forces,' in *The Politics of Democratic Spain*, 183-184.

22. Many of these points are raised in the essay by Maxwell, in *The Politics of Democratic Spain*, 256-273.

23. Coral Bell, *The Diplomacy of Detente: The Kissinger Era* (London: Martin Robertson, 1977), 164.

24. Kohler, *Political Forces in Spain, Greece and Portugal*, 223.

25. U.S. Senate, 'Legislative Origins of the Truman Doctrine,' *Hearings held in Executive Session before the Committee on Foreign Relations*, 80th Congress, 1st Session (Historical Series), made public on 12 January 1973, p. 82. Quoted in Theodore Draper, 'American Hubris: From Truman to the Persian Gulf,' in *The New York Review of Books* (16 July 1987): 41.

The Authors

John Chipman is Assistant Director for Regional Security Studies at the International Institute for Strategic Studies (IISS) in London. This book was prepared by him while he was a Research Associate at the Atlantic Institute for International Affairs in Paris from 1985 to 1987. He is author of *French Military Policy and African Security,* Adelphi Paper no. 201 (IISS, 1985), later revised and expanded as a book in French under the title *Ve République et Défense de l'Afrique,* (Paris: Editions Bosquet, 1986). He is also the author of *Survey of International Relations Institutes in the Developing World,* (IISS, 1987) and of numerous articles and book chapters on European and African security issues.

Maurizio Cremasco is responsible for the department of strategic studies at the Istituto Affari Internazionali in Rome. He has been a visiting professor at the Johns Hopkins University Bologna Centrum. He has done consultancy work for the Italian Ministries of Defence and Foreign Affairs and is a correspondent for politico-military affairs for the daily newspaper *La Stampa* in Turin. He has published four books on security policy including *Il Fianco Sud della NATO* (Milano: Feltrinelli, 1980) and has contributed chapters and articles to several other publications.

Ali Karaosmanoglu is a Board Member and Director of Strategic Studies at the Foreign Policy Institute in Ankara. Previously, he was lecturer and Associate Professor at the Middle East Technical University and Bogaziçi University. He has written much on international relations and strategic issues, contributing to such journals as *Politique Etrangère* and *Foreign Affairs.* Among his books is *Les actions militaires coercitives et non coercitives des Nations Unies* (Geneva: Droz, 1970).

Alvaro Vasconcelos was a founder member and, since 1981, has been Director of the Institute for Strategic and International Studies in Lisbon. Author of numerous articles and papers on security issues, his work has been published in *Europa Archiv* and *NATO's Sixteen Nations,* among other journals.

Thanos Veremis is Associate Professor of Political History in the Politics Faculty of the University of Athens. He has been a visiting fellow at the International Institute for Strategic Studies, Harvard and Princeton. He is author of *Greek Security: Issues and Politics*, Adelphi Paper no. 179 (IISS, 1982) and has published widely on contemporary Greek history and security policy.

Angel Viñas is Director of Latin America and Asia (except the Far East) at the Directorate General for External Relations of the Commission of the European Communities in Brussels. From 1982 to mid-1987 he was Executive Advisor to the Spanish Foreign Minister. He has also been a Professor of Applied Economics at the University of Madrid. He collaborated in writing this chapter with Miguel Angel Martinez (who has been a Spanish (PSOE) deputy since 1977 and is Vice President of the Parliamentary Assembly of the Council of Europe) and with Fernando Alvarez de Miranda (a Christian Democrat who was the first President of the Lower House in parliament after the dictatorship and in 1986 was appointed Spanish Ambassador to El Salvador).

Index

Note: bold page numbers refer to tables in text, 'n' indicates reference to Notes section.

port facilities *see* port facilities
raid on Libya 91, 118, 204, 212,
  215, 216, 226-7, 232, 263,
  336
Rapid Deployment Force 43,
  60, 115, 201, 215, 331
relations *see individual countries*
US Sixth Fleet *see* Naval Forces

Valona Bay, Albania 17, 22
van Fleet, General James 241
Vanizelos, Eleftherios 238
Varna 38
Vasconcelos, Alvaro 86-139
Velez de la Gomera 141
Veneto-Friuli plain 15
Venice Declaration 334
Venizelos, Prime Minister
  Sophocles 241
Veremis, Thomas 236-86
Vicenza 59

Viñas, Angel 140-95

Weinberger, Caspar 271
Western European Union 64, 119,
  166, 337
WESTLANT 95, 117
World Peace Council 108, 120

Yemen 35
Yom Kippur *see* Arab-Israeli wars
Yugoslavia 36, 53, 75, 237, 240,
  243, 253, 263, 272, 278, 294,
  295
  Italy and 200-1
  Soviet facilities in 24

Zaire 115
Zaragoza 59, 115, 190
zero option 262
Zurich Agreement (on Cyprus) 295,
  342